Judaism and Modernity

Philosophical Essays

Judaism and Modernity

Philosophical Essays

GILLIAN ROSE

BLACKWELL
Oxford UK & Cambridge USA

First published 1993

Blackwell Publishers
108 Cowley Road
Oxford   OX4 1JF
UK

238 Main Street
Cambridge, Massachusetts 02142
USA

British Library Cataloguing in Publication Data
A CIP catalogue record for this book is available from the British Library.

Library of Congress Cataloging-in-Publication Data
Rose, Gillian.
Judaism and modernity : philosophical essays / Gillian Rose.
    p.   cm.
Includes bibliographical references and index.
ISBN 0–631–16436–7. — ISBN 0–631–18971–8 (pbk.)
1. Philosophy, Jewish. 2. Judaism—20th century. 3. Jews—
Germany—Intellectual life. 4. Holocaust, Jewish (1939–1945)—
Influence. I. Title.
B5800.R67   1993
    181'.06—dc20   93–15056
                                                        CIP

Typeset in 11 on 13 pt Bembo
by Graphicraft Typesetters Ltd, Hong Kong
Printed in Great Britain by
T.J. Press Ltd, Padstow, Cornwall

This book is printed on acid-free paper

For Jay Bernstein
I wish you a long life

Contents

Preface

A friend has suggested that I preface this book with an *apologia pro vita sua* along the lines in which Franz Rosenzweig tried to explain his return to Judaism in his letter to Friedrich Meinecke declining the offer of a university post. This apology from 1920 seems uncannily to converge with the growing tendency nowadays to present theoretical work with a declaration of one's personal as well as one's academic qualifications and interests: 'I' write 'as a woman', 'as a Jew', and so on.

My trajectory displays no such logic. If I knew who or what I were, I would not write; I write out of those moments of anguish which are nameless and I am able to write only where the tradition can offer me a discipline, a means, to articulate and explore that anguish. Against the self-image of the age, it has been *within the philosophical tradition*, which for me includes social, political and religious thought, that I have found the resources for the exploration of this identity and lack of identity, this independence and dependence, this power and powerlessness. My difficulty is not addressed in any rejection of that tradition which would settle for only one side of my predicament: lack of identity, dependence, powerlessness, or any account of otherness which theorizes solely exclusion and control.

It is this *speculative* account of experience, which persists in acknowledging the predicament of identity and lack of identity, independence and dependence, power and powerlessness, that has led me to Judaism. Or, rather, it is by working through my difficulty in the *ratio* and the crises of modern philosophy that I discover myself in the middle of the *ratio* and crises of modern Judaism.

I have not arrived at Judaism as the sublime Other of modernity – whether as the moment of divine excess from Kant's third *Critique*, as the living but worldless community from Rosenzweig, as the devastating ethical commandment from Levinas, as trace and writing from deconstruction. Nor have I discovered Judaism waiting at the end of the end of philosophy, Judaism *redivivus* out of the ashes of the Holocaust: as the Jewish return into history for Fackenheim, as the issue of modernity for Bauman, and as the terrible essence of the West for Lacoue-Labarthe.

No. I write out of the discovery that both recent philosophy, in its turn to what I name *new ethics*, and modern Jewish philosophy, in its ethical self-presentations, are equally uncomfortable with any specific reflection on modern law and the state, which they assimilate to the untempered domination of Western metaphysics. Rome haunts the *agon* between Athens and Jerusalem, but only the imperial Roman eagle has been admitted, while the Rome which invented private property law, the law of persons, and separated it from citizenship is forgotten because it is so familiar. In the eagerness to eschew the metaphysics of subjectivity, recent philosophy and Jewish philosophy lose the means to discern the structuring of our anxiety, the modern mix of freedom and unfreedom in civil society and the state which continues to contour our subjectivity and which cannot be abjured. Having renounced teleological philosophy of history, general philosophy produces in its place the newly purified polarity of reason and ethics, which Jewish philosophy, scared of the charge of Pharisaical legalism, intensifies with its purified polarity of law and love. Philosophy and Judaism want to proclaim *a New Testament* which will dispose of the broken promises of modernity.

I write out of the violence infecting these philosophical purifications which ignore their own preconditions and outcomes. I write out of the feigned innocence of the 'and' in *Judaism **and** Modernity*. This is my *apologia pro vita sua*: the only way I can approach my life is by attempting to explore how the difficulties with which I engage may articulate that life. The speculative method of engaging with the new purifications whenever they occur, in order to yield their structuring but unacknowledged third, involves deployment of the resources of reason and of its crisis, of identity and lack of identity. This results in what I call *the facetious style* – the mix of severity and irony, with many facets and forms, which presents the discipline of the difficulty.

Since the essay form as well as the style corresponds to the method of speculative engagement, I have kept each essay self-contained at the cost of some repetition of argument. The first three essays ('Is there a Jewish Philosophy?' 'Ethics and *Halacha*', 'The Future of Auschwitz') deal with the difficulties of distinguishing Judaism and philosophy, Judaism and ethics, Judaism and the Holocaust. The second three essays ('Shadow of Spirit', 'From Speculative to Dialectical Thinking – Hegel and Adorno', 'Of Derrida's Spirit') develop the speculative method through engaging with post-modern theology, Adorno and Derrida. The seventh essay, on 'Nietzsche's *Judaica*', examines the connection between Judaism and genealogy as a method in Nietzsche's thinking. The following five essays on Cohen, Rosenzweig, Buber, Benjamin, Weil and Levinas engage with thinkers who are important equally as modern philosophers and as modern Jewish philosophers (in spite of Weil's infamous distaste for Judaism). In each case, methodological innovation and the renewal of ethics are speculatively engaged with the account of modernity and modern law. The final two essays extend the same exploration to recent attempts by architectural theory to take account of Judaism and the Holocaust in architectural history.

In general and when trying to combat widespread misconceptions concerning Judaism, I assume no knowledge of Hebrew terms and I explain them every time they arise. For fundamental and frequently employed terms, such as, Torah, Talmud, Halacha, I have also included the briefest of glosses under the corresponding entries in the Index.[1]

Once again I have had the benefit of much constructive criticism. I owe thanks to the following, who have made substantial comments on particular essays: Keith Ansell-Pearson, Robert Fine, Michael Marrus, Robert Jan van Pelt, Tony Thorlby and Richard

[1] For further introduction to these terms and others pertaining to the Rabbinic tradition, see Adin Steinsaltz, *The Essential Talmud*, trans. Chaya Galai, New York, Basic Books, 1976.

Wolin. Jay Bernstein, Greg Bright, Howard Caygill and David Novak have looked over the whole endeavour with merciless and with generous eyes. This time Greg Bright's cover affords facets of the difficulty of Judaism and modernity. Jim Beckford's works of supererogation have been lavishly drawn on. Iain Liddell has been equally proficient and munificent with computing services and with Classical Greek, while Barbara Gray has saved me at the eleventh hour with her more-than-customary graciousness. At Basil Blackwell, I would also like to thank my editor Stephan Chambers, for his good judgement and support, and also, especially, Andrew McNeillie and Marguerite Nesling for their perspicacity as well as sheer efficiency in preparing both this book and *The Broken Middle*. When *The Broken Middle* had not yet been bound, Judith Harvey arranged for one copy to be hand-bound and delivered by special courier in time for me to take it to James Fessenden in New York before he died.

All my friends, old and new, and perhaps, now, most of all, those who have passed out of friendship and who would not usually be acknowledged in the prefaces to books (but why should they not be? – they are the ones who cause the most pain and despair) have enriched this enterprise. For, just as Rosenzweig said, 'Disillusionment keeps love in practice', so I find, 'Disillusionment keeps love of wisdom in practice.' And it was David Groiser who formulated that and much else for me.

Acknowledgements

The author and publisher wish to thank: T. & T. Clark Ltd for permission to quote from *I and Thou* by Martin Buber; The Balkin Agency and Routledge for permission to quote from *Between Man and Man* by Martin Buber; Gordon and Breach for permission to reprint 'Hermann Cohen – Kant among the Prophets', from the *Journal of Jewish Thought and Philosophy*, vol. 2, no. 2; Robert-Jan van Pelt, C. W. Westfall, and Yale University Press for permission to reproduce the diagram on p. 248, from *Architectural Principles in the Age of Historicism*.

1
Introduction

Athens and Jerusalem

Jerusalem against Athens has become the emblem for revelation against reason, for the hearing of the commandments against the search for first principles, for the love of the neighbour against explanation of the world, and for the prophet against the philosopher. When the common concern of Athens and Jerusalem for the establishment of justice, whether immanent or transcendent, is taken into consideration, these contrasts of form and method lose their definitive status. Yet, suddenly, in the wake of the perceived demise of Marxism, Athens, for a long time already arid and crumbling, has become an uncannily deserted city, haunted by departed spirits. Her former inhabitants, abandoning her justice as well as her reason, have set off on a pilgrimage to an imaginary Jerusalem, in search of difference or otherness, love or community, and hoping to escape the *imperium* of reason, truth or freedom.

This exodus, originally prepared by Nietzsche and Heidegger, has been led over the succeeding decades by thinkers across the spectrum of philosophy. From Buber and Rosenzweig to Weil, Benjamin, Adorno, Arendt, Levinas and Derrida, all are Jews with a deeply problematic relation to Judaism and to philosophy, which is more or less thematized in their thought. It will be argued in this book that their different ways of severing existential eros from philosophical *logos* amounts to *a trauma within reason itself*. This trauma is explored in its effect of making both modernity and Judaism incomprehensible to each other and to themselves; and, each essay seeks to develop anew the comprehensive and critical reflection of Judaism and modernity by weaving together eros and *logos*, Jerusalem and Athens.

One Mistake has been Replaced by Another

Suppose a friend whom you trust more than any other, who taught you the meaning of friendship, lets you down suddenly, and then, persistently, ceases to fulfil the expectations which, over the years, you have come to take for granted, and which, without your being aware of it, act as the touchstone for all your other friendships. Would you give up all your friends? Would you change your expectations of all your friends? Would you simply avoid that particular friend?

Would you try to have it out with your friend and wait to see if you could discuss the problem together and see what might emerge from a frank discussion? You may discover that you cannot agree on the terms of the discussion: that your friend cannot understand your distress and has a completely different interpretation of events, and of her interests and yours. Or you may discover that you are the one at fault: that, unintentionally, you have failed your friend; you may be able to explain your intentions and both come to see why the misunderstanding arose. Perhaps you were both partly at fault, at cross-purposes. And what if, one way or another, you discover that your friend wants to end the friendship for her sake, for your sake or for both of your sakes as she sees it?

In the latter outcomes, whether they induce contrition or humour or despair, the crisis of friendship results in a changed relationship to oneself as well as to one's friend: a change in my self-identity arising from the change in the friend's relation to herself, just as the change in her self-identity arises from the change in my relation to myself. These changes imply a deepening in the notion one holds of friendship which has been learnt from possibly unintended mistakes, from the interference of apparently extraneous meanings.

On the other hand, the first three responses (giving up all friends, giving up the normal expectations of friendship, or giving up the particular friend) seem to be in the wrong order: the last resort coming first. They impoverish the idea of friendship; they involve acts of destruction and they rest on false inferences concerning the meaning of friendship. To be a 'friend' involves a mutual relationship which presupposes independent but plastic self-identity. One must be able to give and take from others, to acknowledge difference and identity, togetherness and separation, understanding and misunderstanding. You cannot give up all friendship, friendship as such, without damaging yourself – without, as it were, ceasing to be a friend to yourself. Being a friend to oneself involves admitting and accepting meanings, emotions and inconsistencies which you do not consciously intend or desire. Deepened understanding between friends arises from their having enough self-trust and mutual trust to renegotiate the friendship, given the ever-shifting possibility of misunderstanding, of unanticipated difficulty.

Now, if you substitute 'reason' for 'friendship', then you will see that the last resort has become the first response and remedy. Difficulty with reason leads to its being reneged altogether – with disastrous consequences for both reason and its purported Other(s). The perceived failure of reason has led straight away to recourse to the most drastic remedy – the abandonment of reason as such. On this account, 'reason' (no friend) is dualistic, dominant and imperialistic in subordinating its others. This is to commit *the first mistake*: reason, which has acted exclusively, is characterized as intrinsically, necessarily and incorrigibly exclusive. *The second mistake* is to assert the claim of the excluded party against restricting and restricted reason. As a result, alterity – the Other, woman, the body (its materiality, its sexuality), dialogue, love, revelation – whatever is named as dangerous to reason and therefore suppressed or silenced by reason, evidently acquires visibility and voice.

To denounce reason and to exalt its abused Other is to replace one mistake by another in three senses: it misrepresents the alterity of reason; it misrepresents the meaning of reason; and it misrepresents the use being made of reason. First, the meaning of the Other whose claim is redressed against reason is presented as, *ipso facto*, utterly unequivocal and totally justified by the long overdue act of assertion. Once the perennial master, 'reason', with his ambivalence of desire and fear, has at long last been subdued, the implication arises that 'woman', 'the body', 'love', released from the rationality of 'man', 'the mind', 'logic', are no longer equivocal. Their newly achieved franchise imparts a fixity to them, even if, or precisely when, they are defined as *fluid*. For if exclusive and excluding reason was in the wrong, then exclusive otherness, *unequivocally Other*, will be equally so. Far from bringing to light what is difficult out of darkness and silence, difficulty is brought to certainty. Certainty does not empower, it subjugates – for only thinking which has the ability to tolerate uncertainty is powerful, that is, non-violent. This principled otherness sent out to reform the world will expend a violence equal to the violence it accuses (reason) – and with an exceedingly good conscience.

Second, reason is not adequately described when characterized as dualistic, dominant and imperialistic: it is only *demonized*. Reason – as the analogy with the deepened notion of friendship suggests – is relational, responsive and reconstructive. Only its restriction by specific institutions renders it exclusive, oppositional and closed – and even then it must precariously maintain itself as such. The exposition of friendship demonstrated that the most *existential* response to the crisis of friendship, that of negotiation, turns out to be the most *logocentric*: it involves recognizing our mutual implication in the dynamics of the relationship, and it leads to changed self-definition inseparable from the changed mutual definition. Boundaries are transgressed and redrawn and ever-vulnerable. The otherness of the Other could not be discovered without discovering the otherness of the self: friendship is relational, not differential, because it is *always pervaded with meanings neither party intends*, but which are recoverable by reflection when challenged. The concept of friendship which emerges from the pain and lessons of experience is dynamic: it connotes the unanticipated outcome of idea and act; and yields the *actuality* of the concept, not its *alterity*. To present experience, with its unwelcome and welcome surprises *and* with its structure, is the work of reason itself, its dynamic and its actuality.

Third, the use as well as the meaning of reason is misrepresented. For the exposure of reason's limitation is accomplished by the selfsame reason that is simultaneously discredited for its exclusivity and employed in its own enlargement. However, denial of the debt to reason means that an alternative oppositional priority is established; the use of reason is plastic while the outcome is fixed. This debases debate; and it may help to explain why the initial, just grievance against restricted and exclusive reason, in its turn, mutates into dogmas of correctness.

In *Standing Again at Sinai: Judaism from a Feminist Perspective*, Judith Plastow indicts Judaism for silencing women and women's experience; elsewhere in the same book, she praises the Judaic prophetic tradition for providing the notion of transcendent justice on which her perception and judgement is grounded. This simultaneous abuse and use of prophetic reason might suggest a dialectic and equivocation, but instead it founds a new certainty – the innocence and immediacy of 'women's experience'. But all and any experience, however long abused and recently uncovered, will be *actual* and not simply *alter* (Other): the discrepant outcome of idea and act will be traceable to meanings which transcend the boundaries of idea and act – to norm, imperative, commandment and inhibition, that is, to the law and its commotion. To promise anything else, any new righteousness which will not be subject of and subject to the difficulty of actuality, which will never become unjust, is to disempower. Reason that is actual is ready for all kinds of surprises, for what cannot be anticipated, precisely because of the interference of meanings which are structured and reconstructable.

New Ethics

If 'differance' has become the hallmark of theoretical anti-reason, 'the Other' has become the hallmark of practical anti-reason. The *new ethics* of the Other, of alterity (whether total or relative), seeks redress for the false claim of reason to universality and disinterestedness when reason has always been demonstrably interested and totalizing. *New ethics* affects to be equally disillusioned with the morality of the abstract, autonomous individual (which has affinities with Kantian reason), and with ethics conceived collectively and intersubjectively, whether the constitutional state (associated with Hegelian reason), or socialism and communism (associated with Marxist rationalism). Since individual liberty minimalizes political representation, while collectivity implies the fullest political representation, indirect and direct, respectively, these extremes indicate that *new ethics* amounts to the crisis of representation and modern law. Yet investigation into the failures of modern regimes of law, into the unintended outcome of idea and act, is itself outlawed, because critical reflection lost its legitimacy when the self-validating ground fell away from reason. Non-intentional, *new ethics* expiates for the unexamined but imagined despotism of reason. As a result, this non-representational, non-institutional, non-intentional ethics leaves principled, individual autonomy and its antinomy, general heteronomy, unaddressed and effective. *De facto*, it legitimizes the further erosion of political will.

Once again, one perceived mistake is replaced by another. The more or less violent imposition of masterplans for justice on the plurality and diversity of peoples and interests has given way to the sheer affirmation of cultural and political diversity, 'plurality'. *New ethics* is consciously and deliberately *gestural* because it has renounced any politics of principle, any meliorist or revolutionary intentions. In the current context, this involves complete evasion of the confrontation between the structured distribution of resources (investment) and the libertarian *laissez-faire* of markets, and the unintended consequences of both. *New ethics* is waving at 'the Other' who is drowning and dragging his children under with him in his violent, dying gestures. *New ethics* cares for 'the Other'; but since it refuses any relation to law, it may be merciful, but, equally, it may be merciless. In either case, having renounced principles and intentions, *new ethics* displays 'the best intentions' – the intention to get things right this time. In its regime of sheer mercy, *new ethics* will be as implicated in unintended consequences as its principled predecessor.

One mistake has been replaced by another in three senses: the initial mistake is not properly described; 'the Other' is misrepresented; and the remedy proposed is self-defeating. The inadequate formulation of the initial mistake may be highlighted by another analogy. Le Corbusier has been blamed for the failings of modern architecture. His idea of the family house as 'a machine for living in', as well as many other features of his new architecture, have been taken as excessively rationalistic: mechanistic, impersonal, technocratic, with no respect for the inhabitants. However, Le Corbusier's streamlining of the interior as well as the exterior of the home was intended, as he declared, *to liberate women from furniture.* His aims were humanistic and emancipatory, not surveillant and controlling. Yet no examination of the intervening institutions which have determined the meaning of Le Corbusier's architecture has followed its general indictment. This examination would relate the intended meaning (idea) to built form or material configuration in order to comprehend how the outcome of idea and act is effected by the interference of meanings, that is, by institutions, which were not taken into account in the original idea, but which mediate its attempted realization; for example, by changes in the family, the occupational structure, property relations, ratio of public to private space, investment in planning, building and infrastructure.

And now a new architectural humanism has been invented without any exploration of the fate of the humanism displaced. 'Community' architecture also seeks to restore 'people' to the centre of architectural design and practice. As planners, builders and dwellers, 'people' are to be active in the process of architecture, perceived as the hitherto remote and sterile project of modernism, dominated by the interests of the architectural profession. This new immediacy of 'the people' takes no account of how people are formed, individually or collectively. Once again, all the institutions that distribute resources, desires and agency are overlooked at every stage; a new architectural dogma and imperialism results from this *new ethics* of architecture.

Once again, the new plan overlooks the inevitable configuration of its intentions in the course of its interaction with effective institutions. Similarly, non-intentional, *new ethics*, in effect, intends a new transcendence, a purified reason, for it proceeds without taking any account of institutions which are extraneous to its idea, that is, without taking any account of mediation. It intends to affirm 'the Other', but it ignores the actuality of its intentions. With no social analysis of why political theory has failed, *new ethics* will be recuperated within the immanence which it intends to transcend.

'The Other' is misrepresented as sheer alterity, for 'the Other' is equally the distraught subject searching for its substance, its ethical life. If *new ethics* ignores the intermediary institutions which interfere with its intention to affirm 'the Other', then, similarly, it ignores the mediation of the identity of 'the Other'. For 'the Other' is both bounded and vulnerable, enraged and invested, isolated and interrelated. *New ethics* would *transcend* the autonomy of the subject by commanding that I substitute myself for 'the Other' (heteronomy) or by commending attention to 'the Other'. Yet it is the inveterate but occluded *immanence* of one subject to itself and to other *subjects* that needs further exposition. Simply to command me to sacrifice myself, or to commend that I pay attention to others makes me intolerant, naive and miserable. I remain intolerant because the trauma of sacrifice, or the gesture towards the unidentified plurality of others, leaves me terrified of the unknown but effective actuality which forms a large part of myself. I continue to be naive and miserable, because the insistence on the immediate experience of 'the Other' leaves me with no way to understand my mistakes by attempting to recover the interference of meaning or mediation. This will produce an unhappy consciousness, for the immanence of the self-relation of 'the Other' to my own self-relation will always be disowned.

A self-defeating remedy is therefore proposed by the call to 'the Other'. In this case, one mistake is replaced by an equivalent one. For 'the Other' is *unequivocally* 'Other'. The adamantine intransigence of this new meaning will be decisive in determining its effective outcome in a way in which the merely abstract universality of the old ethics could not be. For the difficulty with reason, theoretical and practical (ethical), lies not in its initial, abstract universality; the difficulty of reason rests on whether the initial, abstract universal (the meaning or idea) *comes to learn*: whether *something can happen to it*; whether (to recall the one with a difficult friend, who discovered it was a matter of friends in difficulty) one abstractly universal individual enters into substantial interaction with another abstractly universal individual. For in so doing, each comes up against her own violence, her own abstractly universal self-identity. This violence of each individual towards its 'Other' and towards itself is then discoverable, regardless of whether the original intention of each towards 'the Other' was good, evil or indifferent – for the outcome of the self-relation of each in the relation of the Other to itself cannot be controlled or determined by any intention. *New ethics*, which demands the overcoming of the subjectivity of the agent and denies the subjectivity of 'the Other', produces in this 'Other' the inflexible abstraction it sought to indict.

Reason in modernity cannot be said to have broken the promise of universality – *unless we have not kept it*; for it is only we who can keep such a promise by working our abstract potentiality into the always difficult but enriched actuality of our relation to others and to ourselves. Whether disturbing or joyful, reason is full of surprises.

Angélus Dubiosus

Reason, full of surprises, is not Kantian self-limiting, theoretical reason, nor is it the endless task of Kantian moral rationality, according to which duty ever fails wholly to prevail over inclination; nor does it describe classic self-determination according to the model of Freudian psychoanalysis in the Habermasian vein of *Knowledge and Human Interests*; nor does it presuppose the intersubjective linguistic transparency of discourse ethics in the later Habermas. Negotiating the interference of meanings between idea and act, its isolation and implication, its self-identity and lack of self-identity and not hailing and sacralizing the plurality or irreducible singularity of itself and of 'the Other', reason, full of surprises, is adventurous and corrigible.

The discovery of the difficult, dangerous and irrational impulses and actualities of individual and social life can only be *the work of faceted and facetious reason*, which – like Socratic irony equally beyond irony – is at the same time beyond its facetiousness. Paul Klee's *Angélus Dubiosus* provides an image and name for reason, full of surprises. The 'dubious angel', doubtful and doubting, is distinguished from Benjamin's choice of Klee's angel, *Angélus Novus*, the new angel, his emblem for the traumatized Angel of History; and, equally, from the angry angels which I discern in Weil and in Levinas when they propose a *new ethics* defined against an idealized rationalism; and the facetiousness of the dubious angel is contrary to the ethos of so-called 'ironic liberalism', with its cynical display of indifference towards 'the plurality' of the Other.

The dubious angel, bathetic angel, suits reason: for the angel continues to try to do good, to run the risk of idealization, of abstract intentions, to stake itself for ideas and for others. Experience will only accrue if the angel discovers the violence in its initial idea, when that idea comes up against the actuality of others and the unanticipated meanings between them. Now angels, of course, are not meant to gain experience – in the angelic hierarchies, idea and act at once define the angel, who is the unique instant of its species, without generation or gender. But here is the dubious angel – hybrid of hubris and humility – who makes mistakes, for whom things go wrong, who constantly discovers its own faults and failings, yet who still persists in the pain of staking itself, with the courage to initiate action and the commitment to go on and on, learning from those mistakes and risking new ventures. The dubious angel constantly changes its self-identity and its relation to others. Yet it appears commonplace, pedestrian, bulky and grounded – even though, *mirabile dictu*, there are no grounds and no ground.

The dubious angel as the emblem of the work of facetious reason spoils the opposition between Athens and Jerusalem which *new ethics* has re-invented. It takes issue with the claim that Judaism provides the refuge for thought which has finished with the jaded rationalism of the philosophical tradition. Judaism, deprived of this counter-cultural cachet, 'beyond reason', shares with modernity the same crisis of self-comprehension, the same trauma and actuality of reason. The essays in this volume seek to expose this common fate and – with the *Angélus Dubiosus* as my guardian angel – to begin to find a way through.

2

Is there a Jewish Philosophy?

I am sure that you know the answer to this question. The answer must be *no*: for Torah and Talmud, the Written Law and the Oral Law, instruction revealed and the tradition of commentary, yield no *tertium comparationis* for the question and questing of philosophy, the search for first principles – of nature, of the good, of the beautiful, of the true. There is not even Jewish theology, *logos-theos*, logic of God, even less, ontology or epistemology – logic of being, logic of knowledge. Modern philosophy, which has renounced the search for metaphysical foundations and has become uncertain, empirical, mechanistic, is an even less suitable candidate for comparison, with its resolutely secular, finite and anthropocentric impetus and preoccupations.

A riposte to this denial of the possibility of Jewish philosophy might run as follows: that Maimonides' *Guide of the Perplexed*,[1] just like Samson Raphael Hirsch's *Nineteen Letters on Judaism*,[2] assimilated The Philosopher of his epoch (Aristotle or Hegel) in the course of developing the *apologia* for Judaism for his age – medieval or modern, respectively. Subsequently, these

This chapter was originally delivered as a public lecture at the University of Heidelberg, at the invitation of Julius Carlebach, Rector of the Hochschule fur Jüdisches Studium, Heidelberg, July 1990. I have retained the lecturing style.

[1] Moses Maimonides, *The Guide of the Perplexed*, 1190, vols I, II, trans. Shlomo Pines, Chicago, Chicago University Press, 1963.
[2] Samson Raphael Hirsch, *The Nineteen Letters on Judaism*, 1836, trans. Bernard Drachman, Jerusalem, Feldheim, 1969.

assimilations have never ceased to characterize Judaism's most orthodox self-understanding. The counter-riposte could be that these
strategic, *exoteric* defences are complementary to the ancient custom of translating Torah and Talmud into the *Koine* (Aramaic,
Greek, German, American-English),[3] which, precisely, leaves the
specifically Jewish tradition intact for the great codification of
Maimonides and the great compendium of Hirsch – *Mishneh Torah*[4]
and *Horeb*.[5]

However, perhaps this initial reflection is itself premature. For
the meaning of the question posed in the title of this lecture may
not be unambiguous: 'Is there a Jewish Philosophy?' This apparently innocuous formulation is freighted with equivocalities,
which, taken together, lead in directions which may disqualify
my opening reflections. The question may be interpreted as an
empirical question: *is* there, as a matter of fact, a Jewish philosophy – as there is a Christian philosophy, however problematic its
relation to Christianity may be? Or, second, it may be interpreted
as a conceptual or logical question – which was assumed above
provisionally – *can* there be a Jewish philosophy? Or, third, the
question may bear an imperative, a *Sollen: should* there be a Jewish
philosophy? Or, finally, it may, more modestly, inquire into the
exemplary or illustrative validity of any philosophical reflection
on Judaism – the question of philosophical Judaism rather than
Jewish philosophy, substance and subject reversed.[6]

Paradoxically, even this analysis which attempts to discriminate
between different implications of the initial question is itself intrinsically tendentious, for it has not yet thrown into relief that
the whole problematic of posing the question, *die Fragestellung*,
is not neutral. 'Is there a Jewish Philosophy?' permits philosophy
to identify Judaism, and, in so doing, reduces it to an epithet of

[3] *Koine* is the common language of the Greeks from the close of the classical period to the
Byzantine era and hence of the Jews living in Greek cities; subsequently any common
language becomes a legitimate vehicle for the Hebrew sources.
[4] Completed in 1178. See Isadore Twersky's 'Introduction' to *A Maimonides Reader* (New
York, Behrman House, 1972), pp. 16–19.
[5] Completed in 1835; subtitle, *Essays on Israel's Duties in the Diaspora*, trans. Isidor Grunfeld,
New York, The Soncino Press, 1981.
[6] For a survey of the ways in which this issue has been posed, see Ze'ev Levy, *Between
Yahfeth and Shem: On the Relationship between Jewish and General Philosophy*, Bern, Peter Lang,
1987.

philosophy. Should not Judaism have its own voice in this matter since the voice establishes the matter at stake? Can philosophy be restrained from defining and dominating the very *form* of the approach? A response to the inevitable imposition of the form of the philosophical question would seem to be implied by a recent development. For Judaism is being rediscovered *at the end of the end of philosophy*; and, through this irony of irony for the religion which historically has been denigrated as superseded, the issue of Judaism and Philosophy may re-emerge in terms which do justice to their inherent formal and substantive incomparability.

Two traditions proclaim an 'end' to 'Western' philosophy. From Kant to Heidegger, the end of *metaphysics* is proclaimed: for Nietzsche, will to power would no longer be denied by eternal Platonic form or by Christian salvation; for Heidegger, Being would no longer be concealed and forgotten by beings. From Hegel to Adorno, the end of *philosophy* is conceived: the actualization or realization of philosophy. Without positing any empirical termination, the first of these two 'ends' would revert to and repeat an *origin*; the second would advert to and suspend a *finality*. Yet both traditions seek to illuminate historically the equivocation of the ethical middle in which thinking finds itself immersed.[7] These two *modern* 'ends' are then overtaken and sublated in the third sense of 'end' which is implied in their end: the end of philosophy in the sense of classical, Greek philosophy – the end of free inquiry into beginnings, principles, causes. This third demise has returned thought explicitly to ethics and law, which are no longer understood in terms of inner imperative versus outer imperium but as *commandment*, without the individualistic presuppositions of disinterested autonomy versus interested heteronomy.

[7] Since the irruption of the debate over Heidegger's Nazism, it has become a commonplace to argue that the meaning of his work is ethical, in spite of his well-known denial in the 'Letter on Humanism': 'The thinking that inquires into the truth of Being . . . is neither ethics nor ontology', *Martin Heidegger: Basic Writings*, trans. Frank A. Capuzzi, London, Routledge and Kegan Paul, 1978, pp. 234–5. Derrida does not distinguish these two meanings of 'the end of philosophy' in 'Of an Apocalyptic Tone Recently Adopted in Philosophy,' trans. John P. Leavey, Jr, *Oxford Literary Review*, 6: 2 (1984), pp. 3–37. However, earlier in the same essay (234–5), Heidegger argues 'If the name "ethics", in keeping with the basic meaning of the word *ethos*, should now say that "ethics" ponders the abode of man, then that thinking which thinks the truth of Being as the primordial element of man, as one who exsists, is in itself the original ethics.'

Contrary to their explicit intentions to establish the incomparability of Judaism and philosophy, Leo Strauss and Emmanuel
Levinas have made Judaism available to philosophy in new terms.
Formulated in opposition and in debt to Heidegger,[8] Strauss
contrasts obedient love with the spirit of free inquiry, while Levinas
contrasts a 'passivity beyond passivity' with the order of the ego,
self-consciousness and freedom.[9] Strauss reinforces the opposition
between Judaism and philosophy by employing classical and
pre-modern definitions of philosophy, while Levinas characterizes
philosophy *per se* as 'totalizing' and thus incorporates the whole
history of philosophy in this description. Yet both Strauss and
Levinas are clearly motivated by animosity to the form and content of modern philosophy, especially modern political philosophy.[10] With the aim of renewing the 'theologico-political problem'
or 'ethics', each accentuates one pole of the opposition, *par excellence*, on which modern political philosophy has been based – the
opposition between nature and freedom. For it is this opposition
which they both seek to overthrow. If Strauss is *contra* nature;
Levinas is *contra* freedom: both are hostile to modernity's founding discourse of individual rights – of freedom conceived as natural
or human – but they are equally unsympathetic to the social
and political critics of individual rights, such as Hegel, Marx and
Weber.

Strauss contrasts the Greek concern to discover the good 'by
nature' in the classical sense with scriptural observance and commentary on the tradition, the writings received. He opposes philosophy as speech to Judaism as deed; philosophy as thought to
Judaism as action; philosophy as the quest for wisdom to Judaism
as observance and study; philosophy as the God of Aristotle to

[8] For Strauss, see 'An Introduction to Heideggerian Existentialism', in *The Rebirth of Classical Political Rationalism: An Introduction to the Thought of Leo Strauss*, ed. Thomas L. Pangle, Chicago, Chicago University Press, 1989, pp. 27–46. For Levinas, see 'Metaphysics Precedes Ontology' in *Totalité et infini: essai sur l'exteriorité*, 1961, The Hague, Martinus Nijhoff, 1980; trans. in *Totality and Infinity: An Essay on Exteriority*, Alphonso Lingis, The Hague, Martinus Nijhoff, 1979, pp. 42–8.

[9] For Strauss, see 'Thucydides: The Meaning of Political History' in *The Rebirth of Classical Political Rationalism*, p. 72. For Levinas, see 'Substitution' in *Otherwise than Being or Beyond Essence*, 1974, trans. Alphonso Lingis, The Hague, Martinus Nijhoff, 1981, pp. 99–129.

[10] For Strauss, see 'Progress or Return?' in *The Rebirth of Classical Political Rationalism*, pp. 227–70. For Levinas, see 'Truth and Justice' in *Totality and Infinity*, pp. 82–101.

Judaism as the God of Abraham, Isaac and Jacob – the unmoved mover to the zealous God. To philosophy, the beginning of wisdom is wonder; to Judaism, the beginning of wisdom is fear of the Lord. Philosophy predicts, Judaism promises.[11]

Yet by shifting the focus from the general characteristics, where philosophy is Aristotelian and Judaism scriptural, to the *agon* of Socrates and the Prophets, the still Aristotelian premise that 'man is a political animal' yields a sustainable *tertium comparationis*: 'the society-founding, *state-founding* meaning of Revelation'.[12] From this perspective, both Socrates and the Prophets labour for human perfection; and their mission is to proclaim or teach the law which would achieve it. The abstract differences between philosophy and Judaism – Athens and Jerusalem – now communicate in specific differences to this mutually intelligible goal: Socrates' divine mission concerns human nature; the Prophets' divine mission concerns human conduct; human 'nature' restricts human possibilities; human conduct is 'plastic'. Socrates seeks the best political order; the Prophets predict the Messianic age. For Socrates, the perfectly just man is the philosopher, the lover of wisdom; for the Prophets, the perfectly just man is the faithful servant of the Lord. Socrates addresses individuals; the Prophets address a people. The philosopher quests for knowledge of the good; the Prophet relays what is shown by God himself.[13] Elsewhere Strauss argues that while both the Bible and Greek philosophy concur in their ultimate concern with the divine law, they demur regarding 'what completes morality'. For the Bible completion occurs in the desert and in humility, for the Greeks completion occurs in the city and with nobility.[14] While, according to Strauss, classical philosophy is distinct from Greek political life as truth is distinct from opinion, he fails to distinguish the Bible from the political life of the biblical Hebrews – the Bible as the portable fatherland, as the political memory and aspiration of an exiled people.

Levinas contrasts *knowledge*, intentional or apprehensive, with

[11] Strauss, 'Jerusalem and Athens: Some Preliminary Reflections', 1967, in *Studies in Platonic Political Philosophy*, ed. Thomas L. Pangle, Chicago, Chicago University Press, 1983, pp. 147–73.
[12] Strauss, *Philosophy and Law: Essays Toward the Understanding of Maimonides and His Predecessors*, 1935, trans. Fred Baumann, Philadelphia, Jewish Publication Society, 1987, p. 52.
[13] Strauss, 'Jerusalem and Athens', pp. 171–2.
[14] 'Progress or Return?' pp. 248–51.

responsibility, and the face to face of commandment. His author-ship is explicitly divided between *philosophical* expositions of the overcoming of philosophy by ethics; and *lectures talmudiques*, where he demonstrates the form and content of Judaism by exegesis of and commentary on selected passages from tractates of the *Gemara*. Within the philosophical *œuvre*, ethics is presented as the emer-gent Other of philosophy. 'Totality', 'ontology', 'being', each designate an inclusive realm of the Same which is exceeded by the transcendence of the 'face to face'. This face to face is expressed as the *trace* of God which is discernible in the countenance of the neighbour; hence it is the *social*, not the *sacred* relation. The proximity of the stranger – near and far – reveals the exaltation and height of God and, equally, it reveals the command to ex-punge or assuage the humiliation and suffering of the Other. On the other hand, autonomy, ego, 'investiture' of freedom, be-long to the violence of self-reference, constituted by withdrawal from the face to face, withdrawal from radical openness to the Other, from the primordial command 'Thou shalt not kill'.[15] The Other is not the contrary of the same, not assimilable to the duality: same/other. The distinction between the Other 'beyond' being and the other 'of' being divided into categories or con-traries would seem to be transcendental in the original medieval sense. It is analogous to Heidegger's ontological difference between Being and beings, although Levinas reduces Heidegger's difference within what he designates as the 'order of being'.[16] Ethically, however, the Other is presented as the traumatizing incursion of commandment which results in the substitution of the self as hostage for the neighbour.[17]

In their attempts to find a way to voice commandment and commentary, these rediscoveries of Judaism at the end of the end of philosophy are *deeply* misleading: they misrepresent the ra-tionalism or knowledge against which they define themselves; they misrepresent Judaism; above all, they misrepresent the mo-dernity and the history in which they and Judaism are implicated: the 'nature' and the 'freedom' so cavalierly cashiered in both approaches.

[15] See Levinas, 'Ethics and Spirit', in *Difficult Freedom: Essays on Judaism*, trans. and ed. Seán Hand, London, The Athlone Press, 1990, pp. 3–10.
[16] *Otherwise than Being*, pp. 1–20.
[17] Ibid., pp. 99–129.

Strauss misrepresents Greek rationalism by presenting classical philosophy as if it were simply sceptical or silent regarding the Greek gods.[18] While he discusses the charge of impiety against Socrates and contrasts philosophy and poetry in their import for politics by considering Aristophanes' comic portrayal of Socrates in *Clouds*, he overlooks the connection between the birth and development of philosophy and earlier pre-Olympian Greek religion as presented in classical tragedy.[19] If philosophy begins in 'wonder', then it is a response not to what is 'wonderful' but to what is awe-ful; it begins, too, even if apotropaically, in fear and trembling.[20] Levinas misrepresents 'knowledge', assimilating the Cartesian or Kantian self-contained vessel of consciousness with Husserlian reduction (*epoche*) to intentionality, which was itself an attempt to replace Kantian reconstruction of epistemic possibility by description of meaning. Levinas thus avoids the struggle between universal and *aporia* from Kantian judgement to Hegelian speculative experience; and thus does not acknowledge the predicament of universal and local jurisprudence, which characterizes modern philosophy as much as modern Judaism.

Both Strauss and Levinas misrepresent Judaism. Talmudic argument rehearses a rationalism which constantly explores its own limits without fixing them. While, according to Rabbinic tradition, the Oral Law was revealed at Sinai together with the Written Law, this meant in effect that the early Rabbis, the Tannaim, the Amoraim and the Gaonim, renegotiated knowledge and responsibility under their historically and politically changing conditions. This tradition handed down and renewed by Halachic Judaism obscures its tremendous plasticity by apparent subservience to the original revelation of the Oral Law. Yet both Strauss and Levinas represent Judaism as unchanging and without a history, both as study – *Talmud Torah* – and as observance – the utopian, placeless and eternal, Jewish 'community'.

Under these static presuppositions, both thinkers are staked on opposition to modernity, evident in the defence of Platonic

---

[18] 'The Problem of Socrates: Five Lectures', n.d., in *The Rebirth of Classical Political Rationalism*, pp. 103–83.

[19] F. M. Cornford, *From Religion to Philosophy: A Study in the Origins of Western Speculation*, 1912, Brighton, Harvester, 1980.

[20] Jane Harrison, *Prolegomena to the Study of Greek Religion*, 1903, London, Merlin, 1980, pp. 1–31.

political philosophy by Strauss, the defence of ethics by Levinas; and evident in their opposition, in metaphysical terms, to nature and freedom, in virtual terms, to natural, human and civil rights and the modern state – from the liberal, constitutional state to the Fascist and Stalinist state. In both cases, adversion to the baleful political alternations of modern history lead to a principled dismissal of historical consideration as such.[21] As a result, both represent Judaism or the Jewish community eschatologically as irenic and sequestered – beyond rationalism, violence, the history of the world.

I discern and propose a different *tertium quid*: that the relation between philosophy and Judaism be explored neither in terms which presuppose self-identity nor in terms of mutual opposition but in terms of their evident loss of self-identity – when they are cast into crisis, chronic and acute; when they are exposed at their deepest difficulty.

Modern philosophy is most uncertain about itself in that aspect where it is taken to be most certain about its premises: finitude, secularity, man. For at its heart, lies an equivocation about each of these meanings: mortality, the *saeculum*, and the measure of man. In their modern, Copernican transposition, these categories still evince their abandoned contraries: the infinite, the kingdom, God. The resulting equivocations may be traced to the ambiguous place of Revelation in post-Kantian philosophy. Modern Judaism is most uncertain about itself in that aspect where it is taken to be most certain: concerning the relation between ethics and Halacha. Halacha refers to the legal passages of the Talmud, distinguished from *aggada*, the non-legal passages, or 'Law and Lore'.

The reinsinuation of revelation into philosophy by Hegel and by Kierkegaard keeps open and undecided the question of the historical realization of justice, for the good is not yet accomplished, but it ensures that eschatology *becomes politics* because it puts human interaction at stake in the realization of justice and the good. This resulting combination of uncertainty and systematics or dogmatics has been resolutely cast aside by generations of Hegel and Kierkegaard reception which accuse Hegel of panlogism, or, most recently, of 'totalizing', in deference to

[21] For Strauss, see 'Relativism' in *The Rebirth of Classical Political Rationalism*, pp. 13–26. For Levinas, see his essay on Franz Rosenzweig, 'Between Two Worlds', in *Difficult Freedom*, pp. 198–201.

Levinas' opposition of infinity to 'totality'. The closed Hegelian system is then opposed to Kierkegaardian existential faith. The opposition of system to faith which omits the shared intrigue of revelation and justice indicates that Hegel and Kierkegaard have been read aesthetically and subjectively, without the drama of the *Phenomenology* or the pseudonyms. Deleuze, for example, discovers the basis for *ontology* of repetition in Kierkegaard's thought.[22]

In opposition to Kant's, *Religion within the Limits of Reason alone*[23] and to Fichte's, *Attempt at a Critique of all Revelation*,[24] where reason is purified of revelation and becomes dualistic, the thought of Hegel and of Kierkegaard reintroduce revelation in tension with realization. Hegel's 'speculative Good Friday' and Kierkegaard's 'scandal' act as the third which unsettle the dualisms of philosophy and make it possible to reconstruct the modern political history of unfreedom – above all, the inversions of morality and legality, autonomy and heteronomy.

The ambiguity of Nietzsche's thinking on reason and Revelation is a major cause of the reductive reception of his predecessors. When Nietzsche is read as simultaneously proclaiming the redundancy of all transcendent and ethical values and reinsinuating a cosmology of repetition, then this enthrones *unhealthy* scepticism towards all human, social and political values, assimilates all signification to a general sociology of total control, and then yearns for the raptus of a Singularity which cannot be named, known, or negotiated.[25] Recent philosophy offers us this vacuous revelation which is 'transgressive' of universality, yet which offers neither law nor grace – its theoretical antinomianism matched by its practical anarchism.

Modern Judaism is most uncertain about itself in that aspect where it is taken to be most certain: concerning the relation

---

[22] Gilles Deleuze, *Différence et Répétition*, 1968, Paris, Presses Universitaires de France, 1972, pp. 12–41.

[23] *Die Religion innerhalb der Grenzen der blossen Vernunft*, 1793, trans. *Religion within the Limits of Reason Alone*, Theodore M. Greene and Hoyt H. Hudson, New York, Harper and Row, 1960.

[24] *Versuch einer Kritik aller Offenbarung*, 1792, trans. *Attempt at a Critique of all Revelation*, Garrett Green, Cambridge, Cambridge University Press, 1978.

[25] For example, Georges Bataille's reading of Nietzsche has been taken in this sense, see *The Accursed Share*, vol. III, trans. Robert Hurley, New York, Zone Books, 1991, pp. 365–410.

between ethics and Halacha. Levinas gives priority *not* to the relation between ethics and Halacha, 'but rather [to] the passage
from the non-ethical in general to the ethical', arguing that the
latter 'is truly the necessity of our time',[26] when all authority and
morality is called into question. However, reflection on the relation
between ethics and Halacha, which otherwise preoccupies Jewish
thinkers, reveals the connection between Jewish and non-Jewish
modernity in their equal difficulty in conceiving law and ethics.
To focus on these disputes concerning ethics and Halacha is to
reveal the general dilemma of legitimizing authority, which is
evaded by Levinas' turn to the apparently more general issue of
justifying morality as such. Representations of Judaism gleaned
from Rosenzweig, Buber or Levinas but eschewing its modern
internal contestation, have encouraged that recent philosophical
imagination which idealizes Judaism as a perfect jurisprudence, a
holy sociology, and which post-modernity would adopt to complete its nihilism.[27]

The opposed formulations of the relation between ethics and
Halacha at stake in the dispute between orthodox and conser-
vative (reform) Judaism partake in the general difficulty of relat-
ing law and ethics, which is common to Judaic and non-Judaic
modernity. Aharon Lichtenstein, who represents orthodoxy, asks
'Does Jewish Tradition Recognize an Ethic Independent of
Halacha?'[28] while Eugene Borowitz, who represents conservative
Judaism, inquires into 'The Authority of the Ethical Impulse in
"Halacha" '.[29] Lichtenstein appears to question the legitimation of

---

[26] 'Ideology and Idealism', 1975, in *The Levinas Reader*, trans. and ed. Séan Hand Oxford,
Blackwell, 1989, p. 236.
[27] Consider Jean-François Lyotard's relating of Buber's presentations of Hassidic Judaism
to Levinas' Halachic readings in *The Differend: Phrases in Dispute*, 1983 (trans. George Van
Den Abbeele, Manchester, Manchester University Press, 1988). Lyotard, in *Heidegger and
'the jews'*, 1988 (trans. Andreas Michel and Mark S. Roberts, Minneapolis, University of
Minnesota Press, 1990) and Julia Kristeva, in *Powers of Horror: An Essay on Abjection*, 1980
(trans. Leon S. Roudiez, New York, Columbia University Press, 1982) argue, respectively, that Judaism has a special metaphysical or psychological insight into reality which
may account for anti-semitism.
[28] 1975, reprinted in Marvin Fox (ed.) *Modern Jewish Ethics: Theory and Practice*, Columbus,
Ohio University Press, 1975, pp. 102–23.
[29] 1981, in Norbert M. Samuelson (ed.), *Studies in Jewish Philosophy: Collected Essays of the
Academy for Jewish Philosophy, 1980–1985*, Lanham, University Press of America, 1987,
pp. 489–505.

Halacha *qua* traditional authority, while Borowitz questions the legitimation of Halacha *qua* legal-rational authority. Lichtenstein asks whether Halacha is *equitable* by inquiry into the status of *equity* within Halacha, while Borowitz asks whether Halacha is *egalitarian* by inquiring into the *flexibility* of Halacha. Yet it is Lichtenstein who demonstrates the flexibility of Halacha while Borowitz demands that ethics be as categorical (unconditioned) as Halacha, not a secondary kind of imperative, in 'its own way', which he attributes to Lichtenstein. Lichtenstein proceeds by delineating the range of *lifnim mishurat hadin*, 'beyond the line of the law', a tradition which allows that the law may need ethical supplementation. By contrast with a formal, categorical and fixed ethic, *lifnim mishurat hadin* is a 'situational' or contextual morality, which balances universal and local factors in any specific case, instead of assimilating them to a category with strict deduction of judgement. On the other hand, it is Borowitz who argues that this supralegality is insecurely grounded, and tends to eliminate ethical supplementation in practice. Instead of proposing to render both ethics *and* law more flexible, or questioning the conditions which drive them apart and rigidify them, Borowitz attempts to import the categorical Kantian ethic back into Judaism, with its qualities of absoluteness, unconditionality, formality and imperativeness – which he deplores in the law itself, and to which Lichtenstein does not adhere.

This discovery that orthodox formulations of the relation between ethics and Halacha stress flexibility, while conservative or reform formulations stress indubitability, remains paradoxical until its unexamined precondition is exposed: the diremption between the moral discourse of rights and the systematic actualities of power in modern states and societies, which reappears in modern philosophical reflection as the opposition between morality and legality or between ethics and law. The effective opposition between the discourse of rights and the actualities of power is explored by classical sociology: the inversion of intended ethical meaning in its social institutionalization, what Max Weber called the 'unintended consequences' of social action. The idea of Halachic contestation has recently found favour with general philosophy because it does not posit an end to law within or beyond history, and does not resolve or aim to resolve law and ethics. This interest on the part

of philosophy utterly overlooks the dispute within Judaism over
law and ethics. Both this persistent overlooking and the continuing dispute arise from the modern predicament of rights and power
which is not addressed by the parties to the dispute, nor by their
selective philosophical idealizers. Judaism and philosophy idealize
the *potentialities* of each other and fail to locate their own uncer-
tainties and fate in the *actual* discordances of modern political and
intellectual life. This rediscovery of Judaism at the end of the end
of philosophy can be witnessed therefore as a convergent aspiration *without a third – tertium quid* – on which to converge.

This converging in turn has unintended political and philosophical consequences: the interest in Halacha as substantial not
formal law and as infinitely disputable destroys what it would
propagate. For the project of idealizing a living law is contradictory: it involves abstracting its substance and this must turn
it into procedure. Furthermore, the meaning of law and ethics is
not determined by what is posited or intended, or even how it
is posited, but by how positive meaning is *configured* within the
prevailing modern diremption of morality and legality, autonomy
and heteronomy, civil society and the state. Otherwise an idealized Judaic ethic will inevitably become as discredited as any other:
made into procedure and set within the prevailing diremption, its
meaning will be inverted in the social and political fate which it
already attests.

The division of labour between modern philosophy and social
theory itself displays their infection with the diremption between
ethics and law. This diremption afflicts our most urgent orientation: to comprehend the relation between the Holocaust and
modernity. Emil Fackenheim and Zygmunt Bauman attempt to
develop, respectively, a theology and a sociology of modernity
and the Holocaust. Fackenheim's Holocaust 'philosophy' argues
for the *uniqueness* of the Holocaust;[30] Bauman's Holocaust sociology argues for its *normality* – its continuity with the main features of bureaucratic, technocratic rationalization, shored up by
the scientism of sociological reflection.[31] Fackenheim refuses
knowledge as such, while Bauman claims too much monocausal

---

[30] Emil Fackenheim, 'The Holocaust and philosophy', *Journal of Philosophy*, LXXXII, 10 (1985), pp. 506–14.
[31] Zygmunt Bauman, *Modernity and the Holocaust*, Oxford, Polity Press, 1989.

knowledge. In spite of this diametrical divergence in diagnosis and method, both Fackenheim and Bauman indict all previous apprehension for being implicated in what made the Holocaust possible, and both call for redress by means of a pre-social morality: Bauman, drawing on Levinas, calls for responsibility for the Other 'beyond' socialization; Fackenheim issues a new commandment – the 614th – to the Jews. This new commandment forbids Jews to grant Hitler yet another, posthumous victory by either falling into despair over Auschwitz, or, equally, by forgetting it.[32]

Because both Fackenheim and Bauman judge that the tradition, philosophical or sociological, represents complete implication in total domination, they both fail to explore the inversion of meaning into contrary institutions – the predicament of ethics and law – even though it was first explored by Hegel and Weber, the main reduced, discredited and plundered intellectual presence in each, respectively. With sublime consistency, they both issue – without irony or humour – a new commandment or moral imperative. In the hubris of their equally severe transcendence, each reproduces the clash of unthought actualities which configure the modernity they seek to transform.

Reflection on the question whether there is a Jewish philosophy leads either to post-modern scepticism completed by a phantasized Judaism, or to these earnest prophets completed by an imperative Judaism. Reflection uncovers the suppressed equivocations at stake in the self-identity of Judaism, philosophy and sociology. This is not to refer to a chronic 'crisis' in modernity or its apprehension but to systematic diremption in the structure of modern ethics and law which conditions equally its academic interrogation.

Is there a Jewish Philosophy? I hope that by now you *no longer know* the answer to this question. Against the scandal and confusion of the convergence between philosophy and Judaism is here discerned the diremption of law and ethics it attests. Diremption between the moral discourse of rights and the actualities of power is reproduced in the intellectual division of labour and in the recent attempts to overcome this division. These overcomings, from Strauss to Bauman, in their haste for normative renewal, proceed

---

[32] 'The 614th Commandment', in *The Jewish Return into History: Reflections in the Age of Auschwitz and a New Jerusalem*, New York, Schocken, 1978, pp. 19–24.

without recognition of their continuing and further implication in the predicament of modernity they would conjure away. I therefore have not given an answer to the question but have tried to open a reflection on the divergences and convergences at stake. Is *this* a Jewish philosophy? If it is, it offers no consolation of philosophy, even less the soteriology of theology, but only *ein neues Unbehagen* – a new discomfort in our culture.

3

Ethics and *Halacha*

In Jerusalem, July 1988, Emil Fackenheim convened the first 'Continuing Workshop on University Teaching of Jewish Philosophy'. Entitled 'From Modernity to Contemporaneity', the general aim was to discuss the relation between political modernity and the Holocaust. The second substantive in the title of the workshop mobilizes not the now normal but sacralizing holophrasis 'holocaust' but the idea of *contemporaneity* in order to reassess political philosophy and philosophical methodology on the basis of Fackenheim's view of the Holocaust as actually and imperatively definitive of intellectual and political life – non-Jewish and Jewish. In the original rationale for the workshop which was circulated to the prospective participants, the difficulties besetting such reassessment were linked to the mutual ignorance between general philosophy and modern Jewish thought. The opening session of the proceedings, which were to continue for ten days, took the form of a staged confrontation between Aharon Lichtenstein, the eminent Halachist and philosopher, and the present author, who had been chosen, it was conveyed to me, as a scholar and philosopher 'outside Halacha'. I was asked to respond to Lichtenstein's famous article on ethics and Halacha, on which Lichtenstein himself elaborated and expanded in his lengthy opening address. However, once on the platform, with Lichtenstein, representative of the ancient Yeshiva world, to my left and with Fackenheim, representative of the modern philosophical

Halacha refers to the legal passages of the Talmud distinguished from *aggada*, the non-legal passages.

academy to my right, I took it that my hidden but implied brief was to work my way through all the structuring and successive discontinuities which had called the thirty-five participants from all over the world to Jerusalem.

The issues raised in the question of whether there is an ethics 'beyond Halacha' has been broached in two fundamentally different forms: 'Does Jewish Tradition Recognize an Ethic Independent of Halacha?' which is the title of the now famous original article by Lichtenstein;[1] and 'The Authority of the Ethical Impulse in "Halacha"' by Eugene Borowitz which is partly a reply to Lichtenstein.[2] The differences between the formulation of the initial question posed from *within* Judaim reflects, I shall argue, the breakdown of ethics *outside* Judaism. Therefore I propose an inversion: there may be law beyond Halacha and only then 'an ethics'. The argument – to which I devote the elaboration it requires elsewhere[3] – will be sketched here in four stages. First, the breakdown of ethics in the modern state and the conceiving of law in modern philosophy will be outlined. In the second and third place, the two formulations of the question will be compared and contrasted: the question of tradition and the question of authority – the types of question as well as their content will be foregrounded. Finally, the meaning of the proposition that there may be law beyond Halacha and only then an ethics should emerge in a way which is no longer perplexing.

The development of the modern state has led to the breakdown of ethics and the conceiving of law generally. If we view modernity in the light of contemporaneity, using 'contemporaneity' as Fackenheim proposes, to mean the Holocaust and its aftermath, natural law has been replaced by natural rights, just as civil society is separated from the state. 'Natural' and 'human' rights do not protect their bearers but leave them vulnerable to the dictates of the state.[4] If we view contemporaneity in the light of modernity,

---

[1] Op. cit., repr. in Marvin Fox (ed.) *Modern Jewish Ethics: Theory and Practice*, Columbus, Ohio University Press, 1975, pp. 102–23.

[2] Op. cit., 1981, in Norbert M. Samuelson (ed.) *Studies in Jewish Philosophy: Collected Essays of the Academy for Jewish Philosophy, 1980–1985*, Lanham, University Press of America, 1987, pp. 489–505.

[3] Gillian Rose, *Dialectic of Nihilism: Post-Structuralism and Law*, Oxford, Blackwell, 1984; and *The Broken Middle: Out of Our Ancient Society*, Oxford, Blackwell, 1992.

[4] See Hannah Arendt, *The Origins of Totalitarianism*, 1951, New York, Harcourt Brace Jovanovich, 1973.

modern philosophy has been superseded by social theory. This conceptual split leaves both philosophy and social theory without intellectual initiative precisely because it separates ethics from the conceiving of law. The political and intellectual predicament outlined here characterizes the non-Judaic situation as much as the Judaic. Therefore the implicit assumption of the initial question that Judaism is concerned with law (Halacha), while general philosophy is concerned with ethics, is unsustainable.

This double thesis needs developing. First, I offer a brief excursus on the conceiving of law since Kant. In his practical philosophy, Kant separated 'morality' from 'legality', so that morality is the realm of autonomy, legality the realm of heteronomy. The will is autonomous or moral when it is utterly disinterested and obeys the law out of sheer reverence for it; it is heteronomous or legal when it obeys the law out of interested motives, such as fear of punishment or hope of reward, whether material or spiritual. 'Morality' belongs to the law of freedom; 'legality' to the laws of necessity. *Law* in Kant is split demonstrably in these two ways into four meanings: morality/legality; necessity/freedom. These antinomies in the conceiving of law in Kant may be said – quite simply but dramatically – to have led to the breakdown of philosophy and the development of social theory.

In philosophy, Hegel's phenomenological philosophy of history shows how Kant's categorical, unconditioned split between morality and legality is conditioned. Kant's opposition presupposes the modern state which itself separates inner morality from the development of ethical life so that greater moral or subjective freedom invariably develops together with less objective or ethical freedom. In classic sociological theory, Max Weber demonstrates that the increase in individual rights in modern societies may be accompanied by an increase – not a decrease – in domination. In his great work, *Economy and Society* (1922), Weber distinguishes between types of domination as modes of authority to which social action is typically and meaningfully oriented as long as their legitimacy is maintained or routinized. The three main types of authority, traditional, charismatic, and legal-rational, are analytically distinct but always co-present to a greater or lesser degree. Modern bureaucracy, the main exemplar of legal-rational authority, with its inherent tendency to rationalization, separates instrumental means from the evaluation of substantive goals and, increasingly, inhibits any fresh formulation of ethical and political ends. Durkheim, in his main works, *The Division of Labour in Society* (1893) and *Suicide* (1895), attributes the breakdown of social, that is, ethical, cohesion in societies based on contract and administrative law to what he calls *anomie: a-nomos*, without a law – a condition from which he judged, on the basis of statistics, that Jewish communities were exempt.[5]

Now Steven Schwarzschild has argued in more than one place[6] that the priority of practical reason in post-Kantian philosophy demonstrates that Judaism is qualified to lead the way in the convergence of philosophy and Judaism on ethics. But, as the argument here seeks to establish, it is Kant's emphasis on the priority of practical reason or subjective freedom which has itself *undermined* ethics. There is a *disjunction* between the moral discourse of rights and the systematic actualites of power in the modern state and in modern society which gives rise to the separation of philosophy and social theory, and this is both overlooked and presupposed in Schwarzschild's argument. Even within sociology, the disjunction is evident and perpetuated in the spectrum of competing approaches to the conceiving of law and the reinsinuating of ethics into science: from 'law' defined normatively as 'sanction', to 'law' defined ideal-typically as meaningful orientation.

My argument is therefore that the relation of law and ethics is as problematic 'outside' Judaism as it is within it. As this short excursus has, I hope, begun to argue, outside Judaism, the disjunction of law and ethics arises from the modern idea of freedom, inherited by sociological reason from philosophy. This modern idea of 'freedom', according to which man belongs to freedom: freedom does not belong to man[7] (that is, human potentiality is

[5] Max Weber, *Economy and Society: An Outline of Interpretative Sociology*, 1922, 2 vols, ed. Guenther Roth and Claus Wittich, Berkeley, University of California Press, 1978. Émile Durkheim, *The Division of Labour in Society*, 1893, trans. Goerge Simpson, New York, The Free Press, 1964. Émile Durkheim, *Suicide: A Study in Sociology*, 1895, trans. J. A. Spaulding and G. Simpson, London, Routledge and Kegan Paul, 1952, p. 160.
[6] 'Authority and Reason Contra Gadamer' 1981, in Samuelson (ed.), *Studies in Jewish Philosophy*, pp. 161–90; 'Modern Jewish philosophy', in Arthur A. Cohen and Paul Mendes-Flohr (eds), *Contemporary Jewish Religious Thought*, New York, The Free Press, 1987, pp. 629–34.
[7] Martin Heidegger, *Schellings Abhandlung über das Wesen der Menschlichen Freiheit [1809]*, 1936, trans. *Schelling's Treatise on the Essence of Human Freedom* Joan Stambaugh, Athens, Ohio, Ohio University Press, 1985, p. 9.

discerned within the actuality of freedom – which is what Hegel meant by 'the rational is the real and the real is the rational') is different from the traditional inquiry into free will versus determinism, where freedom is an attribute or capacity of the will.

However, it will be objected that neither the subjective nor the holistic notion of modern freedom are relevant to Rabbinic and Halachic Judaism. Yet, I would argue that the major statements of Judaic modernity from Samson Raphael Hirsch's *The Nineteen Letters on Judaism* (1836), the founding work of cultural neo-orthodoxy, to Joseph Solveitchik's *Halachic Man* (1944), the philosophical presentation of the Lithuanian *mitnaggid* idea of Halacha – the former work profoundly neo-Hegelian, the latter, a work of profound Cohenian neo-Kantianism – have struggled with, and, in both form and content, incorporated the modern problematic of freedom into their respective arguments for Halacha. These paradoxes are equally at work in the current debate over ethics and Halacha.

When Lichtenstein asks 'Does Jewish Tradition Recognize an Ethic Independent of Halacha?' while Borowitz questions 'The Authority of the Ethical Impulse in Halacha', two quintessentally different modes of address are at stake. Using Weber's distinctions, it appears that Lichenstein questions the ethical legitimation of Halacha *qua* traditional authority, while Borowitz questions the ethical legitimation of Halacha *qua* legal-rational authority. Prima facie, Lichtenstein asks whether Halacha is *equitable* by inquiring into the *status* of equity within Halacha, while Borowitz asks whether Halacha is *egalitarian* by inquiring into the *flexibility* of Halacha. Lichtenstein focuses on the ethical potential *within* Halacha, while Borowitz focuses on the ethical potential *of* Halacha. Yet, paradoxically, it will be Lichtenstein who demonstrates the flexibility of Halacha, while it will be Borowitz who demands that ethics be as 'categorical', or unconditional and unconditioned, as Halacha, and not a secondary kind of imperative 'in its own way' which is the argument he attributes to Lichtenstein; and it is Borowitz who inquires into the *status* of women.

Conversely, it is the appeal of Halachic contestation which does not posit an end to law, within or beyond history, which is not categorical or unconditioned, that increasingly attracts the attention of general philosophy, not an idea of Judaism which would treat ethics as categorically as Halacha. General philosophy, under the influence of 'reflective' judgement from Kant's third *Critique*, and not practical judgement from the second *Critique*, picks up an idea of Halacha which does not resolve the relation of law and ethics but leaves it precisely fractured or open. Reformed Jewish thinking, on the other hand, aspires towards a Kantian ethic which is itself unstable and unresolved in its relation to law. Each idealizes the potentialities of the other, and fails to locate its own fate in the disjunction between the moral discourse of rights and the systematic actualities of power in the modern state. As a result, we have become witnesses to a convergent aspiration which has no third on which to converge. In view of the ethical interest shown by general philosophy in Halacha, it makes just as much or just as little sense to ask if the idea of Halacha might found ethics, as it does to ask if there is an ethic independent of Halacha.

In the now famous article under discussion, Lichtenstein considers three preliminary definitions of ethics: *lex naturalis, derekh eretz*, natural morality. Although the Rabbis were opposed to natural law thinking, Lichtenstein concludes that all rationalizing of Halacha implicitly presupposes natural morality. The contemporary concern is whether Halacha, either *din*, specific statute, or the whole of Judaism as an ethical system, needs an additional ethical supplement. To avoid the simple equation of law with morality, which would imply that no instance of uncertainty, no question 'What ought I to do?' need arise, Lichtenstein proceeds to consider *lifnim mishurat hadin*. This means, literally, 'beyond the line of the law'. It was transformed by Nahmanides from implying the negative condemnatory judgement that destruction would befall those who, within the limits of Torah, failed to act 'beyond the line of the law', into the suprapositive counsel of perfection: 'Ye shall be holy' and act beyond the line, that is, beyond the strict demands of the law. This morality of aspiration is supralegal but not optional. Lichtenstein scours the traditional sources to highlight the range of connotations of this unique idea of 'supralegality', from an actionable obligation to supreme idealism. *Lifnim mishurat hadin* is gradually delineated as a situational or contextual morality. By contrast with a formal ethic which is categorical and fixed, *lifnim mishurat hadin* balances universal and local factors in any specific case instead of assimilating each case to the mean average of the category or class under which, strictly speaking, it falls. Overall, Lichtenstein defends Halacha as multiplanar and non-deductive. The penumbral regions of *mitzvot* or *din*, specific or strict statute, are continually complemented but not completed with *lifnim mishurat hadin*.

It is with the non-categorical status of this equitable element in Halacha that Borowitz takes issue. He argue that the supralegality of *lifnim mishurat hadin*, presented by Lichtenstein as 'imperative in its own way', amounts to no more than a vague species of command which is all of a piece with Judaism generally by managing to be both highly ethical as a whole, yet leaving the ethical qualified by underqualifying it. He agrees that there are varying levels of authority within Rabbinic Judaism but argues that the ethical impulse is so restricted or denied that it can provide no remedy for issues such as the status of women in Judaism. The muchvaunted flexibility of Halacha is sacrificed when such an issue arises, even though a solution is crucial to its continuing legitimation and future survival. The cumbersome resistance of Rabbinic Judaism proves its formal, outmoded reliance on human not divine authority, which it shares with all other fallible, social institutions.

Borowitz is right to raise the changing status and role of women as a crucial test for Halacha, according to which the category of 'woman' has always been explicit. But the remedy he proposes is bizarre: that ethics 'ought to come as a categorical or unmediated imperative', even though he has argued against Schwarzchild's Cohenian fusing of morality and legality and accuses contemporary Rabbinic Judaism both of excessive formality and of excessive tampering with the imperative quality of the Torah's ethical behests.[8] Instead of searching for a conception that would render both ethics *and* law more flexible, or questioning the conditions which drive them apart and rigidify them, Borowitz imports the Kantian categorical morality into Judaism; that same morality which has itself been fundamentally questioned by philosophical and political modernity, and which displays the qualities of absoluteness, unconditionality, formality and imperativeness, which he otherwise deplores in the idea of Halacha. To demand that the idea of Halacha be enlarged with an ethics which is imperative in an

---

[8] Borowitz, 'The Authority of the Ethical Impulse in "Halacha" ', pp. 495–503.

unquestionable sense is to coincide with the very mode of Halachic judgement rejected by Lichtenstein. Furthermore, Lichtenstein does not subordinate ethics to law as 'imperative in its own way': he sets out the universal and local jurisprudence at stake throughout the sources in a variety of carefully related expositions.

Yet I would continue this dispute by arguing that neither Lichtenstein (on substantial grounds) nor Borowitz (on formal grounds) will be able to remedy, say, the changing 'status' of women without confronting directly the modern problematic of freedom together with its conceptual and political antinomies.[9] Judaism, with its substantial writing of 'women' in the Talmudic tractates of the Third Division, *Nashim (Women)*, cannot dissemble its effective inequalities by employing apparently gender-neutral universals. This does, indeed, constitute a fundamental difference from the way in which general philosophy posits formal equality with the effect that substantial inequalities are veiled and perpetuated, and ethical life is construed in a way which must undermine its own promises.

However, once the Judaic approach is defended as, potentially, a more flexible basis for change, it becomes as formal as the position with which it is contrasted, whether the defence is mounted within Judaism or from general philosophy. For what determines the meaning of law and ethics is not what is posited, nor even how it is posited, by its jurisconsults, Rabbinic or philosophical, but how it is configured within the modern separation of state and civil society. This separation of politics from society reappears in the separation of philosophy and social theory with which both Judaic and general ethics are infected.

To avoid this repeated idealizing and discrediting of ethics within Judaism and between Judaism and general philosophy would involve recognizing the preconditions of these reversals in the political history which they attest. Otherwise this benighted century will end with the same stubborn and sentimental law and ethics from which it seeks to extricate itself. The *status Women* will continue to explode any surety it is made to provide on the way.

[9] See the largely negative conclusions of David Novak's study 'Is There a Concept of Individual Right in Jewish Law?', paper presented to the Jewish Law Association Biennial Conference, Paris, 15 July 1992.

4

'The Future of Auschwitz'

In order to capture and express a difficulty which had already emerged in our opening sessions, viz: Jonathan Webber's reference to the 'innocent' Dutch-Jewish child, symbol of hope; and Anthony Polonsky's relating of the antagonism of a Jewish group visiting Auschwitz to their Polish guide until he shared with them his animosity towards 'Germans': innocent Jew/guilty German; blithe child/malevolent adult – I prefaced my remarks with a 'gnostic' poem:

> I am abused and I abuse
> I am the victim and I am the perpetrator
> I am innocent and I am innocent
> I am guilty and I am guilty

This essay was originally a presentation for the Symposium of Jewish Intellectuals on 'The Future of Auschwitz', which took place in Oxford, 6–8 May 1990. This symposium was initiated by the Polish Commission for the Future of Auschwitz, which had been recently established to take over the control and administration of the site and museum of Auschwitz-Birkenau from the Soviet Union for the first time since the end of the Second World War. It was also an unprecedented decision to invite Jewish participation on an individual basis rather than to invite representatives of Jewish organizations (a few of whom were also in attendance). A second meeting of the Symposium took place in Poland, Krakow and Auschwitz, April 1992. The title of the Symposium and the continuing collaboration owe everything to the pioneering work of the Oxford anthropologist Jonathan Webber, who is extending his 'Holocaust anthropology' to the traces of Jewish life throughout Galicia, Poland. See Jonathan Webber, *The Future of Auschwitz: Some Personal Reflections*, The First Frank Green Lecture, Oxford, Oxford Centre for Postgraduate Hebrew Studies, 1992, pp. 1–30.

To be not only abused and abusing, victim and perpetrator, but 'innocent' in both positions and 'guilty' in both positions yields the *agon* of these four lines – altogether, they imply complicity in tension with any individual or even collective intention – a tension between intention and complicity which might cast light on the traditional opposition between 'faith' and 'knowledge'.

In the second part of the film of Simon Wiesenthal's life, there is a character who does not know if he is a Nazi or a Jew. In Christa Wolf's novel, *A Model Childhood*, we follow a child in the Third Reich, daughter of a 'normal' Nazi family, and share her enthusiasm, fear, energy and perplexity – the verisimilitude of the account intensified by the pain of the recollecting, representing, expiating, narrative voice.[1]

These 'aesthetic' explorations of implication need to be developed and completed by critical reflection. Philosophical reflection and sociological analysis return us, however, to aesthetic questions, questions of representation. For a macabre predicament is ineluctable at Auschwitz as it stands today: former 'site' of mass murder, with lawns where there was mud; well-pointed and well-joined barracks where there were living skeletons; exhibition 'pavilions' where there were Blocks.

However, the intellectual division of labour has, so far, only reproduced an antinomy: Emil Fackenheim's Holocaust philosophy argues for the uniqueness of the event, while Zygment Bauman's Holocaust sociology, developed in his recently published *Modernity and the Holocaust*, much cited and recommended during our proceedings, argues for its normality – its continuity with the main features of bureaucratic, technocratic rationalization, shored up by the scientism of sociological methodology.[2] In spite of this antinomy between philosophy and sociology on the uniqueness and normality of the Holocaust, both positions issue in a call – for a new morality or for a new ethical life.

Utterly lacking in irony, yet indicting all previous apprehension for being implicated in what made the Holocaust possible, this

---

[1] *Kindheitsmuster*, 1979, trans. *A Model Childhood*, Ursule Molinaro and Hedwig Rappolt, London, Virago, 1983.

[2] Zygmunt Bauman, *Modernity and the Holocaust*, Oxford, Polity Press, 1989; Emil Fackenheim, *To Mend the World: Foundations of Future Jewish Thought*, New York, Schocken, 1982.

intellectual division of labour between philosophy and sociology is unable to think the origin of its own diremption, and unable to think a far more dangerous thought: that it is 'morality' itself which has corrupted and which continues to corrupt us.

A brief reflection on 'innocence and modernity', as a prelude to a reflection on 'authoritarianism and morality' would indicate the lines along which this would need to be developed. To Plato, doing wrong could only occur if one lacked knowledge of what was right – one could not wittingly intend wrong; to Aristotle, it was possible to intend and act rightly but unwittingly to incur wrong – a dilemma, but not one of malicious foresight. To modernity, this dilemma of contingency acquires a systemic twist: for, it is possible to mean well, to be caring and kind, loving one's neighbour as oneself, yet to be complicit in the corruption and violence of social institutions. Furthermore, this predicament may not correspond to, and may not be represented by, *any available politics or knowledge.*

The exposition of good intentions imbedded in unknowable preconditions and consequences which this implies would not pursue the theme that modernity made the Holocaust possible because its prevalent socialization – bureaucratic, technological, instrumentally-rational – robs us of moral autonomy and responsibility. Nor would it endorse Levinas' eminence of responsibility 'beyond knowledge'. Instead, it would seek to call attention to a far more difficult thought: that it is the very opposition between morality and legality – between inner, autonomous 'conscience', and outer, heteronomous institutions – that depraves us. Simultaneous possession of inner freedom and outer unfreedom means that the border where cognitive activity and normative passivity become cognitive passivity and normative activity is changeable and obscure. There is a diremption in our agency and in our institutions, which any call to post-natural ethics (Levinas, Fackenheim or Bauman) will reinforce in its imaginary transcendence.

To provoke a child or an adult who visits the 'site' of Auschwitz not only to identify herself in infinite pain with 'the victims', but to engage in intense self-questioning: 'Could *I* have done this?', would be to reinforce the same conscience-stricken *Innerlichkeit* that counts for one half of this diremption in our socialization. Exhibitions at Auschwitz, which are at present divided, lamentably and apparently unnegotiably, into 'national' pavilions, might instead initiate discussion 'How easily could we have allowed this to be carried out?' Are we Germans 'or' German-Jews, French 'or' French Jews, Polish professionals 'or' Polish Jews 'or' Polish peasants? This might contribute to a change in awareness and a questioning of our sentimentality as modern citizens, protected in all 'innocence' by the military might of the modern state. For, in modern dirempted polities, it is the relation between different oppositions – innocence and might, authority and force – between the inner and outer boundaries of our self-identity and lack of self-identity that turns us into strangers to ourselves as moral agents and as social actors.

James Young assured me that no museum curator could permit such a radical questioning of the visitor's identity and agency.[3] This imputed refusal may indicate the necessary rather than contingent reasons for the unavailability of knowledge or politics to explore our implication in the inversion of intentions and institutions. Unless this 'necessity' is confronted, our good intentions will continue to engender new pieties and leave untouched our fundamental – even cherished – complicities.[4]

[3] James E. Young, participant in the Symposium, specialist in Holocaust Monuments and Museums, author of *Writing and Rewriting the Holocaust: Narrative and the Consequences of Interpretation*, 1988, Bloomington, Indiana University Press, 1990.
[4] Compare Berel Lang, *Act and Idea in the Nazi Genocide*, Chicago, Chicago University Press, 1990.

5

Shadow of Spirit

Post-modernism, theological and a/theological, however 'framed' or 'reframed' – whether as ecstasy or as eschatology – is a *trahison des clercs*. For the current sceptical reception of religion is analogous to the former critical reduction of religion: it repeats a historical and political diremption which it refuses to think.

The current sceptical reception of religion, as expressed in the portentous title and subtitle of the original conference out of which this paper grew ('Shadow of Spirit – Contemporary Western Thought and its Religious Subtexts'[1]), has its roots in the erstwhile critical reduction of 'religion'. In both cases the object 'religion' is given as a positivity. To the critical reduction, positive religion is given; to the sceptical reception, positive religions. In effect, the critical reduction knows and posits its *reductee* – 'religion'; while the sceptical reception, although it has renounced knowledge, nevertheless posits integral objects – 'religions'. Criticism, *Kritik*, was quasi-transcendental in its inquiry into the preconditions or possibility of its object, but it was restricted to independently specifiable conditions, and did not address the formation of the object; and it was, of course, negative and destructive. It did not produce a *speculative* exposition of the historical separation of the institutions of Caesar from the institutions of

---

[1] Paper first presented at the conference of the same title, held at King's College, Cambridge, July 1990, and first published under the title 'Diremption of Spirit' in Philippa Berry and Andrew Wernick (eds), *Shadow of Spirit – Post-modernism and Religion*, London, Routledge, 1993, pp. 45–56.

God, which would require neither a sociology nor a philosophy of religion, but an investigation into the changing relation between meaning and configuration, revelation and realization.

Since the original, lyrical title and its academic and expatiatory subtitle resonate with the ethos of post-modernity, they warrant an initial consideration. What do they give us to work with? First, the SHADOW: the shadow of spirit – not the substance, even less the light or, more significantly, the darkness. Second, what casts this shadow – this shadow OF SPIRIT: 'Spirit' is to remain weightless, without *gravitas*, where formerly we discovered the gravity of the material base. Third, RELIGIOUS subtexts takes religions as given, and moreover posit them not as substantives, but as epithets of subtextuality, not even of textuality, even less, actuality. Fourth, SUBtexts: 'sub', does this allude to secret or suppressed predominance – substance not shadow? This would be to reduce the apparently non-religious to a religious substructure. Fifth, subTEXTS: this ontology of the 'text' posits 'Contemporary Western Thought' as its superstructure. It characterizes textual Being as discursive, shying away from its potentiality and its actuality – pardon my metaphysics – from that out of which it arises and that which it effects.

O Shadowy Spirit – whereto your Substance?
O protean and ghoulish Subtext – what is your Text?
O multiple opacity – when is your Actuality?

The post-modern ontology of the text and ethos of the subtext claims that it is sceptical in its acceptance of the demotic plurality of discourses. Yet, I shall show that post-modern scepticism *completes itself as political theology*. The structure of this paradoxical reversal may be rendered explicit by comparing the way in which post-modern theology (Milbank), atheology (Taylor), post-theology (Cupitt) and rediscovered Judaism at the end of philosophy (Strauss, Levinas, Steiner) construe their relation to tradition.

Taylor's post-modern 'atheology' and Milbank's post-modern 'Beyond Secular Reason' offer Christian New Jerusalem for old Athens.[2] These authorships provide evidence of that prodigious, omniscient 'Western' intellectuality that would crown post-modern

[2] Mark C. Taylor, *Erring: A Post-modern A/theology*, Chicago, University of Chicago Press, 1984; John Milbank, *Theology and Social Theory: Beyond Secular Reason*, Oxford, Blackwell, 1990.

theology or atheology – 'queen of the sciences'. Each self-declaredly 'post-modern', their work is comprehensive while decrying comprehension: it disrespects and breaks down further the already lowered barriers between philosophy and literary criticism in the one case, between philosophy and social theory in the other, which are then gathered up and completed as post-modern atheology or theology. Thereby is vindicated an old prognostication: that if we fail to teach theology – we will usurp it. Or, to cite the words of John Henry Newman himself from 1852, in *The Idea of a University*: 'supposing Theology be not taught, its province will not simply be neglected, but will be actually usurped by other sciences'.[3]

In spite of their shared comprehensive scope and fervent ambition for post-modern atheology or theology – what do these two bodies of thought have in common? Nothing – where sources, style, tone and method are apparent. Working closely with Nietzsche and Derrida on that 'shifty [*sic*] middle ground *between* Hegel and Kierkegaard',[4] Taylor inserts Heidegger and recent French thought into the terrain; while Milbank's argument covers the development of secular politics to classic sociology from Malebranche to Durkheim and Weber, from Hegel and Marx to Catholic Liberation Theology, classical philosophy and medieval theology, all oriented, however, by recent French thought, as *trivium* to its ultimate ecclesiology. Stylistically, they are even more diverse: Taylor offers a montage of text and illustration, accruing grammatical, phonetic and graphological juxtapositions and complication, learned, it would seem, from *Finnegans Wake*; Milbank offers a treatise, four books in one, with sober, sustained argumentation, paced temporally and spatially from beginning to end. In tone, Taylor is masked, ironic, transgressive and extravagant; Milbank is straight, logical – in spite of his ontology of narration – severe, authoritative and original. Yet, we are explicitly offered, by the one, a deconstruction of theology; by the other, a deconstruction of classical and modern secularity; by the one, a deconstructive a/theology; by the other, 'Difference of Virtue, Virtue of Difference'.

In *Erring*, Taylor deconstructs 'Death of God', 'Disappearance

---

[3] John Henry Newman, *The Idea of a University*, ed. Martin J. Svaglic, Notre Dame, Indiana, University of Notre Dame Press, 1982, p. 74.
[4] Taylor, *Erring*, p. 99.

of Self', 'End of History', 'Closure of the Book', which are translated into deconstructive atheology in four paratactic 'moves':
'Writing of God', 'Markings', 'Mazing Grace', 'Erring Scripture',
to culminate in Dionysian 'joy in suffering'.[5] 'The "Yes" of an-
guished joy breaks the power of the law and fissures the "Notshall"
of history',[6] while 'The unending erring in scripture is the eternal
play of the divine milieu', for, in play, 'which is interplay', 'the
entire foundation of the economy of domination crumbles'.[7] In
Altarity, the 'middle ground *between* Hegel and Kierkegaard' is no
longer occupied by Nietzsche but by Heidegger and recent French
thinkers. Yet the whole is framed by Hegel as 'Conception' and
Kierkegaard as 'Transgression', titles of the opening and concluding chapters. Hegel is expounded as the identity of difference and
identity, Kierkegaard as the Abrahamic transgression of the ethical
from *Fear and Trembling*. Every other author is then locked into
this opposition between knowledge and faith which Taylor nevertheless knows Kierkegaard invented for his pseudonym, *de Silentio*.
No transgression occurs, for Abraham's arm is stayed by an angel,
but the work concludes by affirming the opposition between 'the
Law' and 'the Call of the Other', an erring in time, where *Erring*
offered a nomadicism in space.

In *Theology and Social Theory: Beyond Secular Reason,* Milbank
demonstrates, by a generic-archaeological reconstruction, that
'secular discourse' is constituted by its opposition to orthodox
Christianity as 'pagan' theology or anti-theology in disguise.[8] In
four 'sub-treatises' the complicity of secular reason with an
'ontology of violence' is rehearsed: first, in eighteenth-century
politics and political economy; second, in all nineteenth-century
sociology which is presented, including Weber, as a positivist
church; third, in Hegel and in Marx, whose impulse towards the
non-secular is 'indecently recruited' for secular science; this
equivocation evident to Milbank is itself, with indecent alacrity,
recruited to 'a gnostic plot about a historically necessary fall and reconstruction of being with a gain achieved through violence under-
gone'.[9] These two treatises conclude with attempts to terminate

[5] Ibid., p. 182.
[6] Ibid., p. 169.
[7] Ibid., p. 134.
[8] Milbank, op. cit., p. 3.
[9] Ibid., p. 4.

the dialogue between theology and sociology and between theology and liberation, respectively. Finally, at the threshold to the
last great treatise, Milbank disentangles his self-declared nihilistic
voice from his Greek-medieval voice to complete nihilism with
Christian *logos* and virtue which know 'no original violence'.[10]
Not the difference of nihilism nor the virtue of the Greeks, not
liberal, of course, but equally 'Against "Church and State"'[11] that
is, without natural rights and without natural law, 'transcendental
difference' is 'encoded' as a 'harmonic peace' beyond the circum-
scribing power of any totalizing reason.[12] Without violence or
arbitrariness, yet with difference, non-totalization and indeter-
minancy, without representation, the Augustinian 'Other City' is
'advocated' as 'the continuation of ecclesial practice', 'the imagination in action of a peaceful, reconciled social order, beyond even
the violence of legality'.[13] The active imagination of 'the *sociality*
of harmonious difference'[14] sketches the peaceful donation of 'the
heavenly city' where 'beyond the possibility of alteration' 'angels
and saints . . . abide in a fellowship [whose] virtue is not the virtue
of resistance and domination, but simply of remaining in a state
of self-forgetting conviviality'.[15] Between this heavenly city and
the sinful city founded on the murder of Abel of the *saeculum*, 'the
interval between the fall and final return of Christ',[16] God sends a
salvation city, the City of God, 'on pilgrimage through this world'
which does not exclude anyone but provides a genuine peace by
its memory of all the victims, its equal concern for all its citizens
and its self-exposed offering of reconciliation to enemies',[17] 'its
salvation . . . "liberation" from political, economic and psychic
dominium'.[18]

This explication of pilgrimage and inclusivity effectively destroys
the idea of a city: its inclusive appeal deprives the city of limit or
boundary that would mark it off from any other city with their
different laws; while its task of salvation deprives it of site: 'the

[10] Ibid., p. 5.
[11] Ibid., pp. 406f.
[12] Ibid., pp. 6, 5–6.
[13] Ibid., p. 6.
[14] Ibid., p. 5, emphasis in the original.
[15] Ibid., p. 391.
[16] Ibid., pp. 391–2.
[17] Ibid., p. 392.
[18] Ibid., p. 391.

city of God is a nomad city (one might say)'.[19] The features of gnostic, demiurgic soteriology in this messenger city, which are otherwise always indicted, and the precondition of violence in this 'peace coterminous with all Being whatsoever' may be decoded in this 'encoded narrative'.

Now the new Jerusalems have emerged: post-modern atheology as nomadic ecstasy – Dionysian joy; post-modern theology as nomadic ecclesial eschatology – harmonious peace; both breaking the frame in their antinomianism, and both reinstating the frame in their dependence on law transgressed – joy 'breaks the power of law',[20] or law subdued – peace 'beyond even the violence of legality',[21] Taylor with joy but without sociality; Milbank with sociality and glimpses of angelic conviviality; both converge on the acknowledgement of difference, but in so doing reinstate the *age-old* oppositions between law and grace, knowledge and faith, while apparently working *without* the *modern* duality of nature and freedom.

Replacing old Athens by New Jerusalem consigns the opposition between nature and freedom to one of any number of arbitrary, binary metaphysical conceits – instead of recognizing it as the index and indicator of the tension between freedom and unfreedom – and then proceeds to complete such 'deconstruction' in holiness. This founding and consecrating of holy cities inadvertently clarifies how that discarded opposition made possible the *critique* which is disqualified by its disappearance. Furthermore, those two Christian holy cities – Protestant (Taylor), Catholic (Milbank) – arise on the same antinomian and ahistorical foundations as the Davidic cities of Leo Strauss and Emmanuel Levinas.

These authorships – Strauss and Levinas – embrace the paradox in presenting Judaic theologico-political prophecy or ethics in *philosophical* terms as the *end of the end* of philosophy. There are, of course two proclaimed 'ends' to philosophy: the end of 'metaphysics' from Kant to Nietzsche and Heidegger which may well found a 'new thinking'; and the end of 'philosophy' from Hegel and Marx to Adorno which raises the question of the *realization* of philosophy. By *the end of* the end of philosophy, I mean the

---

[19] Ibid., p. 392.
[20] Taylor, *Erring*, p. 169.
[21] Milbank, *Theology and Social Theory*, p. 6.

discovery in the long debate between Judaism and philosophy – understood in relation to the Greek quest for the beginning, principles, causes – of the missing middle, the *tertium quid,* ethics, which finds itself always within the imperative, the commandment, and hence always already begun.

Strauss and Levinas present Judaism as solving the theological-political or the ethical problem *without* the opposition between nature and freedom: Strauss is *contra* nature; Levinas, *contra* freedom. Consequentially, both represent Judaism or Jewish history eschatologically: for Strauss, in *Philosophy and Law,* however, 'the prophet is the founder of the [ideal] Platonic state',[22] and while the 'era that believes in Revelation/is *fulfilled*' this is not because of the belief but because what is revealed is a 'divine Law/a simple binding Law/a Law with the power of right'.[23] For Levinas, while the face to face traumatically disturbs the presence of consciousness to itself, this awakening to responsibility for the Other occurs 'beyond being', understood as beyond rationalism, beyond violence – 'war' – in *Totality and Infinity,* beyond the history of the world.[24] In this Judaic Manichaeism Levinas has learned from Rosenzweig's *Star of Redemption,* where Judaism is presented liturgically as 'the holy community' in opposition to the Christian mission of world-imperium.[25]

These philosophical presentations of Judaism which have made Judaism accessible and available to rediscovery at the end of the end of philosophy (*die Ironie der Ironie,* since Judaism is the religion which has been historically denigrated as superseded), are, nevertheless *deeply* misleading. They misrepresent the rationalism or knowledge against which they define themselves; they misrepresent Judaism; and they misrepresent the history and modernity in which they are implicated. Strauss misrepresents Greek rationalism and

[22] Leo Strauss, *Philosophy and Law: Essays towards the Understanding of Maimonides and His Predecessors,* 1935, trans. Fred Baumann, Philadelphia, The Jewish Publication Society, 1987, p. 105.
[23] Ibid., pp. 110, 106.
[24] Emmanuel Levinas, *Totalité et infini: essai sur l'extériorité,* 1961, The Hague, Martinus Nijhoff, 1980; trans. *Totality and Infinity: An Essay on Exteriority,* Alphonso Lingis, The Hague, Martinus Nijhoff, 1979, pp. 21–30.
[25] Franz Rosenzweig, *Der Stern der Erlösung,* 1921, (2nd edn 1930), *Gesammelte Schriften II,* The Hague, Martinus Nijhoff, 1976; trans. *The Star of Redemption,* William W. Hallo, London, Routledge and Kegan Paul, 1971, Part 3, pp. 265ff.

ignores the connection between the birth and development of philosophy and earlier strata of pre-Olympian Greek religion.[26] If philosophy begins 'in wonder' then it is not a response to what is wonderful, but to what is awe-ful: it begins too, even apotropaically, in fear and trembling, in a response to a voice.[27] Levinas assimilates different philosophical accounts of 'knowledge', while alternating between reference to Kantian consciousness as self-contained and to Husserlian reduction (*epoché*) of intentionality. Yet Husserlian reduction presents and describes processes of knowing in opposition to Kantian deductions of validity, that is, without epistemology.[28] By means of this feint, Levinas is able to avoid the struggle between universal and aporia as it is evident from Kantian judgement to Hegelian speculative experience, and thus does not acknowledge the predicament of universal and local jurisprudence which characterizes modern philosophy as much as modern Judaism.

Both Strauss and Levinas misrepresent Judaism. The 'Talmudic argument' rehearses a rationalism which is constantly exploring its own limits – the Oral Law, which was also revealed at Sinai, gives rise within Halachic Judaism to a never-ending commentary on Written Law, according to which knowledge and responsibility are *in effect* renegotiated under the historically and politically changing conditions of both. Yet Strauss and Levinas present Judaism as unchanging and without a history whether internal or external, and as commentary, as law and as community. Strauss gives priority to medieval Judaism, while Levinas' decision to give priority not to 'the relation of ethics and Halacha' 'but rather [to] the passage from the non-ethical to the ethical', arguing that the latter 'is truly the necessity of our time' when all authority and morality are called into question, systematically draws attention away from the mainstream debate within Judaism over ethics and Halacha which, far from being specialized to Judaism, shows the mutual difficulty shared by Jewish and non-Jewish thinkers in

[26] F. M. Cornford, *From Religion to Philosophy: A Study in the Origins of Western Speculation*, 1912, Brighton, Harvester, 1980, pp. 124–53.
[27] See Jane Harrison, *Prolegomena to the Study of Greek Religion*, 1903, London, Merlin, 1980, pp. 1–31.
[28] Emmanuel Levinas, 'Ethics as First Philosophy', 1984, in *The Levinas Reader*, trans. and ed. Séan Hand, Oxford, Blackwell, 1989, pp. 76–87.

the conceiving of law and ethics.[29] It is this evasion which permits post-modern philosophy to allude to a Judaism taken from Rosenzweig, Buber or Levinas, as an open jurisprudence, a holy sociology, instead of confronting the configuring and conceiving of law and ethics in the shared context of modern legality and morality.

Within Halachic Judaism there is fundamental disagreement over the relation between ethics and Halacha, a disagreement which partakes in and reveals the breakdown in the conceiving of law and ethics 'outside' Judaism. Paradoxically, the orthodox inquiry into an ethic independent of Halacha, couched in terms of tradition (Lichtenstein)[30] defends and develops equity, the flexibility of the law, by demonstrating with reference to the Talmudic sources a situational or contextual morality which supplements 'beyond the line of the law', by balancing universal and local factors and not assimilating cases to a strict deduction; while the reform inquiry (Borowitz),[31] suspicious of this supralegality, seeks to import a categorical Kantian ethic with its unconditional and formal character into Judaism in the attempt to make questions not of *equity* but of *equality* unavoidable.

Whether based on the apparent unconditioned immediacy of the face to face or on the idea of Halachic contestation which offers an open jurisprudence and no end to history, recent philosophical 'representations' of Judaism overlook the contestation over law and ethics within Judaism as they overlook it outside Judaism. The rediscovery of Judaism at the end of the end of philosophy is based on mutual idealizations by philosophy and Judaism of each other. It amounts, therefore, to a convergent aspiration without a third, a middle, on which to converge.

However, these nomadic, Christian, and jurisprudential, Davidic, holy cities, consecrated in the shifting sands of ahistoricism and antinomianism, may be compared in the terms made explicit by

[29] Halacha refers to the legal passages of the Talmud, distinguished from *aggada*, the non-legal passages; or law and lore.
[30] Aharon Lichtenstein, 'Does Jewish Tradition Recognize an Ethic Independent of Halacha?', repr. in Marvin Fox (ed.), *Modern Jewish Ethics: Theory and Practice*, Columbus, Ohio University Press, 1975, pp. 102–23.
[31] Eugene B. Borowitz, 'The Authority of the Ethical Impulse in "Halakha"', 1981, in Norbert M. Samuelson (ed.), *Studies in Jewish Philosophy*, Lanham, University Press of America, 1987, pp. 489–505.

the two Christian ones as *post-modern political theologies*. First, they are 'political theology' because they offer a complete solution to the political problem: for Taylor, economies of domination will crumble;[32] for Milbank, salvation must mean 'liberation' from political, economic and psychic *dominium*, and therefore from all structures belonging to the *saeculum*.[33] Second, they are 'post-modern' because their politics and their theology are explicitly developed without the prevalent, guiding, modern contraries of nature and freedom, nature and law, nature and convention. This disqualifies the possibility of *critique* – of recognizing such contraries as indicating the tension of simultaneously possessing freedom and unfreedom. Not therefore representable, they can only be presented as 'holiness': for Taylor, 'the coincidence of opposites extends the divine milieu'; while for Milbank, ecclesial practice extends to the divine.[34] Significantly, both lay claim to the middle: Taylor joins 'the eternal play of the divine milieu', while Milbank distinguishes his ontology from Levinas' by denying that 'mediation is necessarily violent'.[35] So, third, then, the *agon* of post-modernisms: within the holy play, the holy city, holy nomads – beyond nature and law, freedom and unfreedom – they resonate with and claim to do justice to – the unequivocal middle. But where is this middle? Neither ecstatic affirmation vaunting its 'totally loving the world', nor eschatological peace, vaunting its continuity with untarnished ecclesial practice, displays any middle.[36] There are no institutions – *dominium* – in either: Taylor offers no exteriority; Milbank offers no interiority. Without command and without revelation, Taylor's ecstatic affirmation remains exiled in an interior castle; whereas, with Milbank's latinity of 'sociality' and 'charity', how could 'peace' bequeathed as 'harmonious' arise without acknowledgement of the polis intruding into such vapid sociality, and without acknowledging *eros* and *agape* intruding into such tamed 'charity'? In both cases, without anxiety, how could we recognize the equivocal middle? In fact we have here middles *mended* as 'holiness' – without that examination

---

[32] Taylor, *Erring*, p. 134.
[33] Milbank, *Theology and Social Theory*, p. 391.
[34] Taylor, ibid., p. 169; Milbank, ibid., p. 6.
[35] Taylor, ibid., p. 134; Milbank, ibid., p. 306.
[36] Taylor, ibid., p. 169; Mibank, ibid., pp. 6, 433–34.

of the *broken* middle which would show how these holy nomads arise out of and reinforce the unfreedom they prefer not to know.

The dispute between Don Cupitt and George Steiner, which was staged at the original conference 'Shadow of Spirit',[37] displayed the same convergence. Both Cupitt and Steiner declaim their visions in the prophetic mode – the one, prophet of dynamic pluralism; the other, prophet of ancient justice, of a justice which is proclaimable even when unrealizable. The one presents himself as a holy celebrant of the market-place, the other as the zealous guardian of monotheistic absolutism. Yet what they represent displays an inversion: Cupitt glorifies markets – for commodities, languages, political interests and religions – as plural and labile. But the market thus enthroned in the middle becomes a remorseless and authoritarian universal. In high dudgeon, Steiner conjures Deutero-Isaiah for the sake of our futurity – and yet such ferocity in the name of transcendence allows our anxiety and anger to be expressed and hence releases intimations of salvation.

However, these contrary prophecies converge in a powerful complacency which, whether apparently wholeheartedly embracing modernity or stern-heartedly refusing it, reduces modernity to the ineluctable and promiscuous market, which prophecy refuses to know or to criticize. Prophetic exhortation, whether by post-theology or in the name of biblical antiquity, converges with post-modern theology in laying claim to a holy middle elevated without equivocation, and without examination of *the broken middle* which they hold in righteous disdain. This very converging corrupts – for in figuring and consecrating holy cities, such 'holiness' will itself be reconfigured by the resource and articulation of modern domination, knowable to these post-modern ministers only as mute and monolithic sedimentation.

Post-modernism is submodern: these holy middles of ecstatic divine milieu, irenic other city, holy community – face to face or Halachic – and the unholy one of the perpetual carnival market, bear the marks of their unexplored precondition: the diremption between the moral discourse of rights and the systematic actuality of power, within and between modern states. And therefore they

---

[37] See Cupitt, 'Unsystematic Ethics and Politics', in Philippa Berry and Andrew Wernick (eds), *Shadow of Spirit: Post-modernism and Religion*, pp. 149–55.

will destroy what they would propagate, for once substance is presented, even if it is not 'represented', however 'continuous' with practice, it becomes procedural, formal, and its meaning will be configured and corrupted within the prevailing diremptions of morality and legality, autonomy and heteronomy, civil society and state. Mended middles and improvised middles betray a broken middle: antinomian yet dependent on renounced law; holy yet having renounced 'ideals'; yearning for nomadic freedom yet having renounced nature and freedom. This thinking concurs in representing its tradition – reason and institutions – as monolithic domination, as totalitarian. It overlooks the *predominance* of form, abstract legal form in civil society separated from the state, which figures the unfreedom *and* freedom of modern states. Hence it falls into the trap, not of positing another totalitarian ideal, but of presenting a holy middle which arises out of and will be reconfigured in the prevalent broken middle.

This holiness corrupts because it would sling us between ecstasy and eschatology, between a promise of touching our ownmost singularity and the irenic holy city, precisely without any disturbing middle. But this 'sensual holiness' arises out of and falls back into *a triune structure* in which we suffer and act as singular, individual and universal; or, as *particular*, as represented in institutions of the *middle,* and as *the state* – where we are singular, individual and universal in *each position*. These institutions of the middle *represent* and configure the relation between particular and state: they stage the *agon* between the three in one, one in three of singular, individual, universal; they represent the middle, broken between morality and legality, autonomy and heteronomy, cognition and norm, activity and passivity.[38] Yet they stand and move between the individual and the state. It has become easy to describe trade unions, local government, civil service, the learned professions – the arts, law, education, the universities, architecture and medicine – as 'powers'. And then renouncing knowledge as power, too, to demand total expiation for domination without investigation into the dynamics of configuration, of the triune relation which is our predicament – and which, either resolutely

---

[38] For elaboration of this argument, see Gillian Rose, *The Broken Middle: Out of Our Ancient Society*, Oxford, Blackwell, 1992, chs 5 and 6.

or unwittingly, we fix in some form, or with which we struggle, to know, and still to misknow and yet to grow. Because the middle is broken – because these institutions are systematically flawed – does not mean that it should be eliminated or mended.

This elimination of the middle will be the unintended consequence when the tradition is construed as 'Platonism' or 'Monotheism', or as any age-old domination of binary oppositions. It becomes impossible to distinguish between the intellectual tradition – whose resources, nevertheless, are being drawn upon at the very point of their indictment – and the institutional inversions which attend reformations of the kind being attempted yet again here. It becomes impossible to know which of these two paradoxes represents domination and which emancipation.

The analogy drawn once again from the history of architecture may illustrate this.[39] Le Corbusier is the scourge of the Modern Movement, held responsible for its anti-humanism and functionalism and rationalization, apparently captured by his infamous dictum: 'A house is a machine for living in'. But what did he intend? He intended, as he also declared, *to liberate women from furniture*.[40] Since the much-vaunted scepticism of post-modernity indicates *nolens volens* an ethical impulse to overthrow the 'idealizing narratives' of the 'Western intellectual tradition', it will suffer the same fate as Le Corbusier's good intention if it simply represents the tradition as unequivocal domination instead of attempting to comprehend how ideals and anti-ideals may be reconfigured in their historical and political realization. Postmodernity may, as it were, continue earnestly to try and liberate women from furniture, and in so doing, manufacture new, unanticipated lumber.

Holy middles corrupt because they collude in the elimination of the broken middle by drawing attention away from the reconfiguration of singular, individual and universal that is at stake. Cupitt, for example, calls for voluntary associations, for plural politics 'of issues and causes', without mentioning that civil society is the Janus-face of the modern state. This is to draw attention away from the ways in which under the promise of enhanced

[39] See Introduction, pp. 6–7.
[40] See Le Corbusier, *Towards a New Architecture*, 1923, trans. Frederic Etchells, London, Architectural Press, 1982, pp. 210–47.

autonomy – whether for individuals or communities – the middle is being radically undermined in a process of *Gleichschaltung* which, unlike the Nazi version, is quite compatible with the proclamation and actuality of civil society, with the proclamation and actuality of plurality, with the proclamation and actuality of post-modernity.

> This public person, so formed by the union of all other persons, formerly took the name of *city*, and now takes that of *Republic* or *body politic*; it is called by its members *State* when passive, *Sovereign* when active, and *Power* when compared with others like itself.[41]

Before we reorient our theology, let us reconsider the relation between the city and philosophy. Neither politics nor reason unifies or 'totalizes': they arise out of diremption, out of the diversity of peoples who come together under the aporetic law of the city, and who know that their law is different from the law of other cities – what Rousseau called 'power' and we now call 'nation'. Philosophy issues, too, out of this diremption and its provisional overcoming in the culture of an era. Without 'disowning that edifice', philosophy steps away to inspect its limitations, especially when the diremptions fixated in the edifice have lost their living connections.[42] We should be renewing our thinking on the invention and production of edifices – cities – apparently civilized within, dominion without – not sublimating those equivocations into holy cities. For the modern city intensifies these perennial diremptions in its inner oppositions between morality and legality, society and state, and the outer opposition, so often now inner, between sovereignty and what Rousseau called 'power' and we call 'nations and nationalism'; and which recurs, compacted and edified, in Levinas as 'war', as the spatial and temporal nomad in Taylor, as the nomadic city which 'remembers all the victims' in Milbank.

[41] Émile Rousseau, *Du contrat social, ou principes du droit politique*, 1762, ed. C. E. Vaughan, Manchester, Manchester University Press, 1962, p. 14; trans. *The Social Contract and Discourses*, G. D. H. Cole, London, Dent, 1973, pp. 89–90.
[42] See Hegel, *Differenz des Fichte'schen und Schelling'schen System der Philosophie* (1801), Hamburg, Felix Meiner, 1962, pp. 12–13; trans. *The Difference between Fichte's and Schelling's System of Philosophy*, H. S. Harris and Walter Cerf, Albany, State University of New York Press, 1977, pp. 89–90.

A final look at the labyrinth, setting of this spatial and temporal nomadicism: on the cover of *Erring* we look down on a maze, and are placed not in joyous disempowerment but in panoptic dominion, even though in the text the maze is celebrated as 'the horizontality of a pure surface', and we are situated 'in the midst of a labyrinth from which there is no exit'.[43] Towards the end of *Theology and Social Theory* we are told that the nomad city means that 'space is revolutionized' and no longer defensible.[44] It is worth looking more closely at these festive vulnerabilities. Taylor has put a unicursal maze on his cover – which offers no choice of route – as opposed to a multicursal maze – with choice of route. In either case, it is the beginning and the end which give authority to the way, and meaning to being lost – especially to any conceivable relishing of being lost. If the beginning and the end were abolished, so that all were (divine) middle – *Mitte ist Überall* – we would not achieve joyful erring; nor pure virtue 'without resistance'; we would be left helpless in the total domination of the maze, every point equally beginning and ending. We encounter not pure freedom but pure authority and become its complete victim.

We cannot think without freedom because we are thought by freedom and unfreedom, their insidious, dirempted morality and legality. Let us not be holy nomads; let us invent no theologies, mend no middles – until we have explored our own antiquity. Otherwise we blandish a new idolatry – unholy cities, idols of the theatre, masking the idol of the market-place.[45]

[43] Taylor, op. cit., p. 168.
[44] Milbank. op. cit., p. 392.
[45] For 'idols of the theatre' and 'idols of the market place', see Francis Bacon, *The New Organon and Related Writings*, 1620, ed. Fulton H. Anderson, Indianapolis, Library of Liberal Arts, 1979, pp. 47–50.

6

From Speculative to Dialectical Thinking – Hegel and Adorno

I

The True is thus the Bacchanalian revel in which no member is not drunk; yet because each member collapses as soon as he drops out, the revel is just as much transparent and simple repose. Judged in the court of this movement, the single shapes of spirit do not persist any more than determinate thoughts do, but they are as much positive and necessary moments, as they are negative and evanescent. In the *whole* of the movement, seen as a state of repose, what distinguishes itself therein, and gives itself particular existence is preserved as something that *recollects* itself, whose existence is self-knowledge, and whose self-knowledge is just as immediately existence.[1]

However, such dialectic is no longer reconciliable with Hegel. Its motion does not tend to the identity in the difference between each object and its concept; instead, it is suspicious of all identity. Its logic is one of disintegration: of a disintegration of the prepared and objectified form of the concepts which the cognitive subject faces, primarily and directly. Their

This paper was first prepared for 'The Frankfurt School Today' Conference held at UCLA, March 1987.

[1] Hegel, *Phänomenologie des Geistes* 1807, ed. Eva Molden Lauer and Karl Markus Michel, Frankfurt am Main, Suhrkamp, 1973, pp. 46–7; trans. *Phenomenology of Spirit*, A. V. Miller, Oxford, Clarendon, 1979, pp. 27–8.

identity with the subject is untruth. With this untruth, the
subjective pre-formation of the phenomenon moves in front
of the nonidentical in the phenomenon, in front of the
individuum ineffabile.[2]

Dialectic is the self-consciousness of the objective context of
delusion; it does not mean to have escaped from that context. Its objective goal is to break out of the context from
within . . . the absolute, as it hovers before metaphysics,
would be the nonidentical that refuses to emerge until the
compulsion of identity has dissolved. . . . It lies in the definition of negative dialectic that it will not come to rest in
itself, as if it were total. This is its form of hope.[3]

'Truth' for Adorno is a Bacchanalian revel where the alternation
of drunkenness and repose seems to be marked and matched by
'farewells' and 'welcomes' to Hegel.[4] Yet from the court of
Adorno's judgement, the whole is denied any rest, and this inconsistency – for judgement must arrest – reveals that the judge is not
compos mentis. For he thereby refuses to acknowledge that in his
act 'particular existence . . . *recollects* itself, whose existence is self-
knowledge, and whose self-knowledge is just as immediately
existence'.[5]

Whereas in the passage from Hegel we have the 'revel' and the
'judgement', and the 'particular' recollecting 'the whole', in Adorno
we have but *the judgement*. In this paper I shall discuss how Adorno
reduces *speculative* to *dialectical* thinking, replacing recollections of
the whole by judged oppositions. I shall argue that in *Dialectic of
Enlightenment* (1944)[6] he employs Nietzsche to repudiate Lukacs'
Hegelianism, and subsequently in *Negative Dialectic* (1966) he
repudiates Hegelian speculation directly.

This argument turns on the distinction between 'speculative'
and 'dialectical' thinking, which will itself be developed in the
course of this paper *abstractly*, *dialectically* and *speculatively*. In this

---

[2] Theodor Adorno, *Negative Dialectics*, 1966, in *Gesammelte Schriften*, VI, ed. Rolf Tiedemann,
Suhrkamp, Frankfurt am Main, 1973, p. 148; trans. E. B. Ashton, London, Routledge and
Kegan Paul, 1973, p. 145, amended.
[3] Adorno, ibid., p. 398, trans. amended.
[4] 'Die Lossage Von Hegel', p. 148, trans. 'The Farewell to Hegel', ibid., p. 144.
[5] *Phenomenology of Spirit*, pp. 46–7, trans. pp. 27–8.
[6] Max Horkheimer and Theodor W. Adorno, *Dialectic of Enlightenment*, 1944, trans. John
Cumming, New York, Herder and Herder, 1972.

way Adorno's position may itself be comprehended within the whole and within the tradition as he adjudicatively retrieves and undermines it.

If, nowadays, it has become *de rigueur* to call on Nietzsche as a witness against Hegel, Adorno bears a special responsibility for inaugurating this trial of wits both within critical theory and in rival camps.[7] Yet both the repudiation of Hegel and the representation of Nietzsche as a radical alternative rest on partial and one-sided characterizations of their thinking instead of comprehensive reconstructions.

The positions imputed to Nietzsche against Hegel may be listed under the following headings: genealogy to progressive philosophy of history; 'values' to the concept; the singular to the universal; perspectivism to the 'whole is the true'; repetition to reflection; will to power to philosophy of right. While Hegel is said to have disposed absolute, closed, teleological, reappropriated knowledge, Nietzsche is said to propose plural, open, differential creation of new values. Instead of further defining and challenging these exclusive, polar oppositions, the issue here is to discern a *tertium comparationis* from which the endeavour of Hegel and of Nietzsche may be comprehended and not dogmatically contrasted.

Both the form and the content of Hegel and of Nietzsche's thinking may be grasped as a response to the oppositions of Kant's practical philosophy: autonomy–heteronomy; morality–legality; freedom–necessity. I would suggest five beginnings for comprehension on this basis.

First, both Hegel and Nietzsche trace Kant's oppositions to *die Sittlichkeit der Sitte*, to 'ethical life', or 'the custom of morality',[8] which anticipates the apparently categorical moral imperative. In

[7] Although Habermas does not espouse Nietzsche's thinking, he represents it as diametrically opposed to Hegel's, see *Knowledge and Human Interests*, ch. 12, 'Psychoanalysis and Social Theory: Nietzsche's Reduction of Cognitive Interests' (trans. Jeremy J. Shapiro, London, Heinemann, 1972, pp. 274–300), and *The Philosophical Discourses of Modernity*, ch. 4 (trans. Frederick G. Laurence, Oxford, Polity, 1987); Gilles Deleuze, *Nietzsche and Philosophy*, trans. Hugh Tomlinson, London, Athlone, 1983; Michel Foucault, 'Nietzsche, Genealogy, History', in *Language, Counter-Memory, Practice*, ed. Donald F. Bouchard, Ithaca, Cornell, 1977, pp. 139–69; Jean-François Lyotard, *Le Postmoderne expliqué aux enfants*, Paris, Galilée, 1986.

[8] Friedrich Nietzsche, *Werke III*, ed. Karl Schlechta, Frankfurt am Main, Ullstein, 1976, pp. 800, 801, translated misleadingly and severally as 'the morality of mores' and 'the morality of custom' by Walter Kaufmann, *On the Genealogy of Morals*, 1887, New York, Vintage, 1969, p. 59.

both cases, the self-declaiming, unconditioned 'penetrating iron voice'[9] of the categorical imperative turns out to be the result of a long, historically and linguistically determinate conditioning. In the second place, both Hegel and Nietzsche represent this discipline of morality in terms of *Bildung*; that is, they expound or 'narrate', if you wish, the culturing of history and the history of culturing. This accounting for the development of morality opens up the apparently unconditioned oppositions which have been formed by negotiation or lack of it, that is, by experience; it addresses and would school the negotiating potential of the reader. In the third place, the modality of this exposition – its 'justification' in Kant's terms, its 'phenomenology' in Hegel's, its 'genealogy' in Nietzsche's – depends on the legal language in which experience and discourse is ineluctably couched. Exposition takes the form of the history of juxtaposed – simultaneous and successive – legal epochs. Fourth, in both cases, it is the enabling and the constricting consequence of this legalism for human agency and human self-understanding which is expounded; especially the power and the impotence, the politicizing and the depoliticizing, of 'persons', bearers of legal rights and duties. Finally, this attempt to know – and to acknowledge the implication of the knower – is ironic: expressed by Nietzsche's 'conscience of *method*',[10] and by Hegel's 'absolute method';[11] equally self-cancelling phrases, for an 'immoralist' could have no conscience, while no 'method' could be absolute. In these ways, *die Gerechtigkeit*, justice, is insinuated but not 'posited' (Hegel), not 'legislated' (Nietzsche).[12]

If the thinking of Hegel and of Nietzsche is construed comprehensively and speculatively, then the original project of critical

[9] Kant, *Lectures on Ethics*, trans. Louis Infield, London, Methuen, 1979, p. 51.

[10] Expounded in *Beyond Good and Evil: Prelude to a Philosophy of the Future*, section 36, (*Werke III*, 'Zuletzt ist es nicht nur erlaubt, diesen Versuch zu machen: es ist, vom Gewissen der Methode aus, geboten', trans. Walter Kaufmann, New York, Vintage, 1966, p. 48).

[11] 'Absolute Method [die absolute Methode, p. 491]' is expounded in 'The Absolute Idea', the third and last chapter of the third and last part of vols Two of the *Science of Logic, Wissenschaft der Logik*, 1812–16, Hamburg, Felix Meiner, II 1969; trans. A. V. Miller, London, Allen & Unwin, 1969, p. 830.

[12] For *die Gerechtigkeit* in Nietzsche, see *Thus Spoke Zarathustra*, Part II, 'Of Redemption', trans. R. J. Hollingdale, Harmondsworth, Penguin, 1961, p. 162; *Werke II*, p. 395. On the basis established here, further points of comparison emerge: nobility and ignobility with *ressentiment*; faith and enlightenment with active and passive nihilism; self-perficient scepticism with self-perficient nihilism.

theory, following Marx, to reassess the stance towards the Hegelian *dialectic* for its age, may take on a different complexion.

II

After Marx, it was Lukacs who defended and developed the analysis of the capital/wage-labour relation by turning it into the speculative and comprehensive exposition of capital*ism* as a social structure.[13] His famous apology for Marxism 'as a method' even imagining 'all its theses' disproved, was not a version of the 're-turn to Kant' current at the time, but a speculative presentation of 'the whole is the true' – of what he called 'the totality' and its 'mediations'.[14] For Lukacs, the commodity, universal and conditioned, focus yet fragment of the whole, corresponded to the type of legal-rational domination expounded by Weber. Since Weber's sociology of domination and its legitimization is rooted in Nietzsche,[15] Lukacs' mobilization of it brought 'will to power' into the speculative exposition of capitalism as a social system and as a culture.

In Weber, the predominance of modern bureaucracy is the nub of the analysis of the social and political paralysis engendered by rationalization. However, bureaucracy is only an exemplar of the type of legal-rational authority – for there can be traditional bureaucracies, and there are other examples of legal-rational authority. From the central essay of Lukacs' *History and Class Consciousness*, 'Reification and the Consciousness of the Proletariat', it

[13] Fernand Braudel reminds us that 'the awkward word *capitalism* . . . (coined at the latest about 1870) only became current in political, social and then scientific discussion at the beginning of the present century. Karl Marx did not use it' (*Capitalism and Material Life 1400–1800*, trans. Miriam Kochen, Glasgow, Fontana, 1974, p. xiii).

[14] Lukacs, 'What is Orthodox Marxism?', in *History and Class Consciousness*, trans. Rodney Livingstone, London, Merlin, 1971, pp. 1–26.

[15] 'One can measure the honesty of a contemporary scholar, and, above all, of a contemporary philosopher in his posture towards Nietzsche and Marx. Whoever does not admit that he could not perform the most important parts of his own work, without the work that those two have done swindles himself and others. Our intellectual world has to a great extent been shaped by Marx and Nietzsche', cited by Arthur Mitzman in *The Iron Cage: An Historical Interpretation of Max Weber*, New York, Alfred Knopf, 1970, p. 182, from Edward Baumgarten, *Max Weber, Werk und Person*, Tübingen, 1964, pp. 554–5.

emerges that if money is taken as the commodity of commodities then it is qualified exactly to fulfil the ideal-type of legal-rational authority. Weber's criteria for this 'type' of universality, impersonality and rationality, correspond, respectively, to the four functions of money enumerated by Marx: standard of price, medium of exchange, and measure of value and means of payment. In turn, the 'universality' of the standard arises out of particular concrete relations; the 'impersonality' of the medium of exchange requires 'persons' as legal bearers; the 'rationality' or calculability of the measure of value and means of payment depends on the actual inequality of people or on the 'irrationality' intrinsic to the capitalist mode of production.

Lukacs shows that exposition of the universalization of commodity relations and of legitimate domination complement each other; they are not metaphysically or sociologically incompatible. The ineluctable confrontation with legal forms is at the heart of this speculative exposition: the commodity has and is the form of *legal*-rational domination. Furthermore, Lukacs shows not just that capitalism 'reifies' social relations, but that capital posits people as 'persons' and as 'things': it reifies *and* it 'personifies' them. Every individual is a bearer of legal rights and obligations, and hence of commodities and money – a 'person'; but those who do not own the means of production are also 'things' – they have to treat their own labour-power as a commodity, as a thing. Things, in their turn, also become personified – the phantasmagoria of the market-place. 'Reification' and 'personification' imply each other – they are legal categories and social correlatives.[16] This mode of exposition does not presuppose a subject–object dichotomy nor any utopian perspective: it comprehends legal dichotomies speculatively – as the illusory third term in a contradictory and changing relation.

In Lukacs' book as a whole, however, the speculative exposition of capitalism is harnessed with a universalist subject–object theory of proletarian politics which is alternately voluntarist and

[16] Although Marx does not use the word *Verdinglichung* (reification) in the *Grundrisse* or in the first vol. of *Capital*, he does employ *als Personifikationen* in the first vol. of *Capital* and in the *Grundrisse: der Kritik der politischen Ökonomie* (Wien, Europa, n.d., p. 356; trans. Martin Nicolaus, Harmondsworth, Penguin, 1973, p. 452).

'partyist'. It is this weakness of its strength which discredited the work in the eyes of those – such as Ernst Bloch and Adorno – who had been introduced by it to the possibilities of extending the analysis of capitalism as a culture by the converging of motifs from Hegel with motifs from Nietzsche and Weber.[17]

In *Dialectic of Enlightenment*, Adorno and Horkheimer develop an account of domination which owes its credentials to a Nietzscheanism itself reduced from speculative to chiastic propositions which elaborate the main thesis: 'myth is already enlightenment; and enlightenment reverts to mythology'.[18] Expressing the dilemma of enlightenment and domination has priority over presenting speculative exposition or *Bildung* – the relation of universality and particularity as it is actually and potentially negotiated by the singular. Even though the original proposition in effect declares its investment in a vigilant enlightenment by balancing enlightenment's reversion to myth with an insistence on myth's cognitive powers, the one-dimensional view of domination is born: 'culture now impresses the same stamp on everything'; or, with respect to Bacon and Luther, 'Power and knowledge are synonymous'.[19]

This is not to overlook the dialectical strategy of *Dialectic of Enlightenment* – the exaggeration in such propositions designed to release potential reflection and action. Nor is it to overlook the propitious *negative* in the dialectic – the refusal of utopia bought at the cost of overstating unfreedom. On the contrary, Adorno's subsequent strategy of 'negative dialectic' is perfectly consistent with his confessed limitation of thinking to 'dialectic'. What needs developing, however, concerns the way in which the stress on the epithet 'negative' has detracted attention from the larger issue: that 'dialectical' thinking is not 'speculative' thinking.

[17] See Gillian Rose, *The Melancholy Science: An Introduction to the Thought of Theodor W. Adorno*, London, Macmillan, 1978, pp. 35, 40f.
[18] Horkheimer and Adorno, *Dialectic of Enlightenment*, p. xvi. The chapter on 'The Concept of Enlightenment' may be mainly attributed to Horkheimer while 'Excursus I: Odysseus or Myth and Enlightenment' and 'The Culture Industry: Enlightenment as Mass Deception' may be attributed to Adorno (based on interview with Alfred Schmidt by the author in Frankfurt am Main, 1978). However, on internal evidence, it seems highly probable that Adorno also wrote the chapter on the concept of enlightenment.
[19] Ibid., pp. 120, 4.

III

In a letter to Friedrich Immanuel Niethammer of 23 October 1812, Hegel takes up the difficult question of how to introduce gymnasium boys to philosophy – the dialectic, as it were, *expliqué aux enfants*:

> Philosophical content has in its method and soul three forms: it is 1, abstract, 2, dialectical and 3, speculative. It is abstract insofar as it takes place generally in the element of thought. Yet as merely abstract it becomes – in contrast to the dialectical and speculative forms – the so-called understanding which holds determinations fast and comes to know them in their fixed distinction. The dialectical is the movement and confusion of such fixed determinateness; it is negative reason. The speculative is positive reason, the spiritual, and it alone is really philosophical. . . .
>
> The second stage [the dialectical] . . . is more difficult [than the first] . . . The [Kantian] antinomies contain deep fundamentals of the antinomical [content] of reason. Yet these antinomies lie concealed and are recognised in the antinomies so to speak unthinkingly and insufficiently in their truth. . . . Nothing beyond tortuous antitheses.
>
> The third form is the truly speculative form, i.e. knowledge of what is opposed in its very oneness, more precisely the knowledge that the opposites are in truth one. Only this speculative stage is truly philosophical. It is naturally the most difficult; it is the truth. It is itself present in twofold form: 1 in its common form, when it is brought nearer to representation, imagination and the heart . . . [l]aw, self-consciousness, the practical in general already contain in and for themselves the principles or beginnings of the speculative. And of spirit and the spiritual there is, moreover, in truth not even a single nonspeculative word that can be said; for spirit is unity with itself in otherness. As a rule when one uses the word 'soul', 'spirit', or 'God' one is speaking all the same only of stones and coals.

What is philosophical in the form of the concept is exclusively what has been grasped conceptually, the speculative proceeding out of the dialectic.[20]

Adorno, true to Hegel's distinction, confines himself to 'dialectic', which is the second, negative stage of reason. Yet he denounces 'Dialectic cut short by Hegel' – a section heading from *Negative Dialectics*.[21] In passage after passage of *Negative Dialectics* Adorno represents Hegel in terms of oppositions – between individual and ideal, or between particular and universal – which Hegel is alleged to have invariably reconciled in favour of the latter term of the opposition against the former:

Hegel's transposition of the particular into particularity follows the practice of a society that tolerates the particular only as a category, a form of the supremacy of the universal.[22]

It sounds as if Adorno has taken his lessons from the form not the content of Hegel's letter to Niethammer – a letter in which the three stages of thinking are themselves stated abstractly and somewhat dialectically but not speculatively – except as a beginning. . . .

It is the speculative proposition which opens up the irony of history for Hegel: the exposition of the speculative identity and non-identity of the state and religion. This identity and non-identity shows in the craft of his works: as the inversion of substance into subject, that is, the inversion of ethical life into modern legal status and morality, which occurs when the state is separated from civil society.[23] Adorno, by contrast, remains with the dialectical antinomies of subject and object, particular and universal, individual and state. While claiming that Hegel is 'siding with the universal',[24] Adorno does not relate these oppositions to each other as they come to light in a dynamic historical development but argues that they are frozen – 'regression under the spell'.[25] He

---

[20] Hegel, *The Letters*, trans. Clark Butler and Christine Seiler, Bloomington, Indiana University Press, 1984, pp. 280–2.
[21] Op. cit., pp. 328–31, trans. 334–8, p. 8, pp. 328–331.
[22] Ibid., p. 328, trans. p. 334.
[23] See Gillian Rose, *Hegel contra Sociology*, London, Athlone, 1981, pp. 48ff.
[24] *Negative Dialectics*, pp. 320–2, trans. pp. 326–9.
[25] Ibid., pp. 340–3, trans. pp. 347–9.

thereby preserves them under the spell and brings mediation to a standstill. This stasis is justified by reference to its historical pre-condition, which is to dehistoricize that condition. Overall, Adorno construes Hegel as a dialectical dogmatist.

Adorno commits the injury which he has himself identified in *Minima Moralia*: 'The harm is done by the *thema probandum*: the thinker uses the dialectic instead of giving himself up to it.'[26] Even the thesis of reification is undermined *dialectically*:

> The category of reification, which was inspired by the wist-ful image of unbroken subjective immediacy, no longer merits the key position accorded to it, overzealously, by an apolo-getic thinking. . . . Pure immediacy and fetishism are equally untrue. The insistence on immediacy against reification re-nounces (as perceived in Hegel's institutionalism) the moment of otherness in dialectics – as arbitrary a procedure as the later Hegel's unfeasible practice to arrest dialectic in something solid beyond it. Yet the surplus over the subject, which a sub-jective metaphysical experience will not be talked out of, and the element of truth in reity – these two extremes touch in the idea of truth: for there would no more be truth without a subject freeing itself from illusion than there could be truth without that which is not the subject, that in which truth has its archetype.[27]

The circularity of this passage acts as a warning: it begins by undermining the speculative implications of reification, indicting it as nostalgia for immediacy, yet it ends up by affirming the metaphysical archetype. It itself has the form of dialectical reason which is arrested Platonically – in the elusive 'archetype'. By refusing to comprehend the antinomy which he enunciates – the move from dialectical to speculative thinking – Adorno is caught in the illusion with which he will only juggle: that is, he repeats the antinomy and will not comprehend it. This may explain why there is no recognition of law, of the third, of development, of *Sittlichkeit* in *Negative Dialectic*. It may also explain why, under

[26] Adorno, *Minima Moralia: Reflexionen aus den beschädigten Leben*, 1951, Frankfurt am Main, Suhrkamp, 1969, p. 333; trans. *Minima Moralia*, E. F. N. Jephcott, London, New Left Books, 1974, p. 247.
[27] *Negative Dialectics*, pp. 367–8, trans. p. 367, amended.

the heading 'Law and Equity', law is presented solely in terms of the dichotomies of natural law and positive law, abstract legal norm and equity, 'compulsion of the universal' and 'defiance of absorption'.[28] There is no concept of law because there is no configuration in a third, no law of the concept and its development.[29]

The reception and fate of Adorno's work is itself a chapter in the culture of Marxism and of philosophy. At first, ignored, dismissed or misconstrued, it is now – like Nietzsche's – hailed as the gospel of aporetics, of non-identity, with a dying fall of *euporia*. This smothers any attempt to recognize the universal in the aporia and the lack of identity in its specificity. Adorno's judgement tries to prevent the Bacchanalian revellers from collapsing with exhaustion so that while he judges '*No* repose!' – and thereby reposes illicitly, making an exception of himself – we continue gabbling about 'stones and coals'.

Adorno's *œuvre* has broadcast the judgement that Hegel justifies totalitarian politics and that Nietzsche's will to power amounts to omnipotencies but no potentiality. Adorno does not *use* the dialectic, but he does judge it; he cannot 'give himself up to it' – for then his thinking would become *speculative*. For reasons he gives himself, he is 'under the spell', which accounts for the remorselessly judgemental tone and style of his writing. Adorno kept the dialectic spellbound so that when later, post-modern generations insist again on revel without repose, their inevitable judgements may arrest their own inconsistency. If, even only abstractly and dialectically, this paper has begun to undo the spell – speculative beginnings may be released and coaxed to take up the labour of the concept. After the debilitations of the dance, the labour – which is equally repose – may refresh us.

---

[28] Ibid., pp. 305–6, trans. pp. 310–12.
[29] In the section of *Negative Dialectics* entitled 'Against Personalism' the concept of self-alienation – and by implication 'the ideological inessentiality [*Unsesen*] of the person' – is said to play no part in Marx's *Capital* (p. 274, trans. p. 278, amended). Adorno thus overlooks the importance of 'personification' as the legal correlation of the commodity form throughout *Capital* (but see, especially, the beginning of the second chapter (*Capital*, trans. Ben Fowkes, Harmondsworth, Penguin, 1976, vol. 1 ch. 2, pp. 178–9)). This may be why Adorno treats reification as the correlate of immediacy.

7

Of Derrida's Spirit

Should we not be concerned as to whether this fear of error is not just the error itself?[1]

I propose to return the pathos of Derrida's *De l'esprit* to its *logos*; to expose the *logos* lurking in its *elegeia*; to argue that the simultaneous disavowal and displacement of the predicament of diremption results in the 'ontologizing'[2] of Violence as Revelation, as what is 'laid bare'. I shall argue in opposition to Derrida's intention and aim that Heidegger's thinking does not bear the *lapsus* and new beginning he reconstructs in it, but that, on the contrary, it is quite consistent from the *Rectoral Address* to the 'final reply' in 1953 in the *Gespräch* with Trakl.[3]

If *De l'esprit* contains Derrida's *apologia* for Heidegger, it has also come to provide the *Urtext* – the originary text – for Derrida's continuing *expiation of the singular* which emerges from his recent

---

[1] Hegel, *Phänomenologie des Geistes*, 1807, ed. Eva Moldenhauer and Karl Markus Michel, Frankfurt am Main, Suhrkamp, 1973; trans. *Phenomenology of Spirit*, A. V. Miller, Oxford Clarendon, 1979, p. 47. This paper was first prepared for a conference on Derrida's *De l'esprit*, held at the University of Warwick, 1990. It was first published in *New Literary History*, vol. 24, 2 (1993), pp. 447–65, and in David Wood (ed.) *Derrida, Heidegger and Spirit*, Chicago, Northwestern University Press, 1993, pp. 56–72.

[2] By 'ontologizing' I mean to pose 'x' as the Event of Being, *das Ereignis*.

[3] *De l'esprit: Heidegger et la question*, Paris, Galilée, 1987, pp. 131–59, trans. *Of Spirit: Heidegger and the Question*, Geoffrey Bennington and Rachel Bowlby, Chicago, Chicago University Press, 1989, pp. 83–98.

explorations of what he calls 'the *Judeo-German psyche*' in commentaries on texts by Hermann Cohen and Walter Benjamin, and from his recent definition of 'deconstruction' as *justice*.[4] In an extended 'Note' to my discussion of *De l'esprit* I shall show the continuity between Derrida's defence of Heidegger and his own approach to modernity, Nazism and the Holocaust as it has been developed in these later commentaries.

I shall speak of ghost [revenant], of flame, and of ashes.[5]

I shall speak of this opening announcement and of four footnotes; of a passage in Chapter 5 on this *revenant* – of what it is that is said to return, to haunt; and of the imaginary discourse with which the final chapter concludes between Heidegger and the theologians – of the flame and the ashes.

First, 'the ghost' – *le revenant* – at the threshold, also called 'the phantom' (*le fantôme*), and addressed as the equivalent of *Geist* in Hebrew, Greek, Latin and French, in the sense of the Scriptures, as the Holy Spirit, the *logos* of the holy breath. *Geist*, however, bears another set of meanings which, prima facie, are nowhere evident in this work yet which have been displaced from the main text to the footnotes.

I speak of 'modern' spirit – of spirit in the sense which accompanies the strivings of modernity at its inception, and which has been developed analytically to expound the institutional inversion of meaning inherent to modernity: in the former case, Montesquieu, *De l'esprit des lois* – *Of The Spirit of the Laws*, 1748[6]

---

[4] A whole issue of the *Cardozo Law Review* is entitled 'Deconstruction and the Possibility of Justice' (vol. 11, 5–6 (1990)); it opens with Derrida, 'Force of Law: The "Mystical Foundation of Authority"', in two Parts (pp. 919–73; 973–1039). The second Part comprises the commentary on Benjamin's essay 'Zue Kritik der Gewalt' (1920–1, in *Walter Benjamin: Gesammelte Schriften*, vol. II.1, ed. Rolf Tiedemann and Hermann Schweppenhäuser, Frankfurt am Main, Suhrkamp, vols I–VI, 1974–85, pp. 179–203; trans. 'Critique of Violence', in *One Way Street and Other Writings*, Edmund Jephcott and Kingsley Shorter, London, New Left Books, 1979, pp. 132–54). It concludes with a 'Post-scriptum' (pp. 1040–5) which speculates on how the reading of Benjamin might be extended to 'the final solution'; and the appended introduction to the original lecture links the commentary to a seminar on 'Kant, the Jew, the German' (p. 977, n. 1), which is also the subtitle of Derrida's commentary on Cohen's essay 'Deutschtum und Judentum' (1915): 'Interpretations at War: Kant, the Jew, the German', in *New Literary History*, 22 (1991), pp. 39–95.
[5] *De l'esprit*, p. 11, trans. p. 1.
[6] *The Spirit of the Laws*, 2 vols, trans. Thomas Nugent, New York, Hafner, 1949.

– in the latter case, Weber, *Die protestantische Ethik und der Geist des Kapitalismus* – *The Protestant Ethic and the Spirit of Capitalism*, 1905.

The 'spirit' of the laws covers the customs and manners of a people associated with its written, legislated, or codified law – its 'ethos' in the inclusive sense; or, as sociology would conceive it, all the different kinds of norms in a society which are general and sanctioned, and taken to be universal and imperative. The 'spirit' of capitalism captures the extraordinary inversion of incipient modernity: that the development of the Protestant soteriology of inwardness resulted in the methodical and instrumental organization of everyday life; so that, to Weber, modern 'rationality', subsequently broken into 'formal' and 'substantive', *means* that combination of inner anxiety and outer ruthlessness originally displayed by the Protestant individual which made capitalism possible. This is a combination which Durkheim implicitly acknowledged and analysed further in *Suicide*, when he hypothesized that the highest rate of suicide and the lowest degree of social cohesion is found in Protestant communities – the erstwhile courageous, entrepreneurial Protestant spirit becomes most vulnerable to *anomie* and self-destruction. Both Weber and Durkheim link their analysis of this central social paradox to the political paralysis of modern societies as they conceive it. According to Weber, the fate of modern spirit has decreed that the light coat of the Protestant this-worldly saint should have become an 'iron-cage'.[7]

It is in this context of exploring the original development of modern capitalist society that I raise 'spirit' in Hegel, which (to shoot from a pistol[8]) means, phenomenologically, the struggle for recognition in its changing configurations of misrecognition. Between two self-consciousnesses, recognition is presented as the struggle between lord and bondsman, which is subsequently internalized in the duplicated 'unhappy consciousness'; while in the historical world, it is presented as 'legal status': the misrecognitions attendant on abstract legal personality, private property and the decay of public and political life. Hegel also expounds this as 'the

[7] Max Weber, *The Protestant Ethic and the spirit of capitalism*, 1905, trans. Talcott Parsons, London, Unwin, 1968, p. 181.

[8] This is Hegel's phrase – it refers to an abstract summary of a philosophical position in place of its exposition.

spiritual-animal kingdom' – *das geistige Tierreich* – which results when abstract, universal consciousness, unimpeded by others, appears to treat others as ends in themselves, universally, but in effect treats others and itself as means.[9] This exposition of the *spiritual*-animal kingdom corresponds to the exposition of the separation of civil society from the state in the *Philosophy of Right*. In both places the exposition delimits the freedom and unfreedom accompanying 'individual rights'. It may be seen to elaborate Rousseau's account in *A Discourse on the Origin of Inequality* of the interest which dominates people in a society based legally on protecting private property and self-consciously on guarding their social status in appearing to be what they really are not, in scheming and deceiving.

'Spirit' in this sense of 'spiritual-animal kingdom' pervades Hegel's phenomenology, his exposition of modernity and the paradoxes of subjectivity. Kant's inner, moral autonomy is seen to be quite compatible with its purported contrary – outer, legal heteronomy. Viewed dynamically, an increase in subjective freedom and autonomy may mean a *decrease* in objective freedom, that is to say, an increase in heteronomy. It is this dynamic and predicament of modernity according to which social actuality tends to undermine and to invert overt moral and political intentions that post-Kantian philosophy and social theory have sought to expound – without trying to overcome these meanings and their inversions, whether metaphysically or post-metaphysically, as long as they continue to be generated by their legal and political and productive preconditions.

'Spirit' also means the attempt to reconstruct and present these inversions of subject and substance without allowing dominant authorial authority to intensify the inversions expounded: hence the *Phenomenology of Spirit* is a drama of discursiveness which ironizes its passages and its *aporiae* so as to leave its reader exposed to the recognition of being already engaged in the struggle for recognition. In this light, any hypostatizing of 'Spirit' in Hegel is, *a fortiori*, implicated in the drama of misrecognition, the pathos of the concept; while to attribute the discourse of spirit to 'the metaphysics of subjectity' is to universalize the historically specific

---

[9] *Phenomenology of Spirit*, trans. pp. 237–52.

paradoxes of modern subjectivity and to exalt them as 'a continuous tradition' – when they arise out of the discontinuity between modern substance and its inverted subjects.

There are four significant references to Hegel in *De l'esprit* which
are elaborated in the attached footnotes. Three of these footnotes
refer back to the passage from Hegel that is cited in the first:[10]

'Introduction' to *The Philosophy of Spirit*, in the Encyclopedia, #378. In the same introduction, Hegel defines the
essence of spirit as *liberty* and as the capacity, in its formal
determination, to support *infinite suffering*. I think I must quote
this paragraph to anticipate what will be said later about
spirit, liberty, and evil for Heidegger: 'This is why the essence of spirit is formally *liberty*, the absolute negativity of
the concept as self-identity. According to this formal determination, it can abstract all that is exterior and its own
exteriority, its own presence: it can support the negation of
its individual immediacy, infinite *suffering*: that is, conserve
itself affirmative in this negation and be identical for itself.
This possibility is in itself the abstract universality of spirit,
universality which-is-for-itself' (#382).[11]

Not commented on, this passage is conjured as a warning about
the dangers of *pneumatology*, but also about the danger that liberty
of spirit risks 'a merely formal liberty and . . . an abstract universality'.[12] The fourth reference in text and note by contrast im-
plicates Hegel in *holy fire*:

And one of the most obsessing ghosts among the philosophers of this alchemy would again be Hegel who, as I have
tried to show elsewhere, situated the passage from the philosophy of nature to the philosophy of spirit in the combus-
tion from which, like the sublime effluvia of a fermentation,
Geist – the gas – rises up or rises up again above the decom-
posing dead, to interiorize itself in the *Aufhebung*.[13]

[10] Émile Rousseau, *Du contrat social ou pricipes du droit politique*, 1762, ed. C. E. Vaughan,
Manchester University Press, 1962; in, trans. G. D. H. Cole, *The Social Contract and
Discourses*, London, Dent, 1973, p. 86.
[11] *De l'esprit*, n. 1 to ch. 3, p. 33, trans. pp. 15, and 118; n. 3 to ch. 5, p. 65, trans.
pp. 40, and 119; n. 2 to ch. 10, p. 163, trans. p. 99, and 137.
[12] Ibid., p. 65n., trans. p. 119.
[13] Ibid., pp. 161–2, trans. p. 99.

In the note,[14] Hegel is cited from the Lectures on the History of Philosophy to appear as the collective guardian of the 'sacred fire' which the World-Spirit passes from nation to nation, while one of the listed passages from Glas also attributes procession and synthesis to spirit, 'one . . . must proceed from spirit as the synthesis of the singular and the universal'.[15] Without respecting the difference between phenomenological witness and philosophical reconstruction between and within Hegel's texts, and hence without commentary on struggle and misrecognition, such citation can only serve as precession and thematics:

> Given that we are trying to mark the continuity of a tradition in those places where the thematics of fire, hearth, guard, and nation cross, it is appropriate to quote Hegel once again.[16]

Comparison of the two Hegel passages in the text with the passage from Hegel called up thrice in the notes gives us two representations of 'Spirit' in Hegel: the one, an exposition of the abstract, one-sided, negative effect of formal self-identity; the other, conflagration – sacred fire and noxious effluvia.[17]

I discern here (and *passim*) three truncated thoughts. First, 'Spirit' is cited as 'abstract universality' without any reference to what it has been abstracted from and to what it returns, without, that is, any reference to the substance of modern ethical life. Abstract legal right in turn gives rise to the culture of the 'spiritual-animal kingdom'. Second, 'Spirit' as abstract universality is cited 'to anticipate what will be said later about spirit, liberty, and evil for Heidegger'.[18] An anticipation never to be fulfilled. For, when it later emerges that Heidegger takes a metaphysics of evil and origin from Schelling's *Of Human Freedom*, the confrontation between Hegel and Schelling's radically incompatible commitments never occurs. Third and finally, 'the continuity of a tradition' is evoked to justify citing Hegel on 'the nations' and to imply continuity with Heidegger's nationalism. This evocation

---

[14] Ibid., pp. 161–2, trans. pp. 136–7.
[15] Ibid., p. 162, trans. p. 136 and Derrida, *Glas*, Paris, Galilée, 1974, p. 21, trans. John P. Leavey, Jr, and Richard Rand, Lincoln, University of Nebraska Press, 1986, pp. 14–15.
[16] *De l'esprit*, p. 161, trans. p. 136.
[17] Ibid., pp. 33, 161, trans. pp. 118, 99.
[18] Ibid., p. 33, trans. p. 118.

fails to distinguish between 'a people' in Rousseau's sense, where bounded sovereignty and universal citizenship define the nation (Hegel), and the notion of inherited 'ethnicity' which serves as an exclusive criterion for political membership (Heidegger) – between a people (the polity) defining the nation, and 'the nation' defining a people (the polity). Arendt has linked the change from the 'nation-state' to the 'so-called totalitarian state' to the twin contradictions of universal rights dependent on national sovereignties, and universal equality dependent on systematic class inequality.[19] Instead of following through the history of the abstract *form* of dirempted 'Spirit' and its violent overcomings, Derrida offers – 'thematics'.

The second of these textual references to Hegel that I wish to discuss occurs in the second passage in Chapter 5 of *De l'esprit*. It sets out the third and most inclusive 'protocol of interpretation' for reading Heidegger's *Rectoral Address*:

> The force to which Heidegger appeals, and again in conclusion when he speaks of the destiny of the West, is thus a 'spiritual force' (*geistige Kraft*). And we will find this theme of spirit and of the West again, though displaced, in the text on Trakl.
>
> What is the price of this strategy? Why does it fatally turn back against its 'subject' – if one can use this word, as one must, in fact? Because one cannot demarcate oneself from biologism, from naturalism, from racism in its genetic form, one cannot be *opposed* to them except by reinscribing spirit in an oppositional determination, by once again making it a unilaterality of subjectity [*subjectité*], even if in its voluntarist form. The constraint of this program remains very strong, it reigns over the majority of discourses which, today and for a long time to come, state their opposition to racism, to totalitarianism, to nazism, to fascism, etc., and do this in the name of spirit, and even of the freedom of (the) spirit, in the name of an axiomatic – for example, that of democracy or 'human rights' – which, directly or not, comes back to this metaphysics of *subjectity*. All the pitfalls of the strategy of

[19] Hannah Arendt, *The Origins of Totalitarianism*, 1951, New York, Harcourt Brace Jovanovitch, 1973, Part I, ch. 2, pp. 11–28.

establishing demarcations belong to this program, whatever
place one occupies in it. The only choice is the choice between the terrifying contaminations it assigns. Even if all
forms of complicity are not equivalent, they are *irreducible* . . .

In the *Rectorship Address*, this risk is not just a risk run. If
its program seems diabolical, it is because, *without there being
anything fortuitous in this*, it capitalizes on the worst, that is on
both evils at once: the sanctioning of nazism, and the gesture
that is still metaphysical.[20]

Later, in Chapters 9 and 10, Derrida argues that, in his writing on
Trakl, Heidegger fails towards an alternative notion of spirit:
one which is not oppositional but *originary* (or 'heterogenous-
originary'). Given the source of this notion of spirit in Schelling,
the issue becomes whether it overcomes or reinvents and replays
Christian-metaphysical pneumato-spirituality. However, what is
most disturbing in the long passage cited here is the structuring
elision presented, nevertheless, in the name of the *irreducible*. For,
it is claimed, that whether one speaks for Nazism or strives to
oppose it, both positions are equally 'terrifying contaminations'.
This stipulation would deflect investigation from Heidegger's
defence of Nazism as a 'spiritual force' by attributing any conceivable basis for such investigation to a 'metaphysics of subjectity',
and then by indicting any and all conceivable opposition to
Nazism for being ineluctably cast in the same 'metaphysics of
subjectity', which is extended to cover 'all the pitfalls of the strategy of establishing demarcations', 'for example, democracy or
"human rights"'. Derrida diagnoses this paralysing dilemma by
arguing that if metaphysics always returns, it returns doubly in
the discourse of *Geist* which becomes in effect ghost to the notion
of ghost (*Geist*).[21] Furthermore, if metaphysics is redeployed to
sanction Nazism, this is said to occur '*without there being anything
fortuitous about it*'. Compressed in this accentuation is the idea of
the *continuity* of the tradition construed as the metaphysics and
politics of 'voluntarist' 'unilaterality of subjectity'.

Since to establish demarcations is coterminous with conceiving
as such, this reasoning disqualifies all thinking, including its own.

[20] Op. cit., pp. 65–6, trans. pp. 39–40.
[21] Ibid., p. 66, trans. p. 40. n. 3 and p. 119.

It prohibits any and all political discrimination between inclusive and exclusive political ideals, and forecloses any perception or judgement that inclusive political promises may presuppose and perpetuate exclusivity – in short, it destroys the possibility of critique and leaves only 'thematics', which amounts to *listings*.

However, the passage from Hegel cited for the second time in the note to this passage concerns *discontinuity*, abstract subjectivity broken off from its substance, its political community. Far from being posited as a unilateral or subjective *voluntas* or nisus, abstract subjectivity is exposited as the response of infinite suffering to the gain and loss of formal freedom. If 'Spirit' haunts those who would overcome it, this is not because they are still bound within the 'metaphysics of subjectity', which is to limit the problem (while disowning limits) to some cerebrality of positing and demarcation. It is because spirit is still dirempted by the dual character of modern legality – the simultaneous autonomy and heteronomy of the legal person separated from the law of the state – and would mend such diremption with pseudo-holistic phantasms of 'race', 'ethnicity', 'community'. These can begin to be *opposed* for the political history of diremption and of the violent attempts to overcome it are reconstructable. To do so requires commitment to comprehension and critique of the formal legality of subjective agency and the 'infinite suffering' it conjures. But this modern culture of political fate becomes invisible and unspeakable beside the elevation and generalization of the 'metaphysics of subjectity'.

If the elision of 'contaminations' may thus indeed be challenged, and forbidding irreducibility 'reduced', then it becomes possible to distinguish between Heidegger's defence of Nazism as a 'spiritual force' and opposition to that defence which draws on some notion of rights – because the latter may itself be comprehended and criticized. On the other hand, in this light, the change in Heidegger's use of *Geist* from 'spiritual force' to 'originary Spirit' has a consistency from which Derrida labours to detach it.

In Chapters 9 and 10, Derrida stages the argument that Heidegger moved from cautioning against *Geist*, to defending Nazism in terms of *Geist*, to overcoming this succumbing by a defence of *Geistlich*, either as a metaphysics of evil or as an archi-original alternative to any metaphysics. Derrida concedes that the distinction between Geist which is implicated in metaphysical opposition and *Geistlichkeit* which is the pre-historical Event of Being[22] may be, in effect, a distinction without a difference (*sic*). For 'spirit-in-flames', the verbal and visual icon for this 'original' spirit, which is both gentleness and destruction, and in which Evil has its provenance, reintroduces in its very distancing fundamental motifs of Platonized Christianity.[23] This equivocality is argued out in a concluding imaginary dialogue between Heidegger and the Christian theologians to whom is given the final, unresolved judgement of convergence, as the curtain falls on chapter and book – to whom is granted, beyond judgement, the integrity of failing towards what would be ' "the entirely other, inevitably" '.[24]

Lack of integrity, 'irreducible contamination', is reserved for us. All our 'inherited' thinking remains incapable of this return 'towards the most originary'.[25] The 'scene' between Heidegger and the theologians is announced and then briefly held up so that, once more, the irreducibility of contamination may be hammered home:

> And as, since the beginning of this lecture, we have been speaking of nothing but the 'translation' of these thoughts and discourses into what are commonly called the 'events' of 'history' and of 'politics' (I place quotation marks around all these obscure words), it would also be necessary to 'translate' what such an exchange of places can imply in its most radical possibility. This 'translation' appears to be both indispensable and for the moment impossible. It therefore calls for quite other protocols, those in view of which I have proposed this reading. What I am aiming at here is, obviously enough, anything but abstract. We are talking about past, present, and future 'events', a composition of forces and discourses which seem to have been waging merciless war on each other (for example from 1933 to our time). We have here a program and a combinatory whose power remains

[22] Ibid., pp. 166–7, trans. p. 101.
[23] Ibid., pp. 167, 157, trans. p. 102, 97.
[24] Ibid., p. 184, trans. p. 113.
[25] Ibid., p. 177, trans. p. 108.

abyssal. In all rigor it exculpates none of the discourses which can thus exchange their power. It leaves no place open for any arbitrating authority. Nazism was not born in the desert. We all know this, but it has to be constantly recalled. And even if, far from any desert, it had grown like a mushroom in the silence of a European forest, it would have done so in the shadow of big trees, in the shelter of their silence or their indifference but in the same soil. I will not list these trees which in Europe people an immense black forest, I will not count the species. For essential reasons, the presentation of them defies tabular layout. In their bushy taxonomy, they would bear the names of religions, philosophies, political regimes, economic structures, religious or academic institutions. In short, what is just as confusedly called culture, or the world of spirit.[26]

No sooner has the 'impossibility' of 'translating' thoughts and discourses into the 'events' of 'politics' and 'history' been proclaimed than, 'like a mushroom', they are uninhibitedly translated into the nourishing matrix of sylvan silence, and then imbedded as archi-original pre-history. The inarticulate trees defy taxonomy; instead, in terror of contamination, they are set out as a haphazard list, as *thematics*, thereby skirting the issue of any *tertium quid*, which might introduce some logic, some order, some comprehension. With evasive haste, this untheorized and casual list of *institutions of the middle* (religions, philosophies, political regimes, economic structures, religious or academic institutions) is set aside in order to return to the dialogue between Heidegger and the theologians over the 'archi-origin'. Yet the contrast between the 'contamination' of any beginning in the middle, of any demarcation, and 'the promise [of] the *origin-heterogeneous* to all the testaments, all the promises, all the events, all the laws and assignments which are our very memory'[27] casts the issue of *Geist* as a question of meta-metaphysics (even if the latter turns out to converge again with Christian Revelation, reborn – but only aesthetically – precisely as repetition of 'this entirely other',[28] but not as 'the

[26] Ibid., pp. 178–9, trans. pp. 109–10.
[27] Ibid., pp. 176–7, trans. p. 107.
[28] Ibid., p. 184, trans. p. 113.

scandal', to suggest Kierkegaardian terms). Moreover, the promise of promises, archi-promise, becomes the emphatic and no longer casual *form* of any middle, distinguished from all promises, all events, all laws and assignments. In addition, to speak 'of' Heidegger, 'of' spirit, 'of' the question, requires highly structured form, including a 'narrative' of Heidegger's development, a 'dialogue' between Heidegger and imaginary theologians, and an 'elegaic' use of Heidegger's relation to Trakl's poetry as the search for a primeval matutinality. Yet form, which is the middle *qua* social institutions and *qua* their principle of cohesion, is merely offered as *thematics*, as the two lists cited above, without even minimal taxonomic distinction.[29]

All Derrida's *poiesis* draws attention away from Heidegger's *phronesis* or evident lack of it. For if Heidegger's employment of *Geist* and its cognates is set in the more general context of his *systematic* disqualification of any consideration of diremption of spirit, of subjectivity as abstract civil law separated from the modern state, then the consistency of Heidegger's concerns in spite of his changing conceptuality can be reconstructed.

In his commentary on Schelling's *Of Human Freedom* (1936) which is considered in *De l'esprit* as the source of the putative 'metaphysics of evil', which pervades the 1953 Trakl discussion, Heidegger explicitly distinguishes Schelling's notion of freedom as the sixth meaning which 'shatters'[30] the fifth inclusive one, that of Hegel, the 'formal concept of freedom':[31]

> Schelling raises the question of human freedom anew, in a direction to which Idealism especially obscures the way at first. Idealism understood freedom as the determination of the pure ego, as self-determination for the law, as self-legislation in good will. Only this will is good.
>
> On the contrary, freedom is understood by Schelling as the capability of good and evil (sixth concept of freedom). Evil is not an addition and a complement; rather, freedom

[29] Ibid., p. 161, trans. p. 136. For 'institutions of the middle' see Gillian Rose, *The Broken Middle: Out of Our Ancient Society*, Oxford, Blackwell, 1992.
[30] Heidegger, *Schellings Abhandlung über das Wesen der menschlichen Freiheit* [*1809*], Tübingen, Max Niemeyer, 1971, p. 117; trans. *Schelling's Treatise on the Essence of Human Freedom*, Joan Stanbaugh, Athens, Ohio, Ohio University Press, 1985, p. 97.
[31] Ibid., p. 106, trans. p. 88.

changes through it in its very nature. The question of freedom must be asked as a question.[32]

The original unity, indissoluble in God but dissoluble in man, 'constitutes the possibility of good and evil', and man's· inner necessity as freedom, man's being as 'essentially *his own deed*'.[33] Schelling's historicizing of 'the original unruly element' according to the different ages of the world is quickly passed over[34] with the following nonchalant remark:

> What corresponds to the essential historical meaning of evil in Schelling, but is not merely identical with it, is in Hegel what he calls the diremption of unhappy consciousness.[35]

In this vague but loaded comparison is suppressed the difference between metaphysics and phenomenology – between Schelling's Revelation of essential evil in historical stages, and Hegel's exposition of the inversions of self-consciousness which result from the denial of otherness, desire and work, from the duplication of lord and bondsman within one self-consciousness, and which corresponds to the world of legal status and to its spiritual-animal sociality – ancient and modern.[36]

This notion of 'archi-original' evil in Heidegger's Schelling commentary (1936) emerges in the archi-original language of Revelation and Violence in two other texts – the *Rectoral Address* (1933) and the lecture *Introduction to Metaphysics* (1935) – where it is deployed equally to discuss the origin of the Greek polis by commentary on the chorus of *The Antigone*, and to inspire the German people in their Nazi *aubade*. In *An Introduction to Metaphysics* the commentary on the *Antigone* chorus reads 'Man is the violent one [*Gewalt-tätig*]. He gathers the power [against the overpowering: *gegen das Über-wältigende*] and brings it to manifestness [*lässt es in*

[32] Ibid., p. 120, trans. p. 99.
[33] Friedrich W. J. Schelling, *Of Human Spirit*, trans. James Gutmann, Chicago, Open Court, 1936, pp. 37, 39, 63.
[34] 'Since this historical construction is the common property of German Idealism, there is all the less reason to go into detail here', Heidegger, *Schelling's Treatise on the Essence of Human Freedom*, p. 180, trans. p. 150.
[35] Ibid., p. 181, trans. p. 150.
[36] See Hegel, *Phenomenology of Spirit*, trans. pp. 119–38 and cf. pp. 290–4.

eine Offenbarkeit ein]';[37] in the *Rectoral Address* may be found the controlled apostrophe: 'This people shapes its fate by placing its history into the openness of the overwhelming power [*in die Offenbarkeit der Übermacht*]'.[38]

Heidegger's thinking is quite consistent in its deployment of archi-original reduction. 'Power', 'violence', like 'spirit-in-flames', 'evil', each pre-original Event of Being, laid bare, manifest or revealed, are all notions of pre-legitimate or non-legitimate, anthropomorphic participation in cosmic force; they void by pre-dating all the equivocalities of legal constitution and its fate. They make it possible to evade the predicament of finding ourselves always *in the middle* not 'of things', according to Heidegger himself (and in any case, 'things' are always litigious), but of the reflexivity arising from the tension of the freedom and unfreedom, of the legitimacy and non-legitimacy, of the form of modern law. Heidegger is consistent in refusing the conceptuality and conflicts of modern political theory. His *œuvre* is haunted not by *Geist*, metaphysics of subjectity *redivivus* – but by the unacknowledged but evident diremption which he refused from start to finish, from origin to origin, to think.

Derrida's *De l'esprit* has a special dishonesty: a text in quotation marks, it offers a drama or playing out, throughout, and openly at the end. His actors have an author who, in his refusal of any delimitation – for all 'demarcation' is 'contamination' – replays the whole tradition 'in its continuity' and with overweening authority. His auditors are locked in the disgrace that Heidegger and his 'Christian' interlocutors struggle to overcome – with originary and abyssal flames and ashes, 'Is ash the Good or Evil of flame?'[39] – with repetition in thought towards 'the entirely other'.

Yet this sublimity of originary equivocation bars any investigation 'of' abstract universality, 'of' political history. The modern

[37] Heidegger, *Einführung in die Metaphysik*, Tübingen, Niemeyer, 1987, p. 115; trans. *An Introduction to Metaphysics*, Ralph Manheim New York, Anchor, 1959, trans. p. 126.
[38] *Die Selbstbehauptung der deutschen Universität: Das Rektorat 1933/34*, Frankfurt am Main, Klostermann, 1983, p. 15; trans. *Rectoral Address, Review of Metaphysics*, Joan Stambaugh, XXXVIII, 3 (1985), p. 476.
[39] Op. cit., p. 158, trans. p. 97. Compare 'That is why this event – the Extermination – is for the West the terrible revelation of its essence', Philippe Lacoue-Labarthe, *La fiction du politique*, Paris, Christian Bowgetis, 1990; trans. *Heidegger, Art and Politics*, Chris Turner, Oxford, Blackwell, 1990, p. 37.

fate of *Geist* – the law of civil society and state producing its diremption and violent overcomings thereof – will erupt again and again as long as this structure persists. Fear of 'contamination' is just the contamination itself – collusion by not comprehending what *can be* reconstructed. In the place and time of diremption and *logos*, we are given sublime origin and its pathos: systematic violence is bathed in this *serein* of originary violence.

In fine, the gauntlet here taken up disputes 'the continuity of the tradition': since the eighteenth century, 'spirit' and 'subjectivity' have been exposed and expounded as the form of the law and its inversions, and not as presupposing the *irreducible* 'metaphysics of subjectity'. Furthermore, Heidegger is utterly consistent in avoiding any acknowledgement of this modern predicament in the works from 1933 to 1953 under discussion, and in general. May this consistency not begin to explain the attraction of Nazism? That it seemed to offer a way out of the unbearable modern diremption between subject and substance, between the forms of legal equality and the actuality of systematic inequality, out of that combination of insecurity and authoritarianism in economic, political and social institutions which is quite contrary to liberal and democratic concepts of freedom and which generates the phantastical desire for the security of imaginary origins? Heidegger's concentration on the translation of Western *technē* back into its essence left him without *phronesis* but with great unironized authority. In this light his subsequent turn from *Geist* to *Geistlich* marks a further 'retreat' from an unbearable political and social actuality that he still would and could not think – and which Derrida, after him, will not and cannot reconstruct.

Note

In addition to attempting an *apologia* for Heidegger's thinking in the face of his Nazism, *De l'esprit* provides the philosophical foundation for Derrida's subsequent attribution of an ethical meaning to 'deconstruction'.[40] Given his commitment to the ineluctable and irreducible contamination of all thinking, this

[40] 'Force of Law', pp. 919–1045 (see note 4 *supra*).

attribution and its justification has taken the form of commentaries on individual texts by Cohen and by Benjamin in which their 'contamination' by German nationalism is explored.[41]

In the course of these commentaries Derrida's own Heidegger-ianism has deepened. Like Heidegger, the process of whose thinking changed from ontological difference to *das Ereignis*, the Event of Being, Derrida's thinking seems to have changed from *differance* to originary event. Between the text and the now famous long footnote in *De l'esprit*, 'originary evil' and 'pre-originary pledge' or promise, prior to language and responsibility, are separately discerned by Derrida to pertain to a layer of Heidegger's thinking which lies deeper than 'the question' – that residue of Enlightenment.[42] It is only in Derrida's later commentaries that this originary after-thought is systematically connected with originary violence, which in Heidegger's *Introduction to Meta-physics* (and echoed in the *Rectoral Address*) founds the polis while remaining *hypsipolis* – without the city and its law.[43] In the Benjamin commentary, 'beyond Benjamin's explicit purpose' and under the title 'Force of Law', Derrida defends the inseparability of the violence which founds law from the violence which con-serves it by defining both as *the promise of iterability*.[44] Since even the origin is now contamination, *universal* contamination acquires a '*différantielle* representivity' which consigns the originary vio-lence to oblivion.[45] This Heideggerian reading – which Derrida consistently applies in what he concedes in relation to his Cohen commentary is 'a stategically motivated attention', itself one of a number of examinations of what he calls '*the Judeo-German psyche*' – must be challenged.[46] It must be challenged on a number of scores:

[41] Ibid. Benjamin's essay 'Zur Kritik der Gewalt', in *Gesammelte Schriften*, vol. II.1 ed., Rolf Tiedemann and Hermann Schweppenhäuser, Frankfurt am Main, Suhrkarm, 1977, pp. 179–203, is translated as 'Critique of Violence' in *One Way Street and Other Writings*, Edmund Jephcott and Kingsley Shorter, London, New Left Books, 1979, pp. 132–54; Cohen's essay 'Deutschtum und Judentum' (1915), is reprinted in his *Jüdische Schriften*, ed. Bruno Strauss, Berlin, C. A. Schwetschke und Sohn, 1924, vol. II, pp. 237–301.
[42] *De l'esprit*, pp. 147–54, 148–9, 150, trans. pp. 129–36, 130, 131.
[43] Heidegger, op. cit., 116–17, trans. p. 128; see *supra* nn. 35–6.
[44] Derrida, 'Force of Law', p. 997.
[45] Ibid., pp. 997, 1015.
[46] Ibid., p. 977, n. 1; 'Interpretations at War', p. 48.

1   as 'close' readings of Cohen and of Benjamin which are not close at all, for they rest on the opposition between archeo-teleological and originary-eschatological metaphysics;

2   as a style of argument: the perspective of universal 'contamin-ation' seems to legitimize universal elision so that affinities between fundamentally different political philosophies may be insinuated in ways which effectively *prevent* issues of com-plicity or collusion being raised;

3   because Derrida is presenting 'deconstruction' as *justice*. This 'justice' is the mirror image of justice discredited as Hegelian-Marxist 'grand narrative': deconstruction offers violence be-fore the law, where grand narrative is said to have offered peace after law; and if, it may be protested, the 'before' is not temporal but foundational, then the 'after' was never simply temporal but potential.

Deconstructive 'justice' leaves us with a universal but general piety: primal violence may erupt through any legitimation. The per-spective of originary iterability of law-founding and law-conserving violence confirms the 'mystical foundation of authority' to be the force of law, instead of demystifying it by showing how precarious legitimations always appear in historically specific configuration – *form* which relates universal, particular and singular – and by showing how any justice, including deconstruction as justice, can only reform universal, particular and singular, however much it proclaims its 'full negotiation' in the singularity-because-iterability of founding violence figured as conserving violence. 'Decon-struction at work' *is* founding violence: 'It inscribes iterability in originarity, in unicity and singularity.'[47]

Here I can only give some indications of how such a challenge might proceed:

1   To Cohen's argument in his essay 'Deutschtum und Judentum' are imputed affinities with national socialism;[48] to Benjamin's argument in his essay 'Zur Kritik der Gewalt' are imputed affinities

---

[47] Derrida, 'Force of Law', p. 1003. Derrida would seem to have inherited Heidegger's Scotist God. See Gillian Rose, *Dialectic of Nihilism: Post-structuralism and Law*, Oxford, Blackwell, 1984, p. 104.

[48] Derrida, 'Interpretations at War', pp. 79, 84.

with other thinkers hostile to parliamentary democracy.[49] These 'contaminations' are not treated in the same way. Clearly distanced from Cohen's logism, Derrida betrays a special affinity with Benjamin's insight into the force of law, into law-founding and law-conserving violence, and with the perspective of language and representation as a fall from an originary language. These affinities lead in their turn to serious doubt about their structuring contraries when Derrida judges by extrapolation in an appended conclusion that Benjamin's opposing of divine, annihilating, undecidable violence to mythic, deciding violence of right would have led him to sacralize the Holocaust by thinking it to be a manifestation of divine, bloodless, expiatory violence.[50]

However, the affinity of Benjamin's *Ursprung* with Cohen's logic of *Ursprung* and with the latter's Messianic ethics, and the grounding of origin and Messianism *in both cases* in a socialist politics is absent from either discussion. Yet in the thought of both Cohen and Benjamin it is the socialism which defines the Messianism and the logic of origin, and, *a fortiori*, any 'nationalism' or divine violence. For the Nazis it was racist transnationalism which determined the meaning of their 'socialism'.

2   Derrida's description of Cohen's essay as 'hypernationalist'[51] repeats the elision between Heidegger and Hegel on nations discussed above.[52] It overlooks the distinction which Cohen makes between 'nations' and 'nationalities', that is, between a universal polity and an 'ethnic' or racist exclusive entity. Cohen condemns the latter, here and elsewhere, and argues that each nation will contain many nationalities.[53]

3   Derrida's attributes a 'delirious' syllogism to Cohen: the middle term of Philo's Hellenistic *logos* justifies the kinship

[49] Derrida, 'Force of Law', p. 977 n.

[50] Ibid., pp. 975, 1040–5.

[51] Derrida, 'Interpretations at War', pp. 47, 50.

[52] See above, pp. 70–1.

[53] Cohen, 'Deutschtum und Judentum', pp. 271–4; compare Cohen's essay from 1907, 'Religiöse Postulate', in *Jüdische Schriften*, vol. p. 7; see, too, Paul Mendes-Flohr, '"The Stronger and the Better Jews": Jewish Theological Responses to Political Messianism in the Weimar Republic', in *Studies in Contemporary Jewry*, VII (1991), pp. 159–85, especially p. 177, n. 28 and p. 179, n. 50 and Steven S. Schwarzschild, '"Germanism and Judaism" – Herman Cohen's Normative Paradigm of German-Jewish Symbiosis', in David Bronsen (ed.), *Jews and Germans from 1860–1933: The Problematic Synthesis*, Heidelberg, Carl Winter, 1979, pp. 129–72.

between the German-Lutheran and the German-Jewish 'psyche' or spirit.[54] However, in Cohen's argument this 'middle' serves to subordinate logic to ethics. Here and elsewhere, the middle is urged to Jews (all Jews, not just American Jews): to argue against Zionism and for the mission of the Jews to spread a universal ethical life by commitment to the states in which they find themselves and not by nationalist exclusivism. But Derrida does not begin to attempt to do justice to Cohen's address to the predicament of universalism and particularism in the idea and mission of Judaism.[55]

4 It was Cohen's scarcely veiled definition of *Deutschtum* in terms of *Judentum* and not the other way round (of *Judentum* in terms of *Deutschtum*, as Derrida would have us believe) that led to the numerous critical reviews of the essay, and to his writing a second essay of the same title which he published the following year (1916) in order to try and correct the impression he had conveyed that everything good in German life was owed to the spirit of Judaism.[56] Derrida does not mention this second essay or its rationale.

5 Contrary to several of Derrida's other claims, Cohen's idea of the universal mission of Judaism means that he did recognize other national Jewries, e.g. Spanish-Arabic; he did provide specific historical arguments for the importance of the German-Jewish communities, e.g. their strategic position, after the expulsion from Spain, between the Western and Eastern communites; and elsewhere he frequently discusses Spinoza in these historical and political contexts. Reference to Spinoza is not necessarily to be expected in an essay devoted to the relation between German and German-Jewish history; while the extended discussion of Mendelssohn's

---

[54] 'Interpretations at War', pp. 50–3.

[55] See Cohen, 'Deutschtum und Judentum', pp. 277–82; Cohen wrestles with the argument that Judaic universalism and internationalism will not decompose or dissolve (*zersetzen*) peoples and races, p. 278; compare 'Religiöse Postulate', pp. 8–9.

[56] 'Deutschtum und Judentum', 1916, pp. 302–18; reviews of original essay listed, p. 476. In a letter of 20 September 1917, Franz Rosenzweig argued that in his original essay Cohen had in effect exchanged what he considered European for *Deutschtum* and defined that in terms of his own philosophy of universal responsibility. Rosenzweig himself wrote an immediate reply to Cohen also entitled 'Deutschtum und Judentum' which was not fully published until 1984 (see Franz Rosenzweig, *Der Mensch und sein Werk, Gesammelte Schriften*, The Hague, Martinus Nijhoff, vol. I, 1979, *Briefe und Tagebücher 1900–1918*, p. 444; vol. III, ed. Reinhold and Anne Marie Mayer, *Zweistromland*, pp. 169–75).

contribution to German and Jewish Enlightenment shows Cohen's acknowledgement of the complex issues raised by the Spinozist inheritance.[57] Overall, Derrida mystifies Cohen's relation to Spinoza by not discussing Cohen's thought as a system of freedom.

6   Of the relation between Cohen's exposition of Judaism and, after all, not Kant but the neo-Kantianism of his own three-Part *System*, where Kantianism is itself transformed into productive origin and a Messianic ethic of time and counterposed to an historical exposition of capitalist exploitation of labour-power, Derrida shows no knowledge whatsoever.[58]

7   Similarly any attempt to predict the shape of Benjamin's response to the Holocaust would have to locate his essay on language and his Messianism in the scope of his socialism. How can the judgement that Benjamin would have sacralized the Holocaust be sustained in the light of his 'Theses on the Philosophy of History' where the *Angélus Novus*, caught in the storm from Paradise propelling him backward to the future, saw even what was called progress as 'one single catastrophe', and where a Messianic history would proclaim that '*even the dead* will not be safe from the enemy if he wins. And he has not ceased to be victorious'?[59] These 'Theses' were written in 1939–40, and they, too, were strategic: they were designed to induce an intellectual break with the quietist triumphalism of the Marxisms prevalent at that time.

8   Even if one remains within the confines of Benjamin's essay 'Zur Kritik der Gewalt', Derrida misrepresents its operation. For the contrast between divine, bloodless violence and mythic violence of right is only introduced at the end. It is not correlative to the distinction between law-founding and law-conserving violence as Derrida implies by setting out these sets of oppositions at the beginning of his commentary. In spite of the caution against

[57] Derrida, 'Interpretations at War', pp. 54, 66; Cohen, 'Deutschtum und Judentum', pp. 267–70; compare 'Religiöse Postulate', pp. 10–11. See Cohen's essay on Spinoza, 'Spinoza über Staat und Religion, Judentum und Christentum', 1915, in *Jüdische Schriften*, vol. III, pp. 290–372.

[58] For further discussion of Cohen's thought, see 'Hermann Cohen – Kant among the Prophets', in *infra*, pp. 111–25; on Cohen's *Logic*, see, Rose, *Hegel contra Sociology*, London, Athlone, 1981, pp. 2–13; and on Cohen's *Ethics*, see, Rose, *Dialectic of Nihilism*, pp. 25–49.

[59] 'Über den Begriff der Geschichte', *Gesammelte Schriften*, vol. I.2, pp. 697–8, 695; trans. 'Theses on the Philosophy or History' in *Illuminations*, Harry Zohn, London, Fontana, 1973, pp. 260, 257.

translating *Gewalt* as violence[60] – for *Gewalt* carries tones of
power and governance, albeit not legitimate – the impression
conveyed by the use of 'violence' is libertarian and anarchic. On
the other hand, the translation of *Recht* as 'law' instead of 'right'
confers a legitimacy on what is founded or conserved not intended by Benjamin but which Derrida seeks to foreground as
formal law *per se*. As a result of these translation decisions, it
becomes easier for Derrida to develop an eschatological and
originary reading of Benjamin's essay by projecting on to it his
own Heideggerian ontology.

However, the essay presupposes Max Weber's definition of the
modern state as claiming '(successfully) the *monopoly of the legitimate use of physical force* within a given territory'.[61] Challenges
to that monopoly are explained by a *functionalist* argument on the
uses of force, not by an eschatological reflection on originary
violence. The concession of some of that force by the state, such
as the guaranteed right to strike, serves paradoxically to preserve
its own monopoly of legitimate force. Furthermore, far from
equating non-violence with pure, divine violence, Benjamin discusses several forms of non-violent resolution of conflict – between private persons and by diplomats between states.[62]

9   As a result of Derrida's originary approach to law-founding
and law-conserving violence, Benjamin's account of modernity
can only appear reactionary: cast solely in political terms, the hidden
yet overblown law-founding violence of the police in modern
democracies is beyond the control of parliaments. Derrida insists
that this position is reactionary, even if it is also revolutionary, for
it implies a degeneracy from, and return to, a purer origin. However, Benjamin's political reflections presuppose a social theory of
capitalist institutions, and amount to the search for a theory of
revolutionary practice which will be neither reformist nor justify
force as a *means* of right-making. The evocation of divine force,
which can never be a *means*, is returned to the modern context so

---

[60] Derrida, 'Force of Law', 927, 981.
[61] Weber, 'Politics as a Vocation', 1918, *From Max Weber: Essays in Sociology*, trans. and
ed. H. H. Gerth and C. Wright Mills, London, Routledge and Kegan Paul, 1967, p. 78.
[62] Derrida, 'Force of Law', pp. 979, 991: Benjamin, 'Critique of Violence', pp. 195, 191;
trans. pp. 147, 143. Compare Rose, 'Walter Benjamin – Out of the Sources of Modern
Judaism', *infra*, pp. 175–210.

that the educative 'philosophy of history of violence' may demonstrate that as long as force is used 'mythically', as right-making
means, it will prevent the abolition of state power.[63] Here as
elsewhere, and comparable to Rosa Luxemburg, Benjamin is exploring the relation of theory and practice for a truly democratic
revolution which will inaugurate radical democracy at every
moment and not postpone it to a post-revolutionary future when
force, the 'means', will have achieved its 'ends'.

10   Derrida's misconstrual of Benjamin's essay leads him,
however, to a series of paradoxical formulations of deconstruction
which culminate in a crisis for deconstruction itself. Deconstruction
participates in what Derrida nominates 'two violences': the divine
which is 'the decision without decidable certainty' and the state
which is 'the certainty of the undecidable but without decision'.[64]
In the 'Post-scriptum' the consequence that the opposition between these two laws (which is also the opposition between divine
violence and the order of representation, parliamentary democracy, and fallen language) would result in thinking the Holocaust in the biblical sense as indeed a *holocaust*, a divine manifestation and sacrifice, leads Derrida implicitly to refute the whole
eschatological originary and 'contamination' employed to define
deconstruction as justice, when he insists that 'we must think,
know, represent for ourselves, formalize, judge the possible complicity between all these discourses and the worst (here the final
solution)'.[65]

This is precisely what deconstruction can never do because it
has been defined as justice (divine?): 'Justice in itself, if such a
thing exists, outside or beyond law, is not deconstructible.'[66]
'Deconstruction is also the idea of – and the idea adopted by
necessity of – this *différantielle* contamination.'[67] Such claims are
declarations; they leave their authority and legitimacy a mystery
– and leave it open for a false Messiah to proclaim a tyranny.
They leave us with the dilemma of mysterious, primeval violence
versus mythical, formal law, between incomprehensible end and

[63] Ibid., pp. 200, 202–3, trans. pp. 151, 153–4.
[64] Derrida, 'Force of Law', p. 1035.
[65] Ibid., p. 1045.
[66] Ibid., p. 945.
[67] Ibid., p. 997.

bloody means. When what needs investigation is the *fate* of modern law – the diremption and discrepancy between its formal promises and the social actuality they presuppose and reproduce. Then the violent acting out of the nationalist or racist phantasies engendered by these discrepancies may be comprehended instead of being exalted to a pure originary violence or degraded to the violence of pure formal law as such. This would be to demystify law without compensatory myth and without hallowing history as *holocaust*. Only if we resist the temptation of the ontology of 'originary contamination' can we begin to discern the complicities of our political history. To do that we need to be able to represent, to formalize, to think, to know, to judge – all the activities from which Messianic deconstruction would disqualify us.

8

Nietzsche's *Judaica*

In the end not only is it permitted to make this experiment; the conscience of method *demands it.*[1]

It has been a great and barely resistible temptation to introduce this paper with highly charged but quite contrary epigraphs from Nietzsche's various works selected to emphasize the seemingly incompatible extremes of what Nietzsche had to say about Judaism and the Jews. From the most hyperbolic philo-Hebraism to the most profound anti-Hebraism,[2] it might not be too difficult, although perhaps unprecedented, to demonstrate that here, too, *'les deux exces se touchent'*.[3] The extremes meet in indicating the rage underlying Nietzsche's cathexis of the Jews,[4] now declaimed with

[1] 'The Free Spirit', *Beyond Good and Evil: Prelude to a Philosophy of the Future*, 1886, trans. Walter Kaufmann, New York, Vintage, 1966, § 36 p. 48; *Werke*, III, ed. Karl Schlechta, Frankfurt am Main, Ullstein, 1976, p. 601, emphasis in original.

[2] I use 'anti-Hebraism' to refer to philosophical criticism of Judaism projected on to the imagined religion and people of the Hebrew scriptures, known to Christianity as the Old Testament; I use 'anti-Judaism' to refer to Christian religious and social prejudice against the Jews prior to 1870; and I use 'anti-semitism' to refer to racist political opposition to the Jews since 1870. For discussion of the development of 'anti-semitism', see Peter Pulzer, *The Rise of Political Anti-Semitism in Germany and Austria*, London, Peter Halban, 1988, pp. 47–57.

[3] Rousseau, *Du contrat sociale, ou principes du droit politiques*, ed. C. E. Vaughan, Manchester, Manchester University Press, 1962, p. 84; trans. *The Social Contract and Discourses*, G. D. H. Cole, London, Dent, 1973, trans. p. 241, 'Extremes meet'.

[4] Hannah Arendt has cautioned against the convergence between philo- and anti-Judaism, see *The Jew as Pariah: Jewish Identity and Politics in the Modern Age*, ed. Ron H. Feldman, New York, Grove Press, 1978.

supererogatory admiration, now with paradoxically rancorous animosity against, precisely, 'Jewish' *ressentiment*. They meet in the further sense that Nietzsche – or his *personae* – uses the *same* arguments concerning the history of Judaism, now to attribute to it the salvation of European culture through its medieval Dark Ages and through the dark ages to come; now, expunging 'the Christian limit',[5] to attribute to it the original corruption of the priestly mode of evaluation, which has never ceased to trouble Western man. By launching the holistic indictment of 'Judaeo-Christian civilization', Nietzsche is said to have cleared the soil, first for Nazi paganism, and, more recently, for Gaia, Greek goddess of the earth, adopted by New Age paganism.[6]

The temptation to begin in this way has been overcome because the paradoxes of Nietzsche's *Judaica* cannot be elucidated by adopting this eminently rational approach. Such a sceptical but tempered procedure would produce coherence out of Nietzsche's apparent contrariness by reconstructing his changing views; it would presuppose that he always *means* 'Judaism' when he *refers* to 'the Jews', and that he always speaks 'for' or 'against' it. Here, instead, the wildly differing evaluations of Judaism in Nietzsche's works will be shown to be paradigmatic and emblematic of the equivocation which lies at the heart of Nietzsche's thinking – the equivocation with which he identified the depths of his own formation so that the drama of his authorship is devoted to its exploration. The contrary judgements of 'Judaism' and the 'Jews' will be deduced from 'the conscience of *method*'.

What is at stake in these two different approaches is clarified by a recent study which provides an excellent exemplar of *the approach towards judgemental coherence*. Michael F. Duffy and Willard Mittelman attempt to produce judicious consistency from Nietzsche's scattered and various discussions of Judaism by introducing a distinction between what he says about 'pre-prophetic', 'prophetic' and 'modern' Judaism. Employing these distinctions,

---

[5] The phrase is taken from Conor Cruise O'Brien, who argues that, by implicating Christianity so deeply in the inverted values of Judaism, Nietzsche contributed to destroying Christian respect for Jews as the continuing witness of the superiority of Christianity, and hence paved the way for 'anti-Christian (unlimited) anti-semitism' of the Nazis (*The Siege: The Saga of Israel and Zionism*, London, Paladin, 1986, pp. 56–9).

[6] See James Lovelock, 'Gaia', in William Bloom (ed.), *The New Age: An Anthology of Essential Writings*, London, Rider, 1991, pp. 164–7.

the authors survey most of the relevant passages, and conclude that Nietzsche's views on Judaism changed from the commendation of 'prophetic' Judaism and of modern Judaism in his early writings to his condemnation of 'prophetic' Judaism in his mature writings. However, there is an alliance between the inadequacy of these distinctions and the enterprise of addressing 'Nietzsche's attitudes toward the Jews' – which is the title of their article and which indicates the non-philosophical impetus of their argument.[7]

The authors advance three claims for the originality of their approach. First, they rectify the failure on the part of previous commentators to deal systematically with the whole spectrum of Nietzsche's writings on Judaism by making a conspectus of those writings from the earliest letters to the last notes of the *Nachlass*. Second, they chart an ostensible *change* in Nietzsche's views by distinguishing not simply between ancient and modern Judaism, but also between his persisting 'admiration' for pre-prophetic Judaism of the Pentateuch and the historical books of the Bible, and for the Jews of nineteenth-century Europe, and his emergent focus on 'the Jewish prophets as inaugurating the slave rebellion in morals', with Christianity as 'nothing less than the logical outcome of this rebellion and revaluation'.[8] Third, they explain this combination of unchanging 'admiration' and increasing 'antipathy' *biographically*: Nietzsche's early and lasting favourable reassessment of modern and pre-prophetic Judaism is attributed to his emancipation from his friendship with Wagner and his subsequent closeness to Paul Rée, an assimilated Jew; his adversion to anti-semitism is connected to his insistent opposition to his sister's marriage to Bernhard Forster, an active anti-semite; while his later 'harshness and bitterness' towards the Jews of the prophetic era and their revaluation of values is said to 'represent *inter alia* a

[7] Michael F. Duffy and Willard Mittelman, 'Nietzsche's Attitudes Toward the Jews', *Journal of the History of Ideas*, XLIX, 2 1988, 301–17. (Compare, too, Jacob Golomb, 'Nietzsche's Judaism of Power', *Revue des études juives*, 147 (1988), pp. 353–85; and Sander L. Gilman, 'Heine: Nietzsche's Other', and 'Heine, Nietzsche, and the Idea of the Jew: The Other and the Self', in *Inscribing the Other*, Lincoln, University of Nebraska Press, 1991, pp. 99–119, 121–42.) Essays by Newman, Eldad, Solaquarda and Baeumer on Nietzsche and 'Jewish Instinct', the Old Testament, Paul, and Luther, explore the depths of Nietzsche's identifications (see James, C. O'Flaherty, Timothy F. Sellner, and Robert M. Helm (eds), *Studies in Nietzsche and the Judaeo-Christian Tradition*, Chapel Hill, University of North Carolina, 1985).

[8] 'Nietzsche's attitudes toward the Jews', p. 310.

settling of accounts with Paul Rée', from whom he had become disaffected since he had been supplanted by Rée in the affections of Lou Salomé.[9] Finally, the authors solve the quandary which they have invented themselves of why Nietzsche selected 'prophetic Judaism', as the target of his wrath while continuing to praise both pre-prophectic Judaism and modern Jews:

> The answer seems clear. Nietzsche exhibits continually an antipathy towards both Christianity and the Christian culture of his time. He certainly knew that Christianity was in many ways a Jewish development [*sic*], and thus it was natural for him to extend his thinking on the morality of Christianity to the milieu out of which it arose.[10]

The distinctions and arguments proposed by Duffy and Mittelman concerning Nietzsche's 'attitudes' towards the Jews unwittingly but ignorantly perpetuate wide-spread and long-standing false notions about the history of Judaism, and risk creating a new myth concerning Nietzsche. They must be confronted before the meaning of Nietzsche's *Judaica* can be posed.

First, in one place only Nietzsche refers to the prophets;[11] in every other instance he attributes 'the slave revolt in morality' to *priests*. Second, Nietzsche refers to Judaism as the *religion* of the people of the Old Testament, when, *as a religion*, Judaism is a post-biblical development. Talmudic Judaism prevailed as a result of the political success of the rabbis, who, *in opposition to the priests*, claimed to have inherited the mantle of prophetic authority in interpreting the word of God.[12] After the fall of the Second Temple, the legitimacy of the institutions of the priesthood was eroded, and the rabbis created the positive religion we refer to as 'Judaism'. In the third place, the reference to 'modern' Jews is extremely vague: Nietzsche refers to rabbis – 'scholars' – and he refers to secular, assimilated Jews. In sum, Nietzsche refers to priests not prophets, and Judaism, the historical religion, is a

---

[9] Ibid., p. 314; this explanation is taken by the authors from Rudolf Binion (*Frau Lou: Nietzsche's Wayward Disciple*, Princeton, Yale University Press, 1968, pp. 81–111).
[10] Ibid.
[11] *Beyond Good and Evil*, Werke III, p. 653, trans. p. 108.
[12] See Stuart A. Cohen, *The Three Crowns: structures of communal politics in early Rabbinic Jewry*, Cambridge, Cambridge University Press, 1990.

religion of rabbis (scholars) not priests (every adult Jew is expected to minister to their neighbours).

Now this distinction between historical Judaism, the religion formed by the rabbis and maintained by Rabbinic culture, and the biblical suzerainty of priests, is not intended to introduce a rival explanation by further qualifications of Nietzsche's 'attitudes' to the Jews. It is intended to point out that *as a matter of fact* Nietzsche's animus was not directed at the Hebrew prophets – about whom (with the one exception noted) he seems to have had nothing to say – and that he characterizes Judaism as a religion of priests when *in fact* Rabbinic Judaism grew out of the demise of priestly authority. Furthermore, the question of possible connections between Jesus, Paul and Pharisaic and apocalyptic institutions of the intertestamental period remains fraught with scholarly dispute.[13] This should dispel the idea, which Duffy and Mittelman also purvey, that Christianity was 'a Jewish development', and that it was 'natural' for Nietzsche to extend his excoriations of Christianity to 'the milieu out of which it arose'.

In this light, Nietzsche's representation of Judaism as a *priestly* 'religion', which effected the slave revolt in morality, provides the key to the *agon* of Nietzsche's authorship: the predicament of power and impotence which is his obsession as a psychologist. The 'priest' is presented as the author and actor of this predicament; and this sets the strategy of Nietzsche's exposition of 'Judaism' and of 'Christianity'. Now the Priest of priests is Paul, the Jew, epistolary definer of evangelical Christianity. It was Paul who established the necessary chiasmus of law and sin: sin and grace. It was Paul who developed the idea of 'justification by faith alone' which released Luther from his vain attempts to fulfil the law. (Pauline salvation, it now appears, has its roots in the popular Hellenism of his time.[14]) Paul and Luther are closely linked throughout Nietzsche's *œuvre*; for it was the Lutheran Reformation which revived a moribund Christianity and re-established it on the foundation of 'the priesthood of all believers'.[15]

[13] See W. D. Davies, *Paul and Rabbinic Judaism: Some Rabbinic Elements in Pauline Theology*, London, SPCK, 1970; Samuel Sandmel, *Judaism and Christian Beginnings*, New York, Oxford University Press, 1978; E. P. Sanders, *Paul and Palestinian Judaism: A Comparison of Patterns of Religion*, London, SCM Press, 1981, *Jesus and Judaism*, London, SCM Press, 1985.
[14] See Davies, *Paul and Rabbinic Judaism*, p. xiii.
[15] See Roland Bainton, *Here I Stand*, Tring, Lion, 1978, pp. 137, 152, 154, 248.

When, in the first essay in *On the Genealogy of Morals*, Nietzsche seems to indict Judaism for inventing the slave revolt in morality, and, in the third essay on the meaning of ascetic ideals, to idealize the Jews for their achievements, this flagrant contrariness should not be weeded out – its bloom should be cultivated methodologic- ally. Under the subtitle 'A Polemic', in the first essay, the priestly mode of evaluation invents *ressentiment*; in the third essay, the priest is crafty, canny, creative; and in the middle essay, the key to the equivocation – which includes *polemically* completely contrary assessments that are yet no contradiction – is developed. This equi- vocation expresses the contrary inner formation of modern man which founds *genealogy* as a method.

The meaning of Nietzsche's *Judaica* is not 'the priest', but the antinomy of that cultivation which produces both *ressentiment* and *Übermensch*. Which of these two characters – the man of ressenti- ment or the overman – will emerge cannot be known in advance: for morality may undershoot the imperative or overshoot it by self-legislating. More often morality produces that mixture of under- and overcoming which is *asceticism*. Asceticism is the discipline of morality – reactive and active, destructive and crea- tive, derivative and original, powerful by power against itself. This is why Nietzsche could understand morality both as the 'slavish' invention of the Jews *and* as the source of their tremen- dous capacity to create good out of suffering. This is not to make sense of Nietzsche's 'attitudes' to the Jews, but to propose that the logic of morality demands *genealogy*, demands the reconstruction of the deepest equivocation of under- and overman, which is ima- gined out of the paradigm of 'the priest' who is the emblem of contrary character. This is the 'method' of Nietzsche's *Judaica*: it may account for the tension of his authorship but it may never claim to know anything about his 'attitudes'.

The method proposed here is to comprehend Nietzsche's *Judaica genealogically* – where, against recent interpretations, 'genealogy' is not presented as the alternative to the teleology of omniscient philosophy of history. *Genealogy* is understood as *failing towards* securing a coign of vantage from which the mutual implication of *ressentiment* and overcoming of the authority of morality, which has been the breeding of modern man, may be addressed – without arrogating the discredited authority of morality to itself. Whereas for Hegel and Weber the entanglement of subjective freedom with unfreedom is the correlate of change in the structure of objective freedom, for Nietzsche the entanglement of psychological rancour and spiritual sublimity which is the meaning of ascetic ideals has no such objective referent and hence no alleviation. The intensity of Nietzsche's *agon* of authorship which knows it owes both its strengths and its weaknesses to what it deplores, and yet adores, has its source in this difference.

In *Human all too Human*, Judaism is associated with Christianity, for they are both contrasted with the measure and symmetry which holds between the Greeks and their gods. Christianity is characterized by its 'pathological excess of feeling': Christianity

> crushed and shattered man completely and buried him as though in mud: into a feeling of total depravity it then suddenly shone a beam of divine mercy, so that, surprised and stupefied by this act of grace, man gave vent to a cry of rapture and for a moment believed he bore all heaven within him.[16]

It is the institutional organization of this combination of personal abjection and transpersonal exultation that preoccupies Nietzsche. In section 114, the abjection induced by Judaism and Christianity is described as Asiatic, barbaric, un-Hellenic; whereas, in section 475, Judaism is said to have rescued Christianity throughout the Middle Ages from its orientalizing by the activity of its 'Jewish freethinkers, scholars and physicians'. This passage also argues that modern nationalism is the source of literary anti-semitism, and attempts to square the account with

> a people who, not without us all being to blame, have had the most grief-laden history of any people and whom we have to thank for the *noblest* human being (Christ), the purest sage (Spinoza), the mightiest book and *the most efficacious moral code in the world*.[17]

In *Human all too Human*, Judaism is simultaneously represented as the epitome of orientalizing and occidentalizing, of *ignoble*

---

[16] *Human all too Human: A Book for Free Spirits*, 1878–80, trans. R. J. Hollingdale, Cambridge, Cambridge University Press, 1986 p. 66; *Werke I*, 1979, p. 526.
[17] Loc. cit. *Werke I* 686, trans. p. 175, emphasis added.

degradation and *nobility*, purity and moral efficacy, while Christianity displays only 'the pathological excess of feeling'. This is the procedure of *genealogy*, which eschews any teleology of triumphant progression in the present and future: it presents the all-encompassing *agon* of the present, the entangled actuality of which is projected into the past; displaying its pathological excess of feeling, its nobility and its ignobility, in the process. And because the genealogical projection is noble *and* ignoble, it is both owned and disowned in the process. In section 171 of the appended 'Assorted Opinions and Maxims', a glimpse is caught of this projection of the *agon* of Lutheran Protestantism on to Judaism that Nietzsche otherwise will disguise and dramatize: 'It was only in the music of Handel that there sounded the best that the soul of Luther and his like contained, the mighty Jewish-heroic impulse that created the whole Reformation movement.'[18]

In *Daybreak*, which is subtitled 'Thoughts on the Prejudices of Morality', the genealogy of Paul as the source of the priestly mode of valuation emerges in tandem with increasingly contrary evaluations of the Jews. However, the two aetiologies are not yet fused, so that the critical role of Paul in the strange syllogism to come is all the clearer: Paul is both Jew and Christian; Paul is the priestly moralizer of early eschatological Christianity; therefore, Judaism is the original, priestly religion.

The importance of Paul, who appears under the heading *The first Christian*, and with the soubriquet 'the Jewish Pascal',[19] cannot be over-estimated:

> But without this remarkable history, without the storms and confusions of such a mind, of such a soul, there would be no Christianity; we would hardly have heard of a little Jewish sect whose master died on the cross.[20]

Paul's theology of redemption is the exemplar of the germinal argument of *genealogy*: that the assertion of power may arise out

---

[18] Loc. cit., *Werke I* 801, trans. p. 253.

[19] Weber refers to 'the deep hatred of Pascal . . . for all worldly activity, which he was deeply convinced could only be understood in terms of vanity or low cunning' (*The Protestant Ethic and the Spirit of Capitalism*, 1905, trans. Talcott Parsons, London, Unwin, 1968, p. 81). However, Weber contrasts Pascal's position with Luther's conception of the calling, and pursues the development of 'worldly asceticism' as a *paradoxical* result of the positive Protestant valuation of quotidian activity and reality, not the renunciation of it.

[20] *Daybreak*, *Werke II*, 1979, p. 1055, trans. W. Kaufmann, New York, Vintage, 1979, Book I, § 68, p. 39.

of the degradation of life; that in circumstances of political defeat or when political agency is completely curtailed, power may be asserted psychologically by the self-imposition of the sinful nature of one's existence. This surrender of self-esteem, without any consciously interested motive, might be called 'the cunning of the irrational':

> Oh, how much superfluous cruelty and vivisection have proceeded from those religions which invented sin! And from those people who desired by means of it to gain the highest enjoyment of their power![21]

The conversion of Paul is analogous with the conversion of Luther: the interminable suffering in trying to fulfil the law, the sudden realization of the impossibility of succeeding, and the daring to proclaim that 'the torture of the unfulfilled law cannot be overcome'. This moment turns fanatical self-hatred – the lust for power against, precisely, lust – into power: for instead of abolishing the propensity to sin, the law is abolished or fulfilled by Christ's redeeming death. Now 'Even if it is still possible to sin, it is not possible to sin against the law.'[22] Nietzsche interprets Paul's idea of atonement with Christ to mean the abolition of guilt, because the carnality in which the law dwelt is 'dying constantly away'. However, although 'If I were now to accept the law again and submit to it I should be making Christ an accomplice of sin',[23] the structure of law is left intact, while it is proclaimed fulfilled or abolished by redemption. In this way, Paul transforms fanatical vigilance against, and attraction towards trangression of the law – the doomed attempt to *fulfil the law* – into 'the intoxication' and 'importunity' of the *law fulfilled*, which removes 'all shame, all subordination, all bounds' in the idea of 'becoming one with Christ'.[24] Lust is turned, as it were, into gratification: 'the intractable lust for power reveals itself as an anticipatory revelling in *divine* glories'.[25]

This ambivalence of law and sin – preserved and abolished – is parallel to the ambivalence of Christianity and genealogy towards

[21] Ibid., *Werke II*, p. 1048, trans. § 53 p. 34.
[22] Ibid., *Werke II*, p. 1057, trans. § 68 p. 41.
[23] Ibid.
[24] Ibid., p. 1058.
[25] Ibid., *Werke II*, p. 1058, trans. pp. 41–2.

Judaism, the people of the law, capable of the moral sublimity which eluded Paul and, after him, Luther. In section 72, Christianity needs Christ's redeeming death, whereas the Jews are 'as a people firmly attached to life'. The result of Paul's teaching of the unfulfillability of the law, and death as the consequence of sin, is that, while Christ's redeeming death is open to all, it only avails the select few – with eternal damnation for all others.[26] Nietzsche lays out as Pauline theology the inner, scarifying landmarks of Protestant *faith*.

Lacking this Pauline internalization, the modern Jews are able to be creative out of their revenge: 'they have known how to create for themselves a feeling of power and of eternal revenge out of the very occupations left to them'. Here the feeling of power is not the aftermath of revenge but precedes it, and constraint provides the opportunity for overcoming adversity so that self-respect is enhanced not renounced, and courage is hidden 'beneath the cloak of miserable submission'.[27] As a result of their wide experience of society arising from frequent changes of residence, passion and liberality temper each other in the achievements of the Jews:

> And whither shall this assembled abundance of grand impressions which for every Jewish family constitutes Jewish history, this abundance of passions, virtues, decisions, renunciations, struggles, victories of every kind – whither shall it stream out if not at least into great men and great works![28]

This apostrophe to the spirit of Judaism is quite compatible with the judgement that enthusiasm is the indulgence of our deficiencies. On these occasions the unstable balance between creative power and destructive fanaticism is being taught and the fundamental impossibility of any general judgement of which outcome may be expected in specific cases. The command to 'love thy neighbour' may express the hateful refusal to take arms against a sea of troubles, or it may express the urbane equanimity of self-confident power.

---

[26] Loc. cit., *Werke*, pp. 1059–61, trans. pp. 43–4.
[27] Ibid., *Werke II*, p. 1153, trans. Book III, 205, p. 124.
[28] Ibid., *Werke*, p. 1154, trans. p. 125.

The difference between Christian pathological excess of feeling and Jewish overcoming of disability is at stake in *The Gay Science*, when Nietzsche contrasts sons of Protestant ministers, who base their cause on vigour and warmth, with Jewish scholars, who depend solely on the power of logic to combat prejudice against them. Logic provides a true democracy of the intellect which acts as the only 'ancestor in the blood and instinct of the scholar', while others rely on inherited and partial passion for classification, or the sheer force of conviction.[29] Once again, the authority of morality is either succumbed to or overcome in the contrasts elaborated in this rumination.

In the light of the lack of predictability concerning overcoming and succumbing, it is no longer so surprising when, in the same work, the Jews are presented as both noble and ignoble. When Christianity is contrasted with the Greeks, the invention of 'sin' is attributed to Jewish 'feeling'. God is interested, his honour tarnished by sin: sin is an offence against him, not against humanity. '"Only if you *repent* will God show you grace". . . . The Christian presupposes a powerful, overpowering being who enjoys revenge'.[30] Every deed is to be considered '*solely with respect to its supernatural consequences* . . . that is what Jewish feeling demands, for what is natural is considered *ignoble*'.[31] However, this projection of the revenge of sin on to the Jewish heritage is immediately contrasted with the prodigiousness of Jewish power. The relation of the Jews to their God is illustrated by the way in which the French nobility surrender their power to the monarch and receive it back by gaining access to 'the plenitude of power *without equal*' of the divine monarch – from whom 'one did not not hold back the last remaining stones of one's own power'.[32]

In the first case, Nietzsche reduces the idea of divine power to finite, interested vengeance; in the second case, he translates finite, courtly power into the idea of absolute surrender to infinite power and hence to gain of disinterested powerfulness; the first makes power petty, the second makes pettiness into power – divine munificence. The Jews become the signification in which this

---

[29] Op. cit., *Werke II*, pp. 213–15, trans. § 348 pp. 290–1.

[30] Ibid., *Werke,* pp. 131–2, trans. § 135 p. 187.

[31] Ibid., *Werke,* pp. 132–6, trans. p. 188, latter emphasis added.

[32] Ibid., *Werke,* p. 133, trans. § 136 p. 188.

ambivalence is figured, whereas Christ is said to be obsessed with sin and Paul with his evil eye for the passions.[33] In sum, while the Greeks are invariably noble, Paul ignoble, the Jews are presented as both noble and ignoble and then again noble. The Jews seem to express Nietzsche's riven integrity – the compassion of his ambivalence.

In *Beyond Good and Evil*, the art of this compassion almost produces confession:

> What Europe owes to the Jews? Many things, good and bad, and above all *one thing* that is *both of the best and of the worst*: the grand style in morality, the terribleness and majesty of infinite demands, infinite meanings, the whole romanticism and sublimity of moral questionabilities – and hence precisely the most attractive, captious, and choicest part of those plays of colour and seductions to life in whose afterglow the sky of our European culture, its evening sky, is burning now – perhaps burning itself out. We artists among the spectators and philosophers are – grateful for this to the Jews.[34]

At this grandiloquent point, Nietzsche's *agon* of authorship, its *equivocal* relation to the authority of morality it presupposes, converges with his *Judaica*. The only omission is any reference to Protestant Christianity – the genealogical deliverance from which arouses Nietzsche's gratitude towards the Jews. When this genealogy is elaborated *univocally*, then the Jews are represented as the priestly people, and compassion takes on the hue of castigation.

In both the first and the third and last essay of *On the Genealogy of Morals*, 'priests' and the priestly mode of valuation are the focus of Nietzsche's argument: in the first essay, the priestly-*noble* versus the knightly-aristocratic mode of valuation; in the third essay, the ascetic priest and ascetic ideals. In both cases, the passages on the Jews can only be assessed from the entanglement of creating and decreating: adversity can be used for overcoming and *nobility*, or it can be used for *ressentiment* and *ignobility*. The second and central essay provides the *tertium a quo* for both of these outcomes by exploring historically the psychological effects of that strict Pietist morality which receives its philosophical justification in

---

[33] Ibid., *Werke*, pp. 133–4, trans. § 138, 139, p. 189.
[34] Op. cit. *Werke III*, p. 716, trans. § 250 p. 185, emphasis added.

Kant. Not only 'Jews' and 'Christians', but everyone exists in the borderland between nobility and ignobility – for to be creative one must put the negative emotions to work, and therefore one always runs the risk of allowing them to dominate.

Many commentators assume that when Nietzsche contrasts noble and slave modes of evaluation, he is harshly judging the oppressed and commending a return to warrior aristocracies; they assume, that is, that he is employing established social statuses and referring to historical stratifications. Duffy and Mittelman go further: they try to defend biblical prophets and priests from the accusation that they demeaned the strong and idealized the poor: 'they [the prophets and priests] were by no means antipathetic towards the strong and the noble per se, and they hardly viewed all of the poor as being virtuous and blessed'.[35] Far from introducing radically new values, the prophets and priests, Duffy and Mittelman insist, reasserted traditional values. Once again, this attempt to read Nietzsche's 'attitudes' shows no understanding of *the method* of the genealogy of morals, and it therefore fails to understand that Nietzsche is not concerned with the *attitudes* of biblical prophets and priests to the poor and to the nobility. Even less is he concerned with warrior aristocracies and enslaved peoples:

> it almost determines *the order of rank how* profoundly human beings can suffer. . . . Profound suffering makes noble; it separates.[36]

Nietzsche is exploring *what the meaning of 'nobility' might be.*

Nobility and ignobility are always what is at stake in the response to misfortune and constraint; they determine whether the outcome will be free – the freedom of willing the difficulty and overcoming it by self-assertion – or unfree – the unfreedom of inverting the difficulty into an evil deed of an other. 'Nobility' is keenly equivocal: for rancour may galvanize a creative response if the adversary is imagined as worth opposing, as noble; or it may anchor a negative response and become sheer *ressentiment*, if the adversary is imagined as evil, and the self credited with good. The first response creates distance – it is the pathos of distance;

---

[35] 'Nietzsche's attitudes toward the Jews', p. 313.
[36] *Beyond Good and Evil*, *Werke III*, p. 744, trans. p. 220, first four emphases added.

the second response destroys barriers and assimilates the degraded evil to the contaminated triumph of its author.

Futhermore, there is ample evidence that all the pseudo-historical presentations of Judaism and Christianity occur in the context of the contraries of modern, Protestant morality: the Thirty Years War between Protestants and Catholics after which *cuius regio, eius religio* was firmly established in Germany; Luther's Wedding, when, amidst the celebrations of the former monk and former nun as they renounced celibacy and legitimated matrimony, hints of this-worldly asceticism are already discernible; the structure of Kantian, inner, categorical morality as the result of a long process of cultivation.[37]

In the middle essay of *On the Genealogy of Morals*, the psychology and historical sociology of Kantian morality is explored without any reference to Judaism or the Jews. In Kant, the 'sovereign individual' is self-legislating and autonomous when the law is obeyed out of sheer reverence for it and not out of any interested motive. Never achievable, the attempt to overcome natural desire and inclination for the sake of disinterested reverence for the law is an endless task. Nietzsche argues that the constant practice of such overcoming would produce a supramoral individual, who is able to set the law himself, to guarantee his own promises and who is conscious of his freedom and power. This is to accept the justifications of Kantian morality as an accurate account of the moral life and to explore the psychological consequence of learning to overcome natural desire and inclination. For the endless exercise of morality cultivates power and impotence, 'the whole of asceticism belongs here'.[38] It cultivates deeply-invested impotence when the attempt to obey the law against natural desire and out of no interested motive – not even fear – overwhelms the individual and produces the resort to *ressentiment*, the culture of reaction. Both active power and reactive power arise out of the same structuring of moral energy:

> All events in the organic world are a subduing [*ein Über-wältigen*], a *becoming master* [*Herr-werden*], and all subduing and becoming master involves a fresh interpretation.[39]

[37] *On the Genealogy of Morals, Werke III*, trans. W. Kaufman, New York Vintage, 1969, 1:4, p. 775 trans. p. 28, 3:2 p. 840 trans. p. 98, p. 840, 2:2 pp. 800–1 trans. pp. 58–60.
[38] Ibid., *Werke III*, p. 802, trans. 2:3 p. 61.
[39] Ibid., *Werke III*, p. 818 trans. 2:12 p. 77.

Nietzsche is not condemning the overcoming of 'nature' or natural desire, on the contrary, he commends it, but he objects to its *moralization* – when it is justified as disinterested submission to categorical law. For Nietzsche, the law is interested, which is not to deny that it is 'sovereign' or 'universal', but to imply that the meaning of sovereignty depends on the outcome of the struggle to overcome, which, on his view, is to overcome the law itself and the opposition of disinterested reverence and natural desire.

This psychology of morality provides the mathesis for the presentation of 'the priest'; the first essay of *On the Genealogy of Morals* is best understood in the light of the third. In one and the same passage in the third essay, the Jews and the Old Testament are simultaneously said to be noble by contrast to the ascetic priest (who ruins psychical health), and to have devised the piety of fussing over one's own spiritual lapses: 'the appalling taste of this perpetual familiarity with God! This Jewish and not merely Jewish obtrusiveness of pawing and nuzzling God!'[40] The consistency of these prima-facie contrary valuations derives from the distinctions maintained by nobleness and the murkiness of priestly authority. This is confirmed by the examination of Luther's emphasis on the direct and intimate relation of the individual to God which immediately follows. Luther's attack on 'the mediating saints of the church' amounts to an attack on 'the *good etiquette* of the church, that reverential etiquette of the hieratic . . .' because 'he wanted above all to speak directly, to speak himself, to speak "informally" with his God. – Well, he did it.' Hieratic asceticism is here contrasted with loutish asceticism.[41]

The attack on the priest in multiform guises covers the priesthood of all believers (Luther), the priest as mediator (Catholic church), and biblical priests from 'Israel' to Paul. The priestly form of existence is introduced as '*essentially dangerous*';[42] it has branched off from the knightly-aristocratic form and come to oppose it. Priests make '*the most evil enemies*' but are not capable of war, because their revaluation of their enemies is impotent, 'an act of the *most spiritual revenge*'.[43] The evidence for this inversion

[40] Ibid., *Werke*, p. 885 trans. 3:22 p. 144.
[41] Ibid., *Werke III*, pp. 885–6, trans. p. 145.
[42] Ibid., *Werke III*, p. 778 trans. 1:6 p. 33.
[43] Ibid., *Werke III*, p. 779, trans. 1:7 p. 34.

of aristocratic values and spiritual revenge is given in a parody of
the beatitudes of the Sermon on the Mount:

> the wretched alone are the good; the poor, impotent, lowly
> alone are the good; the suffering, deprived, sick, ugly alone
> are blessed by God, blessedness is for them alone – and you,
> the powerful and noble, are on the contrary the evil, the
> cruel, the lustful, the insatiable, the godless to all eternity;
> and you shall be in all eternity the unblessed, accursed and
> damned![44]

Nietzsche concludes that with the Jews, 'there begins *the slave revolt
in morality*'.[45]

A further inversion has to occur for Christianity to develop:
Jewish vengefulness and hatred ('the profoundest and sublimest
kind of hatred') is inverted into Christian love. 'This secret black
art of truly grand politics' is seen as 'Israel's' revenge in the face
of defeat. By means of the crucifixion 'all the opponents of Israel'
come to accept the salvation of man prepared out of the political
and spiritual defeat of Israel.[46] This idea of 'truly grand politics',
of propagating revenge as love, the triumph over nobler ideals,
Christianity as the sublimation of the political institutions of
Israel, this authorial rant and lament, is suddenly interrupted by
an unnamed interlocutor who, in an epilogue in inverted commas
to 'my speech' which had no inverted commas and only retrospectively turns into a speech, accepts the idea that ' "the people
have won" – or "the slaves," or "the mob" or "the herd," or whatever you like to call them – if this has happened through the Jews,
very well! in that case no people ever had a more world-historic
mission" '.[47] Thus speaks a 'free spirit', who is also said to be
'honest' and 'a democrat'. This free spirit has exposed the authorial silence ('for at this point I have much to be silent about') with
humour and irony by his admission that 'we, too, love the poison',
the poison which has spread through 'the entire body of mankind'.[48]

This inner dialogue between the ignoble voice and the noble
voice lies at the heart of what Nietzsche means by 'genealogy':

[44] Ibid., *Werke III*, pp. 779–80, trans. p. 34.
[45] Ibid., *Werke*, p. 780
[46] Ibid., *Werke III*, p. 781, trans. 1:8 p. 35.
[47] Ibid., *Werke III*, p. 781, trans. 1:9 pp. 35–6.
[48] Ibid., *Werke III*, pp. 781–2, trans. p. 36.

it is 'the conscience of method'; the art of compassion of his own – and our – riven integrity. Formed by both Christianity and morality, the second, noble voice is honest about loving his poison – his redemption from the master, from power as such – and thus he is truly democratic – prepared to overcome his *ressentiment* and to form his power with the power of others; the first, ignoble voice, by refusing to forget, cherishes in silence his lack of power; in *ressentiment* he invents his evil enemy, and thereby affirms a division of impotence between imagined demonic powers and righteous indignation which preserves his own innocence and indignity.

These implications become clear from the two sections which follow the dialogue. The man of *ressentiment* 'understands how to keep silent', whereas the noble man 'lives in trust and openness with himself';[49] the noble man is reckless, impulsive, in anger and love, he forgets his mistakes and respects his enemies, and rapidly discharges his *ressentiment* towards them; the man of *ressentiment* is clever, scheming, and secretive, he cherishes his memory of offence, and fixes and idealizes his evil enemy as his own deed.[50]

From here on, by their fascination in the tales of this text, both author and reader are themselves implicated in the inner dialogue between the ignoble and the noble voice, between *ressentiment* and the free, democratic spirit. 'Judea's triumph over Rome' can only be proclaimed by the intense voice of *ressentiment* not by the light voice of the democrat; so that when the Renaissance, the reawakening of the noble mode of evaluation from Judaized Rome, is declaimed to have been destroyed because 'Judea immediately triumphed again, thanks to that thoroughly plebeian (German and English) *ressentiment* movement called the Reformation', it is all to be taken in the inverted commas of the canny, scheming author who, knows how to be silent amidst his personified vociferousness.[51]

'The conscience of method' illuminates *The Anti-Christ* – which still requires that gloves should be worn.[52] The book begins and ends with the scandal of Luther and Kant, restorers of priesthood,[53]

[49] Ibid., *Werke III*, p. 784, trans. 1:10 p. 38.

[50] Ibid., *Werke III*, p. 785, trans. p. 39.

[51] Ibid., *Werke III*, p. 796, trans. 1:16, p. 54.

[52] '[O]ne does well to put gloves on when reading the New Testament' (*The Anti-Christ*, 1895, *Werke III*, p. 1210; trans. R. J. Hollingdale, Harmondsworth Penguin, 1968, 46 p. 161).

[53] Ibid., *Werke III*, pp. 171–2, trans. § 10, 11 pp. 121–2; pp. 1233–4, trans. § 61 p. 185.

but it focuses on Paul, paradigm and emblem of Protestant Christianity. The reflection on Paul is preceded by three genealogies which demonstrate the ambivalence towards the notion of 'the priest' itself. First, priestly power is traced through the history of Israel:[54] after the exile the priests revalued 'the pre-exilic great epoch' so that the exile comes to appear merited as a punishment. The priest thereby makes himself *'everywhere indispensable'*.[55] Christianity continues this 'Jewish negating of reality'. Second, however, Christianity is fundamentally distinguished from Judaism. Christian evangelism destroys Jewish ecclesiology: '"Sin," every kind of distancing relation between God and man, is abolished – *precisely this is the glad tidings'*.[56] The life of the Redeemer exemplifies this unconditioned nature: 'blessedness is not promised, not tied to any condition: it is the only reality'.[57] Christ did not offer any resistance to his enemies, did not defend himself, did not distinguish between others, did not seek the protection of the law:[58]

> It is *not* 'penance,' *not* 'prayer for forgiveness' which leads to God: *evangelic practice alone* leads to God, it *is* God! – What was *abolished* with the Evangel was the Judaism of the concepts 'sin,' 'forgiveness of sin,' 'faith,' 'redemption by faith' – the whole of Jewish *ecclesiastical* teaching was denied in the 'glad tidings.'[59]

Once this refusal to take any stance is transferred from Christ to the individual Christian, its meaning changes: 'True life, eternal life is found – it is not promised, it is here, it is *within you*: as life lived in love, in love without deduction or exclusion, without distance'.[60] This religion of love is interpreted as an evasion of pain – physiological and psychological – by refusing any contact, any resistance as such. 'The fear of pain, even of the infinitely small in pain – *cannot* end otherwise than in a

---

[54] Ibid., *Werke III*, pp. 1185–86, trans. § 25 pp. 135–6.
[55] Ibid., *Werke III*, p. 1188, trans. § 26 p. 138.
[56] Ibid., *Werke III*, p. 1195, trans. § 33 p. 145.
[57] Ibid.
[58] Ibid., *Werke III*, pp. 1195–6, trans. § 33 pp. 145–6.
[59] Ibid., *Werke III*, p. 1195–6, trans. § 33 p. 146.
[60] Ibid., *Werke III*, p. 1191, trans. § 29 p. 141.

religion of love'. Arising from excessive sensibility, from decadence, love becomes the sole, the last, possibility of life which will not live.[61]

Third, the purported inheritance from Judaism of denying reality and the purported substitution of formless evangelic 'love' for Judaic resistance explain why 'Christianity negates the Church – it is the priestly instinct which can no longer endure the priest as reality'.[62] The 'Jewish instinct' of the priest, which is to deny reality in the interests of priestly rule, is developed by Christianity to deny the very idea of the priest itself. The progressive internalization of resistance becomes the refusal of all and any actual resistance.

Paul, genius of hatred, achieved this completion: '*His* requirement was *power*'.[63] He denied what had happened for the sake of the lie of the resurrected Jesus. The lie of the immortality and salvation of the soul teaches that '"The world revolves around *me*,"' it 'wages a war to the death against every feeling of reverence and distance between man and man':[64]

In Christianity, as the art of holy lying, the whole of Judaism,
a schooling and technique pursued with utmost seriousness
for hundreds of years, attains its ultimate perfection.[65]

Paul perfects the cloaking of 'the cold-blooded cynicism' of the rule of priests as the will of God, 'to call one's own will "God," *Torah* – that is quintessentially Jewish [*urjüdisch*]'.[66] If Paul is said to display 'that rabbinic insolence which characterizes him in every respect';[67] he also represents '"the priest in himself"' who projects on to God what he wants to control.[68] Paul is hatred not love incarnate, 'the Jew, the *eternal* Jew *par excellence* . . . .'.[69]

[61] Ibid., *Werke III*, p. 1192, trans. § 30 p. 142.
[62] Ibid., *Werke III*, p. 1187, trans. § 27 p. 139.
[63] Ibid., *Werke III*, p. 1204, trans. § 42 p. 155.
[64] Ibid., *Werke III*, p. 1205, trans. § 43 p. 156.
[65] Ibid., *Werke III*, p. 1206, trans. § 44 p. 157.
[66] Ibid., *Werke III*, p. 1212, trans. § 47 p. 163, compare pp. 1186–87, § 26 p. 137.
[67] Ibid., *Werke III*, p. 1203, trans. § 41 p. 154.
[68] Ibid., trans. § 48 p. 164, '*Priester an sich*', inverted commas in original. In these passages, Nietzsche seems to be using 'rabbi' and 'priest' interchangeably.
[69] Ibid., *Werke III*, p. 1230, trans. § 58 p. 181.

What he divined was that with the aid of the little sectarian movement on the edge of Judaism one could ignite a 'world conflagration,' that with the symbol 'God on the Cross' one could sum up everything down-trodden, everything in secret revolt, the entire heritage of anarchist agitation in the Empire into a tremendous power.[70]

It is German, Protestant Christianity which has restored this Pauline faith. Insisting, therefore, on the contemporaneity of the priestly religion, *The Anti-Christ* concludes its 'eternal accusation' against Christianity, 'the *one* great curse',[71] with an eschatological commandment:

> And one calculates *time* from the *dies nefastus* on which this fatality arose – from the *first* day of Christianity! – *Why not rather from its last? – From today?* – Revaluation of all values![72]

What kind of conversion could this be? It would be the eternal return – the renunciation of *ressentiment* against time. 'Reverence for oneself; love for oneself; unconditioned freedom with respect for oneself'.[73] This revaluation would surely involve 'the invention of an even more abstract form of existence . . . than one conditioned by an organized Church'.[74] For how can the eternal return be distinguished from justification by faith alone? Unless such love *appears in the world*, with reverence for the boundaries between man and man, it would be indistinguishable from hate. No wonder *The Anti-Christ*, like the first and third essays in *On the Genealogy of Morals*, resounds with such cherished hatred! It has been composed by a great, resentful genius, who would force these intense, fictional rememberings of evil deeds; who, in the 'Foreword', admits that he seeks posthumous power.[75] How much this work has in common with its quarry – Paul!

Yet if the 'last' word on that last day of the last and first man

---

[70] Ibid.
[71] Ibid., *Werke III*, p. 1235, trans. § 62 p. 186.
[72] Ibid., *Werke III*, p. 1235, trans. p. 187, *dies nefastus* means 'unlucky day'.
[73] Ibid., 'Forword', *Werke III*, p. 1163, trans. p. 114.
[74] Ibid., *Werke III*, p. 1189, trans. § 27 p. 139.
[75] Ibid., *Werke III*, p. 1163, trans. p. 114.

belongs to the honest democrat, who neither loves nor hates without distancing relationships, who is not frightened to have boundaries or to lose them, who is able to resist and willing to be vulnerable and hurt . . . And if *this* has happened through the Jews, very well! in that case no people ever had a more world-historic mission. And in that case, the date of the last day of Christianity would not depend on the inner conversion of some Paul *redivivus*, as the peroration of *The Anti-Christ* must imply, for the advent of the kingdom would be configured in the world of man and man.

'The conscience of method' is also the method of the last word of Nietzsche's authorship, 'Why I am a Destiny', at the end of *Ecce Homo*. For it would explain the contrariness of simultaneously proclaiming glad tidings and disowning believers: 'I am a bringer of glad tidings like no one before me/I *want* no believers.'[76] The proclaiming voice insists that its evangelism must become a great politics and not found a religion. Zarathustra appears here as the name of 'the self-overcoming of morality', the one who has created morality, 'this most calamitous error', and transposed it into metaphysics, and who must overcome the morality and its metaphysical transposition by telling the truth about it.[77] In this way, Zarathrustra turns into his opposite ' – into me – '.[78] The concluding cry of 'Dionysus versus the Crucified' is itself overcome by the reference to Persian truth and virtue, to a fictive character and destiny beyond the contamination of Hellenism and Judaism. Yet, throughout *Ecce Homo*, Nietzsche nominates his enterprise the *psychology of morality*, rising to the crescendo: 'There was no psychology at all before me.'[79] The deepest identifications and analyses throughout Nietzsche's authorship belong, as indicated here, to Christian morality and its overcoming; but he knew that he could do nothing to prevent his teaching from becoming another Pauline peril of petty politics or from being pronounced holy. By comparison with this dangerous investigation, this temptation, the general preoccupation from Heidegger

---

[76] Op. cit., *Werke*, p. 1152, trans. *On the Geneology of Morals and Ecce Homo*, W. Kaufman, New York, Vintage, 1969, pp. 327, 326.

[77] Ibid., *Werke III*, p. 1153–4, trans. § 3 p. 328.

[78] Ibid., *Werke III*, p. 1154.

[79] Ibid., *Werke III*, p. 1156, trans. § 6 p. 331.

to post-modernity with Nietzsche's opposition to metaphysics has mistaken the transposition of morality – metaphysics – for its aetiology. Nietzsche's new-founded psychology unabashedly requires new-founded truth and imagines new-founded virtue. 'The Jews' and 'Judaism' afforded the only historical and living intimation of ways out of and ways into this truth and this virtue.

9

Hermann Cohen – Kant among the Prophets

The selective reception by general philosophy and social scientific methodology in the European tradition of the mode of neo-Kantianism founded by Hermann Cohen (1842–1918) has contributed to the widespread undermining of conceptual thinking in favour of the hermeneutics of reading.[1] To assess Cohen's thought as a reading and re-originating of the Jewish tradition involves a predicament of circularity: for the question of reading and origin is not neutral but derives from the partial reception of the object addressed. The task of reassessment changes from a methodologically independent survey to a challenge posed by current thought, unsure of its modernity or post-modernity, to re-establish contact with a formative but long-forgotten part of itself.

[1] This chapter was first published in *The Journal of Jewish Thought and Philosophy*, vol. 2, 2 (1993). It is reprinted with permission. It was originally prepared for the Symposium, 'The Playground of Textuality: Modern Jewish Intellectuals and the Horizon of Interpretation', First Annual Wayne State University Press Jewish Symposium, held in Detroit, 20–22 March 1988. Each of the eight participants elected to reassess an individual thinker by focusing on that thinker as a *reader* of the tradition – ancient and modern. In addition, we were asked to consider the following issues:

1 What is the contribution of Jewish intellectuals/writers to what is characteristically modern and post-modern in how we read texts?
2 How have Jewish intellectuals/writers in the twentieth century created new ways of thinking and employed new ways of reading?
3 How has this new way of reading re-originated what it means to be a Jew in the modern and post-modern world?
4 Have these Jewish thinkers and writers – some at the centre and others at the margin of Judaism – created a new modern Jewish hermeneutic theory and tradition?

No longer solely academic, this exercise will have to confront two especially difficult aspects of Cohen's thought. First, he did not 'read' Kant, he destroyed the Kantian philosophy. In its place, he founded a 'neo-Kantianism' on the basis of a logic of origin, difference and repetition. As a logic of validity, this neo-Kantian mathesis is often at stake when its practitioners prefer to acknowledge themselves as the progeny of Nietzsche, Heidegger or Benjamin.[2] Second, as I hope to demonstrate in this paper, Cohen's logic is inseparable from his ethics and his philosophy of Judaism. This implies that, since Cohen, the connection between the philosophy of Judaism and general philosophy has been *fundamental*, in a sense that has not hitherto been imagined or explored.

Moses Mendelssohn – so Altmann, his biographer, relates – eventually managed to write a letter to Kant, and tell him that he could not fathom the *Critique of Pure Reason*.[3] In *Morgenstunden* (1785), however, Mendelssohn refers to 'the all crushing Kant [*der alles zermalmende Kant*]', and implores him to rebuild, 'with the same spirit with which he had torn down'.[4] Hermann Cohen renews Mendelssohn's Judaic Enlightenment by embracing Kant's destructive method, but, paradoxically, he employs it against the critical philosophy itself. Although Cohen's invention of a philosophy of Being as 'productive origin', developed in his three part *System*, remains largely unknown and is not available in English translation,[5] its panlogism has released, and continues to release generations of thinkers who remain beholden to Kant from the critical philosophy as such, as well as from engagement with any

[2] In his comment 'Vertauschte Fronten', on the Davos Disputation between Ernst Cassirer and Martin Heidegger in March 1929, Rosenzweig himself argued that Heidegger, successor to Cohen's chair at Marburg, furthered the spirit of Cohen's thought more than Cassirer, the more orthodox neo-Kantian (op. cit. May 1929, in *Zweistromland: Kleinere Schriften zu Glauben und Denken, Gesammelte Schriften,* III (Dordrecht, Martinus Nijhoff, 1984), 235–7; for an English translation of the Davos Disputation, see 'Appendices' to Heidegger, *Kant and the Problem of Metaphysics*, trans. Richard Taft, Bloomington, Indiana University Press, 1990, pp. 71–85).
[3] Alexander Altmann, *Moses Mendelssohn: A Biographical Study*, London, Routledge, 1973, pp. 705–6 and 629.
[4] Ibid., p. 673, trans. amended; see Moses Mendelssohn, *Morgenstunden oder Vorlesungen über das Dasein Gottes*, 1785, ed. Dominique Bourel, Stuttgart, Reclam, 1979, pp. 5, 7.
[5] For *Logic der reinen Erkenntnis* (1902), see Gillian Rose, *Hegel contra Sociology*, London, Athlone, 1981, pp. 1–47; for *Ethik des reinen Willens* (1904), see Rose, *Dialectic of Nihilism: Post-Structuralism and Law*, Blackwell, Oxford, 1984, pp. 25–51. The third part of Cohen's *System* is *Ästhetik des reinen Gefühls*, 2 vols, 1912 (Berlin, Bruno Cassirer).

of the forms of critique which succeeded it.[6] If, as I hope to show, Cohen's *Religion of Reason out of the Sources of Judaism*, which he wrote after resigning from his chair at Marburg in 1912, where he had founded the northern school of neo-Kantianism, *completes* his *System*, then this must lead to a reassessment of the mutual implication of logic and Judaism in twentieth-century thought. This argument would refute Leo Strauss' claim that 'the return to Judaism' requires the overcoming of philosophy;[7] and it will open up new points of comparison between Cohen's *System* and Rosenzweig's *Star of Redemption*.

Cohen made it clear that whether the source of his thinking was Kant or Judaism, it was *the concept which he laid out as a foundation* and not the authority of those sources which determined what they would yield. This declaimed autonomy, which is fully in the spirit of Kant's *Religion within the Bounds of Reason Alone*,[8] reveals Cohen in effect to be heir to the antinomies of Kantian thinking. For, although Cohen's logic of productive origin would seem to overcome the Kantian antinomies, and his ethics is completed as prophecy, Cohen's difficulty with the Judaic notion of law, Talmud Torah or Halacha, returns him to an unexplored heteronomy.

Cohen and Rosenzweig are systematic thinkers, and their two 'systems' present Janus-faces of modern thinking which claims, nevertheless, that it has abandoned the *System*. No less than four meanings of 'system' need to be distinguished. First, the Kantian system of the deduction of all valid a priori principles of pure theoretical and pure practical reason. Second, Hegel's system of the Absolute, which includes the history of its development and the development of its history, and which is, therefore, universal and aporetic in its exposition of the identity and difference of subject and substance, the rational and the real. The third meaning is that

[6] Compare the discussion of Cohen and Marburg neo-Kantianism by Steven S. Schwarzschild, 'Authority and Reason contra Gadamer', 1981, in *Studies in Jewish Philosophy: Collected Essays of the Academy for Jewish Philosophy, 1980–1985*, ed. Norbert M. Samuelson, Lanham, University Press of America, 1987, pp. 161–90; and the remarks on Cohen and jurisprudence by the same author in 'An agenda for Jewish Philosophy in the 1980s', 1980, in Samuelson, *Studies is Jewish Philosophy*, p. 106.

[7] See his 'Preface' to the English translation (1962) of *Spinoza's Critique of Religion*, 1930, trans. E. M. Sinclair, New York, Schocken, 1982, pp. 8–9.

[8] *Religion der Vernunft aus den Quellen des Judentums*, 1919, Wiesbaden, Fourier, 1978, pp. 4–5; trans. *Religion of Reason out of the Sources of Judaism*, Simon Kaplan, New York, Frederick Unger, 1972, p. 4.

of Cohen's neo-Kantian *System* which propounds validity and origin according to the 'method' of prophecy. The fourth meaning will be Rosenzweig's: it freezes a dialectical world-history by mobilizing Schelling's eschatological world-epochs. While Cohen acts in the spirit of Kant and Rosenzweig declares himself opposed to Hegel, Cohen changes the meaning of Kantianism fundamentally, while Rosenzweig's relationship to Hegel's thought is more systematic than he is willing to concede.[9]

In his 'Introduction' to the three-volume edition of Cohen's *Jüdische Schriften* (1924), Rosenzweig argues that Cohen transmutes the severe logic of origin on which his System is based to the mutuality of the 'correlation' (*Korrelation*) between God and man in his Jewish writings.[10] In the 'Introductory Essay' to the English edition of the *Religion of Reason*, Leo Strauss argues more ambiguously that the *Religion of Reason* forms the 'crowning part' of Cohen's *System*.[11] Eva Jospe, editor and translator of *Reason and Hope: Selections from the Jewish Writings of Hermann Cohen*, argues that Cohen's turn to Judaism occurred after his three-part *System* was complete.[12]

In Cohen's own 'Introduction' to the *Religion of Reason out of the Sources of Judaism*, he contrasts the 'lazy reasoning [*faule Vernunft*]' of ethics, which posits a rigorous God as a mere guarantor of its arguments, with the compassionate God and the sufferer in religion.[13] In the *Ethics of Pure Willing*, the second part of his *System*, and in the *Religion of Reason*, Cohen distinguishes 'ethics' as a discipline and as the principles of action from 'ethical life' (*Sittlichkeit*), the reconstruction of the customary life of a people

[9] However, Robert Gibbs has shown how Rosenzweig employs Cohen's creative logic of origin in the first Part of *The Star of Redemption* (see Gibbs, 'The Limits of Thought: Rosenzweig, Schelling and Cohen', *Zeitschrift für philosophische Forschung*, 43 (1989), pp. 618–40).

[10] 'Einleitung in die Akademieausgabe der Jüdischen Schriften Hermann Cohens' 1924, in *Zweistromland, Gesammelte Schriften*, III, Berlin, Schocken, 1937, p. 208.

[11] Leo Strauss, 'Introductory Essay', to Cohen's *Religion of Reason*, pp. xxiv–xxv. However, Nathan Rotenstreich has stressed the importance of the doctrine of creation in Cohen's System (see 'Hermann Cohen: Judaism in the Context of German Philosophy' in Jehuda Reinharz and Walter Schatzberg (eds), *The Jewish Response to German Culture: From the Enlightenment to the Second World War*, Hanover and London, University Press of New England, 1985, pp. 51–63).

[12] Cohen, *Reason and Hope: Selections from the Jewish Writings of Hermann Cohen*, ed. and trans. Eva Jospe, New York, W.W. Norton & Co. 1971, pp. 16–17.

[13] *Religion of Reason*, p. 24, trans. p. 21, amended.

in its totality and with its contradictions. The English translation, however, renders *Sittlichkeit* as 'morality' under the illusion that this is justified by Cohen's insistence that he is not engaged in *ethics*.[14] As a result, Cohen's concern with ethical life *as opposed to* morality is lost. Yet Cohen, like Hegel, sets Kant's categorical moral imperative, which is heard as the inner voice of individual conscience, against the holistic, historical and communal notion of ethical life. In his *System*, he expounds the historico-juridical development of individualistic morality (*Moralität*), and in the *Religion of Reason* he expounds the suffering individual. All these distinctions and developments are lost when *Sittlichkeit* is translated as 'morality'. Further, the analogy between Cohen's transformation of theoretical philosophy into 'validity' and 'origin' and his transformation of practical philosophy into 'ethical life' and 'origin' cannot be discerned. In short, this mistranslation makes it impossible to follow how Cohen concludes or destroys the Kantian problematics of theoretical and practical reason by fusing the synthesis of appearances with the moral law.

In the third chapter of the *Religion of Reason*, on 'Creation', Cohen discusses Maimonides' claim that the creation of the world out of nothing is as 'rational' as Aristotle's 'claim of reason' for the eternity of the world. Cohen argues that Maimonides advanced 'the claim of reason' by connecting God's 'negative' attributes with 'privative' ones, which, nevertheless, yield and affirm positive implications. Above all, the denial of God's 'inertia' amounts to grounding 'a new positivity', to the idea of God as 'the origin of activity [*der Ursprung des Aktivität*]'. Cohen goes on to emphasize that this 'logic of creation' had been developed as the 'logic of origin' in the first Part of his *System*, the *Logik der reinen Erkenntnis*.[15] This explicit conceptual connection between the *Logic* and the *Religion of Reason* bears out the programmatic statement in Cohen's *Concept of Religion in the System of Philosophy* that 'true religion is based on the truth of systematic philosophy'.[16]

The fundamental connection attested by Cohen between the

---

[14] Ibid., pp. 37–9, trans. pp. 32–3.
[15] Ibid., p. 73; trans. p. 63.
[16] *Der Begriff der Religion im System der Philosophie*, Giessen, Alfred Töpelmann, 1915, pp. 137–8.

logic of origin and the logic of creation may be discerned more generally: for not only 'origin', but all the key notions of the *Religion of Reason* draw on the *System*. Furthermore, the organization of the *Religion of Reason* recapitulates the *System*, and, *pari passu*, the *System* is only fully intelligible in the light of the *Religion of Reason* – in its method and in its content. The first three chapters of the *Religion of Reason* on the 'Uniqueness' of God, on 'Image-Worship' and on 'Creation', expound 'origin' from the *Logic*. Chapters 4 to 7 on 'Revelation', 'Creation of Man in Reason', the 'Attribute of Action', and 'The Holy Ghost', expound 'purpose' from the *Ethics*. Chapters 8 to 10, 'The Discovery of Man as Fellowman', 'The Problem of Religious Love', 'The Individual as I', expound *Sittlichkeit* from the *Ethics* as the correlation of God and man. Chapters 13 to 15, 'The Idea of the Messiah and Humanity', 'Messianism in the Prophets', Chapter 16 on 'Law', Chapters 18 to 22 on the 'Virtues', which include justice (*die Gerechtigkeit*) expound time, history and the prophetic method from the *Ethics*.

The following selective discussion of these interrelations between what I deem to be the 'four' parts, as it were, of Cohen's *System* is designed to demonstrate, first, how the *Religion of Reason* depends on the *Logic* and the *Ethics*, and, vice versa, the *Logic* and the *Ethics* presuppose the *Religion of Reason*; second, that Cohen does not *read* his sources in the sense of modern biblical hermeneutics, nor does he provide a commentary on them in the sense of traditional rabbinics: he *thinks* them, that is, he brings them under a concept – whether his procedure is followed from the 'sources' (Kant, Judaism) to the *System*, or from the *System* to the 'sources'. In both cases, *System* and 'source' are expounded as 'creative origin'. Third, this creative or productive origin abolishes all the finely balanced dualisms of the Kantian philosophy, between theoretical and practical reason, between appearances and things in themselves, between necessity and freedom, between autonomy and heteronomy. Both Kant and Judaism are redefined as 'doctrine' (*Lehre*), instead of critique and as teaching or Torah, respectively. This conflating of logic and Judaism into 'doctrine' is easily overlooked in the English translations.

In his *Logic*, Cohen turns Kant's transcendental logic into *pure* logic. In Kant, the imagination synthesizes appearances, but the mind is unable to know things in themselves; Cohen establishes an independent realm of validity, which is ultimate and underivable. Accordingly, for Cohen, all thinking is the thinking of Being; and Kant's essential distinction between immanent and transcendent knowledge is abolished. In the *Logic*, Cohen justifies this discarding of Kant's most fundamental distinction by arguing that Kant, like Plato, appeals to the given validity of mathematics – the principles of which are pure, underived and underivable, and do not refer to any empirical employment. He argues that Kant's idea of 'synthesis' is misconceived, for it implies an independent plurality or manifold which is formed into a unity, when both plurality and unity must themselves be produced or created by thinking. This productive activity, prior to plurality and unity, Cohen calls 'the origin'. It precedes unifying and diversifying, differentiating and repeating, thought and being. It follows that the validity of propositions is independent of perception and representation. Contrary to Kant, all thinking is cognition, or the doctrine of cognemes (*Erkenntnisse*); it is not synthetic, nor does it require critical justification. Science is the activity of unifying and diversifying, of differentiating and repeating – a never-ending task based on the unity of creating. Even in his *Logic*, Cohen relies on religious and moral ideas and terminology: 'origin' and 'creation', 'activity' and 'task'. In my work on the perdurance of neo-Kantian barriers to engagement with Hegel, I understood Cohen to be providing a Fichtean *Tathandlung*, original act, as the solution to the Kantian antinomies.[17]

The *Religion of Reason* extends this notion of originality (*Ursprünglichkeit*) to ground the claim that Judaism is the religion of reason, the *original* religion, against the Hegelian exposition of Christianity as the *absolute* religion.[18] Reason, Cohen argues, is originally productive or creative in God, not in man (Kant); it is not mediatory (Hegel); nor pantheistic (Spinoza).[19] 'Origin' is the unique, creative, active God: man is created as the *correlation* (*Korrelation*) of this reason; that is, he co-responds to Revelation, which is the continuation of creation in the world and ethical reason in man.[20] Cohen argues that it is these definitions of man as 'response', and creation as continuous, which distinguish Judaism from

---

[17] See Rose, *Hegel contra Sociology*, pp. 1–47.
[18] Op. cit., pp. 9–10, 39, trans. p. 8, 34.
[19] Ibid., pp. 55–6, 47–8, trans. pp. 47–8, 40–1.
[20] Ibid., pp. 41–57, 95, 99–108, trans. 35–49, p. 82, 85–89.

pantheism, 'communication', participation and causality.[21] Conceding that *correlation* cannot be traced in the Judaic 'sources', Cohen proposes instead that an antinomy may be found there, which may be 'purified', following Maimonides, to expose its rational core: the antinomy is the combination of the motifs of universal love and justice with their specific national-political bearer; the rational core, the ethical mission, which *correlation* and continuous creation attest.[22]

'Creation' grounds *correlation*, while Revelation is its execution; but it is the third, traditional category of theology, Redemption, as prophecy and as Messianism, which completes the three and the *System* as a whole. Much greater emphasis is given to this third notion of redemption than to Torah – the gift or giving of which is said to be 'the technical expression' for the Revelation of eternal law, and which is distinguished from the authority of the unwritten natural law of the Greeks, and from law as *Gesetz* or 'specific commands' (perhaps *Mitzvot*).[23]

Rosenzweig is therefore wrong when he argues that Cohen's development of *correlation*, the co-response from man, represents a mitigating of the remorseless logism of 'origin'.[24] *Correlation* is an extension of the kingdom or realm of ends or purposes (*Endzwecke*) from Cohen's *Ethics*; it transforms the meaning of Kant's categorical imperative so that the practical purpose of the will becomes man's response to the ethical challenge of good and evil. 'The kingdom of ends' for Cohen does not refer to Kant's subjunctive command to act *as if* one is a member of the kingdom of ends, but refers the will repeatedly to futural Messianic time.[25] In the *Ethics*, the will is not oriented, as in Kant, to an eternal, that is, to an endless or never-ending, task because it has always to overcome natural desire and inclination, but to the task of the eternal – the kingdom; and in the *Religion of Reason*, this becomes the drawing of *Holiness*.[26]

[21] Ibid., pp. 47–57ff, trans. pp. 40–9.
[22] Ibid., pp. 84–7, trans. pp. 72–5.
[23] Ibid., p. 97, trans. pp. 83–4.
[24] Rosenzweig also argues that *Korrelation* first appears in *Aesthetics of Pure Feeling*, the third Part of the *System* (see Rosenzweig, 'Einleitung in die Akademieausgabe der Jüdischen Schriften Hermann Cohens', pp. 209–10).
[25] See Cohen, *Ethik des reinen Willens*, Berlin, Bruno Cassirer, 1904, pp. 376–7.
[26] *Religion of Reason*, p. 112, trans. pp. 96–7.

This interconnection between the two works clarifies the title of the sixth chapter of the *Religion of Reason*: 'The Attributes of Action', which sits oddly among the conventional, theological headings of the other chapters. In this chapter, Cohen argues that Maimonides refers all divine attributes to divine action, and all action to the realm of ends or purposes (*Zwecke*), the practical equivalent of the theoretical realm of validity.[27] This realm, beyond Being – the task of God, or, equally, God's task for man – is Holiness: the 'Holy Spirit' *means* the drawing or endeavour of Holiness, whereby man and God co-respond. This *correlation* is presented without the categorical imperative addressed to the individual (Kant), and without any mediation (Hegel).[28] It follows from this idea of Holiness as the community of God and man in the execution of *correlation*, that 'the Other' is discovered as 'fellow' (*Mitmensch*), not as 'neighbour' (*Nebenmensch*).[29] As God's love for the stranger precedes His love for oneself, so fellowship precedes individuality.[30]

It is Prophecy which energizes and completes the whole *System*, and which raises the question of its method as well as its telos. The chapters in the *Religion of Reason* on the 'Messianic Idea of Humanity' and on 'Justice' imply and presuppose the role of prophecy in the *Ethics*. For it is Prophecy which makes known the inner *correlation* between God and man by proclaiming that judgements of good and evil do not exhaust ethics because pain and suffering arise from poverty.[31] While the exposition of 'poverty' is general in the biblical setting of the *Religion of Reason*, in the *Ethics*, poverty is traced to the legal fictions which make it possible to alienate and appropriate human activity by dividing it into persons, things and obligations.[32] The preconditions and limits of these legal fictions are expounded in the *Ethics* according to what Cohen calls 'the control of actuality'. In the *Religion of Reason*, this criterion or control of actuality is revealed to be the social ethic of prophetic Messianism. Whereas the *Ethics* is

[27] Ibid., pp. 109–110, trans. pp. 94–5.
[28] Ibid., pp. 116–117, trans. pp. 100–1.
[29] Ibid., p. 133, trans. pp. 114–15.
[30] Ibid., pp. 144–8, trans. pp. 124–8.
[31] Ibid., pp. 152–6, trans. pp. 131–4.
[32] See Cohen, *Ethik des reinen Willens*, pp. 570–2, 591.

concerned with mutually opposed fictions, the *Religion of Reason* is concerned with all individuals beyond the fictions – the judge as well as the criminal.[33] Similarly, the virtue of justice (*die Gerechtigkeit*), which in the *Ethics* culminates the *System* in equity,[34] is the point at which in the *Religion of Reason* method and content – the control of actuality and the task of Holiness – fuse in the prophetic proclamation which concludes on the note of universal peace.[35]

The 'Sources' are in these unhesitating ways transfigured by the *System*. Cohen issues his apologia for this procedure in the 'Introduction' to the *Religion of Reason*:

> [E]ven if I am referred to the literary sources of the prophets for the concept of religion, those sources remain mute and blind if I do not approach them with a concept, which I myself lay out as a foundation in order to be instructed by them and not simply guided by their authority.[36]

While the idea of 'the creativity of reason' legitimizes this concept, Cohen admits that 'wrestling' occurs between the universality of reason and the history of a particular people.[37] Yet, he argues, Judaism is 'the source of sources' and thus the 'original' source.[38] In this way, the contingency of 'source' and the fundament of 'origin' are reconciled.

This arrogation of authority by 'a concept' is prevented from becoming arbitrary because of another 'wrestling' which Cohen fails to address yet which configures his *System* – the concept of 'law' with its multiple meanings in Kant and in Judaism. In the *Religion of Reason*, 'law' (*Gesetz*) is defined narrowly as 'ritual', and a chapter is devoted to it separately from the chapter on 'Revelation'. Cohen argues that the predominance of ritual law in Judaism protects atonement from any easily accomplished redemption and preserves Messianic universalism.[39] This reductive biblicism omits any distinction between commandment, law and ritual,

---

[33] *Religion of Reason*, pp. 195–6, trans. pp. 167–8.
[34] Cohen, *Ethik des reinen Willens*, p. 587; and see Rose, *Dialectic of Nihilism*, pp. 47–8.
[35] *Religion of Reason*, pp. 515–33, trans. pp. 446–62.
[36] Ibid., pp. 4–5, trans. p. 4.
[37] Ibid., p. 9, trans. p. 8.
[38] '[S]ie wird zu einer Urquelle für andere Quellen', ibid.
[39] Ibid., pp. 425–30f, trans. pp. 366–70f.

and any reference in general to Rabbinic Judaism and the institutions of Halacha.[40] Furthermore, Cohen seeks to overcome the Kantian antinomies by forced reconciliation of the multiple and rich equivocations of the meaning of law in Kant's theoretical and practical philosophy. In general, the original conceptuality of the *System* displays what appears to be a resolute refusal to address the meaning of commandment, teaching, law and Halacha, yet these unaddressed meanings fracture its ethical and Messianic longings.[41]

Kant's critical philosophy aims to justify categorical morality on the basis of possible knowledge, which is thereby circumscribed so that God, the thing-in-itself, the transcendental subject, and morality itself, are validated practically, heuristically or as postulates, but remain unknown and unknowable themselves. Cohen's 'neo-Kantian' *System* demonstrates that God is knowable as justice (*die Gerechtigkeit*). Yet, in an essay of 1910, 'The Inner Relations of Kantian Philosophy to Judaism', Cohen attempts to assimilate Kant's philosophy and Judaism on seven scores.[42]

According to Cohen, both the philosophy of Kant and Judaism affirm the sovereignty of reason, and both concur that reason and Revelation are the two sources of religion.[43] Yet, Kant does not admit the credentials of Revelation, and Cohen redefines 'reason' to mean 'Revelation'. According to Cohen, for both Kant and Judaism, reason is sovereign against the senses;[44] yet, such sovereignty is strictly limited in Kant, so that concepts without intuitions are empty and intuitions without concepts are blind. According to Cohen, for both Kant and Judaism, God is the source and motive of ethics;[45] yet, in Kant, the essence of morality is the autonomy of the will, which becomes heteronomous if referred to desire or fear of God. According to Cohen, for both Kant and

---

[40] Compare Paul Mendes-Flohr, 'Rosenzweig and Kant: Two Views of Ritual and Religion', in *Divided Passions: Jewish Intellectuals and the Experience of Modernity*, Detroit, Wayne State University Press, 1991, pp. 283–310.

[41] Compare 'Ethics and Halacha', *supra*, pp. 25–32.

[42] 'Innere Beziehungen der Kantischen Philosophie zum Judentum', in *Hermann Cohens Jüdische Schriften*, vol. I, *Ethische und religiöse Grundfragen*, ed. Bruno Strauss, Berlin, C. A. Schwetsche und Sohn, 1924, pp. 284–305; incomplete trans. 'Affinities between the Philosophy of Kant and Judaism', in Jospe, *Reason and Hope*, pp. 77–89 ('affinities' is less precise than 'inner relations').

[43] Ibid., pp. 287–9, trans. pp. 78–9.

[44] Ibid., p. 298, trans. pp. 79–80.

[45] Ibid., pp. 292–3, trans. p. 81.

Judaism, God is 'the idea' of God;[46] yet, in Kant, God, immortality, and freedom are 'postulates' of practical reason not ideas, whereas, in Cohen, 'the idea' becomes a mathesis or realm of validity.[47] According to Cohen, Kant's emphasis on the son as the meaning of the Trinity is matched by his (Cohen's) emphasis on the Messianic idea of humanity.[48] Yet, while Cohen's idea of universal peace has affinites with Kant, elsewhere he is at pains to show that trinitarian mediation is different in kind from Judaic *Korrelation* of God and man.[49]

According to Cohen, both Kant and Judaism affirm the priority of autonomous practical reason over theoretical reason.[50] Yet, Cohen does not simply 'affirm a priority' – he redefines logic, creativity, and ethical reason so that they imply each other. According to Cohen, Kant and Judaism share the three postulates of God, freedom and immortality even though Cohen has disqualified the need for 'postulates'.[51] However, although Cohen includes a chapter on 'Immortality and Resurrection' in the *Religion of Reason*, these ideas do not have the critical place in Judaism that they hold in Kant or in Christianity.[52] 'Freedom' in Kant implies autonomy of the will, and the injunction to treat 'persons' as ends in themselves; in Cohen, 'freedom' is ethical, holistic and prophetic, and does not pertain to the legal fiction of 'persons' but to the actuality of 'fellowship'. Furthermore, if, as Cohen insists, God is 'unique', and knowable, there is no need for 'postulates'.

Cohen concludes this apparently straightforward but deeply perplexing essay by proclaiming that Messianic optimism is the ultimate idea of his philosophy of history, and provides the

---

[46] Ibid., p. 293, trans. p. 82.

[47] I disagree, therefore, with Guttmann that the meaning in Cohen's thought of 'the idea of God . . . never goes beyond the character of a postulate' (see Julius Guttmann, 'Hermann Cohen', in *Philosophies of Judaism: A History of Jewish Philosophy from Biblical Times to Franz Rosenzweig*, trans. David W. Silverman, New York, Schocken, 1973, pp. 405–6).

[48] 'Inner Relations', pp. 294–5, trans. p. 83.

[49] *Religion of Reason*, pp. 121–2, trans. pp. 104–5.

[50] 'Inner Relations', pp. 295–6, trans. p. 84.

[51] Ibid., pp. 296–8, trans. pp. 84–6.

[52] See 'The Thirteenth Principle: Resurrection', in David J. Bleich, *With Perfect Faith: The Foundations of Jewish Belief*, New York, Ktav, 1983, pp. 619–88; and Arthur A. Cohen, 'Resurrection of the Dead', in Arthur A. Cohen and Paul Mendes-Flohr (eds), *Contemporary Jewish Religious Thought*, New York, The Free Press, 1987, pp. 807–13. See, too, David Daube, *Appeasement or Resistance and Other Essays on New Testament Judaism*, Berkeley, University of California Press, 1987, pp. 4–16.

common ground of Kant's philosophy and Judaism: 'a philosophy whose truth is its methodology and a religion whose truth is
its God'.[53] In the destructive but not the critical spirit of Kant,
Cohen treats the letter of the critical philosophy as prophetic augury
of Messianic redemption. For Kant, the critical method superseded
dogmatic metaphysics which failed to question the capacity of
human reason to have knowledge of God; for Cohen, the method
of prophecy re-originates the doctrine of justice.

Cohen would appear to proceed as if the many critical responses
to Kant's philosophy have not occurred:

> *Reason is the organ of laws*/it means positively lawfulness [*die
> Gesetzlichkeit*], the archetype of all lawfulness. Religion cer-
> tainly cannot be deprived of the lawfulness [*Gesetzlichkeit*] of
> its origin and of its development . . . lawfulness becomes the
> foundation of the primary origin.[54]

The status of the copula in the opening proposition of this passage is ambiguous, as it always is in Cohen's thinking. It could
be predicative, or imperative, or even speculative. After all, in the
Ethics it is the discrepancy not the identity of reason and law,
of substantial freedom and legal subjectivity, which is the central
point of address, and which is traced to the history of private law
notions of obligation as they are surpassed by the prophetic 'control of acuality'. This 'control' reappears towards the end of the
Religion of Reason as the virtue of justice (*die Gerechtigkeit*) which
proclaims 'the suffering call to world history'.[55] In the *System*
as a whole, fictions of legal obligation are set off against Holiness, and this procedure yields the speculative proposition at the
hidden and untouched heart of Cohen's thinking: the lack of
identity between subject and substance – between legal obligation
and the kingdom – which affirms the speculative identity of the
rational and the real, the revealed and the Holy. Cohen does not
bring, as he argued, 'a concept' or method to bear on the sources:
he brings *the concept* of the identity and difference of the real and
the rational, the speculative proposition, to bear on the sources.

---

[53] 'Inner Relations', p. 305, trans. p. 89.
[54] *Religion of Reason*, pp. 11–12, trans. p. 10 amended. By *Gesetzlichkett*, Cohen means
'Lawlikeness' not 'lawfulness'.
[55] Ibid., p. 503, p. 439. The distinction in the Gospels between *kerygma* (proclamation) and
didache (teaching) would appear to be irrelevant to Cohen's exposition of 'prophecy'.

The apparent equation of the doctrine of the logic of origin and the teaching of Judaism, 'the truth of methodology', opens out the difference between the call and the course of world-history. This becomes Cohen's version of Talmud Torah, the repetition of the teaching: 'a religion whose truth is its God'.

This re-examination of Cohen's *System* suggests possible responses to the questions posed by the original Symposium. To the question of the contribution of Cohen 'to the characteristically modern and post-modern in the reading of texts', the response must be that because Cohen's 'productive origin', and its differentiating and repeating, has been received from the *Logic*, but the rest of the *System*, the *Ethics* and the *Religion of Reason*, remain unknown, it is a form of neo-Kantianism which reduces signification to 'productive origin' or, equally, to difference and repetition, yet simultaneously deletes the idea of truth, that has itself contributed to *our loss of all sureness of metaphysical discrimination*, and to the characteristically post-modern emphasis on 'reading' as opposed to *thinking*. This development is 'all-crushing', but not constructive: it disowns tradition – when Cohen, knowingly and creatively, reinvents one.

To the question whether Cohen has 'created new ways of thinking' and 'employed new ways of reading', this essay has demonstrated that, judged *as a reader* of Kant, Cohen destroys critical Kantianism, while as a *reader* of the sources of Judaism, he appears to overlook commandment and law, that is, the sources of Rabbinic Judaism, but apprehended *as a thinker*, who brings the sources 'under a concept', he inherits the antinomies in the conceiving of law in Kant and expounds them as the prophetic speculative proposition. To the question how this 'new way of reading re-originates what it means to be a Jew in the modern and post-modern world', this needs to be rephrased. For if we have already been formed by selective assimilation of Cohen's thought, then this familiarity will have to become unfamiliar in order to be recognized. This essay has attempted to begin to recover the challenge of Cohen's Judaic speculation in its fractured entirety.

Before the final question concerning 'a new modern Jewish hermeneutic theory and tradition' can be addressed, it would be necessary to resume and develop an earlier reflection concerning Cohen's and Rosenzweig's thought as Janus-faces by comparing

Cohen's exposition of Judaism as the ethical religion of world mission with Rosenzweig's exposition of Christianity as the religion of world mission. At first blush, this contrast would seem to follow from the difference between Judaism presented as utopian universality (Cohen's Kant among the Prophets), and Judaism presented as sublime, worldless community (Rosenzweig's inversion of the coercive state, imputed to Hegel). Yet if, as I have argued here, both Cohen and Rosenzweig present a *speculative* exposition of the meaning of Judaism and universal history, so that in both cases the equation of Judaism and world-history allows comprehension of the discrepancy between them, then why, in the moments of their ideal equation in the *Religion of Reason* and *The Star of Redemption*, are Revelation and love expounded in different chapters or books from the world and from redemptive justice?[56]

---

[56] For further discussion, see *infra*, 'Franz Rosenzweig: From Hegel to Yom Kippur', pp. 127–54; and 'Violence and Halacha', in Gillian Rose, *The Broken Middle: Out of Our Ancient Society*, Oxford and Cambridge, Mass., Blackwell, 1992, pp. 247–77.

10

Franz Rosenzweig – From Hegel to Yom Kippur

That the world, this world, is created and withal in need of the future redemption is a dual idea whose disquieting character is quieted in the unity of the law [in der Einheit des Gesetzes]. *For considered as world it is law* [Gesetz] *not what it is as the content of revelation and demand to the individual: commandment* [Gebot].[1]

I

Many scholars, drawing on the work of Nahum Glatzer, envisage Rosenzweig in 1913 wresting his eternity from time on the eve of a conversion to Christianity, which he ardently desired and which he had carefully planned.[2] Beginning with what was to have been a valedictory passage through the nine Days of Awe to the fasting and liturgy of the Day of Atonement – Yom Kippur – Rosenzweig, who, according to his own later account, would have been 'clothed in his shroud', the raiment of death, and 'utterly alone . . . confronts the eyes of his judge . . . as if he were beyond the grave in the

[1] *Der Stern der Erlösung*, 1921, 2nd edn 1930, *Gesammelte Schriften*, vol. II, The Hague, Martinus Nijhoff, 1970, p. 451; trans. *The Star of Redemption*, William W. Hallo, London, Routledge and Kegan Paul, 1979, p. 405, amended. See Paul Mendes-Flohr, 'Rosenzweig and Kant: Two Views of Ritual and Religion', in *Divided Passions: Jewish Intellectuals and the Experience of Modernity*, Detroit, Wayne State University Press, 1991, pp. 283–310.
[2] Nahun N. Glatzer, *Franz Rosenzweig: His Life and Thought*, New York, Schocken 1961, pp. xvi–xx; Stéphane Mosès, *Système et Révélation: la philosophie de Franz Rosenzweig*, Paris, Editions du Seuil, 1982, p. 30.

very fullness of living'.[3] However – the standard story continues – instead of proceeding to Christian Baptism, as he had intended, Rosenzweig's participation in the Jewish rites of repentance and forgiveness precipitated his own return to Judaism – as a *Ba'al Teshuvah*.[4]

This unexpected and unanticipated 'event' when, in conversion as in 'actual conversation', 'something happens' (which is how Rosenzweig later punctuated his presentation of 'dialogue' as *the new thinking*[5]), is also commonly interpreted as the inspiration for Rosenzweig's subsequent 'converting' of general and idealist philosophy – metaphysics, logic and ethics – to existential 'dialogue' and theology of creation, revelation and redemption in his great and main work, *The Star of Redemption*.[6] The well-established convention of these two conversions is dramatized in the title, 'From Hegel to Yom Kippur', which compacts Rosenzweig's path and aporia – his lack of path – from his doctoral dissertation on the development of Hegel's philosophy of the state, to his return to Judaism, and the danger of the 'mortification of the world' (*Weltabtötung*,[7] the third, Jewish 'danger', expounded in the third and final Book of the third and final Part of *The Star of Redemption*).[8]

In opposition to this tradition of the two conversions, it will be argued here that in *The Star of Redemption*, Rosenzweig succeeded neither in making the transition from idealist philosophy to 'existence', nor in making the transition from Christian theology and *Weltanschauung* to a complementary 'representation' of Judaism. The affection for 'love' and the equivocation towards 'the world of law', on which the second and third Parts of *The Star of Redemption* are based, mean that the work retains a predominantly

---

[3] *The Star of Redemption*, p. 363, trans. pp. 326–7.

[4] See Joseph B. Soloveitchik, *On Repentance*, ed. Pinchas H. Peli, Jerusalem, Oroth, 1980.

[5] 'Das neue Denken', 1925, *Zweistromland: Kleinere Schriften zur Glauben und Denken, Gesammelte Schriften*, 1984, p. 151, trans. p. 199.

[6] Written 1918–19, published 1921.

[7] Ibid., p. 452, trans. p. 407.

[8] See Mendes-Flohr, 'Franz Rosenzweig and the Crisis of Historicism', pp. 138–61; Nathan Rotenstreich, 'Rosenzweig's Notion of Metaethics', pp. 69–88; Otto Poggeler, 'Between Enlightenment and Romanticism: Rosenzweig and Hegel', pp. 107–23; and Alexander Altmann, 'Franz Rosenzweig on History', pp. 124–38, in Mendes-Flohr (ed.), *The Philosophy of Franz Rosenzweig*, Hanover, University Press of New England, 1988.

Christian orientation; while Hegel's absolute idealism presented in the form of subjective idealism is translated into eschatological realism, drawn from Schelling's negative and positive theology. Political freedom is exchanged for theosophical freedom while remaining on the terrain of idealist philosophy.[9]

It is from the political theology of the Kingdom, developed in the third Part of *The Star of Redemption*, that the fault lines of the whole work may be traced. In this Part, Rosenzweig in effect overturns 'the two testaments' of Judaism and Christianity, the Old and the New.[10] Judaism becomes the ever-New Testament – its eternally reissued commandment of love continually and continuously fulfilled, the community blessed with perpetual *grace* – whereas Christianity becomes the bearer of the Old Testament – implicated in the coercion of state and the world, its mission riven by imperium and *law*. In principle, Judaism, understood as 'life', and Christianity, with its residue of paganism, as 'way', are to converge in 'truth', the eschatological community, with their differentiated dangers certified 'harmless'.[11] Yet, in the course of Rosenzweig's exposition, Judaism and Christianity emerge as 'torn halves of an integral freedom, to which however they do not add up'.[12] Extrapolating this proposition from Adorno to *The Star of Redemption*, the freedom whose integrity is rent ultimately belongs to God. Freedom in tatters intrudes into the poetic triumph of the Kingdom: for the realization of redemption implies the politics of the third, the middle, which is condensed into the multiform concept of 'the world' – whose 'disquieting' dualism is not quieted in 'the unity of law'.

This is to propose a twofold challenge to *The Star of Redemption*: to the project of expounding redemption and the Kingdom by elevating Judaism as 'life' beyond the political history of 'the

[9] See Else Rahel-Freund, *Franz Rosenzweig's Philosophy of Existence: An Analysis of The Star of Redemption* (1933), trans. Stephen L. Weinstein and Robert Israel, The Hague, Martinus Nijhoff, 1979; and Robert Gibbs, 'The Limits of Thought: Rosenzweig, Schelling and Cohen', *Zeitschrift für philosophische Forschung*, 43 (1989), pp. 618–40.

[10] Op. cit., pp. 460–1, trans. p. 414.

[11] See Mendes-Flohr, ' "The Stronger and the Better Jews": Jewish Theological Responses to Messianism in the Weimar Republic', in *Studies in Contemporary Jewry*, VII (1991), pp. 154–85.

[12] Adorno to Benjamin, 18 March 1936, in *Aesthetics and Politics*, trans. Ronald Taylor, London, New Left Books, 1977, p. 123.

world', which remains the theatre of operation for Christian and pagan fate; and to the project of developing the existential passion of creation, revelation and redemption by elevating the metaphysical, metalogical and metaethical beyond philosophy and the concept. Constructively, this is to propose that the political theology of existence which Rosenzweig requires would have to be developed *immanently*, from within the third, the concept, and not be overworked as the exulted and denigrated 'world', third to God and man. For to inaugurate the Kingdom by depositing two sets of triple dangers is to admit the persistence of finite, 'worldly' *dominium* – and not to fulfil the promise of salvation.

The dilemma of how to conceive the ineluctable third is raised in the letter which Rosenzweig wrote to Rudolf Ehrenberg on 18 November 1917, which has subsequently become known as 'the germ cell' (*die Urzelle*) of *The Star of Redemption*.[13] In this letter Rosenzweig develops the opposition between philosophy and revelation but he does not complete revelation with redemption, or the Kingdom as hypercosmic configuration. What is evident, therefore, even more clearly than in *The Star of Redemption*, is that the opposition between philosophy and revelation requires a third, a *tertium comparationis*, which is *freedom*. Not 'systematic' or relational freedom, which, according to Rosenzweig, is the freedom of philosophy; the notion of freedom sought – in deep equivocation – is both *memorial* and *prophetic*. This notion of freedom, while it is presented in opposition to philosophy, is discerned by Rosenzweig in a recognizable, Marburg neo-Kantian argument in Kant: 'the anamnesis' or memory of freedom is equally 'the miracle' or 'wonder' intervening in the world of appearances.[14] This is to bestow the prophetic twist, familiar from Cohen, on the critical philosophy, which suffers thereby the Platonic depredation.[15] 'Freedom' comes to mean not the endless task of morality, but the eternal miracle of revelation, the commandment and the Kingdom. The sublunary presupposition of this idea of freedom, which either looks back to its archetype or forward to redemption, is the actuality of unfreedom, unfreedom of the world and hence of God and man. Because it haunts *The Star of Redemption*,

[13] '"Urzelle" des Stern der Erlösung', *Gesammelte Schriften* III, pp. 125–38.
[14] Ibid., pp. 129–30.
[15] See 'Hermann Cohen – Kant among the Prophets', *supra*, pp. 111–26.

where it remains unmourned and unmournable, this 'freedom' will be called here 'freedom bereaved'.[16]

Political theology redefines *politics* so that freedom and the city appear as 'the world'; and it redefines *theology* so that creation, revelation and redemption are acts of *love*. *Love* becomes the principle of justice: it is to solve the political as well as the theological problem – to dissolve the *dominium* of the *saeculum*, to overcome all worldly power. *Love* shall accomplish redemption *and* realization, which is the hypercosmic meaning of the Kingdom – for otherwise there may be realization without redemption, and there may be redemption without realization. Transcendent, love is the reality and operation of divine grace; immanent, love of the neighbour is the way that the world as third to God and man, and as *imperium*, shall be translated into the Kingdom, the City of God. Rosenzweig's attempt to exorcise power from love, and love from power, to substitute love for 'freedom', as the third which redeems 'the world', spoils his theology, his anthropology and his cosmology – his ideas of God and man and world. The exorcised political history of modernity is projected backwards to the far shore of what Rosenzweig calls *1800 – Goethe* and *Hegelzeit* – but it reappears in the six 'dangers' divided between Judaism and Christianity, and in the illegitimate modes by which the Kingdom may be entreated which introduce the final Part of *The Star of Redemption*.

II

In the *Urzelle*, the germ cell, the difference between philosophy and revelation is summarized as the difference between 'the freedom of the philosophers' and 'whole freedom', between the Goethean imperative 'Become what you are [*Werde, der du bist*]', and the biblical commandment 'Do my will. Effect my work [*Tue meinen Willen! wirke mein Werk!*]'.[17] While the difference

---

[16] By analogy with 'beauty bereaved – bereaved of truth', in Kant's *Critique of Judgement* (see the argument in J. M. Bernstein, *The Fate of Art: Aesthetic Alienation from Kant to Derrida and Adorno*, Oxford, Polity, 1992, p. 4).

[17] Op. cit., p. 133.

implies contrasting conceptions of God and man and world, it is the idea of 'the world' which acts as the *tertium comparationis* by which philosophy and revelation are distinguished from each other, and which is the middle to God and man. To the philosopher, all points in space and time are potentially middle, because the middle is relative to 'where I am'; whereas revelation is itself the fixed, unmovable, middle-point.[18] To the philosopher, the neutrality and interchangeability of all points in space guarantees the fraternity or brotherhood of man: the predictable, universal order of 'the world' is the foundation of ethical universality or freedom; whereas to revelation, love of the neighbour is not based on interchangeable middle points: love of the neighbour concerns specific events which occur *in the Lord*.[19]

However, revelation, 'a wedge in the world', *in the specific sense*, depends on order *in the universal sense*. For if 'the world' were 'A = C', the expression of chaos, the work of revelation in the world would not be possible.[20] At the point in the *Urzelle* where the use of symbolic notation has been most thoroughly undermined by the contrast between philosophical generalization and the event of revelation, this very inadequacy annunciates the dual third – 'the world'. For 'B = B' is to express both abstract, interchangeability of objects *in space*, the identity and difference of a relation which is always already implicitly 'A = B', that is, the agreement of a representation (A) with its object (B), or always already the power and order of world-relation,[21] AND, prior to any relation, any identity and difference, 'B = B' stands for the descent of God into the named and incomplete human creature, into its sheer factuality at every miraculous moment *in time*. In this latter event, the implicit 'A = B', or the Goethean aspiration towards 'A = B', is reversed by the propulsion of prophecy: every 'A = B' fails towards 'B = B' where '*es gibt kein Sein mehr Gott gegenüber* [there is no more being in opposition to God]', where every individual would be translated from human telos to redemption.[22] 'The world' is dual: the world of mathematical space and time and the world

[18] Ibid., pp. 126, 131, 132–3.
[19] Ibid., pp. 131–2, 132–3.
[20] Ibid., pp. 135–6.
[21] Ibid., pp. 131, 133, 127–8.
[22] Ibid., p. 136.

of specific, named, human creatures and events – the world of relations, of 'A = B', and the real world, *ecce realitas*.[23]

The inadequacy of the symbolic notation, 'B = B', to express the singularities which correspond to the theological concepts of creation, revelation and redemption is reprieved by the insistence on the necessity of the ordered world-relation for the accomplishment of revelation, 'the work of revelation [*die Arbeit der Offenbarung*]':[24] 'A = B' represents the ordered world of law, where the object corresponds in identity and difference to its concept; 'A = C', on the other hand, would allude to chaos not world, where there is no rule for agreement or identification of any object with any concept or any other instance of itself. By contrast with this lack of communication between world and chaos, the incomparability of 'B = B' *qua* philosophical expression and 'B = B' *qua* theological impression comes into a relation which presupposes the relation of their non-relation. Since Rosenzweig will not expound the dual meaning of 'the world', the duality has to be displaced to the apex of the triangle which surmounts the two explicated triangles of God and man and world, one of philosophy and one of revelation; the duality of the world, that is, has to appear in the representation of God: 'A = A/A = A', relational and real, absolute identity and wisdom – theosophy, which combines *theo*logy and philo*sophy*, Rosenzweig concedes, but not without a grimace.[25]

By transposing the duality and equivocation in 'the world' to the duality in God, Rosenzweig avoids *the speculative proposition* which such duality evinces. He asserts simultaneously that 'B = B' is already an idealization or spiritualization of 'A = B', or it may be an aspiration to become 'A = B' (Become what you are), *and* that 'B = A' is prophetically already 'B = B', already redeemed – the labour of revelation accomplished. Yet had he expounded 'A = B' as simultaneously 'B/A', 'B is not A' (without that meaning 'A = C', for the proposition 'B is not A' implies that 'A is both B and not B' without contravening the law of non-contradiction: not 'both B and not-B'), then the proposition would yield the exposition of time and space and of creation and

[23] Ibid., p. 137.
[24] Ibid., pp. 135–6.
[25] Ibid., p. 137.

redemption *as the history of the commandment and the city*. The duality of 'the world' read speculatively implies that 'the rational is the real *and* the real is the rational'; read by Rosenzweig, it implies that 'the world' is expressed as the relation of law *and* 'the world' is impressed as name and event. In Rosenzweig's version the connective 'and' can only be projected on to the mystery of the identity of God.

Rosenzweig refuses to acknowledge *the negation* which 'the world' as he compounds it nevertheless implies: that 'A = B' yet 'B/A' (B is not A). This makes use of the proffered symbolism but would relieve it of the absurdity of employing 'B' and '=' to stand for both any relational point, and for the intrinsic, named creature. 'A = B' and 'B/A' hold the lack of identity of 'A' and 'B' in a way which preserves and changes the meaning of both 'A' and 'B' from abstract to singular and eternal. 'A = B' and 'B/A' together affirm the eternal identity of identity and non-identity and may refer to any specific or singular lack of identity without attempting to bring that defiance into representation and so 'universalizing' it, as Rosenzweig does by employing 'B = B' for pre-relational, human creaturehood.

Instead of lament for the negative, for the loss of Zion, Rosenzweig keeps the loss on Platonic and Christian terrain: memorial freedom intervening in the world of appearances is attributed to Kant and the resulting duality in God is attributed to the hybrid of 'theosophy'. Like Cohen, he would translate ancient freedom into prophetic revelation: 'the new world of revelation is discovered by berthing in the harbour of the ancient logical world'.[26] But by failing to reconstruct the political history of revelation's realization and lack of realization, Rosenzweig immortalizes the gap between revelation and its work in the duality and equivocation of 'the world'. In spite of the brackets which will qualify the use of formal symbolism for creation in *The Star of Redemption* (and its abandonment for revelation), the dual and equivocal 'world' carries the burden of unacknowledged political testimony and remains 'freedom bereaved', overlaid by the prophecy of the kingdom.

How else than in these terms of the difficulty with the world

[26] Ibid., p. 130.

and with method can this letter sustain the reputation of being the *Urzelle* of *The Star of Redemption*? For it conveys nothing of the central *agon* of the work: the passion of love expounded as the meaning of revelation and the configuration of redemption – the Kingdom. However, in the *The Star of Redemption* the central presentation of the passion is triangulated with the fundamental paradoxes of 'the world' and method evident in the *Urzelle*: that 'the world' is divinely created and yet in need of redemption is elaborated in the third Part; that philosophy is presupposed in the metadiscourses of Part I (metaphysics, metalogic and metaethics) and superseded by the discourse on miracles and the prophetic grammatology of Part II.

III

The Star of Redemption is a magnificat to the lover (God) and the beloved (man), who becomes *love* (man for man as neighbour). In the eternal renewal of Part II, 'the ways' of *love* – its ups and downs – are *inseparable* from 'the life' of the *commandment* – whether instant fulfilment or legal coercion – so that disillusionment keeps both love *and* law in practice. However, these renewed meanings of revelation are configured for redemption in Part III: *love* is placed as the self-perficient 'life' of Judaism, and kept *separate* from law and coercion, which is 'the way' of the Christian 'world'. But love is made lifeless if it is sequestered from its errant way – if the ways of love lose their time and their place to exercise and be exercised by the life of the commandment. Nevertheless this eschewal of violence-in-love and coercion-in-commandment cannot prevent them from reappearing in the temptation to entreat or coerce the Kingdom and in the two sets of dangers, which are attributed singly to Judaism and to Christianity and judged 'harmless' when they are in effect double for each. But, without violence-in-love and coercion-in-commandment, Judaism and Christianity are deprived of their political history and hence of their sacred history; without coming to know his will to power, man is deprived of finding faith through his ambivalent love, and God is deprived of his freedom. If – as *The Star of Redemption*

Elements (*Protocosmos*)	Course (*Cosmos*)	Configuration (*Hypercosmos*)
God	Creation	Fire
Metaphysics	Enduring	Life
World	*Revelation*	Rays
Metalogic	Renewal	Way
Man	Redemption	Star
Metalogic	Future	Truth

metaethics? [handwritten marginal note beside "Metalogic"]

Figure 10.1　Main divisions of *The Star of Redemption*

evinces – the concept of God yields the concept of ourselves and of our possibilities, then the freedom of God and thence of man remains bereaved.

Revelation, the midpoint, is architectonically and logically as well as spiritually the third in the structure and argument of *The Star of Redemption*: the patterned repetition of three on three – three Parts, three Introductions, three Books within each Part. Taking cross-sections of each Part, each Book corresponds in terms of protocosmos, cosmos and hypercosmos to its two counterparts (Figure 10.1). Revelation occurs at the centre of the horizontal and vertical axes with 'the world' at either side. To the left, 'the world' is midpoint of God and man; to the right, it is midpoint of life and truth; its meaning, to the left, world-order; to the right, in its dual meaning of law, the way of the world, and salvation. Rosenzweig insists on the absence of any dialectical relation between God and man and world, and in *The Star of Redemption* he employs brackets to mark the difference in kind between 'A' of divinity, '= A' of world-order, 'B = A' of world from the perspective of man, and the logic of creation 'A (= A)/ A (= B)'. 'B = B' is now restricted to the expression of classical or Goethean, pagan independence of the human self.[27]

'The world' understood as 'order' is closely guarded and affirmed philosophically and theologically until *love* is defined as 'commandment', commandment as love, for then fallen love is less than fulfilled commandment (*Gebot*), it is coercion or law (*Gesetz*), and, *ipso facto*, the world is unredeemed. But 'the world' is not

[27] *The Star of Redemption*, pp. 47–8, 67–90, trans. pp. 44, 62–82.

necessarily unredeemable – for Christianity, with its threefold fate, the three Churches, will redeem love fallen into the world of law, coercion, the state, whereas 'Islam' cannot. By translating unfulfilled commandment and love into the political theology of world-history, the definitions of love as fulfilled commandment, as ever-renewed law, and unfulfilled commandment, as coercion of old-law, become deeply problematic. If the defining opposition of fulfilled commandment as the blessing of love and unfulfilled commandment as the coercion of law were presented solely as *formal* and therefore applicable to any historical people, providing the criterion of their ethical freedom, then, the opposition may be disputable, but at least it would provide an even-handed criterion: 'world' would indicate law unaccomplished and unredeemed. But the threeway distribution of love, law and book (commandment to 'worldless' Judaism; coercion and unredeemed world to the state and Christianity; obligation and unredeemable world to 'Islam') leaves 'the world' with a triple equivocation, dogmatically attributed to three peoples.

Although the political theology of Judaism and Christianity is not expounded until Part III of *The Star of Redemption*, the derogating of the political theology of 'Islam' is, however, interspersed throughout Part II. 'Islam' is excluded from the sacred mission, with distinct roles shared by Judaism and Christianity (which carries the residue of the pagan world with it); and, therefore, 'the world' in the sense corresponding to its mores is excluded from redemption and the Kingdom. In two ways *The Star of Redemption* reaffirms the abyssal opposition of *grace* and *law* which is the legacy of the self-definition of Christianity against Judaism: by inverting their bearers so that Judaism qualifies for eternal grace while Christianity struggles with the state and law, and by furnishing 'Islam' as a humiliated 'Other' to both. But this leaves a legacy too – the degraded world and people without hope.

IV

Part II of *The Star of Redemption* expounds the logic and grammar of creation, revelation and redemption by means of an existential phenomenology of God and man and world as lover, beloved and love.

Initially, 'the world' as third to God and man is closely integrated with philosophy and theology, cognition and miracle, for
prophecy is expounded as the prediction of portents and not
as unlawlike event: 'miracle . . . demonstrated . . . the predestined
lawfulness of the world. . . . Thus the idea of natural law . . .
comported excellently with miracle', and 'philosophy contains
the entire contents of revelation, not, however, as revelation'.[28]
The Event, the Real, emerges from 'the real language of grammar, to which the language of logic is prognostication'.[29] Philosophy and cognition are precursors and latecomers to miracle,
revelation, redemption and living-speech. 'The world' presupposed here is 'the world' of the *Urzelle*: either lawlike or singular
– which mode is illuminated depending on whether pedantic philosophy or promise and prophecy hold their torch to it. The logic
of creation shares an ordered world with the logic of the idea:
their *tertium comparationis* is the conception of unity which is presupposed by the multiplicity and the order of the world.[30] Only
the idea of creation guarantees the reality of 'the world' as opposed to the form of its ideality. 'Creation' implies God's eternally creative power: 'And only for this reason [the world] exists
and is yet renewed with each morning.'[31] *The Star of Redemption*
returns here to the God of the philosophers for whom 'the world'
is eternal and not created, for creation has been presented both as
eternity and as beginning in time so that 'the metalogical image
of the world loses its last obscurities through creation'.[32] Thus far,
without man, 'the world' or cosmos is almost already revealed and
redeemed by being eternally created, although the logic of creation can only be accepted in the light of revelation.[33] But between
Book II, revelation, and Book III, redemption, 'the world', the
middle, will begin to take two different courses: as love, commandment, the Kingdom, and as coercion, law, the state.

To expound the relation of God and man by the erotic analogy
of lover and beloved is to court two theological difficulties: to

[28] Ibid., pp. 106, 120, trans. pp. 95, 108.
[29] Ibid., p. 121, trans. p. 109.
[30] Ibid., pp. 53–4, trans. pp. 138–90.
[31] Ibid., p. 146, trans. p. 132.
[32] Ibid., p. 149, trans. p. 134.
[33] Ibid., pp. 119–20, 149, trans. pp. 108, 134–5.

introduce desire and hence lack and possessiveness into the idea
of God; to introduce indifference into the idea of man's relation
to God. These implications are deftly allayed: God's love for man
is excess, giving away, not lack or want; while the beloved,
man's love for God, consists in being awakened and awakening to
God's prior love by obeying the commandment to love. Man, the
beloved, 'dies his way into the lover'.[34] The commandment can
only be heard and obeyed anew in every instant and this makes
love *free*, not obliged. Whether desired or not, 'the instant that
awakens love is its first instant'; man's love of God is God's love
'resurrected' in man; the beloved becomes the lover in this instant
of knowing herself loved.[35]

Man's defiant, individual *self* becomes *soul* in the instant in which
it becomes both beloved and love, being loved and loving. Man
receives love in the instant: he responds not with gratitude but
trusts it eternally. This is 'requited love: the faith of the beloved
in the lover'.[36] In overcoming the initial difficulties of the erotic
analogy – that it implies interest in God and indifference in man
– the discourse of erotic love has given way to the grammar of
faith: love as lack has become resource – not a thing at hand, but
the eternal renewal of the source. From the beginning, however,
the analogy was strained: for Greek Eros does not himself love;
and the god Anteros, 'love returned', is insinuated as the meaning
of 'the beloved', so that both love and the beloved are defined as
loving.[37]

At this moment of love between God and man 'the world' does
not exist: 'Once overcome by the tremors of being-loved, [the
beloved] remains in them to the end. She is content to be loved:
what does she care about heaven and earth? . . . Her requital is
only that she allows herself to be loved.'[38] However, the grammar
of eros, its dialogue, is not 'I' and 'Thou', but man's response,

---

[34] Ibid., p. 182, trans. p. 163. *The Star of Redemption* argues that man and woman are equally
lover and beloved; for the purpose of the divine erotic analogy, the beloved is woman,
whose capacity for eternity man is to acquire: 'Once touched by Eros, a woman is what
man only becomes at the Faustian age of a hundred: ready for the final encounter – strong
as death' (pp. 189, 174, trans. pp. 169, 156).

[35] Ibid., p. 182, trans. p. 163.

[36] Ibid., pp. 191, trans. p. 171.

[37] Ibid., p. 17, trans. p. 156.

[38] Ibid., pp. 188–9, trans. p. 169.

'Here I am', to God's inquiry, 'Where art thou?'[39] The grammar
of eros is *the commandment*: only in the uttering of the commandment and not in the bald and barren declaration of love can love
be bestowed, and only in the instant of obeying can man's reponse
of prostration be free and not forced. Either the commandment to
love uttered by the lover (the one who loves) is obeyed immediately, or *else* the commandment is proclaimed, is *law* – and man
has arrived too late for love: 'The imperative of the commandment makes no provision for the future; it can only conceive the
immediacy of obedience. If it were to think of a future or an
Ever, it would not be, not commandment nor order, but law.
Law reckons with times, with a future, with duration.'[40]

'The world', and the future, held off in this instant of love
consummated – commanded and obeyed – insists on its due. The
sublime passivity of the beloved who has forgotten 'the world' by
virtue of her surrender is herself *love*; and as her love overflows,
eros becomes sibling, and sisterhood seeks neighbourhood. She
wants to be heard 'in the street', in the future, eternally, 'in the
presence of all the world'.[41] Venturing into 'the world' with her
word, where 'being loved does not count', she aspires, 'to the
realm of brotherliness, the bond of a supernatural community,
wholly personal in its experience yet wholly worldly in its existence'.[42] The frantic equivocation of this *Kehre* devolves on 'the
world': 'personal' implies both singular and with legal status; 'the
realm of fraternity' implies both universal and sect; 'supernatural
community' implies eschatological and traditional; and 'wholly
worldly' implies lawlike, street-wise, and yet hypercosmic.

V

The Star of Redemption has rediscovered two quintessential Christian paradoxes. At the end of the second Book of Part II, the paradox of 'the world': 'the world is needed for renunciation and for
the exercise of love' (Troeltsch); to which the third Book will add

[39] Ibid., pp. 195–6, trans. pp. 175–6.
[40] Ibid., p. 197, trans. p. 177.
[41] Ibid., pp. 227–8, trans. pp. 203–4.
[42] Ibid., p. 228, trans. p. 204.

the paradox of the Kingdom: 'the saints are ever failing from the earth and Christ is all but coming' (John Henry Newman). The Kingdom of God is already, not yet, forever; it is present, future, eternal. 'The world' shall become the Kingdom; it is still world; it is already kingdom: 'the kingdom . . . its growth is essential. It is always yet to come – but to come it is always. It is always already in existence and at the same time still to come.'[43]

The secluded soul of the beloved which has been commanded to love God is also commanded to love man, for God's love is man loving. The erotic discourse of love which stresses the sublime passivity of the beloved *makes the transition to the active love of the neighbour difficult to motivate.* The commandment to love the neighbour returns God and man to their third, 'the world', for this love is not the total affirmation in which the beloved dies into love and is without otherness, boundary or freedom. The neighbour is the third party, the other, and cannot be expounded in turn as 'the beloved'.

The movement from love renewed in each instant to love oriented, love with a future, seems contrived when the commentary on the *Song of Songs* is made to end on the note of brotherhood as hollow as the end of Lessing's *Nathan the Wise.* Unlike the transition in Rousseau's *Social Contract* from unbounded state of nature to the bonds of civil society which is effected by the boundary stakes of private property, *The Star of Redemption* is reluctant to negotiate boundaries – it implies them and then revokes them. For 'love of the neighbour' is introduced as an act, as configured, as aware of the otherness of the other, but then the neighbour is to be melted down with *love.* Although mysticism, since it is without configuration, is condemned, the transition from love of God to love of the neighbour is effected either eschatologically, or by drawing on the residue of paganism whereby the soul prostrated in love may don *daimon* and acquire 'character', or by the argument that the love of neighbour is the only other love which unites the momentary love awakened by God with ethical volition rooted in God's love. By contrast with the formal morality of Kant, this 'contentful' love is allegedly rooted in 'freedom'. However, the formulation of the categorical imperative

---

[43] Ibid., p. 250, trans. p. 224.

which enjoins treating persons as ends in themselves and never as means, is a version of 'love of the neighbour' *except* that it recognizes that 'persons' are bounded, are 'other'.[44]

Under the heading 'Love in the World', love of the neighbour is redefined so that like the love of God it must be eternally renewed. Although it requires *series* of acts and is not momentary, it 'always erupts anew'. 'Disillusionment keeps love in condition. . . . Otherwise it would become rusty, it would harden into a schematic, an organized act.'[45] This would make love instrumental and unfree, for it would become conclusive, subservient to God – it would become 'Islam'. Only under this heading is the disillusioning world expounded in which love hardens but has no perdurance. To 'Islam' is attributed the violence-in-love and coercion-in-commandment that *The Star of Redemption* does not explore in Judaism or in Christianity, nor in the as yet non-denominational presentation of love of God and love of the neighbour. When God's love is given once and for all, and not commanded in every instant, it becomes *past, material, the Book*; to which corresponds not man's soul but his incessant obligation; and the issue is not freedom but works.[46] 'Islam's' way into the world 'assumes' the 'inherent dangers' of obedience, 'it is a way of subservience', 'pure obedience toward a law imposed on the will once and for all'.[47] Love of the neighbour can lead to religious wars when obedience is 'imposed on the will once and for all'. In this way, love of the neighbour accomplished by 'the world-act' of incalculable love which is wholly free, is contrasted with 'the world-act' of 'Islam' which is obedience to law and wholly constrained.

Yet how could one distinguish between love disillusioned and renewed in every moment and love imposed and constrained without specifying the meaning of the middle, the yielding and recalcitrant world? In the midst of its discourse on eternal love and faith, *The Star of Redemption* introduces bald historical allusions to the violence of 'Islam', the world-act of which is Holy War, and relies on this eschatology of war and peace. *The Star of Redemption*

[44] Ibid., pp. 232–3, 236–9, trans. pp. 208–9, 212–14.
[45] Ibid., p. 240, trans. p. 215, 191–3.
[46] Ibid., pp. 183–6, trans. pp. 165–6, 171–3.
[47] Ibid., pp. 240–1, trans. p. 216.

opts for the Kingdom, the eternity of which will be the accomplishment of Judaism, while Christianity struggles with its 'not yet'. This is to overlook the connection between political and sacred history for both, and, especially for Judaism. For it ignores the formation of Talmud Torah – the changing relation between 'the three crowns' of prophet, priest and king, and the subsequent *political* success of the rabbis in inheriting the mantle of power – the right to interpret the relation between renewed commandment and imposed law as the fundamental political institution of Judaism.[48]

Only under the title of the Kingdom, only eschatologically, can *The Star of Redemption* acknowledge that 'the neighbour' is bounded, is Other; not the beloved, 'not loved for his own sake', but because 'he just happens to be standing there . . . only a representative . . . the all-inclusive concept of all men and all things . . . the world'.[49] The duality of 'the world' becomes the duality of two kingdoms – of God and of the world. The kingdom of the world is to *become* the kingdom of God: it is variously identified as the world of natural law, as the pagan world, as idealism's 'life', as 'Islam', and as the history of Christianity: 'the kingdom of God could only begin to emerge into the world in the world-wide principiate of the Emperor Augustus, the political realization of paganism's plastic image of the world'.[50] 'The inevitable growing of the kingdom' draws its 'citizens' from 'life' by assuring life of immortality.[51] The circularity and evasiveness of these arguments is again assuaged with a turn to 'Islam': 'The Religion of Progress'. This description amounts to the judgement that 'Islam' is incapable of growth, of the idea of the future as 'eternal'; instead the future is 'interminable'. This *obscurus per obscurius* is little more than a denigration of 'Islam's' imputed 'worldliness', and of its imputed dogmatic infallibility.[52]

The Kingdom of God and the Kingdom of 'the world' are reaffirmed as presupposing each other for the idea of love's free

[48] See Stuart A. Cohen, *The Three Crowns: Structures of Communal Politics in Early Rabbinic Jewry*, Cambridge, Cambridge University Press, 1990.
[49] *The Star of Redemption*, p. 243, trans. p. 218.
[50] Ibid., p. 230, trans. p. 224.
[51] Ibid., p. 251, trans. p. 225.
[52] Ibid., pp. 251–4, trans. pp. 225–7.

act to have meaning but as utterly different in kind for redemption to have meaning. 'The world' is endless chaos and 'the world' is the law of its growing life;[53] love's anarchic, unanticipated act presupposes law, interconnection, articulation and growth, for this is the medium of its freedom.[54] 'The world' is blind and deaf to redemption, and 'the world' is animated by the awakened soul of man.[55] The Kingdom of the world 'grows in itself, apparently according to its own law'; the Kingdom of God 'originates with God, and man knows neither the day nor the hour. He only knows that he is to love always the nighest and the neighbour'.[56]

The two kingdoms – of God and of 'the world' – imply two contrasts of 'the world' with love: love versus (natural) *law* is split off from love versus *Law* (obligation), and the latter is projected on to 'Islam', the mythical political history of which is diverted from the central trajectory of the argument. While the exposition of 'Islam' is concluded at the end of the second Part, the dilemma of love's meaning and its political configuration has barely begun.

VI

This dilemma of love's configuration is accentuated in the great political theology of the third Part of *The Star of Redemption*. No longer projected on to 'Islam', the violence-in-love and the coercion-in-commandment are related in the conjoint, so-called 'messianic politics' of 'the peoples of the world': 'the eternity of realization' (*die Ewigkeit der Verwirklichung*).[57] The dilemma is more evident because it is distributed between Judaism and Christianity.

> Thus the commandment [*Das Gebot*] is purely the present ['Love me!']. . . . The imperative of the commandment makes no provision for the future; it can only conceive the immediacy of obedience. If it were to think of a future or an Ever, it would be, not commandment or order, but law [*Gesetz*]. Law reckons with times, with a future, with duration. . . .

[53] Ibid., pp. 267–8, trans. p. 240.
[54] Ibid., p. 268.
[55] Ibid., pp. 266–7, trans. p. 239.
[56] Ibid., p. 269, trans. p. 241.
[57] Ibid., p. 373, trans. p. 336.

But while every other commandment could easily well have been law if one viewed it from without and, so to speak retroactively, the sole commandment of love is simply incapable of being law; it can only be commandment. All other commandments can pour their contents into the mold of the law as well.[58]

While the Christian Church is separated from the state but implicated with it because of their competing universal claims and worldly jurisdictions, the Jewish people, who has 'left its holy wars behind in its mythical antiquity' and has 'already reached the goal towards which the nations are still moving', has no need of the state.[59] For, as preservers of 'the vision of the ultimate community',[60] the Jewish people 'is bound to be outside the world'. It has the inner unity of faith and life, which Augustine ascribed to the Church as the unity of *fides* and *salus*, but which remains a dream to the nations of the world, 'constantly involved in a holy war'.[61]

Although its borders are perpetually embattled, the state is defined eschatologically as 'the ever changing guise under which time moves step by step towards eternity'.[62] Law (*das Recht*) in the state attempts to preserve the fluidity of the life of the people and to form it to its eternal end. But life defies law in its fecundity, and therefore law requires coercion or force (*die Gewalt*) to supplement it and coercion implements the renewal of law.[63] It is coercion that renews old law: 'In the coercive act, law constantly becomes new law.'[64] Paradoxically, it is this coercion which makes it possible for the state to keep abreast of the changing life of the people by instituting new law which may equally be to renew old law. There is no perpetual law (*Recht*) without coercion (*Gewalt*), which is to define new law as the 'forceful assertion of the moment',[65] that is, temporally, as present. The coercion in law or

[58] Ibid., p. 197, trans. p. 177.
[59] Ibid., pp. 390–2, 368, trans. pp. 352–3, 331.
[60] Ibid., p. 369, trans. p. 332.
[61] Ibid., p. 368, trans. pp. 331–2.
[62] Ibid., p. 369, trans. p. 333.
[63] Ibid., p. 370, trans. p. 333.
[64] Ibid., p. 370, trans. p. 333.
[65] Ibid.

right is argued, legitimized, made explicit. The state is the refuge and the source of law. 'Coercion provides life with legal redress against law.'[66]

Unless this simply means that new law must have enforceable sanctions to be operative, prima facie, it flies in the face of what one would expect: that old law which is no longer appropriate to life would lose its traditional legitimacy and therefore be perceived as coercive; while new law, representative of the current interests of 'life' would be legitimized: its domination accepted as authority. Old and new law are equally domination, equally dangerous, but the former is perceived as coercive, the latter as legitimate authority. Contrary to this, *The Star of Redemption* argues that new life understood from the standpoint of eternity requires the perceived application of coercive domination to distinguish it from the habituation of tradition and from the anarchy of changing life.

Formerly the only commandment that must be obeyed in the instant is love's commandment, commanded by *love* – distinct from old, declared love and from any concern for the future. So for *love* to be new, to be renewed, it must be commanded against the waywardness of life which has forgotten how to love or which relies on a 'once and for all' commandment become law and fixed for the future.[67] According to the analogy between right and coercion, in order to be renewed, *love* must coerce, because it has form. There is violence in any effective love.

On the one hand, love has *form* – it has the form of commandment: 'Love me'! or the form of the interrogative: 'Where art thou?' or the form of the canticle: the middle voice of the verb reconciles subject and substance in the choral reciting of the greatest We-psalm, Psalm 115.[68] On the other hand, consummated love dissolves the boundaries of these forms – it prostrates itself, it *dies* into love, it obliterates heaven, earth, world. The creative violence in effective form which makes possible the free act is always displaced by the destructive violence of this effacing love – this is *the gnostic moment*, at the heart of *The Star of Redemption*, its grammar of pathos, which makes it so difficult to sustain a politics.

---

[66] Ibid.
[67] Ibid., p. 197, trans. p. 177.
[68] Ibid., pp. 280–1, 258, trans. pp. 251–3, 281.

VII

That violence may be the outcome of love is addressed at the effective 'threshold' to the Kingdom which is entitled: 'On the Possibility of Entreating the Kingdom', with one of the sub-headings, 'On the Coercion of the Kingdom' (*Die Erzwingung des Reichs*).[69] Prayer can be a way of tempting God; for man attempts to impose his law [*Gesetz*] on the love of the Revealer when the freedom of his act of love 'seeks to intervene tyrannically in the course of the world'.[70] For, *enlightened* love may become 'pur-posive', seeing or knowing the goal and the way and the sta-tions on the way; whereas true love is blind, it gives itself to the nighest without premeditation, its effects are 'side-effects', as it were, not intended.[71] Love's sight is dangerous: only love's feel-ing heart is sure. Otherwise the nighest may be unloved for the sake of the farthest, and the eternal future will be forced, with the result of delaying not hastening the Kingdom. This dangerous because purposive love creates 'the sectarian', 'the fanatic', 'the tyrants of the Kingdom of heaven'.[72]

On the contrary, this ideal of non-discriminating love – super-natural community but wholly worldly – this community of feeling, captures uncannily the ethos of the Pietistic sect. The banishment of all judgement and discrimination returns the love of the neighbour to the love of the beloved: it revokes the promise to respect the boundary of person and world. For the neighbour was *not* to be beloved, *not* to be 'loved for his own sake', but for 'the all-inclusive concept of all men',[73] that is, as universal. But non-discriminating love cannot be all-inclusive, for it recognizes no boundaries, no others, and therefore cannot know any universal, any comprehension of the self-relation of other as the middle of its own identity. The exploration at the threshold of the Kingdom of the potentially violent outcome of love is stopped by a regress to Pietist violence in love.

The equation of all enlightenment with fanaticism and diabolical

[69] Ibid., p. 297, trans. p. 267.
[70] Ibid., p. 299, trans. p. 268.
[71] Ibid., pp. 300–1, trans. pp. 269–70.
[72] Ibid., p. 302, trans. p. 271.
[73] Ibid., p. 243, trans. p. 218.

messianism means that a greater danger is ignored. No rational knowledge or politics is permitted; only the divine anarchy of love, and this will leave the world to the tyrants of the Kingdom of darkness rather than the fanatics of the Kingdom of heaven. The only people capable of form and of flexibility to create and to reform political institutions, capable, that is, of an inclusive rationality – are the pagans: the Greeks with their plastic cosmos. Just as the Jewish people are not trusted with the political institutions to negotiate commandment and law, so they are not trusted with the eternal vigilance to wrest their freedom from Torah – law – and Messiah by negotiating the relation of act to goal. Unrecognized, coercion enters into the realization of the Kingdom, deflected as the two lists of dangers attributed, respectively to Judaism and to Christianity when, it will be argued here, the dangers are double for both and inseparable from their political history. *Dominium* stalks this political theology which would divorce eschatology from the history of the polity. 'Danger' has its etymology in *dominium*, Latin for 'lordship' or being in the power of another. This is what *The Star of Redemption* would prefer not to know – that there is no form without power and that man is will-to-power, by virtue of which his love is either actively or reactively engaged.

'Messianic politics' refers neither to the Messiah nor to politics. The Jewish people are 'the eternal people', while the nations of the world are 'the living people'. The living people are not at the goal; they require the state to symbolize eternity, 'the constantly undertaken resolution of the contradiction between old law, the onward course of life and the mighty assertion of the moment' by use of the sword in war or revolution.[74] 'Christendom', double and rival jurisdiction to Empire and then to states, proceeds to eternity 'by making all the points of the way, one by one, into midpoints'.[75] In this way both state and *ecclesia* are translated out of the equivocal middle of 'the world', where, unlike Judaism, they reside, into the holy middle, the eternal in the present: 'Ecclesiastical history is no more the history of the kingdom of God than is imperial history. The eternal can have no history at most a prehistory.'[76] The more unequivocally the eternal begins,

[74] Ibid., pp. 370–1, trans. pp. 333–4.
[75] Ibid., pp. 375–8, trans. pp. 339–40.
[76] Ibid., p. 343.

the more equivocal is the meaning of 'the world' – fallen and holy middle.

Christianity, however, finds its middle in mission: 'Christianity, as the eternal way, has to spread. . . . Christianity must proselytize. . . . It propagates by spreading.'[77] For the individual, one point 'must become . . . middle', but for the Church, the infinite line, 'the very possibility of unrestricted expansion', is *the eternal way* which must bear witness as midpoint at every point.[78] That this imperative is political since it implies shifting boundaries, otherness, and universality, potential and realizable, is implicitly acknowledged by the reminder that the Church, *ecclesia*, was originally the assembly, the deliberation of citizens: 'In the ecclesia, however, the individual is and remains an individual, and only its resolve is common and becomes – *res publica*.'[79] This body politic, holy in its assembly, is determined to cross its outer boundaries: 'The envoys of the successors of Peter have crossed the *limes* [the sacred boundaries]: they have gone forth and taught the nations.'[80] This must mean that they are willing to court danger in relation to the boundaries of the other living peoples of 'the world', to engage in *dominium* by staking their own boundaries.

The three Churches, three epochs of world-history (although they are also said to be equally ancient, 'as age-old as the other two'[81]), are defined by paradoxes of 'split reality' and worldly authority. The Petrine Church (Patristic and Medieval) is imperial: it establishes a worldwide, visible unity, but its *love* battles against pagan reason, and its authority is the Holy Empire.[82] The Pauline (Protestant) Church is invisible: it opposes *faith* to the world, for the *saeculum* now posseses authority, and 'modern life' is conducted in a dual reality.[83] The Johannine Church is completely invisible: heralded by Pietism, by Goethe's life, and by the Russian orthodox Church, its quintessence is *hope*. Goethe's idea of *Bildung* is its elaboration: that the fate of the individual be united

[77] Ibid., p. 379, trans. p. 341.
[78] Ibid., pp. 380–1, trans. p. 343.
[79] Ibid., p. 381, trans. p. 343.
[80] Ibid., p. 310, trans. p. 279.
[81] Ibid., p. 317, trans. p. 285.
[82] Ibid., pp. 310–11, trans. pp. 279–80.
[83] Ibid., pp. 312–13, trans. pp. 280–1.

with the course of the world; and that this basically pagan devotion to becoming what one is be perfected by hope.[84] For it is the
individual who now bears the authority.

The idea of this third Church, the Johannine, with its precursor
in Schelling's adoption of the three ecclesial epochs from Joachim
of Fiore, is the least convincing, historically and eschatologically.[85]
By stressing that the 'Johannine Church itself does not assume a
form of its own',[86] the idea of the individual becoming integrated
with the course of the world collapses, and hope becomes hollow.
For the combination of Piety, invisibility and hope delineates exactly the kind of integration with the world that Goethe himself
explored and deplored as 'the beautiful soul', in Book VI of *Wilhelm
Meister's Apprenticeship.* 'The beautiful soul' expires from a surfeit
of *unbounded* good will, for she can find no form, no middle, no
world, to resist and reform her heavenly hopes.[87]

From their respective dangers, it is clear that all three Churches,
whether with or without authority, remain in a relation to 'the
world' and to *dominium.* The danger of the Johannine Church is
'the spiritualization of God'; the danger of the Pauline Church is
'the humanization of God'; the danger of the Petrine Church
is 'the secularization of God'.[88] These dangers are contrasted with
three Jewish dangers: 'denial of the world, disdain of the world,
mortification of the world'.[89] The three Christian dangers imply
a world-act and world-relation, just as the three Jewish dangers
imply a God-relation. The hope of the Johannine Church denies
the anarchic world and loses touch with the world and the living God; the faith of the Pauline Church deifies man by stressing
the inner life at the expense of the soulless, disdained world; the
love of the Petrine Church aims to convert the legal system of the
world; it wants to mortify the living world by making it divine.[90]
The contrast between the two sets of dangers is summarized as

[84] Ibid., p. 315, trans. pp. 283–4.
[85] Karl Löwith, 'Joachim', *Meaning in History*, Chicago, Chicago University Press, 1949,
pp. 145–59.
[86] *The Star of Redemption*, p. 317, trans. p. 285.
[87] See Gillian Rose, *The Broken Middle: Out of Our Ancient Society*, Oxford, Blackwell, 1992,
pp. 188–92.
[88] *The Star of Redemption*, p. 452, trans. p. 407.
[89] Ibid.
[90] Ibid., pp. 443–7, trans. pp. 399–401.

	Christianity		**Judaism**	
	God	*World*	*World*	*God*
1	spiritualized	anarchic	denied	of redemption
2	humanized	soulless	disdained	of creation
3	secularized	made divine	mortified	imposes law

Figure 10.2 Comparison of dangers of Christianity and Judaism

the difference between externalization, Christianity's turn towards
the world, and inwardness, Judaism's turn away from the world.
However, if their respective dangers are translated into both God-
and world-relation they turn out to have more in common than
the summarized contrast will allow (Figure 10.2). Taking the three
dangers in turn, the first implies that the world is not seen in the
light of God's activity: it lacks divine order. The second danger
implies that the vocation of man is determined in opposition to
the world. The third danger implies that God's law is to be imposed
and the world 'converted' (Christianity), 'regulated' (Judaism).

VIII

The opposition between the eternal people and the living people
breaks down: they court the same dangers, live in the same world,
share the same paradoxes of sacred history because they have
mutually related political histories. But *The Star of Redemption* can
say nothing about the political histories which these sacred histories
attest, for it has left Judaism without its political institutions as it
has left Christianity and Judaism without modern political law
and institutions. God and world and man have no freedom because they have no power to dispose and no knowledge to expose. The world is dangerous for it is to have no *dominium* – it is
to become Kingdom; and man is abyssal but not sinful, for he
has no will to power – and is to be absorbed and to absorb in
love; and God gives and revokes form which means that love
without violence becomes violence-in-love. The Holy Middle is

not witnessed at every point but the terror of power unformed lurks at every point.

There can only be a middle if there is a boundary between two things, the relation to which becomes the third (in time or space, eternal or finite). In *The Star of Redemption, the self* is *contra the soul*: the self is for itself, bounded, enclosed and solitary, it lacks any bridge to other selves; while the soul receives and gives boundless love.[91] 'No community can originate' from selves, even though the defiance of the self is the potential beginning of soul.[92] However, only if the Other's being-for-self – the other's relation to their own boundary – becomes my being-for-self can there be a middle. Redemption would mean not that the Other, the neighbour, is covered by love, is beloved, but that the bounded singularity of both one and the other fail towards the recognition of that sinful self-relation which denies the self-relation of the other in the relation to self – this is the configuration of atonement or forgiveness. Revelation would be the incursion of the unwelcome news of the boundary and of the investment of reactive will to power in its denial, not the effacement of the boundary. 'The world' is that investment, the domination to be found in an apparently independent self-relation which, however, depends on degradation of the self-relation of the other; so that the world, the middle, is dangerous: its *dominium* that of an apparently independent 'power' which is in effect dependent on the defeat of its others, and is therefore rigidly enforced but unstable and reversible. The way through the world – not the hypercosmic Kingdom – is configured by sacred history.

While *The Star of Redemption* is explicit about its ambivalence towards Goethe, its ambivalence towards Nietzsche is deeper and brings its endeavour closer to its hidden but deep despair at man and at God. 'Goethe's life is truly a hike along the precipice between two abysses': the abyss of the sinner who is free to entreat or coerce anything, and the abyss of the fanatic whose devotion to the distant one denies the neighbour.[93] Goethe, the emblematic personification of *hope*, completing Augustine's *love* and Luther's *faith*, is precariously balanced between the futurity of redemption

[91] Ibid., pp. 88, 188–9, trans. pp. 81, 169.
[92] Ibid., pp. 88, 190, trans. pp. 81, 170.
[93] Ibid., pp. 318–19, trans. p. 286.

and a self-seeking, Godless future.[94] Courage to shoulder the burden of this ambivalence is provided by the contrast with another ambivalence which is beyond redemption: Zarathustra 'sinner and fanatic in one', is an 'immoralist who smashes all the law tablets, and a tyrant who overpowers his neighbour as well as himself for the sake of the next-but-one'. The emblem of Zarathustra expresses despair at following Goethe's path and counsel against it.[95]

Now Nietzsche is the author of 'Zarathustra': it is he who recounts Zarathustra's *agon*, the failure of Zarathustra's pedagogy, which consists in its difficult relation to the nighest, to the boundaries of others who do not wish to be loved or to love. Zarathustra teaches *the eternal return*, how to overcome *ressentiment* against time which has its source in a reactive will to power. To will eternally is to institute *new law tables* – which is also how *The Star of Redemption* expounds love in the moment, which does not become old law. Whenever Zarathustra's teaching fails and verges on the fanatic, because the nighest rejects his revelation, he withdraws to the mountain lest his love become tyranny.

Nietzsche, like *The Star of Redemption*, considered Goethe to be the ideal man, but not for the same reasons. To *The Star of Redemption*, Goethe is the last pagan and the first Christian, whereas to Nietzsche, he combined Apollo and Dionysus, renewed form embellishing subterranean power and violence, the perpetual overcoming of reactive will to power to bring destructive force into creative form. This predicament cannot be acknowledged if the idea of man is the inflected into moods of 'to love'. When *The Star of Redemption* claims Nietzsche as the prototype of the metaethics of man, of its singularity and of its life-centred as opposed to world-centred view, 'the one man who knew his own life and his soul like a poet, and obeyed their voice like a holy man, and who was for all that a philosopher',[96] it cannot appreciate Nietzsche as holy man nor Zarathustra, his holy man, for it will not know will to power but separates the bounded, immured self from the boundless, loved and loving soul.

[94] Ibid., p. 316, trans. p. 284.
[95] Ibid., p. 319, trans. pp. 286–7.
[96] Ibid., pp. 11, 9, trans. pp. 11, 9.

The Star of Redemption argues that philosophers from Parmenides to Hegel claim that the painting is painted on the wall; they assert the unity of being and reason, of God and the world. Only *The Star of Redemption* argues that the painting is hung on the wall, and thus recognizes the multiplicity of being as against reason and the non-identity of the world and reason, 'the world is a beyond as against what is intrinsically logical, as against unity'.[97] The world, however, is not alogical; it is created, a plastic cosmos of participation, of the whole in the parts, of universality, and must be so for the work of revelation to be possible. This lack of relation between the relational and non-relational, between law-fulness and non-identity is projected on to God: it is God's project and God is the source of danger and *dominium* – his freedom, like ours, bereaved.

God has an 'existence of his own within him', apart from his relationship with the world, an existence prior to the identity of being and reasoning. God is alive, vital *nature*, but it is his *freedom* to which Nietzsche bears witness in his 'curse' of denial: 'If God existed, how could I bear not to be God?'[98] *The Star of Redemption* does not bear witness to the humility in Nietzsche's irony – the eternally shouldered burden of will to power that casts violence into form and finds violence in form – the boundary that is *love's formation* by being its education.

---

[97] Ibid., p. 15, trans. p. 14.
[98] Ibid., p. 20, trans. p. 18.

11

Søren Kierkegaard to Martin Buber – Reply from 'the Single One'

No generation has learned from another how to love, no generation can begin other than at the beginning, the task of no later generation is shorter than its predecessor's, and if someone, unlike the previous generation, is unwilling to stay with love but wants to go further, then this is simple and foolish talk.[1]

I

The gravamen of Buber's question to 'the Single One' may be introduced as a response to this passage from the 'Epilogue' to *Fear and Trembling*: 'if only, instead of fighting with Hegel's *System*, Kiekegaard *had* addressed the generations, the married ones, and not "the single one" . . . if only he had cherished the *entelechia* of human mutuality within the world and not taught *and* exemplified in his own life renunciation of the world – "the teleological suspension of the ethical."' In Buber's famous essay on Kierkegaard, 'The Question to the Single One,' 'the question' is political: it concerns what Buber calls the 'body politic'. And the meaning of Kierkegaard's life and work is explored within digressions on Stirner, Schmitt and Gogarten, which compare

[1] Kierkegaard, *Fear and Trembling: Dialectical Lyric by Johannes de Silentio*, 1843, trans. Alastair Hannay, Harmondsworth, Penguin, 1985, p. 145. For a recent, outstanding philosophical engagement with Buber's thought, see Nathan Rotenstreich, *Immediacy and its Limits: A Study in Martin Buber's Thought*, Chur, Harwood Academic Publishers, 1991. This chapter was first prepared for the Conference on Martin Buber held at the Hebrew University, Jerusalem, July 1991.

their respective arguments on the modern state, politics and the individual.[2]

This 'Reply' from 'the Single One' will show that Buber understood neither her, nor *de Silentio* (her Director), nor her author, Kierkegaard – God, of course, is her Producer. It will argue that Buber overlooks Kierkegaard's use of pseudonyms, irony, humour and 'Stages', and that he fails to follow the strategy of 'suspending the ethical'.[3] As a result, it will emerge in this 'Reply', that it is Kierkegaard who relates the lesson of love to the lesson of law, 'the generation', while it is Buber who would keep human relations apart from 'the world', understood as the realm of *dominium*. In other words, it is Kierkegaard who acknowledges the ethical and Buber who renounces it.

If Buber's ambivalence towards law and power makes him deny actuality more than Kierkegaard, this arises partly from Buber's lack of attention to the authority of his own authorship; and partly from his failure adequately to theorize modernity, which, in all its brokenness, nevertheless, returns to haunt what he would tell us about the human condition in general, its potentiality and its practical task. The argument, to be developed in this 'Reply', forms part of a more extensive argument, which concerns Rosenzweig and Levinas as well as Buber: the separation in their work of the lesson of love or perficient commandment from the actualities of law or coercion suffuses their ethics with an originary violence that has been borrowed from the political modernity which they refuse to historicize. Their several paths from violence to the Holy will be retraced to *the broken middle* in a reflection which restores the *pathos* of the concept, split between love and law, to its *logos*, and 'the Single One' to her failing towards modernity and towards God.

II

Paul Mendes-Flohr has shown in his important essays on the development of Buber's thought, that Buber overcame his early

[2] 'The Question to the Single One', 1936, in *Between Man and Man*, trans. Ronald Gregor Smith, London, Collins, 1979, pp. 60–108.

[3] Buber does not discuss the idea, which is central to Kierkegaard's aesthetic authorship, of 'the teleological suspension of the ethical', in 'The Question to the Single One'. However, compare his later essay, 'On the suspension of the ethical', 1952, in *Eclipse of God: Studies in the Relation between Religion and Philosophy* ed. Robert M. Seltzer, New Jersey, Humanities Press, 1988, pp. 113–20.

commitment to the mystical *Gesinnung* of the *Neue Gemeinschaft*. He followed the example of Gustave Landauer, who protested against 'its wont to deny in the name of its mystical *Gesinnung* the exigent social contradictions of the real world'.[4] This 'overcoming', on the argument at stake here, was flawed from the very beginning. The inadequacies of Buber's subsequent relentless call to respond to the demands of the world, articulated throughout all his different kinds of work – on the idea of Israel, in his presentation of the Tales of the Hassidim, in his philosophical *œuvre* – can already be discerned here.[5]

Landauer, the 'executor' of whose political testament Buber has been titled, was an anarchist and utopian socialist, for whom 'counter-communities' (*Gegengemeinshaften*) were to nourish a socialist *Gesinnung*.[6] Mendes-Flohr argues that Buber also inherited a deep ambivalence about the nature of the state from Landauer, so that they both understood the state 'to be an institution that by its very nature begets violence'.[7] In spite of adopting Landauer's injunction to examine 'social contradictions and their political effects', Buber fails to differentiate between the violence of the state as such, and the political structure and history of the modern state – the tension between civil society and the state, which arises out of what Hannah Arendt has called 'the twin contradictions' between abstract legal equality and systematic class inequality, and between the promise of universal human rights and the particular national sovereignties necessary to guarantee them – or to abuse them.[8]

[4] Mendes-Flohr, 'Nationalism as a Spiritual Sensibility: The Philosophical Suppositions of Buber's Hebrew Humanism', in *Divided Passions: Jewish Intellectuals and the Experience of Modernity*, Detroit, Wayne State University Press, 1991, p. 184.

[5] Compare Paul Tillich's criticisms of Buber's political theory, cited in Richard Rubenstein, 'Buber and the Holocaust: Some Reconsiderations on the 100th Anniversary of his Birth', in *Michigan Quarterly Review*, September (1978), p. 398.

[6] Mendes-Flohr, 'Nationalism as a Spiritual Sensibility', pp. 185, 186.

[7] Mendes-Flohr, 'The Politics of Covenantal Responsibility: Martin Buber and Hebrew Humanism', in *Divided Passions*, p. 201.

[8] See *The Origins of Totaliarianism*, 1951, New York, Harcourt, Brace Jovanovich, 1973, Part 1, Ch. 2. In a later essay, 'Zwischen Gesellschaft und Staat' (1950), after surveying modern political and social theory in terms of the distinction between society and politics, Buber sets out a solely analytical distinction between *Verwaltung* as the principle of the social sphere, and *Regierung* as the principle of the political sphere. The latter always enjoys a political 'surplus' by which it may shift its boundaries. The vitality of society depends on the spontaneity of the social sphere; and ideally, the political sphere would be absorbed by a multiplicity of regional and local societies (*Gesellschaften*). Buber stressed this idea of

Buber's failure to develop an adequate account of the modern state and of political modernity is allied to his antipathy to *the idea of law itself* – across the range of connotations from 'commandment' to 'coercion'. Aversion to conceiving any idea of regularity, and the desire only to affirm the singular in the instant of its incursion, yields a notion of encounter, 'I and Thou', which expels ambivalence, and abandons modernity to the specific violences which are thereby enshrined.[9]

Scholem has pointed out the affinities with mystical antinomianism evident in the exposition of Revelation which Rosenzweig developed in his correspondence with Buber[10] over 'The Builders', an address, itself in the form of a letter, which Rosenzweig had written in response to Buber's 'Lectures on Judaism'.[11] In order to try to accommodate and synthesize his own intention of distinguishing between commandment (*Gebot*) and law (*Gesetz*) with Buber's refusal to understand Revelation even as a species of command, Rosenzweig posits the content of Revelation to be *the act of Revelation itself* – all else is interpretation.[12] Buber's part in this correspondence is enigmatic; while he apologizes for being succinct and dry, his very inhibition evinces the passion of the pathos to which he succumbs – from abyss to abyss –

3. 6. 1925

Dear Friend

For me the one question which is sounded in my soul from abyss to abyss is: Is the Law God's Law? The other answer to this question is not mere silence. If, however, the answer

---

social federation rather than the idea of a unitary community (see *Werke*, vol. I, *Schriften zur Philosophie*, Munich, Lambert-Schneider, 1912, pp. 1017–20).

[9] See the 'Dialogue between Martin Buber and Carl R. Rogers', 1957. Rogers insists, in opposition to Buber, that the discovery of one's ambivalent self-relation, the discomfort with the otherness in oneself, must precede the encounter between I and Thou, or, the acknowledgement of the difference of the other (in *The Knowledge of Man: A Philosophy of the Interhuman*, trans. Maurice Friedman and Ronald Gregor Smith, New York, Harper, 1966, pp. 166–84.)

[10] 'Religious Authority and Mysticism', in *On the Kabbalah and its Symbolism*, 1960, trans. Ralph Manheim, New York, Schocken, 1969, pp. 166–84.

[11] Buber, 'Lectures on Judaism', 1923, in *On Judaism*, 1909–51, trans. Eva Jospe and I. M. Lask, New York, Schocken, 1972; Rosenzweig, 'The Builders: Concerning the Law', 1923, in *On Jewish Learning*, ed. N. N. Glatzer, New York, Schocken, 1965, pp. 72–92.

[12] Buber, 'Revelation and Law', in Glatzer (ed.), *On Jewish Learning*, p. 118. See Paul Mendes-Flohr, 'Rosenzweig and Kant: Two Views of Ritual and Religion', in *Divided Passions*, pp. 283–310.

were 'Yes', I would not meditate on whether the Law is a force making for the wholeness of life, for such would then be immaterial. On the other hand, no other Yes can replace the missing affirmation. The missing 'Yes' is not quietly absent: its absence is noted with terror.[13]

The trauma of 'the missing "Yes"' registers the anguish of being able to exist neither in the full silence of Revelation ('No'), nor in the equivocation of Law (the missing 'Yes'). Such terror communicates a refusal of the predicament of human freedom: that the meaning of the Law depends on man's freedom, on his response to it. The trauma was overcome by the 'and' of *I and Thou* (1922), and was further elaborated as the 'between' of 'Dialogue' (1929). Yet, these holy paths, from abyss to abyss, betray violation and violence as well as terror, for, instead of providing an antidote to modernity, and 'its hysterical nationalism', the holy 'between' reproduces the features of modernity it has itself fixed.

III

It was in these circumstances [of the Roman Empire and Cult] that Jesus came to set up on earth a spiritual kingdom, which by separating the theological from the political system, made the State no longer one, and brought about the internal divisions which have never ceased to trouble Christian peoples . . . this double power and conflict of jurisdiction have made all good polity impossible in Christian States; and men have never succeeded in finding out whether they were bound to obey the master or the priest.[14]

Unlike Rousseau, Buber judges the idea of the separation of Caesar and God to arise either from 'massive misinterpretations of [Christ's] teaching [over two millenia]', or to be a dualistic Gnostic heresy, recently recycled by Harnack.[15] This misinterpretation

[13] 'Revelation and Law', p. 117.
[14] Rousseau, 'Civil Religion', *The Social Contract*, in *The Social Contract and Discourses*, trans. G. D. H. Cole, London, Dent, 1973, p. 270.
[15] See Buber, 'The Holy Way: A Word to the Jews and to the Nations', 1918, dedicated to Gustave Landauer, in *On Judaism*, trans. Eva Jospe and I. M. Lask, New York, Schocken, 1972, pp. 124–5; 'The spirit of Israel and the world of today', 1939, in *Israel and the World: Essays in a Time of Crisis*, New York, Schocken, 1963, p. 192; on Christ's teaching, see 'Geltung und Grenze des politischen Prinzips', 1953, in *Werke*, I, pp. 1097–108.

has, however, never ceased to trouble the Jewish people, for it has justified the exclusion of both Judaism and 'the spirit of Israel' from preparing the world for the Kingdom of God, and it has legitimized 'the unholy dogma of the sovereignty of nations'.[16] Yet, Buber fails to acknowledge and analyse how the separation of religious from political institutions has formed the historical fate of the West. Even less is he able to account for the way in which the twin contradictions of modernity – of formal equality and class inequality, and of universal rights dependent on particular sovereignties – have become enmeshed with the traditional separation of religion from the state. As a result, Buber's notion of 'the world' becomes overburdened with contrary significations: positively, it means God's sovereignty; while, negatively, it means the sovereignty of the devouring nations.[17]

> A great historian has asserted that power is evil. But this is not so. Power is intrinsically guiltless; it is the precondition for the action of man. The problematic element is the will-to-power, greedy to seize and to establish power, and not the effect of a power whose development was internal. A will-to-power, less concerned with being powerful than with being 'more powerful than,' becomes destructive. Not power but power hysteria is evil.[18]

The contrasts in this passage between power and will to power, immanent development and imperialism, creative will to power and destructive will to power, are not elaborated or consistently maintained by Buber in his essay on 'Nationalism'. He is more concerned to distinguish political state-formation, which precedes awareness of national boundaries and missions, such as the Roman Empire and the French Revolution, from 'modern nationalism', which he defines as 'power hysteria, which disintegrates the responsibility to draw boundaries'.[19] This distinction is then taken to indicate the 'disease' or 'health' of a nation, depending on whether that nation transgresses its limit.[20] This argument is

[16] 'The Holy Way', p. 135.
[17] Ibid., pp. 135–6.
[18] 'Nationalism', 1921, in *Israel and the World*, p. 216.
[19] Ibid.
[20] Ibid., pp. 218–19.

ahistorical and circular, since limit- or boundary-setting defines both types of 'nation'. Buber ignores his own distinction of will to power: active or reactive, creative or resentful, but with all the canniness of *ressentiment*. A sustained analysis of the dynamics of will to power could suggest how internal developments or contradictions may lead a body politic to imperialism – to transgress its limits. Buber's interest in justifying a Jewish nationalism meant that he was not willing to investigate the paradoxes of the idea of popular sovereignty, that is, of democratic institutions, which, since Rousseau first set them out, have never ceased to trouble modern states.

> [R]everence for the absolute, without the use of an intermediary agency, is the principle of Israel. To this day we have not learnt to revere the absolute by our very existence.[21]

While, for Rousseau, citizenship defines 'the people', here the address – Revelation – defines 'the people' and their task (in this sense, there is commandment in Buber's thinking: 'Walk before me').[22] Buber argues that the failure of the Jewish people to revere the Absolute directly and to live the eternal life has made it possible for Christian polities to pay lip-service to the Kingdom, while they deliver themselves into the hands of the Prince. In an excursus on Dostoevsky, Buber reveals his sympathy with the idea of world-redemption commmencing with 'the spiritual, national life of a people'.[23] This compound idea of 'spiritual, national' solves the problem of 'the people' by conflation: the call defines 'the people' – the meaning of their spiritual life; 'the people' defines the nation – national or bounded history. This denies the ambivalence of republicanism and nationalism at the heart of the meaning of the modern nation-state: whether political membership or citizenship defines 'the people', that is, universally and therefore inclusively; or, whether membership of 'a people' – more or less exclusively qualified – defines citizenship. Buber wants to distinguish benign from malfeasant nationalism without dealing either with the general idea of political modernity – representative

---

[21] 'The gods of the nations and God', 1941, in *Israel and the World*, p. 200.

[22] Ibid., p. 209, Gen. 17:1.

[23] Ibid., pp. 208–10.

democracy – or with the discovered contradictions of that ideal: that it presupposes and perpetuates class inequality and arbitrary national sovereignty.

Buber dismisses any intermediary or mediation between God and man or between man and man because it would imply a share in power and domination. This disavowal amounts to an attempt to overcome the predicament of representation (in both its political and aesthetic sense) and of boundary or limit from the definition of God, from the vocation of Israel, and from the mutuality of man. A nihilistic impulse, it is carried over from Buber's political writings to his founding of the existential philosophy of 'I and Thou' and of 'Dialogue'. As a result of such nihilism, the inner life is left at the mercy of a repeated terror, while the outer world is affirmed in its repeated violence and cruelty – 'the whole cruel hour/the hour of the world'.[24] Existentially, a way is presented from terror and violence to the Holy, which lapses back, again and again, to these originary, unmoved movers.[25]

IV

This may be demonstrated by reconsidering two 'dreams': the first may be found at the end of the Second Part of *I and Thou*;[26] the second dream introduces 'Dialogue' in a section entitled 'Original Remembrance':[27]

> At times when man is overcome by the horror of the aliena-
> tion [*Verfremdung*] between the I and world, it occurs to him
> that something might be done. Imagine that at some dread-
> ful midnight you lie there, tormented by a waking dream:
> the bulwarks have crumbled and the abysses scream, and

[24] 'The Question to the Single One', p. 89.

[25] For a study of ambivalence in Buber, see Avraham Shapira, 'A divided heart and a man's double', *Journal of Jewish Thought and Philosophy*, 1, 1 (1991), 115–39.

[26] Buber, *Ich und Du*, (1922, 11th edition 1957), Heidelberg, Lambert Schneider, 1983, pp. 85–6; trans. *I and Thou*, Walter Kaufmann, Edinburgh, T. & T. Clark, 1983, pp. 120–2. *Verfremdung* is translated as 'alienation', which is usually reserved for Marx's use of *Entfremdung*.

[27] 'Dialogue', 1929, in *Between Man and Man*, pp. 17–19.

you realize in the midst of this agony that life is still there and I must get through to it – but how? how? Thus feels man in the hours when he collects himself: overcome by horror, pondering, without direction. And yet he may know the right direction, deep down in the unloved knowledge of the depths – the direction of return that leads through sacrifice. But he rejects this knowledge; what is 'mystical' cannot endure the artificial midnight sun. He summons thought in which he places, quite rightly, much confidence: thought is supposed to fix everything. After all, it is the lofty art of thought that it can paint a reliable and practically credible picture of the world. Thus man says to his thought: 'Look at the dreadful shape that lies over there with those cruel eyes – is she not the one with whom I played long ago? Do you remember how she used to laugh at me with those eyes and how good they were then? And now look at my wretched I – I'll admit it to you: it is empty, and whatever I put into myself, experience as well as use, does not penetrate to this cavern. Won't you fix things between her and me so that I can get well again?' And thought, ever obliging and skillful, paints with its accustomed speed a series – nay, two series of pictures on the right and the left wall. Here is (or rather: happens, for the world pictures of thought are reliable motion pictures) the universe. From the whirl of the stars emerges the small earth, from the teeming on earth emerges small man, and now history carries him forth through the ages, to persevere in rebuilding the anthills of the cultures that crumble under its steps. Beneath this series of pictures is written: 'One and all.' On the other wall happens the soul. A female figure spins the orbits of all stars and the life of all creatures and the whole of world history; all is spun with a single thread and is no longer called stars and creatures and world but feelings and representations or even living experiences and states of the soul. And beneath this series of pictures is written: 'One and all'.

Henceforth, when man is for once overcome by the horror of alienation and the world fills him with anxiety, he looks up (right or left, as the case may be) and sees a picture. Then he sees that the I is contained in the world, and that there really is no I, and he calms down; or he sees that the world is contained in the I, and that there really is no world, and thus the world cannot harm the I, and he calms down. And when man is overcome again by the horror of alienation and the I fills him with anxiety, he looks up and sees a picture; and whichever he sees, it does not matter, either the empty I is stuffed full of world or it is submerged in the flood of the world, and he calms down.

But the moment will come, and it is near, when man, overcome by horror, looks up and in a flash sees both pictures at once. And he is seized by a deeper horror.

The second dream from 'Dialogue':

Original Remembrance

Through all sorts of changes the same dream, sometimes after an interval of several years, recurs to me. I name it the dream of the double cry. Its context is always much the same, a 'primitive' world meagrely equipped. I find myself in a vast cave, like the Latomias of Syracuse, or in a mud building that reminds when I awake of the villages of the *fellahin*, or on the fringes of a gigantic forest whose like I cannot remember having seen.

The dream begins in very different ways, but always with something extraordinary happening to me, for instance, with a small animal resembling a lion-cub (whose name I know in the dream but not when I awake) tearing the flesh from my arm and being forced only with an effort to loose its hold. The strange thing is that this part of the dream story, which in the duration as well as the outer meaning of the incidents is easily the most important, always unrolls at a furious pace as though it did not matter. Then suddenly the pace abates: I stand there and cry out. In the view of the events which my waking consciousness has I should have to suppose that the cry I utter varies in accordance with what preceded it, and is sometimes joyous, sometimes fearful, sometimes even filled both with pain and with triumph. But in my morning recollection it is neither so expressive nor so various. Each time it is the same cry, inarticulate but in strict rhythm, rising and falling, swelling to a fulness which my throat could not endure were I awake, long and slow, quiet, quite slow and very long, a cry that is a song. When it ends my heart stops beating. But then, somewhere, far away, another cry moves towards me, another which is the same, the same cry uttered or sung by another voice. Yet it is not the same cry, certainly no 'echo' of my cry but rather its true rejoinder, tone for tone not repeating mine, not even in a weakened form, but corresponding to mine, answering its tones – so much so, that mine, which at first had to my own ear no sound of questioning at all, now appear as questions, as a long series of questions, which now all receive a response. The response is no more capable of interpretation than the question. And yet the cries that meet the one cry that is the same do not seem to be the same as one another. Each time the voice is new. But now, as the reply ends, in the first moment after its dying fall, a certitude comes to me that *now it has happened*. Nothing more. Just this, and in this way – *now it has happened*. If I should try to explain it, it means that that happening which gave rise to my cry has only now, with the rejoinder, really and undoubtedly happened.

After this manner the dream has recurred each time – till once, the last time now two years ago. At first it was as usual (it was the dream with the animal), my cry died away, again my heart stood still. But then there was quiet. There came no answering call. I listened, I heard no sound. For I *awaited* the response for the first time; hitherto it had always surprised me, as though I had never heard it before. Awaited, it failed to come. But now something happened with me. As though I had till now had no other access from the world to sensation save that of the ear and now discovered myself as a being simply equipped with sense, both those clothed in the bodily organs and the naked senses, so I exposed myself to the distance, open to all sensation and perception. And then, not from a distance but from the air round me, noiselessly, came the answer. Really it did not come; it was there. It had been there – so I may explain it – even before my cry: there it was, and now, when I laid myself open to it, it let itself be received by me. I received it as completely into my

perception as ever I received the rejoinder in one of the earlier dreams. If I were to report with what I heard it I should
have to say 'with every pore of my body.' As ever the rejoinder came in one of the earlier dreams this corresponded
to and anwered my cry. It exceeded the earlier rejoinder in
an unknown perfection which is hard to define, for it resides
in the fact that it was already there.

When I had reached an end of receiving it, I felt again
that certainty, pealing out more than ever, that *now it had
happened*.

These two narrated dreams have several comparable features. First,
while the second dream is called 'the dream of the double cry',
both dream-commentaries display a double and a triple structure:
an answering cry is in turn itself surpassed. In the fictitious, waking
dream of *I and Thou*, the alternate, calming dissolution of the *I*
in the *It-world* and of the *It-world* in the *I* proves to offer only
temporary alleviation, and gives way to a deeper horror which
leads to and can only be assuaged by the 'eternal You' of the
Third Part. In 'Original Remembrance', the usual pattern of the
confessed, recurring dream of a fast and furious molestation
followed by an almost interminable and suffocating cry has been
uniquely superseded by an awaited but unexpected experience,
which comes – but not from a distance and thus beyond the
economy of distance and relation. What happens is a 'noiseless'
osmosis – a complete permeation of the dreamer by the Event as
such. 'It' (not Thou) 'has happened' (perfect continous) without
any sound. The first dream portrays raptus by alien otherness; the
second, raptus by absolute otherness.

Second, the first dream from *I and Thou* occurs after a discourse
on the economy and the state, 'the two chambers of life', and
before the reflection on the eternal Thou, the Holy; it occurs, that
is, in the middle. The second dream occurs at the outset – it is an
original remembrance. Third, both dreams proceed to destroy
and move beyond all barriers and boundaries by the irruption
of paranormal representation. The first dream, conjured to dispel alienation of the I from the It-world, only serves to deepen
the abiding alienation. Opening with 'the bulwarks have crum-
bled and the abysses scream', a female, once playful, now cruel,

appears after the imaginary dreamer has rejected 'sacrifice' as too mythical an expiation. (Is she the *Shekinah*, God's wisdom, disfigured as a Gnostic demiurge, and fallen into a vile creation – 'the world'?) The dreamer desires reconciliation with her, for her to relent, so that his health may be restored. A female figure also spins 'the world' into the I. The two contrasting images and modes of dissolution, alternate then simultaneous, abandon the dreamer to a deeper horror without image or representation. (What would a woman dream?) In the second dream, presented as Buber's own, a small animal resembling a lion-cub (diminutive of the Chariot?) tears the flesh from Buber's arm, an initiation into breaking the barrier of the flesh, which, at the denouement, becomes total penetration.

Fourth, both dreams are initiations; they are anagogical. The first leads from the terror of the solipsistic I in face of the It-world, through the breakdown of the dreamer's ego and representation, to terror deepened at the threshold of the Holy. The second dream leads from initial terror through the breakdown of the dreamer's body and representation to complete anaesthetic permeation – every threshold crossed without painful sensation by the Holy. In the first dream, the terror is abyssal; in the second dream, it is the terror of long-desired holy violation.

Fifth, the original experience is bound to recur: the first dream, 'at times when one is', 'henceforth when one is', overcome by horror of alienation, and so on. The second dream has recurred through all kinds of changes, and after intervals of several years, but, in its new version, it is insinuated, it is unique and total and hence unrepeatable. Sixth, both dreams are implicated in dealings with 'the world': their devastation opens out into the sublime, but it emerges from, and returns to, the mundane. The first dream occupies a chamber which is introduced after reflection on economy and state, 'the two chambers of life'; the second dream implodes prior to immersion in the mundane, and – strange to Judaism – annunciates an unhearable God.

What he does in communal life is no different from what is done in personal life by a man [*Mensch*] who knows that he cannot actualize the You in pure fashion but who nevertheless bears witness of it daily to the It, defining the limit

[*Grenze*] every day anew, according to the right and measure
of that day – discovering the limit anew.[28]

Grenze, 'boundary', implies positing, knowledge of what is beyond the boundary and hence surpassability; while *Schranke*,
'limit', does not imply such knowledge and surpassability. 'Boundary' is therefore the correct translation here. But Buber again
begs the question of the relation of the unbounded to the boundary, and is only able to exhort that the potential for unbounded-
ness should be related to what is intrinsically within the bounds
of measure and right. The unbounded and the bounded might
be negotiable if the discrepant relation between universal and
particular, between promise and actuality, were comprehended.
Instead, we are offered sublime Otherness, alienated *It-world*,
and violated singularity, but no account of how they might modify
the right and measure of the day – except in dumb witness.

These dreams, which wound the subject by the implosion of
radical alterity, opposed to 'the world', understood as 'the order
of Being', provide a response to Levinas' criticism that Buber's
ethics of mutuality, *I and Thou*, derogates the exaltation and
heteronomy of the Other.[29] The 'Reply' to Buber, which is being
developed here, has discovered the dark aspect of Buber's ethics
which is comparable to Levinas' trauma of substitution and
effacement of the ego and hence to the heteronomy and exaltation
of the Other. This 'Reply' may therefore be delivered to both
Levinas and Buber.

V

'The Single One' may be mute, but as *the knight of faith* – knight
of the pedestrian – she is not dumb. It is *the knight of resignation*
who is dumb, preoccupied with loss, and removed from the everyday and the actual. Buber might have been able to produce a
philosophy of praxis, able to relate the unbounded to the bounds

[28] *I and Thou*, p. 61, trans. pp. 98–9.
[29] Emmanuel Levinas, 'Dialogue avec Martin Buber', 1965, in *Noms Propres*, Paris, Fata
Morgana, 1976, pp. 51–5.

of measure and right, if he had read Kierkegaard with a less serious mien but with attention to the irony and humour of the aesthetic authorship. Plundering Kierkegaard's *Journals*, like Brod and Blanchot after him, careless of reference to the specific texts of an author who was rigorous in the theatre of his authorship, Buber produces a 'story' of 'Kierkegaard' as 'the Single One', and elides work and life. Thus, according to Buber, it is 'the Single One' who is resigned to the loss of Regina and renounces the feminine as such, marriage, and all ethical relationships, because only God is essential and everyone else, all otherness, is inessential.[30]

Buber presents his own position by opposing it to this caricature, 'Kierkegaard'. For Buber, marriage is the essential ethical relation, and it leads to the body politic. A section entitled 'The Single One in Responsibility', captures the gravamen against 'Kierkegaard':

> You are not at liberty to select what suits you, the whole cruel hour is at stake, the whole claims you, and you must answer – Him.[31]

Redefined by Buber, 'the Single One', true to the 'historico-biographical hour' (the redeemable world is defined temporally) is to receive 'the word', and, grasping the situation of his people, 'he experiences the boundary. He experiences it in such agony as if the boundary-post had pierced his soul.'[32] Openness to 'the word' here provides a measure – even if qualitative – of the violence of 'the world', of its injurious boundary-posts, but this insight, gained in pain, when 'the word' has priority over 'the world' is not developed into an account of how that 'world' might be transformed. Instead, Buber returns to 'Attempts at Severance', and allows selected political thinkers to misdescribe modernity for him – which is how he judges their arguments. The four considered, Stirner, Spengler, Strauss and Gogarten, all reduce the relation between universal and particular to individual or collective, arbitrary acts of power, and reject any democratic account of

---

[30] 'The Question to the Single One', pp. 60–108.
[31] Ibid., p. 89.
[32] Ibid., p. 90.

modernity or its criticism, from Rousseau to Hegel and Marx. Buber surveys each of these four metaphysicians of political sovereignty, but he omits any consideration of Kierkegaard as a political thinker. Kierkegaard as 'the Single One', is simply declared 'out of court' – for him, 'the objective either has only a secondary existence or, as crowd, is the negative which is to be avoided'.[33]

Finally, the question to 'the Single One' is 'restated'. Buber argues that 'the human crisis' which has transferred sovereignty from the individual to the collective, and has brought about the progressive relativization of truth, means that the recast 'Single One' is called by Buber to stake himself on truth. A concluding apostrophe is instructive: 'There is need of the Single One who stands over against all being which is present to him – and thus over against the body politic – and guarantees all being which is present to him – and thus also the body politic.'[34] Buber employs the language of Revelation, of immediacy, in a discourse on the mediations of modernity. A passage from a chapter of his book on Moses, called 'The Words on the Tablets', clarifies this: 'the words written on the tablets . . . make present . . . what had once become word . . . something spoken to them in this very hour'.[35] Constitution, for Buber, is *allocution*: 'The constitution [of the people of YHVH] appears not as something objective, to be taken at its own intrinsic value . . . but as an allocution by Him, a thing which can be actualized only in and through a living relationship with Him.'[36] 'The word' is constitution, while 'the world' is to be *allocution*, in a reversal of normal meaning, where 'allocution' would mean 'the word', and 'constitution' the formal structure of the body politic. These declarative equations, which try to conjure the *entelechia* into the fallen world, the unbounded into the bounded, leave 'the Single One' impotent and inactive. For they offer no critique of the singular or the world in all their mediations, nor, *a fortiori*, any acknowledgement of implication in power and domination. 'The Single One', forced into this holy

[33] Ibid., p. 95.

[34] Ibid., p. 108.

[35] *Moses: The Revelation and the Covenant*, 1946, ed. Michael Fishbone, New Jersey, Humanities Press, 1988.

[36] Ibid., p. 131; YHVH is the Tetragrammaton, the unpronounceable written name of God.

immediacy, is abandoned to the mercy of his inner terror and of outer violence.

Buber has confused Kierkegaard and his life, Kierkegaard and his authorship, Kierkegaard and his pseudonyms, Kierkegaard and the *Stages on Life's Way*. To 'suspend the ethical' in *Fear and Trembling* is not to renounce relationships for an exclusive devotion to God; it is a test of faith which, if successful, takes place instantaneously, and respects the mediated boundaries of both the ethical and the individual. 'The Single One' is not an empirical category, nor a category of individual experience, and she is presented by *de Silentio*, in an aesthetic authorship, as a *knight of faith*. The *knight of faith* inherits the world in all its mediation and law; it is *the knight of resignation* who renounces the world and the ethical for the sake of a lost love.

Furthermore, Kierkegaard's authorship is premised on the recognition that no author can avoid the arrogation of authority attendant on the use of language as much as on any other institution of domination. Kierkegaard refuses to imply that love and law, commandment and coercion, can be separated. The only consistent response to this dilemma for him was the use of pseudonyms by which he acknowledged unavoidable implication in the form as well as the content of his works. To speak about the paradox when one is always speaking from the ethical, and necessarily employing the resources of aesthetic and philosophical eros, requires irony and humour from one who knows he is neither genius, prophet nor apostle.

Acceptance of this inseparability of love and law, Revelation and coercion, prevents the enshrining of originary and incursive violence. On the contrary, the violence in love is explored: the violence in God's commandment to kill Isaac as much as the violence in Abraham's exclusive love for his own child, and as much as the violence issuing from Jacob's excessive love for Joseph.[37] Faith, aware of the potential encounter with its own violence in any of its intentions, is not traumatized by a violence it disowns. Nor is the potentiality of violence taken out of the

---

[37] There is a magnificent retelling of the *Akedah*, the binding of Isaac, as Jacob's temptation, in Thomas Mann, *Joseph and his Brothers*, 'The Testing', trans. H. T. Lowe-Porter, Harmondsworth, Penguin, 1978, pp. 64–7; for 'violence in love', see Rose, *The Broken Middle: Out of Our Ancient Society*, Oxford, Basil Blackwell, 1992, pp. 147–52.

history of modernity and generalized. The suspension of the ethical may be transhistorical but it is not suprahistorical: it returns the Single One – not in the 'cruel' or 'historico-biographical' hour, but *in the instant* – to her stake in the struggle of particular and universal which is the everyday, the body politic. This stake, according to Johannes Climacus, the assumed name for the philosophical authorship, is simultaneously aesthetic-erotic, ethical and religious, in both the sentimental and the paradoxical senses of religion. The Single One would expect to find love and law in all these places. She does not oppose her faith or love to an alien law or fallen world, but discovers time and time again, how they pervade each other. She is alert to the way that modern institutions invert her intentions, and prepared to begin again and again with the irony, humour and anxiety which recognizes her implication in mediation, in law, and in domination.

Buber evaded Kierkegaard's authorship. He prefers to call the world into Holiness, turning politics into the passion of witness which remains terrified by the universal and its antinomies. Opposed to any law, he fixes what he deplores; opposed to any *logos*, allocution is his *pathos*.

VI

Buber's work has been solicited to endorse the idea of 'postmodernity'. Introduced by Lyotard as a response to scepticism about 'the grand narratives' inherited from foundational critique or philosophy of history,[38] the post-modern alternative has also been presented by Lyotard by exploring the difference, which may be none, between Buber's ethics and Levinas' ethics: between the inavowable community which aspires to cognitive status in a still Kantian sense and the scandal of obligation.[39] A cycle may be discerned here from philosophical scepticism to new political theology. Initially deposing scientific socialism for being utopian, and renouncing universalizing reason, post-modern scepticism

---

[38] Lyotard, *The Postmodern Condition: A Report on Knowledge*, 1979, trans. Geoff Bennington and Brian Massumi, Manchester, Manchester University Press, 1984.
[39] *The Differend: Phrases in Dispute*, 1983, trans. George van Den Abbeele, Manchester, Manchester University Press, 1988.

rediscovers a notion of 'community', which denies the problem of power and its legitimation, and yet claims the middle in holy immediacy. This new aspiration – post-modern theology – draws on that tradition in modern Jewish thought which separates the lesson of love from the actualities of power, 'dialogue' from dialectic, time from history. Turning the *logos* into *pathos*, originary violence returns to bedevil its dreams.

In Buber, the immediacy of dialogue yields the loveful, holy middle, 'between' man and man, while the broken middle appears as the alienated world, law and coercion, and the sovereignty of 'nations'. The individual bears the burden of this equivocation in its tormented phantasy. And Levinas is not as different from Buber as either he or Lyotard think: holy *illeity* (the unbounded) is opposed to 'the just violences' of the state (bounded), while the individual is traumatized by his somnolent auditions of the *il y a*.

Irenic thought remains implicated in the oppositions it claims to transcend. To separate community from sovereignty, dialogue from comprehension, delivers 'the world' to the very violence that can only call forth lamentation. The time has come to retrace such thinking from its *pathos* to the *logos* it so fears. The 'Reply' from Kierkegaard to Buber imagined here offers a propaedeutic for recognizing *the broken middle* instead of remaining submerged in original violence and in terror, from abyss to abyss, only emerging from abyssal abjection to entreat the kingdom – alas, to no avail.

12

Walter Benjamin – Out of the Sources of Modern Judaism

There is nothing as whole as a cleft heart.[1]

I

In a review of Robert Alter's recently published book, *Necessary Angels: Tradition and Modernity in Kafka, Benjamin and Scholem,*[2] S. S. Prawer subtly questions the wisdom of understanding Kafka, Benjamin and Scholem without looking beyond Judaism, with what Alter calls its 'classic triad' of revelation, law and commentary,[3] to the German tradition, especially Goethe and romanticism, which 'they did not shake off' when they turned to French literature or to Jewish mysticism, and further, to the concerns of 'the wider gentile world of tradition and modernity'.[4]

---

[1] Rabbi Menachem Mendel of Kotsk. From Ruth Nevo's 'Introduction' to her translation of *Chaim Nachman Bialik: Selected Poems*, Jerusalem, Dvir and the *Jerusalem Post*, 1981, p. vii. This chapter was originally prepared for the Conference to celebrate the Centenary of Benjamin's birth, organized by Birkbeck College, University of London, 1992. It was first published in *New Formations*, July 1993.

[2] Robert Alter, *Necessary Angels: Tradition and Modernity in Kafka, Benjamin and Scholem*, Cambridge, Harvard University Press, 1991.

[3] Op. cit., p. 17. Alter also refers to 'language, interpretation, tradition and revelation' (p. 23).

[4] S. S. Prawer, 'Review of Robert Alter, *Necessary Angels: Tradition and Modernity in Kafka, Benjamin and Scholem*', *Times Literary Supplement*, 2 August 1991.

In the case of Benjamin, however, Prawer's understated scruple against reductionism is otiose, not only in the face of Alter's own nuanced approach to the paradoxes of language and identification (a central chapter in his book is entitled 'On Not Knowing Hebrew'),[5] but also in view of the rich and substantial body of criticism already in existence in which reference to the Jewish dimensions of Benjamin's life and work helps to clarify precisely the tremendous scope of his interests – from the mourning play to Marxism to Messianism. Moreover, this body of criticism has not assumed that Judaism is itself secure as tradition but has problematized the 'crisis' of Judaism and of Jewish identity. With different emphases, this approach is evident in Scholem's own essays on Benjamin and his Angel, and in his remarkable account of their friendship;[6] in Hannah Arendt's famous essay on Benjamin in *Men in Dark Times*;[7] in T. W. Adorno's essay on Benjamin in *Prisms*;[8] in Jürgen Habermas' essay on Benjamin's 'redemptive criticism';[9] and, more recently, in Irving Wohlfarth's aptly named study, 'On Some Jewish Motifs in Benjamin'.[10]

Nevertheless, it could be argued that none of these studies has distinguished clearly enough how Benjamin related fundamental elements of Judaism – tradition, commentary, Messianism – to specifically *modern* Jewish philosophical reflection on tradition and modernity. While Benjamin's relation to Franz Rosenzweig's great

[5] Alter prefaces the second chapter, 'On Not Knowing Hebrew', with a dream from Benjamin's *One Way Street*: 'In a dream I saw myself in Goethe's study . . . Goethe rose to his feet and accompanied me to an adjoining chamber, where a table was set for my relatives. It seemed prepared, however, for many more than their number. Doubtless there were places for my ancestors' (*Necessary Angels*, p. 25).

[6] Scholem, 'Walter Benjamin', 1964, and 'Walter Benjamin and his Angel', 1972, in *On Jews and Judaism in Crisis: Selected Essays*, trans. Lux Furtmüller and Werner J. Dannhauser, New York, Schocken, 1978, pp. 172–97, 198–236; *Walter Benjamin: The Story of a Friendship*, trans. Harry Zohn, London, Faber and Faber, 1982.

[7] Arendt, 'Walter Benjamin: 1892–1940', 1968, in *Men in Dark Times*, trans. Harry Zohn, Harmondsworth, Penguin, 1973, pp. 151–203.

[8] Adorno, 'A portrait of Walter Benjamin', 1950, in *Prisms*, trans. Samuel and Shierry Weber, London, Neville Spearman, 1967, pp. 227–42.

[9] Habermas, 'Consciousness-Raising or Redemptive Criticism: The Contemporaneity of Walter Benjamin', 1972, trans. Philip Brewster and Carl Howard Buchner, *New German Critique*, 17 (1979), pp. 30–59.

[10] Wohlfarth, 'On Some Jewish Motifs in Benjamin', in Andrew Benjamin (ed.), *The Problems of Modernity: Adorno and Benjamin*, Routledge, London, 1989, pp. 157–216.

Star of Redemption and to Rosenzweig's philosophy of language
and translation have received attention from Stephane Mosés and
others,[11] there exists little study of Benjamin's relation to neo-
Kantianism, especially to his reception of Hermann Cohen's
Platonizing neo-Kantianism.[12] Cohen's mathesis of the origin (*der
Ursprung*), developed in the *Logic*, which forms the first part of
his three-part *System*, also provides the mathesis of his late work,
Religion of Reason out of the Sources of Judaism.[13] While he sought
to overcome the structure of neo-Kantianism, it is this grammar
of origin which Benjamin opposes to the logic of idealism in the
'Epistemo-Critical Prologue' to *The Origin of German Trauerspiel*.
And this is why the title of this paper alludes to Benjamin's
inheritance from Cohen's great work – 'out of the sources of
Judaism'.

In this paper, written to celebrate the centenary of Benjamin's
birth, I hope to develop a new approach to assessing Benjamin's
thought 'out of the sources of modern Judaism'. Here it will not
be a question of referring to Judaism, whether traditional or modern, in order to demonstrate the patterning of Benjamin's complex
work; on the contrary, I shall propose a way of understanding
the complexity of Benjamin's work which will itself yield the
difficulty of his relation to Judaism. This illumination of Benjamin's
thinking will make it possible *to derive the meaning that Judaic categories exhibit in it*. Since Benjamin's thinking will be engaged
comprehensively, the emergence of the Jewish question cannot
diminish the focus of Benjamin's vision. This should also satisfy
Prawer's discretion.

---

[11] Mosés, 'Walter Benjamin and Franz Rosenzweig', *The Philosophical Forum* XV, 1–2
(1983–4), pp. 188–205. Mosés's argument that Rosenzweig's dialogism is fundamentally
different from Benjamin's lapsarian view of communication overlooks the way in which
both Rosenzweig and Benjamin defend a divine 'grammar' of names in opposition to
idealist logic of universals.
[12] Bernd Witte mentions Benjamin's knowledge of Cohen's book on Kant (p. 42); of the
third part of Cohen's *System*, *Ästhetik des reinen Gefuhls* (2 vols, Berlin, Bruno Cassiner,
1912 p. 52); of Cohen's *Religion of Reason out of the Sources of Judaism* (p. 54) in *Walter
Benjamin: An Intellectual Biography*, trans. James Rolleston, Detroit, Wayne State, 1991; see
too, the discussion of neo-Kantianism in Witte, *Walter Benjamin – Der Intellektuelle als
Kritiker: Untersuchungen zu seinem Frühwerk*, Stuttgart, Metzler, 1976, pp. 6–14.
[13] See Gillian Rose, 'Hermann Cohen – Kant among the Prophets', *supra*, pp. 111–25.

II

At the heart of Goethe's novel, *Wilhelm Meister's Apprenticeship*, lies the story of 'the beautiful soul'.[14] Borrowing from Goethe's novel within a novel, Hegel makes her story the pivot of the section of the *Phenomenology of Spirit*, 'Conscience. The "beautiful soul," evil and its forgiveness',[15] which concludes the path of objective spirit. 'The beautiful soul' is a learned but sickly female, who comes to reject marriage, aristocratic courts and the activities of the new class of Burghers. She retires from the world to cultivate her deepening religious piety, but, in spite of her perspicacity, she fails to find any means of public expression, or any bridge back to ethical and political life. In both Goethe's and Hegel's recounting, she pines away in consumption and dies.

This *image* of 'the beautiful soul' (who cannot, in fact, be pictured because her 'beauty' is not aesthetic but *ascetic*) is *dialectical*, for it captures the impotence that results from excessive religious zeal, which opposes the world in the name of an inner, individual protestantism, or, collectively, in the name of the brethren of the common life – a pre-Reformation community of lay celibates, women and men, whose idea and organization were adopted in the eighteenth century by Pietist communities, especially the community of Herrnhut, led by Count Zinzendorf, to which Goethe refers by name in his novel in connection with 'the beautiful soul'.[16] The concentration on the image of 'the beautiful soul' exhibits what Benjamin called *dialectics at a standstill*, for she bears no fruit – her body disintegrates as her soul swells – and she returns in death to fallen nature, neither realized nor redeemed.

[14] Book VI is entitled 'Confessions of a Beautiful Soul'. Thomas Carlyle, in the first English translation of 1824 (still to be recommended) translated *schöne Seele* as 'fair saint' (London, Chapman and Hall, 1899).

[15] *Phenomenology of Spirit*, trans. Miller, Oxford, Clarendon, 1979, pp. 383–409.

[16] Max Weber discusses the connection between the brethren of the common life and Pietist sects in one of the many long footnotes to *The Protestant Ethic and the Spirit of Capitalism* (trans. Talcott Parsons, London, Unwin, 1968), pp. 240–2 note 108; he also discusses Goethe's *Wilhelm Meisters Wanderjahren* and *Faust*, on the relation between deeds and renunciation, pp. 180–1.

This zealous and melancholy profile, caught in a narrative, forms a *constellation* with earlier and later times.[17]

What Goethe, Hegel, Kierkegaard,[18] Weber and, I shall argue, Benjamin, have in common is probably most familiar from Max Weber: the investigation of *the unintended consequences* of the Protestant ethic.[19] Protestant legitimation of one's worldly vocation – a vocation which may demonstrate but which may never *earn* individual salvation – results in 'worldly asceticism'. The Lutheran doctrine of 'the calling' and the Calvinist doctrine of predestination produce the sober, methodical organization of everyday life. Weber explored the connection between the Protestant ethic and 'the spirit of capitalism': the worldly asceticism which establishes the preconditions for the development of rational, capitalist accumulation and investment. Goethe, Hegel and Kierkegaard, and, I

[17] In Goethe's novel, 'the beautiful soul', other-worldly asceticism, is contrasted with the ethic of worldly asceticism; in Hegel's *Phenomenology*, 'the beautiful soul' is contrasted with 'the hard heart of judgement' and forgiveness. For further discussion of 'the beautiful soul' see Rose, *The Broken Middle: Out of our Ancient Society*, Oxford, Blackwell, 1992, pp. 153–246.

[18] Adorno represents Kierkegaard in terms of Benjamin's notion of baroque melancholy (*Kierkegaard: Construction of the Aesthetic*, 1933, trans. Robert Hullor-Kentor, Minneapolis, University of Minnesota Press, 1989, pp. 62–4, 54). For a criticism of Adorno's reading of Kierkegaard, see Rose, *The Broken Middle*, pp. 8–9, 13–16.

[19] The method employed in this paper, which construes the continuity, first, between Max Weber and Benjamin, and, equally, between Benjamin and Carl Schmitt's theories of sovereignty and emergency, which are crucial from the *Ursprung des deutschen Trauerspiel* (where Benjamin links the concept of the baroque and the state of emergency with reference to Schmitt's *Political Theology* (1928, in Walter Benjamin: *Gessamelte Schriften*, vol. I.1, ed. Rolf Tiedemann and Hermann Schweppenhäuser, Frankfurt am Main, Suhrkamp, vols I–VI, 1974–85; trans. *The Origin of German Tragic Drama*, John Osborne, London, New Left Books, 1977, pp. 65–6, and see the reference to further discussion below, note 55)) to the so-called 'Theses on the Philosophy of History' (where Benjamin calls for 'a real state of emergency' to oppose the fascist norm of emergency (see the reference to further discussion below, note 125)), should be compared with the recently published, major study by G. L. Ulmen, *Politischer Mehrwert: Eine Studie über Max Weber und Carl Schmitt*, trans. Ursula Ludz, Weinheim, VCH Acta Humaniora, 1991: and with Norbert Bolz, 'Charisma und Soveränität: Carl Schmitt und Walter Benjamin im Schatten Max Webers', in Jacob Taubes (ed.), *Religionstheorie und Politische Theologie*, vol. 1, *Der Furst dieser Welt: Carl Schmitt und die Folgen*, Munich, Wilhelm Fink, 1993, pp. 249–62. Schmitt wrote a response to Benjamin's *Trauerspiel*, 'On the Barbaric Character of Shakespearean Drama: A Response to Walter Benjamin on the Origin of German Tragic Drama', which is an Appendix to 'The Source of the Tragic', ch. 3 of *Hamlet oder Hecuba: Der Einbruch der Zeit in das Spiel*, 1956, trans. David Pan, in *Telos*, Special Issue *Carl Schmitt Friend or Foe?* 72 (1987), pp. 146–51.

shall argue, Benjamin, explored further *the unintended psychological and political consequences* of Protestant *Innerlichkeit* (inwardness) and worldly asceticism. They followed the way in which the Protestant doctrine of salvation creates hypertrophy of the inner life. Hypertrophy of the inner life is correlated with atrophy of political participation. Eventually, the interest in salvation itself atrophies, but the inner anxiety of salvation persists and is combined with worldly opportunism and ruthlessness; this combination of anxiety and ruthlessness amounts to the combination of inner and outer violence.

To Goethe, Hegel and Weber, eighteenth-century German Pietism represented the attempt to establish a reformation of the Reformation, which, alas, resulted in yet another set of paradoxical or 'unintended' outcomes. In its reaction to burgeoning bourgeois legality with its excessively autonomous individuality as well as in its reaction to the remnants of the aristocratic ethic, Pietism produces a more extreme asceticism – more emotional inwardly, and organized outwardly to render 'the invisible Church of the elect visible on this earth'.[20] In Goethe and Hegel, 'the beautiful soul' offers the image of this kind of piety: intelligent, bookish and intense, she mourns a world which she cannot and will not join; her increased subjective freedom represents a decrease in objective freedom, an incapacity for and a refusal of political participation. She mourns a world which she has no reason to mourn – because it is not lost: it is beginning.

III

Walter Benjamin, it will be argued here, investigates 'the Baroque Ethic and the Spirit of Fascism'. He extends the exploration of the Protestant ethic from Protestant or Pietist inwardness to the inwardness of the Protestantism of the Counter-Reformation, to nineteenth-century French Catholic inwardness, and to the inwardness of Jewish modernity. These forms of inwardness are correlated with the transition from *worldly asceticism to worldly aestheticism*, from worldly renunciation to worldly ornamentation

[20] Weber, *The Protestant Ethic and the Spirit of Capitalism*, p. 130.

(the Baroque ethic of worldly aestheticism persists from the seventeenth century to the twentieth century). They are also correlated with the transition from the end of politics in the spirit of capitalism to aestheticized politics in the spirit of Fascism. While the Protestant ethic leads to *the withering of the interest in salvation without loss of the anxiety of salvation*, the Baroque ethic evinces *a created and creaturely world* with the aspiration but *without the promise of redemption*. In Judaic categories, this spiritual condition gives rise to the Messianic fixation. For the Messianic fixation in Judaism always indicates *a disgrace or disorder in the relation to revelation*. ('Revelation' in Judaism means the Written and the Oral Law, the teaching and its interpretation, not the redeeming death of Christ which effects individual salvation.) Benjamin expresses this disgrace of revelation as 'the decay of aura' or 'transmission without truth'.[21] The object, style and mood of Benjamin's philosophy converge, not in the Christian mournfulness or melancholy, discerned from the Baroque *Trauerspiel* to Baudelaire, but in the Judaic state of desertion – in Hebrew, *agunah* – the stasis which his *agon* with the law dictates.

In philosophical terms, the *spirit* of Fascism does not mean that spiritual value is accorded to Fascism, but that Benjamin derives the meaning of 'Fascism' from the violence of its relation to actuality – this is *spirit* in Hegel's sense of misrecognition of otherness. Fascist violence is itself derived from the change in the structure of experience – the subjectivity which issues from and responds to the atrophy of substance.

Benjamin is the *taxonomist of sadness*, and he adds figures of melancholy to the philosophical repertoire of modern experience: the repertoire which includes stoicism, scepticism, the unhappy consciousness, resignation and *ressentiment*. But his figures of melancholy – baroque, Baudelaire, Kafka, 'left-wing', the angel of history – are not counterposed to recognition, love, forgiveness or faith: and therefore their mourning is not completed; it remains *aberrated* not *inaugurated*. The figures of melancholy are

---

[21] According to Scholem, 'It must be emphasized that later on when he had turned to historical materialism, out of those two categories of Revelation and Redemption only the latter was preserved *expressis verbis* but not the former, closely though it was bound up with his basic method of commenting on great and authoritative texts' ('Walter Benjamin', p. 194). In my view, this was true at all times.

counterposed instead to the Divine, which is characterized by pure violence or pure language, and is approachable in mimesis or correspondences. The accessibility of the Divine in mimesis and correspondences eschews law or mediation or representation. As a result, subjective, fallen, melancholy judgement can only be over-thrown by the expiation of bloodless violence of a new, divine immediacy – the general strike, the distracted cinema audience, a Socialist emergency law (to oppose the Fascist emergency), the Messiah.

If the dialectical image of Pietist melancholy is 'the beautiful soul', then the dialectical image of baroque melancholy is the *agunah* – the deserted wife, who has not been sent a bill of divorce and who does not know if her husband is still alive; she may not remarry nor does she even know whether she may embark on mourning. In the tales of the modern Hebrew writer, S. Y. Agnon, which Benjamin cherished, everybody is in a state of desertion, including the *shekhinah*, the Divine Presence in the world.[22] The aim of this centenary reflection is to move from *aberrated* to *in-augurated* mourning – to break the hard heart of subjective judge-ment; to soften the rigid stare of the *Angélus Novus*, the angel of history.

Strictly speaking, there is no Judaic theology[23] – no *logos* of God – because Rabbinic Judaism, formed in post-biblical times, is the creation of the Rabbis, who, claiming to be the rightful heirs of the prophets, established Talmud Torah at the focus of Jewish life. Talmud Torah means the teaching of the teaching, or the commentary on the law. Its validity derives from the tradition that the Oral Law as well as the Written Law were revealed to Moses on Sinai. The Oral law was handed down to the Elders, and thence to the Rabbis, who eventually wrote it down, first in the *Mishnah* and then in the Talmud.[24] The Oral Law is also called 'the commandment' and 'the interpretation'.[25] Now, if there is,

[22] See 'Agunot', 1908, Agnon's first major tale (in Nahum N. Glatzer (ed.), *Twenty-One Stories*, New York, Schocken, 1970, pp. 30–44).

[23] Even Scholem uses 'theology' loosely when discussing Benjamin's thought.

[24] The *Mishnah* was the first compilation of the Oral Law at the end of the second century of the Common Era; the Talmud, the commentary on the *Mishnah*, compiled in the fourth century of the Common Era.

[25] See Moses Maimonides, 'Introduction' to the *Mishneh* Torah, in Isadore Twersky (ed.), *A Maimonides Reader*, New York, Behrman House, 1972, p. 35.

strictly speaking, no Judaic theology, there can be no theological notions of creation, revelation and redemption. However, to characterize Judaism philosophically, it is often necessary to resort to these notions. The key to the three must be 'revelation', for it is only according to revelation that nature can be seen as created, and that redemption is either proclaimed or promised. In Christianity, the Redeemer lives and the repentant, individual soul is saved. In Judaism, the Messiah is promised and life is lived in view of this deferment; redemption, when it comes, will be universal – it is promised to the whole world, not just to the Jews.

Scholem has shown in many of his studies that while Messianism in its deferment is always an ingredient of Judaic self-definition, it only tends to become urgently and exclusively definitive of Jewish peoples in emergencies when they are politically and mortally endangered – by expulsion, pogrom or persecution. Settled and relatively secure communities are not intensely eschatological; they live within the repetition of the liturgy and the study of the law.[26] Similarly, the Kabbalistic, or mystical tradition, redefines the meaning of the Written and Oral Law so as to bypass the rigorous complaisance of life lived according to Talmud Torah. The black letters of the Written Law are themselves understood as a specification of the whiteness between the letters, so that the Written Law itself is already an interpretation of God's unknowable name. The former divine word is already oral, already transmission.[27] Scholem points out how Martin Buber and Franz Rosenzweig approach this Kabbalistic antinomianism when, in a now famous correspondence, they agree that the meaning of revelation is not ritual, not law – even if understood as commandment – but the sheer event of revelation itself – 'I am I.'[28]

---

[26] See Scholem, 'Towards an Understanding of the Messianic Idea in Judaism', pp. 1–36; and 'The Messianic Idea in Kabbalism', in *The Messianic Idea in Judaism and Other Essays on Jewish Spirituality*, New York, Schocken, 1971, p. 41.

[27] Scholem, 'Revelation and Tradition as Religious Categories in Judaism', 1962, in *The Messianic Idea*, pp. 292–303.

[28] Scholem, *On the Kabbalah and its Symbolism*, 1960, trans. Ralph Manheim, New York, Schocken, 1969, p. 30 n. 3. For the correspondence between Buber and Rosenzweig, see Rosenzweig, *On Jewish Learning*, ed. N. N. Glatzer, New York, Schocken, 1965, p. 118.

IV

From the early philosophical fragments and short essays to the *Arcades* work and to the so-called theses on the concept of history, I shall argue, Benjamin expounds 'the Baroque Ethic and the Spirit of Fascism' – the mournful character, equally creature of subjective judgement and sovereign of the violent politics of law-abolishing emergency. *The disgrace of revelation,* by which I mean a revelation which stamps the creature and the creaturely world of nature as forever lacking grace, that is, with no hope of redemption, this disgrace of revelation, is evident from the beginning in Benjamin's essays on language and mimesis. These essays develop the neo-Kantian metaphysics which unifies religion and philosophy for which Benjamin called,[29] by bypassing the notion of law – whether understood as regularity, imperative (normative), or lawlikeness without law.

In the essay 'On Language as Such and the Language of Man', language is defined as naming, not as verbal, grammatical, propositional, judgemental or logical. 'Linguistic being' consists in the communicability of naming, the unfallen language of man to God.[30] This idea of the universality and intensiveness of names as the condition of communication precedes *meaning*: 'There is no such thing as a meaning [*einen Inhalt*] of language.'[31] 'Meaning' assumes a problematic relationship between the inexpressible and unexpressed mental entity and language, while the thesis of the communicability of names defines *revelation*: 'the inviolability' of the name is 'the only and sufficient condition and characteristic of the divinity of the mental being that is expressed in it'.[32] Revelation, on this argument, is encompassed by the second story of the

---

[29] 'Über das Programm der Kommenden Philosophie', in *Walter Benjamin: Gesammelte Schriften*, vol. II.I, p. 167, *Walter Benjamin: Gesammelte Schriften*, ed. Rolf Tiedemann and Hermann Schweppenhäuser, Frankfurt am Main, Suhrkamp, vols. I–VI, 1974–85, p. 167 trans. 'On the Program of the Coming Philosophy', 1918, Mark Ritter, in *Benjamin: Philosophy, History, Aesthetics*, ed. Gary Smith, Chicago, University of Chicago Press, 1989, p. 8.

[30] 'Über Sprache überhaupt und über die Sprache des Menschen', 1916, in *Gesammelte Schriften*, vol. II.I, 144; trans. Edmund Jephcott and Kingsley Shorter, in *One-Way Street and Other Writings*, London, New Left Books, 1979, p. 111.

[31] Ibid., pp. 145–6, trans. p. 112.

[32] Ibid., pp. 146–7, trans. p. 113.

Creation in the first chapter of the book of Genesis in the gift of language: 'In God name is creative because it is word, and God's word is cognizant because it is name. "And he saw that it was good;" that is He had cognized it through name.'[33]

Created from God's word, the thing in itself is known in its name by a human word which effects the translation of things into the language of man. Through translation God's unspoken word becomes the naming word in the knowledge of man. However, 'knowledge of good and evil abandons name, it is a knowledge from outside, the uncreative imitation of the creative word'.[34] The Fall is the fall of 'the eternal purity of names' into 'the sterner purity of the judging word':[35] it gives rise to a new immediacy, the magic of judgement, to language as a means, as *mere* sign, to abstraction. Judgement is ambiguous: both a new immediacy and the mediation of abstraction: 'This immense irony marks the mythic origin of law.'[36] After the fall, the tree of knowledge of good and evil becomes the emblem of language fallen into judgement.

After the fall, the original bliss of mute nature, now named by man, turns into a deep sadness:

> After the Fall, however, when God's word curses the ground, the appearance of nature is deeply changed. Now begins its other muteness, which we mean by the deep sadness of nature. It is a metaphysical truth that all nature would begin to lament if it were endowed with language.[37]

'This proposition has a double meaning.' It means that nature would lament language, and that nature would lament. Lament, Benjamin comments, is 'the most undifferentiated, impotent expression of sadness'. Nature mourns because she is mute but it is her sadness that makes her mute:

> In all mourning there is the deepest inclination to speechlessness, which is infinitely more than inability or disinclination

[33] Ibid., p. 148, trans. p. 115.
[34] Ibid., pp. 152–3, trans. p. 119.
[35] Ibid., p. 153, trans. p. 120.
[36] Ibid., p. 154, trans. p. 120.
[37] Ibid., p. 155, trans. p. 121.

to communicate. That which mourns feels itself thoroughly known by the unknowable. To be named – even when the namer is Godlike and blissful – perhaps always remains an intimation of mourning. But how much more melancholy to be named not from the one blessed, paradisiac language of names, but from the hundred languages of man, in which name has already withered, yet which, according to God's pronouncement, have knowledge of things . . .

In the language of men, however, [things] are over-named . . . over-naming as the deepest linguistic reason for all melancholy and (from the point of view of the thing) of all deliberate muteness.[38]

Benjamin's distinctions and elisions between 'melancholy', 'mourning' and 'lament' indicate *several specific challenges* to the Judaic tradition apparently recovered here. To the tradition (the Oral Law) the fall is the occasion of loss *and* gain; it delineates the precondition of human passion and action. Lamentation over the condition of exile is not 'impotent': on the contrary, it is the strongest thing: it is the recovery of strength by moving from refusal of loss to acknowledgment and acceptance, 'receiving everything back'. Revelation is not creation, not naming, but commandment and love, the commandment to love the Lord with all one's might. To the tradition, the dominion of the tree of knowledge marks the transition from unitary, unrestrained life to the duality of good and evil. The distinctions of good and evil, commandment and prohibition, holy and profane, pure and impure, are the appearance of Torah in this aspect of revelation which prevails prior to regaining the unity of life.[39] For Benjamin, however, the birthing of law is absolute loss, so he employs Greek terms for its *adventus*: 'This immense irony marks the mythical origin of law.' 'Myth' belongs to Greek religion, 'irony' to Greek philosophy. This inaccessibility of revelation as God's silent language is far more nugatory and abandoned than the secret of revelation in antinomian, apocalyptic Kabbalistic Messianism. No wonder, in sooth, it is so sad. However, to fulfil the promise of the taxonomy of sadness, it is sad in the sense of the mournfulness

---

[38] Ibid., p. 155, trans. pp. 121–2.
[39] See Scholem, 'The Crisis of Tradition in Jewish Messianism', in *The Messianic Idea in Judaism*, p. 69.

of desertion, *agunah*, *aberrated mourning*, not the sadness of true mourning and lamentation, of being 'thoroughly known by the unknowable' – *inaugurated mourning*.[40]

Torah has its origin in God. According to Maimonides, the Torah exists with God in eternity before the creation of the world. To Benjamin, the origin of law in the Fall either provokes the melancholy response of nature and man, the creaturely world, in the face of inexorable judgement; or the response of heroic genius, the speechlessness of the hero in Greek tragedy, who breaches 'the demonic determination of legal statutes'; or the response of comic genius of character in Greek comedy who breaches, in his amoral persistence, the fate of guilt by which the law makes the impersonal into the measure of the personal, the individual.[41] The only complete response to the violence of law-making and law-preserving, the violence in law, would be divine, the law in violence, which is only conceivable as God's anarchy.

Since the Epistles of Paul and the Gospels, Judaism has borne the opprobrium of the evangelical opposition of Christian love to Pharisiacal law. In the modern period, the further connotations of 'positive' or 'human' law (without the Christian criterion of natural law) can accrue to Torah if it is translated as *law*, when it would be more accurately translated as *teaching* or *instruction*. These inherited difficulties in the presentation of Judaic motifs, as well as their ambivalent relation to the tradition of cultural orthodoxy, lead Buber and Rosenzweig to dissociate the idea of the divine from the idea of law. In their thought, the divine is *dialogue*, or *love* in opposition to the fallen world of law; God is diadic not triadic – divine anarchy. As a result, the difference between modern and pre-modern law cannot be conceived by these apologies for Judaism. As boundary-destroying agapic love, this conception

---

[40] In 'Über das mimetische Vermögen', 1933, *Gesammelte Schriften*, vol. II.I, pp. 210–13; trans. 'On the Mimetic Faculty' in *One Way Street*, pp. 160–3 and 'Lehre vom Ähnlichen', 1983, *Gesammelte Schriften*, pp. 204–10, trans. 'Doctrine of the Similar', Knut Tarnowski, *New German Critique*, 17 (1979), pp. 65–9 (see Anson Rabinbach's 'Introduction', pp. 60–4), Benjamin defines the mimetic gift as being able 'to read what was never written' (p. 213, trans. pp. 162–3), such as, stars, entrails, runes, hieroglyphs. This circumscription represents a further derivation of language without regularity or normative force, that is, without any connotation of law.
[41] Benjamin, 'Schicksal und Charakter', 1919, *Gesammelte Schriften*, vol. II.I, pp. 173–9, 'Fate and Character', in *One-Way Street*, pp. 127–30.

of God falls to Nietzsche's criticism of Pauline love: that it is violent in its annihilation of bonds and boundaries.[42]

Benjamin displays the same unease with the traditional conceptuality of Torah. He, too, conceives all law as pagan, mythic violence, as law-making and law-preserving violence; but, to my knowledge, he is the only modern, Jewish thinker who is consistent enough to realize that this violence in law has implications for the idea of God. To avoid transferring the world's violence in law to God's violence in love, Benjamin defines divine sovereignty not as *love* but as law-abolishing *violence*. In his essay the 'Critique of Violence', it is not violence which is criticized, but any notion of the rule of law, the law of the constitution or representative institutions. All visible law is mythic law-making violence which posits and changes boundaries and laws even as it claims to be policing established ones. State power is 'legal violence', 'bloody power over mere life for its own sake'. Only the violence of God or the general strike, which is invisible because total, can counter the partial and bloody violences of the law. This divine or sovereign violence abolishes law by destroying boundaries without making new ones. It is boundlessly expiatory; without demanding sacrifices, it accepts them.[43]

Benjamin comes near to the idea of Talmud Torah when he contrasts the commandment as a guideline (not a criterion) and its educative potential[44] with the versatility of mythic law-making violence, which invests people with guilt not punishment. But he maintains the strict opposition between the pagan feast of law-making violence, ranging from the Greek to the modern state, the violence in law, and divine violence, either invisible in act, visible in outcome, or in the general strike effecting the suspending of violence because it has no programme, no utopia, no law-making.[45] Consequently, the idea of mediation or negotiation which lights up in the idea of commandment is quickly extinguished. There is no way to distinguish law-abolishing violence from law-making violence that *decides* in the state of emergency to usurp divinity,

---

[42] Compare the argument in the essays on Buber, Rosenzweig and Nietzsche *supra*, pp. 155–73, 127–59, 89–110.

[43] Benjamin, 'Zur Kritik der Gewalt', 1921, *Gesammelte Schriften*, vol. II.I pp. 199–200; trans. 'Critique of Violence', in *One-Way Street*, pp. 50–1.

[44] Ibid., p. 200, trans. p. 151.

[45] Ibid., pp. 193–5, trans. pp. 145–7.

because there is no recognizable rule of law and no benign or wise judgement, no *phronesis*. The Tower of Babel triumphant is conceivable.

This outline of the Baroque ethic and the spirit of Fascism is drawn in these early, seminal pieces. The mournfulness of creaturely being, set in language and deserted by God, experiences the world as *excess of signification without salvation*, which is the meaning of worldly aestheticization, not truth as beauty but ornamentation without truth – *the Baroque ethic*. Restricted by its mythic origin to law-making and law-preserving violence, subjective judgement beholds itself in the phantasmagoria of soulless personifications of this mythic law. Seeking in desperation the unobtainable redemption, *the spirit of Fascism* usurps divine violence in the spectacle of war which is to abolish the boundaries of the world. The invisible Church of the elect is to be visible on earth.

To express this in the terms of Benjamin's so-called 'Theologico-Political Fragment', the Messianism prefigured in the cosmic violence of total passing away and the inner man's suffering of misfortune in isolation[46] is appropriated by Fascism for a theocracy of imminent and immanent end. To strive to accept eternal transience is 'the task of world politics', that is, the politics that would abolish the fallen world, a method that 'must be called nihilism'.[47] This politics presupposes the inner man in isolation, able to bear a suffering that promises neither realization nor redemption. *E contrario*, it implies misfortune which is unable to bear this suffering, a thirst for the realization of entreated redemption, for the politics of the world, and total perdition.

V

The baroque writer felt bound in every particular to the ideal of an absolutist constitution, as was upheld by the Church of both confessions.[48]

---

[46] 'Theologisch-Politisches Fragment', 1921, *Gesammelte Schriften*, vol. II.I, pp. 203–4; trans. 'Theologico-Political Fragment', in *One-Way Street*, p. 155.

[47] Ibid., p. 204, trans. p. 156.

[48] *The Origin of German Tragic Drama*, trans. John Osborne, London, New Left Books, 1977. *Ursprung des deutschen Trauerspiels*, 1928, *Gesammelte Schriften*, vol. I.I, p. 45. I retain the German *Trauerspiel* in my translation of the title, and refer to the work by this word alone in the notes.

The *Origin of German Trauerspiel* explores the transition from the Protestant ethic to the Baroque ethic, from Lutheran and Calvinist salvation, with its ethic of worldly asceticism and its outcome in the rational spirit of capitalism, to the loss of salvation, characteristic of German Protestantism and Spanish Catholicism of the Counter-Reformation, with its ethic of worldly aestheticism and its outcome in the violent spirit of Fascism. This is to propose three, potentially disturbing theses: that Benjamin's account of the origin of Fascism is contained in his exploration of seventeenth-century Baroque drama; that our tendency to melancholy, however intellectual and passive, is violent; that Benjamin analyses, or breaks down, but he also fixes what he discerns.

If the Reformation delivered religion from the hands of the Pope to the hands of the Prince, then the Baroque inherits the Princely sovereign, recipient of this absolute power. The double dangers of political authority and of religious authority are concentrated in the Prince, whose melancholy autocracy results in the rule of tyrant, martyr or, most dangerous of all, the intriguer. The complementary Lutheran doctrines of salvation, 'justification by faith alone', and 'the priesthood of all believers', have turned into *the Princedom of all believers*; every unscrupulous action is justified in a world where signification has been separated from salvation. This excess of signification is Baroque ornamentation, worldly aestheticization. The powerless melancholy of the contemplative and feckless Prince bestows on the intriguer the licence to exploit his own melancholy. The loss of salvation, of 'value rationality', together with the instrumental rationalization of the world, transformed the initial Protestant release of worldly energy into what Weber called 'the iron cage', (*ein stalhartes Gehause*), and 'the house of bondage' (*ein Gehause der Horigkeit*) – the biblical phrase for the captivity and enslavement of the Jews in Egypt, who were liberated in the Exodus, in the redemption of hostages by God. The difficulty or end of politics which ensues when that redemption does not obtain was the stasis which preoccupied Weber's authorship; the violence of aestheticized politics which ensues when that redemption does not obtain was the stasis, 'the pile of debris', which preoccupied Benjamin's.

Both the method and the content of *The Origin of German Trauerspiel* display the logic of Baroque mournfulness. The famously difficult 'Epistemo-Critical Prologue' to the book is best read as the text to which the rest of the book provides the introduction. For the 'Prologue', couched in the Platonizing neo-Kantianism of Cohen, speaks of the salvation and redemption of the world of phenomena in a way which *presupposes* the loss of salvation and disgrace of revelation in a world of beings who know themselves to be creatures, not natural beings. This presupposes the account of *Trauerspiel* to come. Both Kantian deduction and Platonic derivation of the phenomenal world are disqualified in the 'Prologue'; method and anamnesis are to be replaced by the truth of names. Names, 'unimpaired by cognitive meaning', are linguistic displays of Ideas, which are not prototypes but 'constellations', 'Faustian mothers'.[49] They 'do not make the similar identical, but they effect a synthesis between extremes'.[50] The name of names is 'the Origin' (*der Ursprung*) which has nothing to do with genesis (*die Entstehung*):

> The term origin is not intended to describe the process by which the existent came into being, but rather to describe that which emerges from the process of becoming and disappearance.[51]

Not fully factual, 'its rhythm is apparent only to a dual insight' of singularity and repetition.[52] This dual insight bears the hallmark of Cohen's 'logic of origin', for Benjamin's 'Idea' and 'phenomena' are not synthesized, but, no longer distinguished from the noumenal world (unknowable things in themselves), they hold in an asymptotic relation whose tenability is given by the origin or mathesis – what Benjamin calls, 'the Faustian mothers'. Cohen's *System* also abolishes epistemology and Kantian *Kritikismus* for an ultimate logic of redemption. The methodological nihilism of names has the same origin as *Trauerspiel* itself – 'the instrument of lamentation and its resonance'.[53]

> The baroque knows no eschatology . . . no mechanism by which all earthly things are gathered in together and exalted

[49] Ibid., pp. 216, 215, trans. pp. 36, 35.
[50] Ibid., p. 221, trans. p. 41.
[51] Ibid., p. 226, trans. p. 45.
[52] Ibid.
[53] Ibid., p. 235, trans. p. 54.

before being consigned to their end. The hereafter is emptied of everything which contains the slightest breath of this world, and from it the baroque extracts a profusion of things which customarily escaped the grasp of artistic formulation and, at its high point, brings them violently into the light of day, in order to clear an ultimate heaven, enabling it, as a vacuum, one day to destroy the world with catastrophic violence.[54]

In the seventeenth century, *Trauerspiel* referred to historical events as well as dramas; it presupposes the new concept of absolute sovereignty which 'marked the final collapse of the theocratic concept of the state', and the need for kings and princes to maintain power, resist harmful counsel and avert the state of emergency power.[55] The tyrant, the martyr and the intriguer, the three faces of the monarch, are the characters this sovereignty may take when regal action 'is no longer integrated into the process of redemption'.[56] The persistence of religious aspiration in spite of the increasing worldliness of Protestants and Jesuits of the Counter-Reformation and the absence of a divine plan of salvation 'lead to a complete revolution of the content of life, while orthodox ecclesiastical forms were preserved'.[57] The king 'proves to be a secularized redemptive power' who may resolve 'the conflicts of a state of creation without grace'.[58]

As its vocational ethic so emphatically proclaims, Lutheran moralism was always intent on bringing together the transcendence of the life of faith and the immanence of everyday life; it therefore never permitted the decisive confrontation between human-earthly perplexity and princely-hierarchical power on which the conclusion of so many of Calderón's dramas depends.[59]

---

[54] Ibid., p. 246, trans. p. 66.
[55] Ibid., p. 246, trans. p. 65.
[56] Ibid., p. 257, trans. p. 78.
[57] Ibid., p. 258, trans. p. 79.
[58] Ibid., p. 260, trans. p. 81.
[59] Ibid., p. 263, trans. p. 84, and see P. Calderón, *Plays: One*, trans. Gwynne Edwards, London, Methuen, 1991.

This ethic of the Spanish Counter-Reformation comes to prevail over the original German Protestant ethic. Lutheran moralism, which correlated inner faith with the everyday world brings about the rise and fall of princes. The tyrant, arbitrary and emotional, combines absolute power of decision with severe indecisiveness;[60] while the martyr is a 'radical stoic' who 'fortifies [herself] against a state of emergency in the soul' and acts regardless of her own downfall – for the martyr is frequently a chaste woman.[61] However, the most dangerous face of sovereignty is the intriguer, 'all intellect and will-power'.[62] This is the Baroque ethic par excellence, 'the unique ambiguity of . . . spiritual sovereignty', which requires 'both strict inner discipline and unscrupulous external action'.[63] This strict discipline in a creature 'stripped of all naive impulses'[64] may produce a saint or an evil genius. The combination of 'icy disillusion' and 'the fierce aspiration of the will to power . . . awakens a mood of mourning', in the intriguer, which is infernal in the Protestant dramas, tranquil in the Spanish Catholic dramas.[65]

The silence of the tragic hero is defiant. It is 'designed not only to bring about the restoration but above all the undermining of an ancient body of laws in the linguistic constitution of the renewed community'.[66] *Trauerspiel*, by contrast, 'are not so much plays which cause mourning [*traurig macht*], as plays through which mournfulness finds satisfaction [*die Trauer ihr Gegnügen findet*]: plays for the mournful [*vor Traurigen*]'.[67] It is the absence not only of salvation but also of revelation which makes not for mourning, which would acknowledge the law, but for mournfulness and melancholy, perplexed by the created world which lacks both law and redemption: 'For all the wisdom of the melancholic is subject to the nether world; it is secured by immersion in the life of creaturely things, and it hears nothing of the voice of revelation'.[68]

[60] Ibid., pp. 250–1, trans. pp. 70–1.
[61] Ibid., pp. 251–3, trans. pp. 72–4.
[62] Ibid., p. 274, trans. p. 95.
[63] Ibid., p. 276, trans. p. 98.
[64] Ibid.
[65] Ibid., pp. 276–7, trans. p. 98.
[66] Ibid., p. 294, trans. p. 115.
[67] Ibid., p. 298, trans. p. 119.
[68] Ibid., p. 330, trans. p. 152.

And 'Melancholy betrays the world for the sake of knowledge. But in its tenacious self-absorption it embraces dead objects in its contemplation, in order to redeem them.'[69]

Melancholy is the logical outcome of Protestantism; in particular, of the antinomic relation to the everyday of Lutheranism: the denial of good works in the doctrine of justification by faith alone affirmed the secular and the political world as the demonstration of obligation, 'but in its great men it produced melancholy'.[70] For life is deprived of all value. Distinct from stoical refusal of emotion, and also from the unhappy consciousness which regards itself as a degraded creature, separated from transcendent actuality, mourning becomes the state of mind which tries to revive the world of alienated objects and deadened emotions.[71] Benjamin summarizes: 'the ethical subject' has 'lost its heart in the beautiful soul'.

Allegory is the *prodigious* outcome of this mournfulness, since 'the most simple object appears to be a symbol of some enigmatic wisdom because it lacks any natural creative relation to us'.[72] If the symbol means the immanence of the moral world in the world of beauty and therefore of perfected individual action within redemption, allegory is the contemplative claim immersed in the depths which separates the visual world from meaning:[73]

Whereas in the symbol destruction is idealized and the transfigured face of nature is fleetingly revealed in the light of redemption, in allegory the observer is confronted with the *facies hippocratica* of history as a petrified, primordial landscape. Everything about history that, from the very beginning, has been untimely, sorrowful, unsuccessful, is expressed in a face – or rather in a death's head . . . This is the heart of the allegorical way of seeing, of the baroque, secular explanation of history as the Passion of the world; its

---

[69] Ibid., p. 334, trans. p. 157.
[70] Ibid., p. 317, trans. p. 138.
[71] Ibid., p. 318, trans. p. 139.
[72] Ibid., p. 319, trans. p. 140.
[73] Ibid., p. 342, trans. p. 165.

importance resides solely in the stations of its decline. . . .
The greater the significance, the greater the subjection to
death, because death digs most deeply the jagged line of demarcation between physical nature and significance.[74]

In allegory, nature is emblematic: torso, rune, ruin, fragment,
monument, piled up with no goal, significations without realization, sacrament or salvation, present the physiognomy of history
as decay not as bloom.[75] Lutheran *Heilsgeschichte*, the presentation of history as the fall and salvation of man, becomes the
allegory of soulless nature eternally separated from the story of
salvation.[76] The meaning of Baroque, allegorical personification is
not the spiritualization of the physical, the ensouling of things,
but, on the contrary, allegorical personifications deprive nature
of a soul while imposing a gravid body on emblems which 'offer
themselves to view in desolate, sorrowful dispersion'.[77] Banal
objects arise from allegory with 'the overbearing ostentation
[which] is soon displaced by its disconsolate everyday countenance . . . succeeded by that disappointed abandonment of the
exhausted emblem'.[78]

    Trauerspiel in its extreme allegorical forms demands a theolo-
gical understanding not an aesthetic one, but this theology would
be a dynamic theology of history not 'a guaranteed economics of
salvation'.[79] For mourning in *Trauerspiel* is really the mournfulness which will not soften and weep in the meekness of genuine
grief,[80] but remains rigid and petrified. It belongs to the theology
of evil: 'the absolute spirituality, which is what Satan means,

---

[74] Ibid., p. 343, trans. p. 166. A note to Adorno's citation of *facies hippocratica*, Hippocratic
face (taken from Francis Adams, 'Introduction' to *The Genuine Works of Hippocrates* (New
York, William Wood, 1886, p. 195)), explains: 'This countenance, suffering from "the
worst", is marked by "a sharp nose, hollow eyes, collapsed temples, the ears cold, con-
tracted and their lobes turned out: the skin about the forehead being rough, distended and
parched; the colour of the face being green, black, livid or lead coloured"' (see Adorno,
Kierkegaard, pp. 151–2, n. 33).

[75] Ibid., pp. 347, 353–8, trans. pp. 170, 177–82.

[76] Ibid., p. 358, trans. p. 182, *Heilsgeschichte*, the Lutheran term for the history of the fall
and salvation of man is incorrectly translated.

[77] Ibid., pp. 361–2, 362–3, trans. pp. 186, 187.

[78] Ibid., p. 361, trans. p. 185.

[79] Ibid., p. 390, trans. p. 216.

[80] Ibid., the text is cited in the translation in German and translated in a footnote,
p. 154.

destroys itself in its emancipation from what is sacred'.[81] The figures of the tyrant and of the intriguer show this at work in 'three
original satanic promises . . . spiritual in kind: What tempts is
the illusion of freedom – in the exploration of what is forbidden;
the illusion of independence – in the secession from the community of the pious; the illusion of infinity – in the empty abyss
of evil.'[82] These are indeed the features of the spirit – of the spirit
which issues from the Baroque ethic of worldly allegory – the
spirit of Fascism, or, *what Fascism means.*

Yet Benjamin offers two unexpected intimations of salvation
before his masterpiece concludes: the allegorical emblems of
Golgotha reinforce the desolation of human existence, the world
abandoned to the spirit of Satan, but, reversing the direction of
allegory, melancholy immersion in the contemplation of bones
'faithlessly leaps forward to the idea of resurrection', which 'clears
away the final phantasmagoria of the objective', and rediscovers itself – without mourning, violence or play – 'seriously
under the eyes of heaven'.[83]

This *seriousness* exposes the theatricality of the Baroque altogether. For the final reminder returns to the substitution of subjective judgement of good and evil for God's initial beholding of
creation and his benison, 'And God saw everything that he had
made, and, behold it was very good.' 'This knowledge [of evil]
as the triumph of subjectivity and the onset of arbitrary rule over
things, is the origin of all allegorical contemplation.'[84] While the
earthly courts are uncertain in their judgements, 'in the heavenly
court the illusion of evil comes entirely into its own'.[85] But here
is the rub – for the whole topography is engineered: 'the display
of manifest subjectivity becomes a formal guarantee of the miracle,
the divine action itself'; just as in the Baroque balcony, 'the constant reference to the violence of the supporting and supported
forces . . . emphasize the soaring miracle above, by drawing attention to the difficulty of supporting it from below'.[86]

[81] Ibid., p. 404, trans. p. 230.
[82] Ibid., pp. 403–4 trans. p. 230.
[83] Ibid., p. 406, trans. p. 232.
[84] Ibid., p. 407, trans. p. 233.
[85] Ibid., p. 407, trans. p. 234.
[86] Ibid., p. 408, trans. pp. 234–5.

In the Counter-Reformation, Protestantism has become melancholy and mournful in the face of a world without salvation. This rigid mourning gives rise to the Baroque ethic of violent display and contemplation of the allegorical, aestheticized world and to the evil genius of the intriguer – the spirit of Fascism, hierarchical and absolute sovereign – who, having destroyed his own impulses and unscrupulous towards the world, rules by emergency and the frenzy of destruction. In developing this *genealogy of morals*, Benjamin insinuates 'seriousness', 'meekness' of the heart that grieves, the actualites abused by the Baroque ethic, but he knows no divine or human law, no Torah, revelation, or democracy, beyond the ancient violence of law in Greek tragedy and the arbitrary subjective rule over things of the judgement of man from the biblical Fall, to the Christian Baroque, and I argue, to the spirit of Fascism.

The *genealogy* of the Baroque ethic and the spirit of Fascism in the *Trauerspiel* book forms a *constellation* with later times. Benjamin's shorter studies offer further explorations of mournful sovereignty. These figures of melancholy in his gallery of sadness exhibit different qualities and degrees of the disgrace of revelation, of the law which is presupposed and rigified in allegory or in the phantasmagoria of commodities.

VI

From the early study of Goethe's late novel, *Elective Affinities*, to his general article on Goethe's life and work, commissioned by a Soviet encyclopedia but rejected by it, Benjamin argues that Goethe's opposition to Christian remorse and to Jacobi's Pietist metaphysics according to which nature conceals God is belied by *the Baroque ethic* of his works.[87] The presentation of marriage as the mythic law and the implication that Ottilie's death displays the muteness of mythic sacrifice in *Elective Affinities* are undershadowed by the emblematic world of fallen nature; and the violence released in the decay of marriage reveals history as

---

[87] 'Goethe', *Gesammelte Schriften*, vol. II.2, p. 719, trans. 'Goethe: the reluctant bourgeois', Rodney Livingstone, *New Left Review*, 133 (1982), p. 79.

Trauerspiel.[88] The second part of *Faust*, the summation of Goethe's experience as a courtier, is not set in an eighteenth-century court but in an idealized Baroque Court and it ends in a vision of Catholic penitence, which arises out of its 'innermost political necessity'.[89] Benjamin derives this necessity from Goethe's unease with bourgeois culture, 'Become what you are', for which he is ostensibly the most lyrical and assiduous advocate. Bourgeois risk is effectively reprieved by the secret *Turmgesellschaft*, the society of the tower, in *Wilhelm Meister's Appenticeship*, and by feudal artisanship and utopian-socialist pedagogy in *Wilhelm Meister's Wanderings*.[90] According to this comprehension, Goethe never overcame the strain of Pietism in himself, so that Herrnhut, the Pietist community, located by the entrepreneurial spirit in the heart of action in opposition to 'the beautiful soul', who withdraws from the world, is, nevertheless, subsequently realized in the *Turmgesellschaft*.

The very form of the novel also represents profound Baroque perplexity. The intrinsic difficulty of communicability in the novel arises from the unravelling of counsel from the fabric of life. Only sects can tell Tales – the Russian legends of Leskov, Buber's reinventing of Hassidic Tales – because only sects retain a vision of salvation which confers meaning on death, so that life can be related with its weave of wisdom.[91] But when sects, too, lose their faith, and relinquish the delicate intimation of redemption in order to attempt realization – to make the invisible Church of the Elect visible on earth – they exhibit *the spirit of Fascism*.

Proust proves a fellow taxonomist of sadness for he found a law for his malady. By submitting to 'the laws of night and honey', he conquered the hopeless sadness within himself.[92] Proust transformed existence into the preserve of memory and overcame 'the incurable imperfection in the very essence of the present'.[93] Out

[88] See 'Goethes Wahlverwandschaften', 1921–2, *Gesammelte Schriften*, vol. I.1, pp. 125–201; see, too, Witte, *Walter Benjamin: An Intellectual Biography*, p. 55.

[89] 'Goethe', p. 737, trans. p. 91.

[90] Ibid., pp. 732, 717, trans. pp. 88, 78.

[91] Benjamin, 'Der Erzähler: Betrachtungen zum Werk Nikolai Lesskovs', 1936, in *Gesammelte Schriften*, vol. II.2, pp. 438–65; trans. 'The Storyteller: Reflections on the Works of Nikolai Leskov', *Illuminations*, Harry Zohn, London, Fontana, 1973, pp. 83–109.

[92] Benjamin, 'Zum Bilde Proust', 1929, *Gesammelte Schriften*, vol. II.2, p. 312; trans. 'The Image of Proust', *Illuminations*, p. 205.

[93] Ibid.

of this abyss of loneliness, Proust recognized Baudelaire's acquiescence in his own distress, his immoderate garrulousness in the face of death.[94]

It is, however, in his commentaries on Kafka's solitariness that what Benjamin calls 'the sickness of tradition', the disgrace of revelation, is most fully diagnosed.[95] 'Tradition' means the Oral Law, the commentary on the Written Law, its transmissibility and hence its truth. Kafka's prose pieces have 'a similar relation to doctrine as the Haggadah does to Halakah', that is, they tell stories and anecdotes to illustrate the meaning and outcome of the laws and statutes.[96] Wisdom is inherent in tradition, 'it is truth in its haggadic consistency'.[97] Kafka's genius lies in his response to the loss of this consistency of truth: 'he sacrificed truth for the sake of clinging to its transmissibility, its haggadic element'.[98] The misery and beauty of his parables arise from their witness of the vacuum at the heart of the tradition. Benjamin's equation of *haggada* and the Oral Law indicates his strange relation to the tradition he seeks to witness in the stations of its decline. For the Oral Law or commentary is not necessarily haggadic; *haggada*, stories or anecdotes, constitutes a small proportion of it.

To capture Kafka's world, Benjamin introduces two versions of the aetiological Talmudic legend which explains the preparation of the Sabbath meal. On receiving a letter from her fiancé, who has not forgotten her, and is on his way to her, a princess, languishing in exile in a village whose language she does not speak, prepares a meal – the only way she is able to express her joy.[99] Benjamin argues that this Messianism (which, to him, will be without law because it is mute) indicates ignorance of the law; this tallies with his emphasis on the predominance of uncompleted

[94] Ibid., p. 321, trans. p. 214.

[95] Letter to Gerhard Scholem, 12. July 1938 in *Briefe*, vol. 2, ed. Gershom Scholem and Theodor W. Adorno, Frankfurt am Main, Suhrkamp, 1966, p. 763; trans. 'Max Brod's Book on Kafka: And Some of My Own Reflections', *Illuminations*, p. 147.

[96] 'Franz Kafka: Zur zehnten Wiederkehr series Todestages', 1939, *Gesammelte Schriften*, vol. II.2, p. 420; trans. 'Franz Kafka: On the Tenth Anniversary of His Death', *Illuminations*, p. 122.

[97] 'Max Brod's book on Kafka', ibid.

[98] Ibid.

[99] 'Franz Kafka', p. 424, trans. p. 126; 'Franz Kafka: Beim Bau der Chinesischen Mauer', 1931, *Gesammelte Schriften*, vol. 2.2, p. 680.

grace in *The Castle*.[100] True to the tradition, Benjamin stresses that Kafka is not asserting law against myth: not the law but the learning is lost – the gate to justice.[101] However, Odradek, Joseph K, and the victim in the Penal Colony, are taken to be engrossed in deciphering the nature of their unknown and unincurred guilt.[102] Benjamin does not raise the possibility that Joseph K. might be guilty (as Orson Welles implies in his film of *The Trial*) and is punished, not because he has lost access to the doorway of the Law, to learning, but because of his refusal to keep his promise to life, to struggle with the doorman who seems to bar the access to the Law, in the parable 'Before the Law', which is included in *The Trial*.

In his introduction to his translation of Baudelaire's *Tableaux Parisiens*, 'The Task of the Translator', Benjamin argues that pure language, which is without the learning and work of law and is mute in the languages of man, is the only mode of access to God: 'In the original [language], language and revelation are one without any tension.'[103] The languages of man represent supplementary intentions towards the pure language.[104] The task of the translator is to find how far the hidden meaning of languages is from revelation.[105] Revelation is here hidden, mysterious, not discernible from surface transmissibility.[106] Benjamin has changed the relation of the Written to the Oral Law by understanding all human signification as removed from revelation so that even the 'original' language is not original, but an interlinear interpretation of pure language.[107] Approach to this pure language is highly charged and dangerous. If the translator succeeds in making two languages proximate to pure language, he will perish; like Hölderlin, who went mad, 'the gates of a language . . . may slam shut and enclose the translator with silence'.[108]

[100] Ibid., p. 678.
[101] 'Franz Kafka', p. 437, trans. p. 139.
[102] Ibid., p. 432, trans. p. 133.
[103] 'Die Aufgabe des Übersetzers', 1923 *Gesammelte Schriften*, vol. IV.1, p. 21; trans. *Illuminations*, 'The Task of the Translator', p. 82.
[104] Ibid., p. 13, trans. p. 74.
[105] Ibid., p. 14, trans. pp. 74–5.
[106] Ibid., pp. 14–15, trans. p. 75.
[107] Ibid., p. 21, trans. p. 82.
[108] Ibid., p. 21, trans. p. 81.

VII

If Protestant salvation gives rise to the ethic of worldly asceticism and its unintended outcome, the spirit of capitalism, then Counter-Reformation Protestant and Catholic loss of salvation gives rise to the Baroque ethic of worldly aestheticization and its unintended outcome, the spirit of Fascism. To Baroque melancholy, the world is allegorical, the phantasmagoria or personification of soulless things. Hyperdisciplined interest in this sorrowful projection results in the destructive rule of the tyrant or the intriguer. In the capital of the nineteenth century, Paris, these two genealogies, the Protestant and the Baroque, form a *constellation*, for the sovereignty of the commodity fetish, expanded form of the spirit of capitalism, becomes the allegorical personification of soulless things. Baudelaire's melancholy lyric is the new Baroque ethic of the commodity fetish, while the Fascist total mobilization of war is its eschatological consummation.

Baudelaire manages to be the last, successful lyric poet in the face of 'the increasing atrophy of experience'.[109] The prevalence of shocks, which characterize collective life and cut it off from remembrance and tradition, and which individual consciousness cannot absorb (unless ready for anxiety) are made into the matter and form of his poetry.[110] This is captured by the shock of love *at last sight*, as it were, in Benjamin's understanding of Baudelaire's poem to a passer-by. The unknown woman, who passes by, arouses the sexual shock that can beset a lonely man: not the rapture suffused with eros which could lead to loss or mourning, but the distraught response to a pale, ghost of a woman, who is dressed in mourning.[111] Benjamin's commentary implies desertion, *aberrated mourning*, not *inaugurated mourning*; not fulfilment and loss, even if only for a rapturous moment, but the inability to engage the other, to know her desire and to be known by her.

---

[109] 'Über einige Motive bei Baudelaire', 1939, *Gesammelte Schriften*, vol. I.2, p. 611; trans. 'On Some Motifs in Baudelaire', *Illuminations*, p. 161. A version of this with the second and third sections incorporated into the first is also included in 'Some Motifs in Baudelaire', trans. Harry Zohn, *Charles Baudelaire: A Lyric Poet in the Era of High Capitalism*, London, New Left Books, 1973, pp. 107–54.

[110] 'On Some Motifs in Baudelaire', pp. 162–3, trans. pp. 162–3.

[111] 'Some Motifs in Baudelaire', p. 623, trans. p. 171.

The woman in mourning is phantasmagorical; embellished by her flounces, to the soulless voyeur, she is without soul.

This melancholy desertion of the shocked poet on the passing of the phantasmagorical woman is *the Baroque ethic* – the mournful fixation on the aesthetic of the untouchable world. The flaneur, by contrast, accepts the condition of phantasmagoric allegory, the deathless but dead-pale Other, and, recognizing himself in this fate, yields the position of observer and 'succumbs to the fascination of the scene which finally lures him outside into the whorl of the crowd'.[112] Baudelaire's theory of correspondances represents his attempt to overcome shock and resume assimilable experience by regaining access to remembrance without any mediation of law or representation. The attempt to bypass law issues in rage: 'it is the very inability to experience that lies at the heart of rage'. This rage gives a sense of 'unfathomable desolation' to Baudelaire's verse.[113] The opposition of *spleen* and *ideal* in *Les Fleurs du Mal*, it might be argued, displays the same mutual implication as the Baroque balcony: violent, tortured supports theatrically emphasize the supervenient miracle.

The loss of the ability to know and be known (which would define the ability to mourn or *inaugurated mourning*), to look and to have one's gaze returned, even nostalgically, by conjuring up lost love in old photographs, is what Benjamin means by 'the decay of aura': 'To perceive the aura of an object we look at means to invest it with the ability to look at us in return.'[114] A look exchanged presupposes the unique manifestation of distance, a ceremonial barrier which entices approach. This separation would be effaced by blank, unseeing eyes, which abolish the distance necessary for relating. In the idea of the repetition of exchanged looks which manifest distance, Benjamin offers a visual image of recognition as repetition: acknowledgement of the relation of the other to herself in my relation to myself. In Baudelaire, *sexus* is detached from *eros*: the eyes of the Other are void, without distance, they have no familiarity, no resemblance, and hence no family, no ethical life.[115] This emphasis on the visual is itself

---

[112] Ibid., p. 628, trans. p. 175.
[113] Ibid., pp. 641–2, trans. 186, amended.
[114] Ibid., pp. 646–7, trans. p. 190.
[115] Ibid., pp. 648–9, trans. pp. 191–2.

derived by Benjamin from the nature of modern life – the decline of listening and the importance of sight to negotiate one's solitary way among the public conveyances of modern transport. Yet Benjamin accepts the terms of Baudelaire's complaint, his desertion by the dead look of the female other, because he shares with Baudelaire the inability to hear the commandment.

> '*Fiat ars – pereat mundus*', says Fascism, and, as Marinetti admits, expects war to supply the artistic gratification of a sense perception that has been changed by technology. . .[116]
>
> In big parades and monster rallies, in sports events, and in war, all of which are nowadays captured by camera and sound recording, the masses are brought face to face with themselves.[117]

In the essay 'The Work of Art in the Age of Technical Reproducibility', the new technology has two contrary implications for Benjamin, which are equally derivable from the destruction of distance. Technology may result in total violence, or in the complete abolition of violence – this was the ambiguity in the idea of 'law-abolishing violence' in the 'Critique of Violence'. Mankind's 'self-alienation has reached such a degree that it can experience its own destruction as an aesthetic pleasure of the first order'.[118] On the other hand, the new technology has 'burst our prison world asunder',[119] and its destruction of traditional boundaries may lead to the general and mild politics of distraction. In the second case, the politics of distraction, the technological abolition of distance bases art on a different practice – politics; but, in the first case, the witness of mankind's own destruction as an aesthetic pleasure, the technological abolition of distance bases politics on another practice – art.

The 'decay of aura' means not just the loss of authenticity or authority, but the loss of the distance from any other, so that one cannot even see oneself looking back. This may result in

---

[116] 'Das Kunstwerk in Zeitalter seiner technischen Reproduzierbarkeit', 1936, *Gesammelte Schriften*, vol. I.2, p. 508; trans. 'The Work of Art in the Age of Mechanical Reproduction', *Illuminations*, p. 244.

[117] Ibid., p. 506, n. 32, trans. p. 253, n. 21.

[118] Ibid., p. 508, trans. p. 244.

[119] Ibid., p. 499, trans. p. 238.

sublime violence, which, seeking to restore grace, does not even recognize itself as the object as well as the subject of destruction. Benjamin prefers to argue that this law-abolishing violence will resemble the general strike in his depiction of the cinema audience, half-hungry for an artistic medium which will embellish shock experiences, yet discovering that their change in apperception can be satisfied by the mode of distraction in the cinema – rather than by retreating into melancholic, judgemental concentration.[120] Yet he seems to realize, too, that the old cult has been replaced by the new, as the old religious ritual is recreated in the spell of movie stars, the phoney spell of commodities.[121]

What Benjamin wants to imply is that 'the tremendous power of bourgeois autonomy', specifically, the Protestant ethic, 'being alone with one's God',[122] free to shake off clerical bondage, and the sad legacy of melancholy which that liberation imposes, have been overcome by technological change. Yet he is equally aware that this overcoming of mournfulness has not occurred. The violence released from Baroque sovereignty would explain why the two contrary outcomes of distraction and destruction emerge, but not solely from changes in technology.[123] Benjamin has taught us better concerning the Baroque ethic and the spirit of Fascism. The Baroque ethic is not superseded; and Benjamin's *œuvre* ends not with Messianic redemption but with another Baroque *Trauerspiel*,

---

[120] Ibid., pp. 503–5, trans. pp. 241–2.

[121] Ibid., p. 492, trans. p. 233.

[122] Ibid., p. 502 n. 27, trans. p. 252 n. 18.

[123] See, too, Benjamin, 'Theorien des deutschen Faschismus: Zu der Sammelschrift "Krieg und Krieger"', 1930, *Gesammelte Schriften*, vol. III, 'Theories of German Fascism: On the Collection of Essays *War and Warrior*, edited by Ernst Junger', in which Benjamin argues that the theory of the German 'post-war war [*Nachkrieg*]' with its combination of Junger's 'total mobilization' and Salomon's 'landscape of the front', displays the features of Baroque ethic, its idealism and its violence: 'Etching the landscape with flaming banners and trenches technology wanted to recreate the heroic features of German Idealism. It went astray. What is considered heroic were the features of Hippocrates, the features of death. Deeply imbued with its own depravity, technology gave shape to the apocalyptic face of nature and reduced nature to silence – even though this technology had the power to give nature its voice. Instead of using and illuminating the secrets of nature via a technology mediated by the human scheme of things, the new nationalists' metaphysical abstraction of war signifies nothing other than a mystified and unmediated application of technology to solve the mystery of an idealistically perceived nature' (pp. 243, 247, trans. Jerolf Wikoff, *New German Critique*, Special Walter Benjamin Issue, 17 (1979), pp. 124, 126–7; see, too, Ansgar Hillach, 'The aesthetics of politics: Walter Benjamin's 'Theories of German Fascism'', *New German Critique*, Special Walter Benjamin Issue, 17 (1979), pp. 99–119).

which is staked on transforming *aberrated* mourning into *inaugurated* mourning in order to overcome the spirit of fascism: this *Trauerspiel* takes the form of the so-called 'Theses on the Philosophy of History'.

VIII

These eighteen theses, entitled in German, 'On the Concept of History' seek urgently to replace the Fascist state of emergency, which (as has been learnt from the tradition of the oppressed), 'is not the exception but the rule', by 'an actual state of emergency'.[124] Real emergency is imagined as a sovereign, divine, law-abolishing violence, which will awaken and boundlessly expiate the dead. This is what the Messiah means: the conception of the present not as homogenous, empty time but as the 'time of the now'; the past is referred to redemption, to a unique not an eternal image of the past, 'a constellation' with the present, both 'shot through with chips of Messianic time'.[125] This attempt to revitalize the struggle of historical materialism against Fascism *exhorts remembrance as both method and outcome* of the revolution: 'it means to seize hold of a memory as it flashes up at a moment of danger'.[126] A great revolution will introduce a new calendar, a sequence of holy days, recurring 'days of remembrance', by contrast with clock-measured time.[127]

The theses on the concept of history grapple with the insinuation and exhortation of divine law-abolishing violence against the partial, pagan, mythical, emergency rule of Fascism, which decides to become sovereign. Unlike law-making and law-preserving violence, which displays the semblance of the rule of law, Fascism exposes its predatory nature. However, the theses on the concept of history grapple even more profoundly with the law-judging violence of Social Democracy, which displays the features of *Trauerspiel*. To overcome this Social Democratic *Trauerspiel*,

---

[124] 'Über den Begriff der Geschichte', *Gesammelte Schriften*, vol. I.2, pp. 694–709; trans. 'Theses on the Philosophy of History', *Illuminations*, p. viii, amended.

[125] Ibid., p. xviii A.

[126] Ibid., p. vi.

[127] Ibid., p. xv.

Benjamin must transform Baroque mournfulness into mourning, *aberrated mourning* into *inaugurated mourning*. However, without a divine law that can appear, he risks deepening the despair he would overcome. This lack of visible law accounts for the mood of exhortation; and the theses culminate in the commandment that is at the heart of Judaism: *Zakhor*, the commandment to remember. This Judaic commandment to remember, which Benjamin would enlist for the method and outcome of revolution, is utterly different from contemplative, Platonic anamnesis.

> Consider the darkness and the great cold
> In this vale which resounds with mystery.[128]

These two lines, with which the seventh thesis on history begins, express the perception, which is characteristic of *Trauerspiel*, of history as fallen and allegorical nature. The second thesis introduces 'the secret [*heimlich*] index which refers the past to redemption', the Messianic idea. As a result of this arcane calibration, the fixed contemplation of the angel of history is all the more mournful; while the presentation of history as a single catastrophe, driven by a storm from Paradise, and the image of the ever-mounting pile of debris, which 'we call progress', reinforce the most remorseless image of a world without redemption: '*even the dead* will not be safe from the enemy if he wins. And this enemy has not ceased to be victorious'.[129] Social Democracy is directly associated with medieval *acedia*, or sadness, 'the indolence of heart which despairs of possessing the genuine historical image as it flares up briefly'.[130] Social Democracy has inherited 'the old Protestant work ethic'; 'it recognizes only the progress in the mastery of nature, not the retrogression of society; it already displays the technocratic features later encountered in Fascism'; and it believes in 'the infinite perfectibility of mankind'.[131] The combination of sadness with this brutal optimism leaves Social Democracy resourceless to oppose Fascism, while it shares some of the most destructive features of Fascism.

This political melancholy is blasted against Messianic mourning,

---

[128] Brecht, *The Threepenny Opera*, ibid., p. vii.
[129] Ibid., pp. ix, vi.
[130] Ibid., p. vii, trans. amended.
[131] Ibid., p. xi, trans. amended.

not the *work* of remembrance but its eschatology: history is exilic not universal; and thinking as well as its object – history – should be arrested not flowing. A 'constellation saturated with tensions' should be shocked into monadic form, which is a sign of 'a Messianic cessation of happening, or, put differently, a revolutionary chance in the fight for the oppressed past'.[132] This is the point at which the argument in this paper might reopen the debate with Adorno. For, to Adorno, 'universal history must be construed and denied'.[133] Instead of crystallizing 'the configuration pregnant with tensions' into a Messianic monad, Adorno would unravel the antinomies of realization before staking everything on the flash of redemption – which could leave everything as it is; restore the old regime; or inaugurate a greater violence.

Benjamin's peroration to the theses on the concept of history acknowledges that the future cannot be entreated, but reminds us that 'the Torah and the prayers instruct [the Jews] in remembrance'. This final reminder becomes the approximation to transforming homogenous, empty time into 'the strait gate through which the Messiah might enter'.[134]

However, in Judaism, the politics of *Zakhor*, remembrance, are equivocal. The ancient commandment of remembrance, the annual renewal of awareness of the exilic condition and of the redemption, has the consequence of devaluing historiographical discernment in different times and places. It encourages eschatological repetition in the place of political judgement.[135] But, for Benjamin, all political judgement is melancholic and violent. Even Benjamin's reference to *Zakhor*, the commandment to remember, has been given an idiosyncratic mystical and Messianic twist. There are six *Mitzvot*, injunctions to remember, in Biblical and Rabbinic Judaism: Remember the day you came out of Egypt;[136] Remember the Sabbath and keep it Holy; Take heed lest you forget the things your eyes saw at Horeb (this commandment

---

[132] Ibid., p. xvii, trans. amended.

[133] Adorno, *Negative Dialectics*, trans. E. B. Ashton, London, Routledge and Kegan Paul, p. 320.

[134] Benjamin, 'Über den Begriflf der Geschichte', pp. 694–709; trans. 'Theses on the Philosophy of History', p. xviii B.

[135] For this argument, see Yosef Hayim Yerushalmi, *Zakhor: Jewish History and Jewish Memory*, Seattle, University of Washington Press, 1982.

[136] Deut. 4:32, 16.3.

refers to the Golden Calf, and the giving of the Second Tablets of the Law, with Moses as mediator); Remember the wrath of the Lord in the desert; Remember what the Lord did to Miriam (she slandered her brother and was smitten with leprosy); Remember what the Amalekites did to you (they attacked from the rear).[137] There is, however, a crucial difference between the first five and the last of these commandments. The first five are not restricted: they may be remembered on any day, because they are constructive; the sixth may only be remembered on a special Sabbath once a year, because it is soul-destroying and destructive. This last commandment, therefore, affords rest from one's enemies, and that is what is not to be forgotten. For Benjamin the enemy – Fascism – had not ceased to be victorious, and must be remembered every instant. Yet, in the 'Critique of Violence', Benjamin emphasized that the commandment, 'Thou shalt not kill', relates to God and the doer, and may be abused neither to justify the ends of killing over the means, nor, on the contrary, to sanctify mere life rather than just existence.[138] The need for Talmud Torah, local jurisprudence, the complex contextuality of the commandment, seems to have been forgotten in his invocation of *Zakhor*.[139]

> the idea of happiness . . . resonates with the idea of redemption. This happiness is founded precisely upon the despair and the forsakenness which were ours.[140]

Agunah, the deserted wife, is the Judaic category and Messianic image of this forsakenness, which I have suggested by analogy with the Christian, baroque image of melancholy. In Judaic terms, I would argue that, in spite of his emphasis on creating new holy

---

[137] Exod. 17:14, Deut. 25:17–19.

[138] 'Critique of Violence', pp. 200–2, trans. p. 153.

[139] For this idea of Halacha and ethics as a local, contextual jurisprudence, see Aharon Lichtenstein, 'Does Jewish Tradition Recognize an Ethic Independent of Halacha?' repr. in Marvin Fox (ed.) *Modern Jewish Ethics: Theory and Practice*, Columbus, Ohio University Press, 1975, pp. 102–23.

[140] From Lotze's *Mikrokosmos*, cited in 'N', a section of the preparatory material for the *Arcades* project, *Gesammelte Schriften*, vol. V.1, p. 599; trans. in *Benjamin: Philosophy, History, Aesthetics*, ed. G. Smith, Chicago, University of Chicago Press, 1989, p. 71. The words with which the second thesis on the concept of history opens are taken from the same source.

days, Benjamin knew no Day of Atonement, no Yom Kippur, although this date is already in the liturgical calendar. In his work, the hard heart of judgment does not melt into grief, into forgiveness, or into atonement.

In philosophical terms, I would argue, Benjamin only knew the dialectical image as a lightning flash, 'the Then . . . held fast', in the Now of recognizability. The rescue that is thus – and only thus – effected, can only take place for that which, in the next moment, is irretrievably lost.[141] It is this unequivocal refusal of any dynamic of mutual recognition and struggle which keeps Benjamin's thinking restricted to the stasis of desertion, *aberrated mourning*, and the yearning for invisible, divine violence. This yearning for divine annihilation finds expression in his lament at being excluded from the ranks of the New Angels, which God creates in immense numbers, and which have the sole purpose of singing His praise before His throne for a moment before they dissolve into nought.[142] Unable to praise God, this is Klee's traumatized Angel, who appears in the ninth thesis – the New Angel. Propelled backwards into the future by a storm from Paradise, he cannot stay and he cannot dissolve, but must impotently watch in horror the single catastrophe of History, the infernal raging caused by the same paradisical storm, as it piles up its debris at his feet.

I prefer another angel of Klee's, *Angélus Dubiosus*. With voluminous, blue, billowing and enfolded wings in which square eyeholes are cut for the expanse of rotund, taupe flesh to gaze through, this molelike angel appears unguarded rather than intent, grounded and slack rather than backing up and away in rigid horror. To me, this dubious angel suggests the humorous witness who must endure.

To celebrate Benjamin is to lament his *aberrated* mourning. *Inaugurated* mourning bears the fruits of forgiveness: it may become silent. I conclude with a passage from Agnon's novel *A Guest for the Night*:

> I do not remember whether we walked and talked, or whether we walked in silence. Perhaps we were silent, perhaps we

---

[141] Ibid., pp. 591–2, trans. p. 64.
[142] See Scholem, 'Walter Benjamin and his Angel', p. 205.

talked. When the heart is full the mouth speaks, but when the soul is full a man's eyes look with affectionate sadness, and his mouth is silent.[143]

---

[143] S. Y. Agnon, *A Guest for the Night*, 1939, trans. Misha Louvish, New York, Schocken, 1968, p. 284. For further discussion of 'aberrated mourning', see Laurence A. Rickels, *Aberrations of Mourning: Writing on German Crypts*, Detroit, Wayne State University Press, 1988.

13

Angry Angels – Simone Weil and Emmanuel Levinas

Simone Weil, you have never understood anything about the Torah.[1]

That Levinas is troubled by Simone Weil's thought is evident in his essay 'Simone Weil Against the Bible' (1952),[2] and in various *obiter dicta* scattered among the pieces gathered in the volume entitled *Difficult Liberty*.[3] Weil's antagonism to the Old Testament, to the God whom she calls 'Jehovah', and to Israel as a world religion, has been thoroughly documented in recent secondary literature on Weil,[4] but, to my knowledge, Levinas' early response

---

[1] Levinas, 'Aimer la Thora plus que Dieu', 1955, in *Difficile Liberté: Essais sur le judaïsme*, Paris, Albin, Michel, p. 192; trans. 'Loving the Torah more than God', in *Difficult Liberty: Essays on Judaism*, trans. and ed. Sean Hand, London, The Athlone Press, 1990, p. 144, amended.

[2] In *Difficult Liberty*, pp. 178–88, trans. pp. 133–41.

[3] The third part, 'Polemics', pits Zachariah against Weil by way of epigraph: '"The Lord of Hosts [*Dieu des armées*]". The history of the Hebrews shows that this has to do not with stars, but also with the warriors of Israel. . . . This blasphemy was unknown to all other (peoples). (Simone Weil, Letter to A. M. Monk) Not by might, nor by power, but by my Spirit, says the Lord of hosts. (Zachariah 4: 6)'. The opening essay of 'Polemics', 'Place and Utopia', in spite of disclaimers, renews the dispute between Christianity and Judaism: 'The man of utopia wishes unjustly. Instead of the difficult task of living an equitable life, he prefers the joy of solitary salvation' (p. 131, trans. p. 101). See, too, 'Jewish Thought Today' (1961), p. 211, trans. p. 161.

[4] See Leslie Fielder, 'Simone Weil: Prophet out of Israel', *Commentary*, 11 (1951), pp. 36–46; more recently, David McLellan, *Simone Weil: Utopian Pessimist*, London, Macmillan, 1989, pp. 149–54; and Thomas R. Nevin, *Simone Weil: Portrait of a Self-Exiled Jew*, Chapel Hill, University of North Carolina Press, 1991.

not only to her animus against the Bible but to her presentation of Christianity and the spiritual life has not been taken up in these later discussions.

It would not be difficult to demonstrate that Levinas has misunderstood the meaning of Christianity in Weil's thought, just as – Levinas is right – Weil never understood the meaning of Talmud Torah, neither the formation nor the ethos of post-biblical, Rabbinic Judaism. However, this blind spot in the projection of their confessional other – Weil on Israel, Levinas on Weil's Christianity – illuminates in turn the weak spot in the *apologia* of each for Christianity and Judaism, respectively.

For both Simone Weil and Emmanuel Levinas are *ethical* thinkers; and they both seek to justify *in philosophical terms* the essentially ethical as opposed to the sacrosanct character of the religious impulse which they elect to present. Moreover, their thought converges at the deepest level: where it exposes the intrinsic violence of the sovereign individual towards herself, her others, and towards God. Both attest the spiritual liberty which such violence implies but refuses: liberty which it is always so difficult to assume – to accept and to exercise – because it effaces the boundaries of sovereignty and dissolves the autonomous individual. In both authorships, violence, the obstacle and alternative to the Good, issues from and returns to the setting of spiritual life in the modern state. Fascist and Communist politics are seen as temptations which arise from the failings of individual rights and from the prevalence of bureaucratic rationality and domination. Political and spiritual life are entwined; and political theology stakes itself on redemption *and* realization.

The aim of this short consideration of Weil and Levinas is to propose that the negative characterization of their respective spiritual Other indicates a residue of violence in their own thought. This residue of violence follows partly from the severe philosophical presentation of themes which require the ethico-religious dissolution of authority. Lacking the humour and irony essential to presenting difficult liberty, Weil and Levinas reproduce by their mode of address the violence prowling the boundaries which they seek to unsettle. Instead of confessing and configuring the paradox of authorship, each accuses the other faith of not allowing for the ever-theatening contamination of the Good by violence.

Divine hubris stalks this absence of authorial humility: Levinas becomes entangled in the coils of unwelcome grace; Weil in the rigours of Talmud Torah, as she battles with the lessons of the *Bhagavadgîtâ*.

In his essay, 'Simone Weil Against the Bible', Levinas seems torn between three strategies of confrontation. One strategy involves conceding that Weil's indictment of biblical cruelty is a revulsion he shares – the commandment to annihilate the Canaanite people, men, women, and children. Levinas argues that the meaning of the Oral Law, that is, of Rabbinic Judaism, is the mitigation of 'the inescapable harshness of Scripture';[5] and 'It is through the Talmud's intelligence that we accede to the Bible's faith.'[6] Another strategy involves dissociation from Weil's attribution of Evil to Israel by arguing that 'she turns the Good into an absolutely pure idea, excluding all contamination or violence'.[7] Levinas attributes Weil's sole exclusion of the Jews from the Divine to her misunderstanding of the speculative nature of prophecy. When Malachi proclaims 'God is both universal and yet not universal', this means 'His universality is not accomplished as long as it is only recognized by thought and is not fulfilled by the acts of men. It remains abstract then.'[8] According to Weil, 'Jews possess only a God for armies – how horrible!'[9] Levinas opposes Weil's idea of the universal Divine rooted in particular nations by emphasizing that the Word cannot root in the arid soil of the desert, and is nowhere fixed because it is not yet universal.[10]

The third strategy develops a Gnostic criticism of Weil's alleged Gnosticism, her imputed radical separation of the purity of the Divine from the Evil which she attributes to the Old Testament.[11]

---

[5] 'Simone Weil Against the Bible', p. 185, trans. p. 138.

[6] Ibid., p. 182, trans. p. 136.

[7] Ibid., p. 179, trans. p. 134, amended.

[8] Ibid., p. 182, trans. p. 136.

[9] Ibid., p. 181, trans. p. 135.

[10] Ibid., p. 183, trans. p. 137. Levinas does not cite any of Weil's words, but he seems to be referring to 'The Three Sons of Noah', included in *Attente de Dieu*, 1950, Paris, Fayard, 1966, pp. 229–46; trans. *Waiting On God*, Emma Craufurd, London, Fount, 1983, pp. 177–91; and *L'enracinement: Prélude à une déclaration des devoirs envers l'être humain*, Paris, Gallimard, 1949; trans. *The Need for Roots: Prelude to a Declaration of Duties towards Mankind*, A. F. Wills, London, Routledge and Kegan Paul, 1978.

[11] For an excellent summary of Weil's affinities with and divergence from Gnosticism, see McLellan, *Simone Weil*, pp. 154–7 and 195–6.

Levinas implies that Weil's statement of outrage, 'To say that God can order men to commit acts of injustice and cruelty is the greatest error that can be committed in his regard', results in a demiurgic conception of God, so that 'From this point on, evil itself can only inspire love.'[12] This proposition is elided to (God's supernatural) love 'can signify only love of evil itself'.[13] Levinas' argument for this elision is that, according to Weil, even the most active charity, 'the perfection of love', cannot overcome the evil of the world, because it presupposes the continuation of evil and the creature loved only as creature. A true action, according to Levinas, would 'give the Other his due . . . within the framework of justice . . . because, in the creature, [man] transcends the creature'.[14]

Negatively, to Weil, Judaism upholds the God of armies, of violence; to Levinas, Christianity is the charity which confirms evil itself. Positively, Weil focuses on the love of God; Levinas, on the justice of God. The negative projections are equally dualistic – the alien theology is characterized as making Evil or Violence into the Absolute as a consequence of the initial assumption that evil is totally separated from good. By contrast, the presentation of their own commitment always involves the mediation of three: God, man and world. 'The world' is defined as the relation of man to man, the love of the neighbour, where *love* passes through God's love for man. Both Levinas and Weil define this relation as justice: for Levinas, it is *Lernen*, the learning of the Torah;[15] for Weil, 'it is for men to see that men are preserved from harm'.[16]

The difficulty they both embrace is this: how to present the demands of infinite justice as alternative to the justified demands of human rights; how to present the cry of other human beings as higher than the claim of the autonomous individual. For the dethroning of the person (Weil) or the ego (Levinas) may always be misunderstood: as if, in the name of an absolute dogma or cultus, the human person, the citizen, the body, indeed, everything finite about human life, is being itself violated; as if just

---

[12] 'Simone Weil Against the Bible', p. 184, trans. p. 138.
[13] Ibid., p. 186, trans. p. 139.
[14] Ibid., pp. 186–7, trans. pp. 139–40.
[15] Ibid., p. 185, trans. p. 139.
[16] See 'Human Personality', 1957, trans. in *Simone Weil: An Anthology*, ed. Sian Miles, London, Virago, 1986, p. 94.

grievances, only recently articulated – for women, minorities, children, the environment, which concern harm done precisely to the person, the ego – would once again be denied a voice. Yet the aim is to make the *hearing* more urgent and effective, by transcending the idea of human rights based on legal fictions and their claims – to substitute cry and response for the contention of the claim. The aim is to strengthen human agency, not to accrue arguments to the grievous history of its undermining.

In his Talmudic reading of the tractate 'Shabbat', Levinas presents the Judaic meaning of 'difficult liberty' without philosophical representation: '*La Tora ou la mort.*'[17] This revelation, prior to liberty or non-liberty, founds a commitment prior to rational choice or deliberation, which, however, opens up the rationality of the Oral tradition.[18] The initial violence of revelation is inseparable from its incursion and immediate dispute by five loquacious, pugnacious rabbis in the drama of dialogue and difference which is the tradition. They share 'wisdom which knows without proof'; and the proceedings evince the irony and humour that accompanies their mix of commitment and aporia.

It is in this Talmudic reading but not in the book entitled *Difficult Liberty* that Levinas finds a representation, an aesthetic, for the very incursion of the law, the teaching, the founding violence. In the first essay included in *Difficult Liberty*, 'Ethics and Spirit', Levinas expounds philosophically the ever-present temptation of individual violence. He describes consciousness or the self as invading reality to possess or seize it. This invasion denies the existence of other individuals, but it enhances the self which is formed and nurtured reflexively both by the resistance it encounters and by the enjoyment of reality.[19] Knowledge has this structure of sovereign and solitary violence. To turn back from this possessive violence is to have the vision of the face, which is already to hear the commandment 'You shall not kill.'[20] This vision or hearing is a moving out of oneself without the recoil of the enhanced sensation of self. It is not *an experience* but contact with 'the uncrossable

[17] Levinas, 'Le Tentation de la tentation', in *Quatre lectures Talmudiques*, Paris, Les éditions de minuit, 1968, p. 82, trans. 'The Temptation of the Temptation', Annette Aronowicz, *Nine Talmudic Readings*, Bloomington, Indiana University Press, 1990, p. 37.

[18] Ibid., pp. 82–3, trans. pp. 37–8.

[19] Levinas, 'Éthique et Esprit', pp. 23–4, trans. pp. 9–10.

[20] Ibid., p. 22, trans. pp. 8–9.

infinite in which all murderous intent is immersed and submerged'.[21] Far from returning to the point of departure with the
spoils of experience, moving out of oneself leads to further em-
barkation: 'It inaugurates the spiritual journey of man.'[22]

Simone Weil is the spiritual psychologist of this difficult liberty
– of this journey with the inevitable recoils of the person to possessive individualism. Her essays on force and on human personality explore the difficult liberty which rests on the response of
infinite justice and not on the claims of individual rights, or of
the collectivities which expunge those rights. She cannot avail herself of the aesthetic or the law available to Levinas. Her denigration
of the ancient Hebrews as 'the chosen people' amounts to a refusal to consider the covenant or revelation which redeemed Israel
from the Egyptian house of bondage and committed it to the
bondage of the law – the difficult liberty of hearing before understanding, and obeying before hearing. Instead, her own spiritual
journey, as recorded in her *Notebooks*, serves as her aesthetic, the
representation of the law, which she finds, above all, in the Hindu
Upanishads. Her declaration that 'The Bhagavad-Gîtâ and Gospels
complete each other'[23] is sustained by the attention she pays
to the *Bhagavadgîtâ* throughout *The Notebooks*.[24] Learning Sanskrit,
the way a Jew might learn Hebrew, Weil undertook to follow the
education of the warrior Arjuna, who, in great despondency and
hesitation in the face of the violence necessary in field of battle
where kin is ranged against kin, is taught by the God Krishna,
incarnate as his charioteer, how even action involving violence
can be accomplished in detachment and be lawful.[25]

The notion of rights, which was launched into the world in
1789, has proved unable, because of its intrinsic inadequacy,
to fulfil the role assigned to it.[26]

[21] Ibid., p. 24, trans. p. 10.
[22] Ibid.
[23] *The Notebooks of Simone Weil*, vol. I, trans. Arthur Wills, facsimile edition London,
Routledge and Kegan Paul, 1956, p. 25.
[24] See ibid., pp. 88–100 and *passim*.
[25] For a commentary, see S. Radhakrishnan, *The Bhagavadgîtâ*, Bombay, Blackie and Son,
1977; for the classic English translation, see Edwin Arnold, *The Song Celestial or Bhagavad-
Gîtâ* (1885), London, Routledge and Kegan Paul, 1972.
[26] 'Human Personality', in *Simone Weil*, p. 71.

In Weil's essay on 'Human Personality' (1942–3), the perception of the passer-by is equivalent not to hearing the commandment, 'You shall not kill' (Levinas), but to hearing the commandment, 'You shall not harm.' 'If it were the human personality in him that was sacred to me, I could easily put out his eyes.'[27] The idea of 'personality' is partial, reductive, a standard of public morality, 'which can neither be denied nor conceived'. The infinite but impotent demand of the person is juxtaposed to the 'indomitable expectation' of every human being, regardless of what they have suffered or committed, 'that good and not evil will be done to him. It is this above all that is sacred in every human being',[28] where nothing is sacred, 'except the good and what pertains to it'.[29] Justice pertains to this profound and unchanging expectation and not to the comparative demand of person to person.

Not freedom but a system of public education is needed which would provide expression for the cry against evil, and 'next, a regime in which the public freedem of expression is characterized not so much by freedom as by an attentive silence in which this faint and inept cry can make itself heard; and finally, institutions are needed of a sort which will, so far as possible, put power into the hands of men who are able and anxious to hear and understand it'.[30] Like Levinas, the emphasis here is on response to the cry provoked by the infliction of evil. Whatever she claims, this is surely in the tradition which Weil has learnt from the Old Testament: God's response to the cry of the children of Israel in the house of bondage – that original redemption, which continues to imply justice beyond the redress assumed by individual rights.

The difference between claims based on persons and the justice which is impersonal cannot be determined in advance; it depends in practice on the difference between *attention* and *force*. *Force* means to seize and possess the world for oneself; *attention* means to move out towards the world and to God without the recoil which is self and possession – to decreate the self. 'The notion of rights is linked with the notion of sharing out, of exchange, of measured

---

[27] Ibid.
[28] Ibid.
[29] Ibid., p. 72.
[30] Ibid., p. 73.

quantity . . . [it] must rely on force in the background, or else it will be laughed at.'[31] Antigone, prototype of Christ, stands for justice against the idea of law as force and measure: 'it was Justice, companion of the gods in the other world, which dictated this surfeit of love, and not any right at all. Rights have no direct connection with love.'[32] Supernatural good is not a sort of supplement to natural good (Aristotle); the only choice is between supernatural good on the one hand and evil on the other. This is why 'middle values', such as 'democracy', 'rights', and 'personality', do not help the afflicted.[33]

To these liberal middles, Weil opposes the icon of the tree, an analogy of the middle which implies the mutuality of gravity and grace:

> It is the light falling continually from heaven which alone gives a tree the energy to send powerful roots deep into the earth. The tree is really rooted in the sky.[34]

This is no mystical image; it represents no heavenward longing; grace comes down and makes for gravity. The tree rooted in the sky offers a representation, an aesthetic, for the law, which is not natural but supernatural, and which belongs to the exposition of invisible justice, which may yet be recovered in its sisters of truth and beauty: 'Justice, truth, and beauty are sisters and comrades.'[35]

Similarly, the annihilation of the soul must be understood supernaturally, not naturally. It means to learn to listen (what Levinas calls *substitution*): 'To listen to someone is to put oneself in his place while he is speaking. To put oneself in the place of someone whose soul is corroded by affliction, or in near danger of it, is to annihilate oneself.'[36] This decreation of the self for the sake of justice means the radical renunciation of the possessive relation to the world, but this does not imply the renunciation of relationship to the world itself: 'To acknowledge the reality of affliction means saying to oneself: 'I may lose at any moment, through the play of

---

[31] Ibid., p. 81.
[32] Ibid., p. 83.
[33] Ibid., p. 86, *E contrario*, Levinas refers to Plato's location of the Good beyond being.
[34] Ibid.
[35] Ibid., p. 93.
[36] Ibid., p. 91.

circumstances over which I have no control, anything whatever I possess, including those things which are so intimately mine that I consider them as being myself. There is nothing I might not lose.'[37] Yet this death of the self, although unmotivated, may be the gain of the universe:

> Even though I die, the universe continues. That does not console me if I am anything other than the universe. If, however, the universe is, as it were, another body to my soul, my death ceases to have any more importance for me than that of a stranger. The same is true of my sufferings. Let the whole universe be for me, in relation to my body, what the stick of a blind man is in relation to his hand. His sensibility no longer resides in his hand, but at the end of the stick.[38]

This image of infinitely extended, impersonal sensibility provides an analogy for the decreation of the self as participation in divine creation.

To put oneself in the place of one who is afflicted 'is more difficult than suicide would be for a happy child'.[39] To do so, however, is justice: attention which is the response to the cry of those who cannot speak. This does not imply, however, that man is loved merely as creature, as infected with evil. For the process of decreation of the self is not a process of destruction; it is the assumption of supernatural love which creates – both for the self and for the one who is afflicted, who may be the same one:

> Everything which is grasped by our natural faculties is hypo- thetical. It is only supernatural love that establishes anything. Thus we are co-creators. We participate in the creation of the world by decreating ourselves.[40]

Weil and Levinas are phenomenologists of the conflict of good and evil, of *attention* and *force* or of *substitution* and *possession*. Neither

[37] Ibid., p. 90.
[38] *The Notebooks*, vol. I, p. 19.
[39] 'Human Personality', in *Simone Weil*, p. 91.
[40] Weil, *Gravity and Grace*, 1952, trans. Emma Craufurd, London, Routledge and Kegan Paul, 1963, p. 29.

does justice to the other, nor to him or herself, when they charge
the other with exclusivity of good or evil (Weil characterizing
Judaism as unalloyed Evil; Levinas characterizing Weil's Christianity as uncontaminated Good). Religious authorships in the medium
of philosophy, they both present justice which is not natural (even
though Levinas claims his perspective is social not sacred). They
cannot therefore be understood if the concepts at stake are taken
naturally, such as 'personality', 'body', 'woman', 'citizenship', for it
is the *supernature* of these concepts which is under examination.[41]
However, phenomenologically, the supernatural must appear.
Amidst Rabbinic humour and in the icon of tree or stick, revelation
(Levinas) and the supernatural (Weil) appear as the middle, the
world – as it would be, were it realized and redeemed, God and
man and world at one.

In both cases, the weakness in the thinking results in a defect of
presentation. This weakness emerges from the configuration of
difficult liberty with, what I shall call, *the difficulty of modernity*. Both
authorships judge that liberal, human rights destroy love of the
neighbour, and result in idolatrous collectivities of Fascism and
Communism. Both, therefore, warn of *the double danger* of external authority and of the inner authority of the autonomous
individual, which calls for difficult liberty. How can Levinas, even
less than Weil, refute the consequence that justice, as he conceives
it to be social not sacred, will nevertheless be utopian? Its intelligibility can only be ideal, for it involves setting aside the character of the modern state, which he describes as 'the alliance of
logic with politics', the just violences of which betray the kingdom.[42] Just as Weil's love and justice must set aside what she
describes as the character of the modern state: the inevitable

[41] Compare, for example, Jean Bethke Elshtain, who argues *contra* Weil, 'We are never not
our bodies', and that Weil repudiates 'the appetitive part of the soul altogether' ('The
Vexation of Weil', *Telos Special Issue on Religion and Politics*, 58 (1983–4), p. 203). Mary
G. Dietz, like Elshtain, draws on Arendt to disparage Weil's lack of politics based on active
citizenship (*Between the Human and the Divine: The Political Thought of Simone Weil*, New
Jersey, Rowman and Littlefield, 1988, pp. 74–5). However, both Elshtain and Dietz
overlook the tension in Arendt's thought arising from her supernatural understanding of
the miracle of human birth and the consequent ambiguity whether the idea of politics in
her late thinking is natural or supernatural.

[42] Levinas, *Autrement qu'être on au delà de l'essence*, 1974, The Hague, Martinus Nijhoff,
1978, pp. 216–17, trans. *Otherwise than Being or Beyond Essence*, 1974, Alphonso Lingis,
The Hague, Martinus Nijhoff, 1981, pp. 170–1.

extension and specialization of the means of domination, especially bureaucatic rationality, according to which both master and slave are equally beholden to force.[43] My argument is that the implicit unease of Levinas as well as Weil with the traditional charge that Judaism is the religion of law whereas Christianity is the religion of grace, has had paradoxical consequences in each case for thinking and representation. For it has left a legacy of reluctance to expound the notion of law, to demonstrate its plasticity, even when its equivocal meaning is clearly at stake. Thus Weil degrades Judaism, but finds a law – *dharma* – she is willing to learn in the *Bhagavadgîtâ*;[44] the justice of which, she claims, would complete the Gospels. Thus Levinas redefines ethics so that Torah, or commandment, means the face, the voice, dialogue or divine anarchy. But the face to face, the commandment, is never mediated and cannot be learnt, that is, it is not law, for any conceivable flexibility of knowledge and experience can only pertain to possession. On this account, difficult liberty cannot be tried and tested. In Levinas' philosophical writings, the phenomenology of the commandment is indistinguishable from the devastating incursion of grace.

Their inhibition with respect to law means that neither Weil nor Levinas is able to bring the sublime into the pedestrian, to suspend and resume the ethical with its features of modern state and society. Their judgement of modernity leaves the middle, the world, untouched supernaturally. For Levinas, the state conveys and betrays 'proximity'. Weil, hating the world at war, her middle, yet reluctantly recognizing its necessity, tried many middles – joining the Durruti column in the Spanish Civil War, exile in the United States, working for the Free French in London – but was unable to achieve the equanimity of Arjuna with the teaching in the field of battle. Perhaps this is the meaning of her dying. Did she not project her failing towards mediation onto Israel, just as Levinas projects his failing towards mediation onto Christianity – both of them claiming violently that violence is cultivated elsewhere?

This perhaps fatal weakness has been dramatized for me for a

---

[43] *Réflexions sur les causes de la liberté et de l'oppression sociale,* 1934, Paris, Gallimard, 1955, pp. 55–6, in *Oppression and Liberty,* trans. Arthur Wills and John Petrie, London, Ark, 1988, pp. 65–6.
[44] See, for example, *The Notebooks,* vol. I, pp. 99–100.

long time by a remark of the Catholic writer, Gustave Thibon, which he made in connection with Simone Weil's arrival to live and work on his farm in the Ardèche, where she went in 1941 in order to avoid the registration of the Jews in the free zone. He was initially reluctant to have her; and, on arrival, she protested immediately at the plain but comfortable quarters prepared for her. He described his first impressions:

> Nor will I dwell on the way she was outfitted and her in-credible baggage – she had a superb ignorance not only as to the canons of elegance but extending to the most elementary practices that enable a person to pass unnoticed.[45]

Contrary to feminist severity concerning Weil's imputed rejection of her body and of her femininity, *of her nature*,[46] I would argue that this inability to pass unnoticed may have been her spiritual, her *supernatural*, failing. For she who has faith – who passes as a knight or lady of faith – would, like Jane Marple, know how and when to pass unnoticed. Jane Marple has also been the subject of recent feminist criticism, which equally overlooks the super-natural dimension of Agatha Christie's creation, and judges that the character of Miss Marple recuperates all the traditional niceties of class and gender.[47] Yet Jane Marple remains the most observant intelligence and the most spiritually free in all manner of woeful situations because she is partly, as it is expressed in *Nemesis*, *exactly what she appears to be*: a proper, fussy, inquisitive, old lady. Her success in establishing justice invariably depends on her being able to pass unnoticed while noticing everything herself. For liberty involves a further difficulty: freed from external authority and inner autonomy, it resumes life in the world as an ordinary person and, equally, as extraordinary and beyond the confines of the person. I do not suggest that Simone Weil should have strategi-cally embellished herself, but that her inability to pass unnoticed

---

[45] Cited in Simone Pétrement, *Simone Weil: A Life*, trans. Raymond Rosenthal, London, Mowbrays, 1976, p. 424.

[46] See note 41, *supra*.

[47] See Marion Shaw and Sabine Vanacker, *Reflecting on Miss Marple*, London, Routledge, 1991; for the genesis of 'Jane Marple', see Janet Morgan, *Agatha Christie: A Biography*, London, Fontana, 1985, pp. 175–7.

is connected with that residue of violence, which she could not own, and which she tried to disown.

Next to Søren Kierkegaard, with his mildly uneven trouser legs, stepping out with jaunty street credibility, knight of the pedestrian, Simone Weil and Emmanuel Levinas, ever at odds with their imaginary adversaries, stand out as angry angels – this *contradicto in adjecto* alerts us to the arrogated authority they meant to give away.

14
Architecture to Philosophy – the Post-modern Complicity

Why is it that so many academic disciplines – literature, philosophy, sociology, anthropology – are posing the question concerning rationality in terms of 'post-modernism', terms which have been taken from architectural history – from the periodization of movements in style – and, yet, at least one school of exponents claim that they herald an 'anti-aesthetic'.[1] In this paper I shall attempt to clarify issues and evasions of the debate over post-modernism by re-examining this conflation of architecture and theory, taking as my recurring *point d'appui* the biblical story of the Tower of Babel and asking why God punishes humankind's invention of architecture with the confusion of tongues.[2]

Once upon a time all the world spoke a single language and used the same words. As men journeyed in the East they came upon a plain in the land of Shinar and settled there. They said to one another, 'Come let us make bricks and bake them hard;' they used bricks for stone and bitumen for mortar. 'Come,' they said, 'let us build ourselves a city and a tower with its top in the heavens and make a name for

This paper is dedicated to the memory of Mary Bottomore, who died on 30 December 1986. It was first published in *Theory, Culture and Society*, 5 (1988), pp. 357–71.
[1] Hal Foster (ed.), *Post-modern Culture*, London, Pluto, 1985.
[2] Steiner only considers the tower as a metaphor for the mutual opacity of language and does not raise the question of the connection between architecture, language, society and God (George Steiner, *After Babel: Aspects of Language and Translation*, Oxford, Oxford University Press, 1975).

ourselves, or we shall be dispersed all over the earth.' Then the Lord came down to see the city and the tower which mortal men had built and he said, 'Here they are, one people with a single language, and now they have started to do this; henceforth nothing they have a mind to do will be beyond their reach. Come let us go down there and confuse their speech so that they will not understand what they say to one another.' So the Lord dispersed them from there all over the earth and they left off building the city – that is why it is called Babel, because the Lord there made a babble of the language of all the world; from that place the Lord scattered men all over the face of the earth.

That version was taken from *The Cambridge Bible Commentary* on the *New English Bible*.[3] To the Christian tradition the Hebrew story tells of punishment for the crime of *hubris*. For the Jewish tradition one may turn to the commentaries on it to be found in: the Talmud, the Babylonian compilation of Jewish law; the *Midrash Rabbah*, the main body of post-biblical Rabbinic exegesis; the *Zohar*, the major work of Jewish mysticism; Rashi, the greatest medieval commentator on Bible and Talmud; and the Hersch *Pentateuch*, a modern compendium of ancient commentaries.

The commentaries on the biblical story in these sources seem to agree that the key to the meaning of the story is the rallying cry – 'Let us . . . make a name for ourselves.' For this implies making and naming a god of their own invention – an 'idol' of brick and bitumen – usurping the name of God because these people desire to become invulnerable and apart from God. The image of the Tower derives from the Assyrian or Babylonian Ziggurat, the Mesopotamian Temple Tower, atop a mound itself erected on a flat plain and surmounted by a shrine of the deity. To the Babylonians they were a gate of God, but to the Hebrews, in exile by the waters of Babylon, they were symbols of impiety, for they appeared to scale or wage war against the heavens.

It is, however, important not to forget that the ambition was to build a city as well as a tower. If the act of building a tower is synonymous with inventing, erecting and worshipping a named

---

[3] Gen. 11:1–9; Robert Davidson, *Genesis 1–11: The Cambridge Bible Commentary on the New English Bible*, Cambridge, Cambridge University Press, 1980, p. 104.

idol and rejecting the Holy Name then the connection between an impious religious architecture and language seems to become clearer. In this light the confusion of tongues may be understood as the way humankind are taught a lesson about the relation between divine and human power.

According to the *Zohar* humankind had not understood that speaking the holy tongue is the source of their own power.[4] Once the tongue is confounded, the rebels are not able to express their desires so that the angels, God's messengers, can understand what they want; nor, it may be added, as a consequence, can they express their desires to each other, and as a result communal labour becomes impossible.[5] The attempt to exercise power independently of God seems to end with loss of power, for they are not able to continue building. This may explain what happens to the tower, but it does not explain the fate of the city. The culture of cities is founded on the need for unity and defence which arises out of the mix of customs, languages and buildings. Is the confusion of tongues a punishment – as both Rabbinical and Christian sources seem to concur? Is it a loss or might it be some kind of gain in power or is it perhaps both?[6]

[4] *The Zohar*, vol. I, trans. Harry Sperling and Maurice Simon, London, The Soncino Press, 1984, p. 256.

[5] Compare Kant's opening to 'The Transcendental Doctrine of Method' of the *Critique of Pure Reason* (A707, B735, p. 573): 'If we look upon the sum of all knowledge of pure speculative reason as an edifice for which we have at least the idea within ourselves, it can be said that in the Transcendental Doctrine of Elements we have made an estimate of the materials, and have determined for what sort of edifice and for what height and strength of building they suffice. We have found, indeed, that although we had contemplated building a tower which should reach to the heavens, the supply of materials suffices only for a dwelling house, just sufficiently commodious for our business on the level of experience, and just sufficiently high to allow of our overlooking it. The bold undertaking that we had designed is thus bound to fail through lack of material – not to mention the babel of tongues, which inevitably gives rise to disputes among the workers in regard to the plan to be followed, and which must end by scattering them all over the world, leaving each to erect a separate building for himself, according to his own design.' (Immanuel Kant, *Critique of Pure Reason*, trans. N. Kemp Smith, New York, St. Martin's Press, 1965.)

[6] Compare the commentary of Samson Raphael Hirsch (1808–88), the arguably Hegelian founder of Jewish neo-orthodoxy: 'If the united community so misuses its authority that, instead of employing it to serve the treasure entrusted to it . . . it will seek to make the individual subservient not to God but only to itself, then the individual must rise up and say, "I do not recognize this community; I recognize only myself." In making this declaration, of course, he pours out the child with the bath water; he cuts himself off from the root through which he was to have absorbed all human wisdom from its Divine source, and flings himself into a vague uncharted subjectivity. . . . This subjectiveness, this

According to the Talmud the rebels who built the tower split up into three parties: one said, 'Let us ascend and dwell there'; the second said, 'Let us ascend and serve idols'; and the third said, 'Let us ascend and wage war [with] God'. The first was scattered; the third was turned into apes, spirits, devils and night demons. The second, however, the Lord did confound the language.[7] But, this account continues, 'A third of the tower was burnt, a third sunk into the earth, and a third is still standing'. Rab concludes, 'The atmosphere of the tower causes forgetfulness'. In this retelling the confusion of tongues is only one and the better one – of a number of less desirable fates. It reminds us that many worse ones are conceivable. Perhaps the atmosphere of that third still standing has made us forget. This Talmud discussion suggests that the story is trying to account for a determining and perennial feature of the destiny of humankind. It is aetiological.[8]

---

self-awareness on the part of the individual which defines things not in terms of the coercion exercised by the community but in terms of the way in which he, the individual, sees them, was the new element . . . which God awakened in the minds of men when He caused their language to disintegrate . . . From that time on it was such factors as obstinacy, wilfulness, mood and even passion that devised names for things — of course no longer in the uniform manner in which God had formerly defined them. And so it came to pass that men no longer understood each other' (Samson Raphael Hirsch, *The Pentateuch*, trans. by Gertrude Hirschler, New York, The Judaica Press, 1986, p. 57).

[7] Seder Nezikin, vol. III, Tractate Sanhedrin 109a, *The Babylonian Talmud*, trans. I. Epstein, London, The Soncino Press, 1935, p. 748. Compare, too, the account in *Midrash Rabba*, vol. I, *Genesis* (Noach), (trans. H. Freedman, London, The Soncino Press, 1983), Ch. XXXVIII 1–12, pp. 302–10.

[8] Compare the American Indian version 'Many generations ago Aba, the good spirit above, created many men, all Choctaw, who spoke the language of the Choctaw and understood one another. These came from the bosom of the earth, being formed of yellow clay, and no men had ever lived before them. One day all came together and, looking upward, wondered what the clouds and the blue expanse above might be. They continued to wonder and talk among themselves and at last determined to endeavour to reach the sky. So they brought many rocks and began building a mound that was to have touched the heavens. That night, however, the wind blew strong from above and the rocks fell from the mound. The second morning they again began work on the mound, but as the men slept that night the rocks were again scattered by the winds. Once more, on the third morning, the builders set to their task. But once more, as the men lay near the mound that night, wrapped in slumber, the winds came with so great force that the rocks were hurled down on them.

The men were not killed, but when daylight came and they made their way from beneath the rocks and began to speak to one another, all were astounded as well as alarmed – they spoke various languages and could not understand one another. Some continued henceforth to speak the oriental tongue, the language of the Choctaw, and from these sprung the Choctaw tribe. The others who could not understand this language, began to

I propose, initially, to think of a tower in relation to a wall, as a special or limiting case of a wall: as a wall that has been made continuous, completed as a circle and then elevated. This idea of the perfected and elevated wall by contrast to the initial linearity of a wall which stands as a barrier, implies that the centre has been appropriated and become radial – the former barrier or limit transgressed by being denied as a limit. Perhaps the rebels have taken control – taken into their own hands what would otherwise be a limit to their own activity. This is surely dangerous. The word 'dangerous' comes from the Latin *dominus,* master, and means to be subject to the domination of another. The idea that human powers and their successful execution are dangerous to their perpetrators is common to many ancient cultures. Pindar's cosmopolitan odes, commemorating and expiating the victors of the Panhellenic games, are another striking instance of this. And this is surely why in Kafka's story, 'The Great Wall of China', the first-person narrative voice explicitly states that the issue is how to rebuild the Tower of Babel on 'a secure foundation'.[9] Yet the secure foundation turns out to consist of building a wall and not a tower, and building it 'piecemeal', so that it never joins up into a continuity.[10] And within the story itself this system of construction is interpreted in terms of what relation to take to an absolute yet absent authority which will best preserve and develop human powers and potentialities.

In Genesis 10:1–32 just before the account of the Tower of Babel a complex genealogy of the 'peoples of the coasts and islands each with their own languages, family by family, nation by nation', is given.[11] This genealogy is resumed – after the Tower

---

fight among themselves. Finally they separated. The Choctaw remained the original people; the others scattered, some going north, some east, and others west, and formed various tribes. This explains why there are so many tribes throughout the country at the present time' (in Stith Thompson, *Tales of the North American Indians,* Bloomington, Indiana University, 1966, p. 263. Thanks to Jacob Murray for this reference).

[9] Franz Kafka, 'The Great Wall of China', in *Metamorphosis and Other Stories,* trans. Willa and Edwin Muir, Harmondsworth, Penguin, 1976, p. 71.

[10] 'How could the wall which did not form even a circle, but only a sort of quarter or half-circle, provide the foundation for a tower? That could obviously be meant only in a spiritual sense. But in that case why build the actual wall, which after all was something concrete. The result of lifelong labour of multitudes of people?' (Kafka, ibid). Compare Steiner's discussion of Kafka's 'uses of Babel', *After Babel: Aspects of Language and Translation,* pp. 5–7.

[11] Genesis, 10: 1–32, pp. 8–9.

of Babel – in Genesis 11:10.[12] It terminates with Abraham – one nomad among nomads – who receives a special call. From this perspective the story of the Tower of Babel clearly presupposes that the plurality of language has already come about. The purported transgression punished by the multiplicity of languages captures or pinpoints the change in self-awareness that occurs when one people encounter another people when, previously, they had only known their own way.[13] Many of the ancient words now translated as 'law' originally meant 'the way': the Hebrew word for law, Halachah, is connected by the Babylonian Talmund with the Hebrew word for 'the going' – the way one should go; the Arabic word for law, *Shari'a*, means, literally, 'the road to the watering place'; the Greek name for the Goddess of Vengeance, *Dike*, means, 'the way things happen'.

As a result of the encounter of one people with another people, 'the' way becomes distinguishable from other 'ways' in terms of law, language and labour; and the relation between law, language and labour becomes problematic. One community has become aware of itself as different from other communities – as having its 'own' ways. These distinct ways of law, language and labour become the third term – or mean or middle – by which the community understands, represents or relates to itself and others.

It would, therefore, be just as wrong to see the confusion of tongues as a punishment or degeneration as it is to see the eating of the fruit of the Tree of Knowledge in the Garden of Eden story as a fall. Instead, both of these stories are the *mise en scène* of a paradox: the semi-elevation of a humanity which understands itself to possess one half of an absolute or divine power – from the Garden of Eden gaining knowledge but not immortal life; from the Tower of Babel deploying that knowledge and the curse of labour inherited from the expulsion from Eden to try to win back immortality and the Adamic gift of naming. The labour and the knowledge how to construct bricks and mortar and plan a city and tower are projected into an architecture designed to defy death by usurping the realm of God who decreed labour and death for humankind in the first place.

[12] Genesis, 11: 10–32, pp. 108–9.
[13] Leo Strauss (1953), *Natural Right and History,* 1953, Chicago, The University of Chicago Press, 1971, pp. 81–119.

In the Garden of Eden story God comments, after the eating of the forbidden fruit, 'The man has become like one of us, knowing good and evil; what if he now reaches out his hand and takes the fruit from the tree of life also, eats it and lives for ever?'[14] In the Tower of Babel story God says, 'henceforth nothing they have a mind to do will be beyond their reach'. The paradox acknowledged in the first story is that of beings with a mind (knowledge) but without the reach – immortality. In the second story the paradox acknowledged is that of beings with the reach to build a city and tower, but without the mind – the confused tongue. In both cases the prodigious combination of power and impotence together with its changing negotiation is being recognized as the narrative unfolds. In the earlier story the scenario consists of individuals in a 'natural', albeit paradisical and walled, setting. In the subsequent story after the Flood, the scenario consists of an ethical community in a social setting, self-aware because of the necessity of labour, and because of the existence of other communities without which there would be no need to build a city, an organization for collective external and internal defence.

'The Lord made a babble.' The confusion of tongues does not simply mean the origin of different languages in the empirical sense: it does not simply imply the plurality of languages, but that language itself is plural. Because 'the way' is now divided into law, language and labour, archetypical speech in which words were deeds – the Hebrew *da'bar* means act, event, deed, thing, word – and in which there is no distinction between thought, word, thing, is replaced by the notion of language itself as a signifying system distinct from law and labour, in which word, thought, thing may not coincide. Architecture, whether the wall around Paradise or the Tower of Babel, exhibits the limit at which human and divine agency encounter each other. It registers in the visible world outcomes of that encounter which would otherwise remain intangible.[15]

The reading thus far developed sees the story as a stage in the development of the potentiality for freedom. In opposition to this

---

[14] Genesis 3:22, p. 46.

[15] I say 'law', 'language' and 'labour' not for their alliteration, but as part of a developing argument that it is their inseparability which gives rise to the philosophical illusion now current that the 'realm of discourse' is our exclusive mode of actuality – which replaces

reading it might be argued, however, that the Tower of Babel
story is a fiction which deals with the metaphysics of discourse in
the setting of omniabsent (*sic*) yet contested powers. The Tower
of Babel story may therefore illustrate some of the key oppositions characteristic of the 'post-modern' debate, and hence help to
explain why the distinction between 'modern' and 'post-modern'
has been adopted in recent theoretical discussion outside the field
of architecture. First, the story concludes with 'plurality' defining
'discourse' as opposed to unity of meaning; secondly, it reveals
itself as an aetiological fiction and does not claim universal validity; third, it may imply that history consists of ineluctable paradox and is not the progressive resolution of dynamic contradiction.

Architecture has come to provide a paradigm for this new
atheoretical nominalism by means of three analogies between philosophy or social theory and architecture – analogies which are
themselves based on dubious characterizations and accounts of
architecture to begin with. In the first place, it is argued that the
history of architecture has been simply periodized into nineteenth-
century historicism, twentieth-century early modern movement,
post-Second World War failure of modernism, and, nowadays,
'post-modernism'. The conclusion is then drawn that a plural
account and a plural alternative will remedy this; an example is
Charles Jencks' *Modern Movements in Architecture* – the 's' is the
crux.[16] Second, it is argued that the meaning of rationality in
architecture is simple, that it may be identified with slogans of the
modern movement, such as 'buildings are machines for living in',
or 'form follows function', misinterpreted, respectively, from Le
Corbusier, *Towards a New Architecture* (1927), and Hitchcock and
Johnson, *The International Style* (1932).[17] By extension it appears
that the failure of that rationality – its dialectic of enlightenment
reduced to the instrumental rationalism which suppresses the

---

the contrary illusion that representations give us access to a reality independent of them.
My argument would stress that all categories or social institutions are *conceptual*: equally
ideal and real they can only be articulated and recognized in legal and linguistic form.
Since architecture illustrates these paradoxes *par excellence* this approach might suggest why
architecture has become the cipher for the post-modern debate.

[16] Charles Jencks, *Modern Movements in Architecture*, Harmondsworth, Penguin, 1973.

[17] Le Corbusier (1927), *Towards a New Architecture*, trans. Frederick Etchells, London: The
Architectural Press, 1982; and Henry-Russell Hitchcock and Philip Johnson, *The International Style*, 1932, New York, Norton, 1966.

totality and the individual – may be easily analysed. Third, it is argued that the theoretical and practical solutions in architecture are available. An example of the practical is Robert Venturi's infamous proposition, 'Main Street is almost alright', which aims to restore signs and symbols to overly functionalized building.[18] The theoretical solution is a 'plural' theory of architectural signs, yet generalized and dehistoricized under the protection of an overarching typological historicism – similar to Comte's 'Law of the Three Stages'. An example of this is provided by Jencks' use of Umberto Eco's architectural semiotics in the former's *The Language of Post-Modern Architecture*.[19]

Instead of developing sociological analysis to cover architecture such as Max Weber's sociology of domination, a 'post-modern' thesis resting on strained analogies with these dubious accounts of the development of architecture is exploited to obscure the way in which *an unexamined opposition of positions within the 'modern' is thereby recreated and perpetuated in both architecture and philosophy*. For the 'modern' has always involved such internal contestations.

In social theory the notions of the 'modern' and the 'post-modern' are, in the first place, fundamentally the same, and, in the second place, are not 'modern' or 'new' – for want of a neutral term. The debate between Jürgen Habermas and Jean-François Lyotard, which has taken over Jencks' terminology into social theory and philosophy, is defined in a way that returns to Hegel's exposition of Kant.[20] This Kantianism is taken from two works by Theodor W. Adorno: Habermas takes his terms from Horkheimer and Adorno, *Dialectic of Enlightenment*;[21] Lyotard takes his terms from Adorno's posthumous *Aesthetic Theory*.[22] Both

---

[18] See Robert Venturi, Denise Scott-Brown, and Steven Izenour, *Learning from Las Vegas: The Forgotten Symbolism of Architectural Form*, Cambridge, MIT Press, 1982.

[19] Umberto Eco, 'Function and Sign: The Semiotics of Architecture', in G. Broadbent, R. Bunt and C. Jencks (eds), *Signs, Symbols and Architecture*, Chichester, John Wiley, 1980, pp. 11–69; Charles Jencks, *Modern Movements in Architecture*.

[20] Jürgen Habermas, 'Moderne und postmoderne Architektur', in *Die Neue Unübersichtlichkeit: Kleine Politische Schriften V*, Frankfurt am Main, Suhrkamp, 1985, pp. 11–29; and Jean-François Lyotard, *The Post-modern Condition: A Report on Knowledge*, 1979, trans. Geoff Bennington and Brian Massumi, Manchester, Manchester University Press, 1984.

[21] Max Horkheimer and Theodor W. Adorno, *Dialectic of Enlightenment*, 1944, trans. John Cumming, New York, Herder and Herder, 1972.

[22] Theodor Adorno, *Aesthetic Theory* (1970), trans. C. Lenhardt, London, Routledge and Kegan Paul, 1984.

Habermas, who defends modernist rationality, and Lyotard, who defends post-modernist plurality, understand themselves to be reviving Kant against Hegel.[23] In spite of Lyotard's emphasis on 'games', this revival arises from *misunderstanding Adorno's speculative play of Kant against Hegel and of Kant against Hegel as a refutation of Hegel*. Habermas defends the notion of 'communicative rationality' which depends on Kant's distinction in the three critiques between three realms of experience – theoretical, practical and aesthetic. Lyotard defends Kant's notion of the 'sublime' from the third critique as a kind of non-determinate judgement which offers the possibility for an aesthetic education which would remain open. Habermas appears to defend discursive critical rationality, Lyotard the sublime beyond formal rationality. Yet it may be argued that both are engaging in an enterprise which has characterized both humanism and anti-humanism in architecture and in philosophy – they seek to enlarge the idea of reason beyond the instrumental so that it may acknowledge the uncontainable, the aporia.

As Reyner Banham argues in an article on the Lloyd's building, whether the new architecture understands itself as 'realizing modernism' for the first time, or as 'postmodern' it shares 'the compulsion to try and make sense of . . . human dilemmas' – even when the dilemma is perceived as aporia and not as ideal.[24] It is this celebration of aporia which makes Lyotard's aesthetic of the 'sublime' comparable to self-styled 'anti-aesthetic' versions of post-modernism.[25] At the 1986 exhibition of New Architecture at the Royal Academy, the first architecture exhibition at that venue for forty years, half of the display was devoted to unbuilt, rejected or still undecided projects for restoring whole areas of London to pedestrians in the wake of the perceived destruction of social life by the values of modern architecture. Yet the only sociological concept used in the exhibition itself and in the scholarly catalogue is 'the creation of a public realm' – a phrase and concept which Habermas has taken over and developed from the work of

---

[23] Jürgen Habermas, 'Modernity versus Post-modernity', *New German Critique*, 22, (1981), pp. 3–14; Lyotard, ibid.

[24] Reyner Banham, 'The Quality of Modernism', *The Architectural Review*, CLXXX, 1076 (1986), p. 56.

[25] Hal Foster (ed.), *Post-modern Culture*.

Hannah Arendt.[26] Architecture, social theory and philosophy seem to be complicit in exchanging each other's most undifferentiated and general concepts and theses.

In the scholarly symposium which accompanied an exhibition held in Berlin in 1984, 'The Adventure of Ideas – Architecture and Philosophy since the Industrial Revolution', may be found a German translation of a discussion between Jacques Derrida and Eva Meyer, 'Labyrinth und Archi/Textur', in which they discuss the Tower of Babel, post-modernism, architecture and philosophy.[27] This discussion exemplifies how the three analogies between architecture and philosophy are employed.

Derrida interprets the Tower of Babel story as a 'defeat' for God. He argues that the attempt of a tribe to give themselves a name, 'the Semites', is the main event. The name 'Semite' means 'name' already, but the Semites want to 'make themselves a name' in order to colonize and dominate the other tribes and their languages from the place they intend to usurp in Heaven. God devastates this undertaking by uttering one word – 'Babel' – meaning confusion. The Semites plan of domination is nullified by the bestowal of a proper name and by the deconstructing of their architectural construction. Accordingly, universal language is terminated; henceforth the plurality of languages cannot be mastered, and there can be no universal translation: language becomes labyrinthine. It also means that there is no single architecture: architecture is also henceforth plural and labyrinthine in spite of its axonometric (*die Axonometrie*) grids of plan and elevation. The Tower of Babel story thus opposes architectural as well as linguistic difference to the unificatory ambition which has been vanquished. Derrida argues that reading the story in terms of

---

[26] Hannah Arendt, *The Human Condition*, 1958, Chicago, The University of Chicago Press, 1973.

[27] Derrida also discusses his 'architectural metaphor' of 'deconstruction' which is not to be understood as retracing the construction of a building or philosophical system, but as 'a questioning of technique', of the 'authority of architectural metaphor', and as a deconstruction of architectural rhetoric itself. 'Deconstruction' is thus not a technique of reversed construction but 'a thinking of the idea of construction itself', in Jacques Derrida and Eva Meyer, 'Labyrinth und Archi/Textur: ein Gespräch mit Jacques Derrida', in *Das Abenteuer der Ideen: Architektur und Philosophie seit der industriellen Revolution*, Berlin, Frölich und Kaufmann, 1984, p. 101.

this plurality is neither anthropocentric nor theocentric. The almightiness of God is undermined when He is forced to intervene and speak the word 'Babel': for 'Babel' means 'confusion' – but it only means that because of the confusion according to which the word 'Babel' sounds like the word for 'confusion' in Hebrew. God is equivocal: he commands and forbids translation of His Name and lapses into the same situation as those he opposes. He cannot dominate this situation which gives rise to the plenitude of architecture as well as the plenitude of language. Post-modernity, Derrida infers, takes off from this 'defeat and beginning'.

Derrida's thesis is here couched in the form of a classic Kantian transcendental argument:[28] 'It is the impossibility of the Tower of Babel which makes it possible for architecture like language to have a history.' This history is *always* to be understood (he claims and I emphasize) in relation to a *divinity which is finite*. Modernity, he continues, is the striving for absolute mastery or domination; post-modernity is the establishment or experience of the end of this plan and elevation for mastery and domination. Post-modernity, he concludes, is a new relation to the divine – not Greek, nor Christian, but *the conditions (sic)* for architectural thinking. This strange phraseology is another transcendental deduction with a metacritical twist. The 'conditions' for architectural thinking are the 'dwelling', the event of place – an idea which comes from Heidegger's famous essay 'Building Dwelling Thinking'.[29] The 'event' of place is the precondition of architectural form: a communal relating of human beings to concrete, unmeasurable dwelling, not to abstract, measured, architectural planning. It is this delineation of the absolute event which Derrida offers as a new idea of our relation to God – and surely it amounts to a new humanism.

How is the account of the Tower of Babel developed above different from Derrida's? There are four main points: history, humanity, God, language and architecture. According to Derrida, the Tower of Babel story narrates the origin of the history of architecture and language. I argue that this reading opens and closes history at the same time: for its notion of history does not

---

[28] Gillian Rose, *Hegel contra Sociology*, London, Athlone, 1981, pp. 1f.

[29] Martin Heidegger (1951), 'Building Dwelling Thinking', 1951, in *Poetry, Language, Thought*, trans. Albert Hofstadter, New York, Harper, 1971, pp. 143–61.

imply development. Derrida argues that the dichotomy of humanity as rebellious and God as sovereign and infinite is dissolved; all dichotomies – human/divine, nature/culture – are replaced by the idea of labyrinthine plurality. I argue that the dissolution of this opposition between human and divine, absolute and relative power, dissolves potentiality too, and cancels the negotiating of the relation between potentiality and actuality through history. Similarly, Derrida's argument that God is defeated and becomes finite apparently offers instant release from the master/slave dichotomy and from humanity's desire for domination and mastery. I would argue, on the contrary, that it robs humanity of any experience whereby that trying of power may be acknowledged and cultured through a third. Derrida's position that history is 'always in relation to a finite divinity' is dogmatic in the pre-critical sense that it implies no dialectic of dependence and independence, no political or spiritual life. Derrida's argument that the plurality of language and of architecture is at stake legislates a current perception into a universal – employing and undermining universal explanation at the same time. The reading developed above expands architecture as the means, the third term, by which a community negotiates its relation to itself and to other communities. Where Derrida deals with dichotomies and their abolition, I propose the changing configuration of two in a third. Then the current experience is not frozen: it is seen as transitory but not as reduced and relative.

A return to the notion of the Tower may concretize this argument. The problem of its meaning may also be encountered in Rodin's 'Tower of Labour' and Tatlin's 'Tower', the Monument to the Third International. The importance of the Tower to the post-modern argument is that it is an exemplar of what Hegel in the *Aesthetics* calls 'Symbolic' architecture so as to distinguish it from 'Classical' and 'Romantic' architecture.[30] Norbert Lynton captures Hegel's meaning when he explains Tatlin's Tower as an image of the forerunner, St John the Baptist who cannot deliver salvation but proclaims it is 'at hand', and calls us to repent.[31]

[30] See Daniel Payot, *Le Philosophe et l'architecte: Sur quelques determinations philosophiques de l'idée d'architecture*, Paris, Aubier Montaigne, 1982.

[31] Norbert Lynton, 'Icon of the Revolution', in *The Times Higher Educational Supplement*, 4 April 1986.

Symbolic architecture is monumental, the dwelling place of the god not of human beings, an external not an interior space; and it arises when meaning (absolute power) and configuration (form) remain ununified. The symbolic form of art or architecture does not present (Classical) nor re-present (Romantic) the absolute, but refers or points to it ambiguously, employing symbols which always also imply things other than the meaning for which they furnish the image. The Tower is analogous to the pointing finger of the Baptist in the Grünewald altarpiece, occupying a different kind of space from the crucified body of Christ.

According to Hegel the sublime is a special instance of the symbolic, 'an attempt to express the infinite without finding in the sphere of finite phenomena an object which proves adequate for this representation'.[32] In this particular passage Hegel is himself citing with approval Kant's distinction of the sublime from the beautiful. However, unlike the postmodern aesthetics for which this very proposition of Kant's cited by Hegel is also the key text, Hegel develops the proposition into a question: 'First the question arises about what character the world situation must have if it is to provide a ground on which a [sublime] event can be adequately presented.'[33] Hegel compares the 'unconscious' symbolism of Oriental and Jewish architecture with later 'conscious' literary symbolism, such as fable, parable, riddle and allegory. It is the unconscious obliquity of meaning and configuration which links the post-modern 'conscious' symbolism with the story and image of the Tower, and with monumental symbolic architecture and with the sublime in art generally.

Yet this is to take a development – a changing relation between form and configuration – and to freeze it. For in Hegel the symbolic may overlap with and change into the Classical and the Romantic and back again. Hegel criticizes – and his warning is peculiarly apposite:

> the extension of symbolism to *every* sphere of mythology and art which is by no means what we have in mind here in considering the symbolic form of art. For our endeavour

---

[32] G. W. F. Hegel, *Aesthetics: Lectures on Fine Art*, 1835, vol. I, trans. T. M. Knox, Oxford, Clarendon Press, 1975, p. 363.
[33] Ibid., vol. II, p. 1051.

does not rise to finding out how far artistic configuration could be interpreted symbolically or allegorically in this sense of the word 'symbol'; instead we have to ask, conversely, how far the symbolic itself is to be reckoned an *art-form*. We want to establish the artistic relation between meaning and configuration insofar as that relation is *symbolical* in distinction from other modes of presentation, especially the classical and romantic.[34]

The Romantic form of art also consists of a lack of unity between meaning and configuration, between the absolute or whole and its representation as form, its appearance in the sensuous medium or means, but the lack of unity is *represented* not *referred to* as in the symbolic. It is illusion *(Schein)* and this illusion is derived from a specific socio-historical experience in which spheres of life – religious and political, or law, language and labour – have become separated from each other.

To conclude this reference to Hegel and the paper in general five points may be drawn out. First, there may be more than one kind of divorce between meaning and configuration, whereas the post-modernism considered here with its focus on the 'sublime' or the abolition of recurrent dichotomy is only able to conceive of one. Therefore a dialectical approach is more open and plural than the modernism or post-modernism arguments themselves. Secondly, it is the form of that divorce or *form* itself in *its specificity* which can be seen to have historical presuppositions, not the divorce *in its generality* as in most versions of post-modernism. In this sense the means of law, language and labour have a changing fate. Third, these changes may be related chronologically and systematically without producing a metanarrative or a progressive teleological philosophy of history; it is not a question of employing discredited metanarratives but of seeing narratives themselves as different kinds of form. In this sense genealogy may be found – in Hegel and Marx as well as in Nietzsche – within aporetic philosophy of history. Fourth, in Hegel and the dialectical tradition, the 'ending' of art has a different history from the 'ending' of religion and politics, and the end of art characterizes modernity. It is the modernist defence of an aesthetic realm and post-modernism's

[34] Ibid., vol. I, p. 312.

aesthetics of the sublime or anti-aesthetics which produce a uniform philosophy of history over all disciplines, not the dialectical approach.

Finally, on the view developed here, configuration is related to confrontation with absolute power and becomes an indicator of human potentiality which is constantly renegotiated. In the Tower of Babel story humanity achieves an *initial* measure or idea of its own potentialities by encountering its limit. That encounter does not arrest it in an endless 'labyrinth', but sets it off on further encounters where what has been learnt or not learnt is tried out again and again, constantly changing both the idea of the potential and the idea of the limit; these encounters cannot be assimilated to the meanings or 'signs' of the first one. This reading is different from pluralism, vernacularism, nominalism: it is not rationalistic nor is it the 'compulsion to make sense of human dilemmas'; it is the human dilemma being represented or referred to.

Paradoxically, the claim advanced formerly by modern and now by post-modern architecture and philosophy, that each alone offers a genuine 'opening' disowns previous openings – attempts to renegotiate potentiality and actuality[35] – by characterizing the other position without differentiation as 'total', 'closed', 'functionalist', 'rationalistic', 'dominatory', instead of drawing on the experience of those openings and their subsequent subversion, instead of comprehending illusion: the relation between the limit of the meaning at stake and its configuration or form. I conclude that the use of architecture in philosophy bolsters a tendency to replace the concept by the sublimity of the sign, which is, equally, to employ an unexamined conceptuality without the labour of the concept.

---

[35] By 'possibility' as employed throughout this paper I do not mean to imply a romantic yearning (*Sehnsucht*), but a severe category: 'possibility' is a translation of Aristotle's *dynamis*. It might be argued that post-Kantian thought is characterized by its transforming of Kantian a priori possibility which debases actuality to a mere empirical instance into 'real possibility' (Hegel), 'will to power' (Nietzsche – a reversal of power to will or faculty), 'scientific' versus 'utopian' possibility (Marx). Lyotard not only overlooks the fate of this category in post-Kantian thought but even in Kant he ignores the connection between 'faculty' as power or possibility and transcendental a priori possibility, (see 'An Interview with Jean-François Lyotard', *Theory Culture and Society*, 5 (1988), pp. 292–3).

15

Architecture after Auschwitz

The title 'Architecture after Auschwitz'[1] has lost its irony as well as its innocence. 'Auschwitz' and 'the Holocaust' have become emblems which bear a philosophical and theological world within them. Synecdoches, they unify and make compact a complex series of events[2] in a way which removes those events even beyond mythic meaning and leaves only dumb witness.[3] The current conflict of the faculties reinforces the dichotomy between explanation and witness even while both parties are also struggling with tainted motivations: on the one hand, the *Historikerstreit*, provoked by the attempt of conservative German historians to relativize Nazi genocide;[4] on the other hand, recent Heideggerian thinking, atoning for the master's silence, presents 'Auschwitz' as 'the Unthinkable'.[5] Lacoue-Labarthe draws on Hölderlin's

---

[1] This chapter was first published in *Assemblage* 21 (1993). Theodor W. Adorno, 'After Auschwitz', in *Negative Dialectics*, 1966, trans. E. B. Ashton, London, Routledge and Kegan Paul, 1973, pp. 361–5; and 'Erziehung nach Auschwitz', 1966, in *Erziehung zur Mündigkeit: Vorträge und Gespräche mit Hellmut Becker 1959–1969* ed. Gerd Kadelbach, Frankfurt am Main, Suhrkamp, 1972, pp. 88–104.

[2] See Marc H. Ellis, *Beyond Innocence and Redemption: Confronting the Holocaust and Israeli Power*, San Francisco, Harper and Row, 1990, pp. 32–3.

[3] This development far exceeds the inevitable dilemma of balancing historiographical and mythological meaning in any reflection on the meaning of Auschwitz. See Jonathan Webber, *The Future of Auschwitz: Some Personal Reflections*, The First Frank Green Lecture, Oxford, Oxford Centre for Postgraduate Hebrew Studies, 1992, pp. 1–30.

[4] See '*Historikerstreit*': *Die Dokumentation der Kontroverse um die Einzigartigkeit der national-sozialistischen Judenvernichtung*, Munich, Piper, 1987; and *New German Critique*, Special Issue on *The Historikerstreit*, 44 (1988).

[5] See Jürg Altwegg (ed.), *Die Heidegger Kontroverse*, Frankfurt am Main, Athanäum, 1988.

interpretation of the Theban tragedies to apply 'the caesura' which interrupts history to 'Auschwitz',[6] while Lyotard argues that 'Auschwitz' is 'the experience of language that brings speculative discourse to a halt', and delegitimizes names and narrative as such.[7]

It is these kinds of philosophical reflection which elevate or denigrate (it becomes impossible to distinguish) their emblematic object beyond even mythic meaning. In both cases, 'Auschwitz' is presented as a 'pure event', which is not assimilable to finitude, history, or meaning as such. There can be no 'after' to 'Auschwitz', for the preposition 'after' is the part of speech which expresses place in time, and 'Auschwitz' on this view has no ascertainable locus in quantifiable or even qualifiable time.

Furthermore, in the title 'Architecture after Auschwitz', the phrase 'after Auschwitz' becomes an adverbial qualification of the activities implied by 'architecture', so that 'after' acquires another set of ambiguities: does 'after' refer temporally to how architecture has been constructed in the wake of 'Auschwitz'; or does it inquire, ethically and prescriptively, into how it should proceed? And then, in turn, does this use of 'architecture' imply reflection about architecture, that is, architectural theory, or does it refer to architectural plans and constructed buildings?

Yet another proposition has emerged from the phrase 'architecture after Auschwitz'; it refers to the southern Polish towns of Oswiecim and Brzezinka, which were renamed 'Auschwitz' and 'Birkenau' and rebuilt by the Nazis: it implies 'Auschwitz' as an architectural object and project, its connections with all of Nazi architecture and planning, and with the history and principles of architecture in general.

Recently but *belatedly*, the investigation into 'Auschwitz', the architectural actuality and project, has been embarked on by Robert Jan van Pelt, a Dutch architectural historian currently working in Canada, who is preparing a major study of the relation between the architectural creation of Auschwitz and the Nazi general plans for the Germanization of the East. The study will also assess the

[6] Philippe Lacoue-Labarthe, *La fiction du politique, Heidegger, Art, Politics: The Fiction of the Political*, trans. Chris Turner, Oxford, Blackwell, 1990, pp. 41–52.
[7] Jean-François Lyotard, *The Differend: Phrases in Dispute*, 1983, trans. Georges van Den Abbeele, Manchester, Manchester University Press, 1988, pp. 88, 155: see, too, Lyotard, *Heidegger and 'the jews'*, 1988, trans. Andreas Michel and Mark S. Roberts, Minneapolis, University of Minnesota Press, 1990.

import of Auschwitz in the history of architecture. Entitled *Architecture of Perdition: Auschwitz in Architectural History*, the publication of this work is planned to precede the Jubilee of the liberation of Auschwitz in January, 1995. Meanwhile this prospective work has been itself preceded by the publication of a treatise, entitled *Architectural Principles in the Age of Historicism* (1991), which, in spite of its venerable title, is developed by van Pelt in dialogue form with a colleague from the University of Virginia, Carroll William Westfall.[8] Since this work with its epochal and fundamental delineation of 'principles' is pervaded by and culminates in a reflection on architecture after 'Auschwitz', in such a way that the 'after' defines all architecture *before* 'Auschwitz', it seems that these studies have been conducted in the reverse of the order which the argument would entail: that is, the historical material on Auschwitz and Nazi plans for Germanization would have been studied before developing the general reflections on 'Auschwitz' and on 'principles'. For such material may provide empirical insight into the relation between the architectural tradition and its conscription to or undermining by Nazi imperialism, which otherwise is determined a priori if the meaning of Auschwitz is made the measure of all other meanings and institutions, especially when that meaning is itself presented as transcendent evil. The whole project is belated both in terms of its internal organization, that is, the relation between its philosophical and archival components, and in terms of the recent intellectual history regarding 'Auschwitz' which seems to dictate van Pelt's approach to Auschwitz.

It is belated in the further sense that the periodization which launched the debate between modernity and post-modernity borrowed its initial definitions from simplified accounts of architectural history without any reference to Nazism, its architecture and its genocide. Westfall and van Pelt claim that their framework of 'the age of historicism' transcends the debate between modernity and post-modernity, but their debate, which rests on the opposition of classical architectural types to classical architecture as crisis and caesura, which they represent, respectively, provides a magnificent and extended dramatization of it.

---

[8] Robert Jan van Pelt and Carroll William Westfall, *Architectural Principles in the Age of Historicism*, New Haven, Yale University Press, 1991.

Belated, but also therefore, lamentably, the work on Auschwitz itself may be *too late*. From the work published so far, 'After the Walls Have Fallen Down' (1989),[9] *Architectural Principles* (1991), 'Into the Suffering City: Considerations of the German Series [by Melvin Charney]' (1991),[10] van Pelt's position has developed from the argument that architecture must be divided into an epoch before and an epoch after 'Auschwitz'[11] to the argument in *Architectural Principles* that the whole history of architecture can only be approached via the event of 'Auschwitz', and he attempts to demonstrate that even the architectural logism of his interlocutor and polar opposite, Westfall, has its unreflected roots in this event.[12] Concomitantly, van Pelt's position has changed from the relative light of 'the singular, numinous and kerygmatic reality of Auschwitz', which prescribes resistance,[13] to the dark despair which issues when he stages his realization that existential repetition and rebirth, on which he relies to define his alternative both to historicism and to Westfall's classicism, could equally describe the path which leads from Heidegger's *Rectoral Address* to the construction of the five-square city of Auschwitz-Birkenau.[14]

Both of these responses, however, oppose the metameaning or spiritual meaning of 'Auschwitz' to its discernible architectural configuration. Yet, given his access to the archives in the museum at Auschwitz and to the related planning departments of the Reich, van Pelt is better placed than anyone else to examine the relation between the architectural, cultural and political meaning of Auschwitz. Indeed he intends to explore the continuity between the Nazis' overall plans for the Germanization and colonization of the East and their roots in the nineteenth-century German civilizing mission based on the interpretation of the history of medieval German–Slav relations in the territories from the Oder to the Bug.[15] This approach should open up the question of the continuity of architecture and Auschwitz and not posit it a priori.

[9] *Queen's Quarterly*, 96, 3 (1989), pp. 641–60.
[10] In Phyllis Lambert (ed.), *Parables and Other Allegories: The Work of Melvin Charney, 1975–1990*, Montreal, Canadian Centre for Architecture, 1991, pp. 35–53.
[11] 'After the Walls Have Fallen Down', p. 656.
[12] *Architectural Principles*, pp. 122–5.
[13] 'After the Walls Have Fallen Down', p. 656.
[14] *Architectural Principles*, 7, pp. 277–8.
[15] *Prospectus: Architecture of Perdition*.

This essay amounts therefore to an attempt to forestall any further philosophical and theological prejudicing of the methodological approach to this material by recovering and questioning some of the assumptions that Westfall and van Pelt have accepted and elaborated in their book *Architectural Principles in the Age of Historicism*. More generally, I shall argue that the alternative between explanation and witness (which recurs once again *within* Bauman's sociology of bureaucratic rationality and his call to morality)[16] can be overcome if and only if the historical and political assumptions underlying this alternative are challenged. Unwittingly, Westfall and van Pelt succeed more than any other work known to me in setting out those assumptions because the alternate chapters dramatize the opposition of classicizing rationality to redemptive crisis in terms of the meaning of citizenship and the built configuration of the city. Their reflection on architecture, unlike the general, unreflected, post-modern adoption of architectural categories, reveals something about recent thinking in general and its continuity with the emblematizing of 'Auschwitz'.

Architectural Principles in the Age of Historicism has been received by architectural historians with a theoretical and philosophical bent[17] according to its own claim that it be taken as the successor to Wittkower's *Architectural Principles in the Age of Humanism* (1949).[18] Wittkower's anti-aesthetic work on the theory of Renaissance architecture stressed that proportion and planning in the Renaissance were the visible materializations of the intelligible mathematical symbols, resulting in an equipoise which revealed 'the perfection, omnipotence, truth and goodness of God'.[19] This orientation notwithstanding, the book had a tremendous effect on post-war British architecture, 'for evil as well as good'.[20] Given the immodest ambition of *Architectural Principles in the Age of Historicism* to be

[16] Bauman, *Modernity and the Holocaust*, Oxford, Polity Press, 1989.
[17] See Joseph Rykwert, 'Review of Robert Jan van Pelt and Carroll William Westfall, *Architectural Principles in the Age of Historicism*,' 1949, *The Times Higher Educational Supplement*, 30 August 1991, pp. 19, 22.
[18] Rudolf Wittkower, *Architectural Principles in the Age of Humanism*, 1949, 3rd edn, London, Alec Tiranti, 1962.
[19] Ibid., p. 29.
[20] Reyner Banham, cited in Wittkower's 'Preface to the third edition', p. v. See, too, Kenneth Frampton, 'New Brutalism and the architecture of the Welfare State: England 1949–59', in *Modern Architecture: A Critical History*, London, Thames and Hudson, 1985, pp. 262–8.

Contents

Prolegomenon

Figure 15.1 Contents of *Architectural Principles in the Age of Historicism*

equally canonical for its time and given that its apparently ency-clopaedic coverage of history and philosophy enhances its aim to provide the definitive handbook for architectural education, it is imperative to expose its selectivity and partiality, which the dialogue form, and even more the apparent breakdown of the dialogue, serve all the more effectively to obscure.

The book is divided into three parts with alternate chapters written by Westfall (even) and van Pelt (odd).[21] However, in the course of the debate, van Pelt withdrew his originally planned Chapter Seven, and, in apparent capitulation to Westfall, merely appends as a dissolute coda the extant Chapter Nine. However, in its application of van Pelt's argument developed up to that point and in its lamentation at the outcome, Chapter Nine proceeds on the same ground or rather in the same abyss that van Pelt initially embraced, and its argument undermines and discredits Westfall's blithe consistency much more ruthlessly than van Pelt's own con-fession of his 'shattering intuition' and 'renunciation' of the debate would have the reader believe. The challenge to be developed here

[21] See Figure 15.1.

concerns the beginning (Chapters One, Two, Eight), the middle (Chapters Four, Six, Five) and the end (Chapters Three, Seven, Nine) of the book. 'The beginning' consists in the characterization of 'the age of historicism' in terms culled from Leo Strauss's indictment of historicism which both Westfall and van Pelt broadly endorse. 'The end' ostensibly registers the difference regarding the validity of architectural principles, which leads to van Pelt's withdrawal from the debate, and to his exposure, paralipomenally, of the consequences for his contribution that Auschwitz-Birkenau fits (awkwardly) the existential typology of the five-square city. Figure 15.2 presents the two kinds of typologies and van Pelt's extension of his typology to Nazi Germany and to Auschwitz.[22]

In effect, however, Strauss's rationalist rejection of modernity as 'historicist' and relativizing has, logically, two possible outcomes – nihilism or arch-rationalism. Nihilism disowns the validity of principles or the inquiry into the nature of things, for it rejects the realm of validity and objective truth as such, whether in philosophy or architecture; arch-rationalism narrows even more the realm of validity to exclude any historical or contingent admixture. Westfall re-deduces the logic of archetypes from the canonical Books of Architecture. Hence, the alternating chapters may be understood not as a debate doomed from the start because of the fundamental incompatibility of the principles embraced by each contesting author, but as *two equally logical outcomes of a doomed starting point*. As a result of this shared starting point, it will become evident that the reflection on politics and polities which otherwise seems confined to Westfall's chapters (Chapter Two 'Politics', Chapter Eight 'Cities') is equally at stake in van Pelt's self-declared 'prophetic' and 'apocalyptic' remembrances which first accrue to civic assurance and then traumatize that assurance

---

[22] The sources for each column are as follows: Westfall, *Architectural Principles*, pp. 155–60, van Pelt, ibid., pp. 169–214, Nazi Germany, Auschwitz, ibid., pp. 348–75 (corrections and additions by van Pelt). Joseph Rykwert has provided two critical comments on these typologies: 1. *Tholoi* in Greece were not invariably sacred buildings; some were civil buildings. Latin *templum*, equivalent to Greek *temenos*, meant separating and fencing ground: Greek *noas*, or Latin *aedes*, would more accurately express Westfall's intention. 2. The five-square city has been found in China, not in the West, and, consequently, van Pelt has to force his evidence in order to make Athens into this type of city. However, this misinterprets van Pelt's claim that Athens may be understood *symbolically* as five-square (Rykwert, Review, pp. 19, 22).

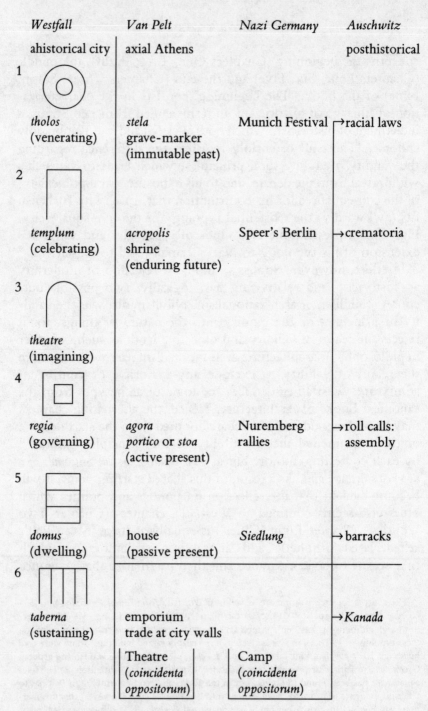

Westfall	Van Pelt	Nazi Germany	Auschwitz
ahistorical city	axial Athens		posthistorical
1			
tholos (venerating)	*stela* grave-marker (immutable past)	Munich Festival	racial laws
2			
templum (celebrating)	*acropolis* shrine (enduring future)	Speer's Berlin	crematoria
3			
theatre (imagining)			
4			
regia (governing)	*agora* *portico* or *stoa* (active present)	Nuremberg rallies	roll calls: assembly
5			
domus (dwelling)	house (passive present)	*Siedlung*	barracks
6			
taberna (sustaining)	emporium trade at city walls		*Kanada*
	Theatre (*coincidenta* *oppositorum*)	Camp (*coincidenta* *oppositorum*)	

Figure 15.2 Typologies and extensions

with existential 'dejection' and 'abjection'. To put it simply, restricted rationalism itself produces its abject remainder.

'The middle' concerns the clash of principles prior to van Pelt's
apostasy from principles as such. The architectural core of the
debate involves the deduction and employment of contrastable
and comparable uses of architectural typology: Westfall's deduction
of types proceeds according to the logic of origin and validity,
while van Pelt, with reference to Christian typology and Greek
historiography, re-deduces types to include axial, actual and existential context, in a way which displays affinities with Rossi's
memorial definition of type as locality and event.[23] Although they
are polar contraries, nevertheless, these two principles of typology *fuse meaning and configuration* in architecture, whether meaning is eternal (Westfall) or incursive (van Pelt). Against this, I
would mobilize Hegel's analysis in the *Aesthetics* of the deficiences
and divergences between meaning and configuration which arise
when architecture assuages the social utopianism that emerges from
different kinds of political freedom and unfreedom.[24] This might
begin to make more precise the burden that architecture bears in
a modern society with its historically specific mix of formal political freedom and chronic social inequality.

> *Architectural Principles in the Age of Historicism* explores the
> identity of what is usually considered as being radically dis-
> tinctive: the purpose of citizenship versus the form and dis-
> position of building.[25]

Westfall and van Pelt's shared commitment to understanding
architecture as the correlate of citizenship is undermined by their
underdeveloped account of both classical and modern politics,
and their overgeneralized gravamen (uncritically adopted from
the thought of Leo Strauss) that intellectual *historicism* counts as
the overwhelming evil of modernity and has destroyed our potential for politics as well as for architecture.[26] This is the
oppositional schema against which Westfall poses eternal 'building

[23] Aldo Rossi, *The Architecture of the City*, 1966, trans. Diane Ghirardo and Joan Ockman,
New York, MIT Press, 1989, pp. 35–41, 106–7.
[24] See Gillian Rose, *Hegel contra Sociology*, London, Athlone, 1981, pp. 121–48.
[25] Loc. cit. 'Prolegomenon', p. 3.
[26] Ibid., pp. 35–41.

types', justified by a general logic of validity[27] (which is neo-Kantian not pre-Kantian as van Pelt insists);[28] and van Pelt poses a soteriological deduction of typological analysis, justified by a logic of crisis and repetition. Van Pelt subsequently argues that Strauss's construal of classical political philosophy was itself subordinated to a religious return when he (Strauss) confronted Schmitt's apologetics for Nazism,[29] and thus Westfall's classicism has its roots in this conversion of Strauss's – which is not to account for the *history* of Westfall's classicism but to point to *its crisis*. Yet this attempt to convert rationality to crisis does not disturb the fundamentally Straussian assumptions on which the whole debate is grounded.

Three basic commitments yield in addition an insinuation which bedevils Strauss's thought, and even more acutely Westfall and van Pelt's architectural embodiment of it. First, the deploring of modern historicism in the name of classical political philosophy; second, the degradation of classical politics by comparison with the life of the philosopher; third, the evasive definition of 'the crisis of modernity' by reference to historicism or to the individual. These exoteric complaints harbour an esoteric political theory of modernity, which Strauss himself could avoid elaborating, but the implications of which Westfall and van Pelt's programme to uncover the principles for building the modern city cannot escape.

Strauss's defence of classical political philosophy against modern historicism turns into an apology for the philosophical life defined in opposition to any political participation. The anticipated case for classical virtue against modern freedom is itself undermined by the argument that political wisdom remains confined to the cave, to *doxa*, mere opinion not truth. Truth is esoteric; it demands 'a real conversion', that is, a total break with the attitude of the beginner: 'a beginner is a man who has not yet for one moment left the cave'.[30] This proclamation of a total break implies the exclusion of any education, development, *paideia*, or any

---

[27] Ibid., p. 139.

[28] Ibid., pp. 75, 115.

[29] Ibid., pp. 122–5.

[30] Strauss, 'Exoteric Teaching', repr. in *The Rebirth of Classical Political Rationalism: An Introduction to the Thought of Leo Strauss*, ed. Thomas L. Pangle, Chicago, Chicago University Press, 1989, p. 68.

realization of virtue from the meaning of Plato's political philosophy. Strauss's degrading of classical virtue in relation to the philosophical life is strangely matched by the subordination of his criticism of modern freedom to the obsession with historicism. Historicism itself first developed in opposition to the French revolution and the idea of abstract human and political rights. Strauss expresses 'the crisis of modern natural right' as 'the appeal from society to an ultimate sanctity of the individual as individual, unredeemed and unjustified'.[31] Acknowledging that historicism arose in order to combat this abstract individualism, Strauss nevertheless argues that both modern natural right and historicism undermine the transcendence necessary in 'the quest for the natural or the best political order'.[32] In this way, Strauss ensures that the crisis of modernity is defined as an intellectual one and not a political one. For, by concentrating definitively on historicism, he elides the critical difference between classical natural law (which he calls 'premodern natural right') and modern human and political rights, which presuppose modern property, legality, sovereignty, inequality and power. Strauss evades any consideration of modern political practice just as he degrades classical political practice.

In addition, Strauss and his architectural mediators, Westfall and van Pelt, ignore that intellectual tradition which cannot be assimilated to either modern rights or to the historical school, but was equally critical of both, precisely because it related the promises of modern liberalism to the actualities of systematic power or domination: with Rousseau as progenitor, this tradition includes Hegel, Marx, Weber. Neither Strauss nor Westfall and van Pelt show any awareness of the independent, critical analysis of modernity developed by these thinkers just as they show no awareness of property, legality, sovereignty, inequality, power and domination in modern societies and cities, nor, consequently, are they willing or able to interpret architecture as a mode of representation of social dynamics arising from these structures.

It is this deficient idea of modern politics and representation

[31] Strauss, 'The Crisis of Modern Natural Right', *Natural Right and History*, 1953, Chicago, Chicago University Press, 1971, ch. 4, p. 294.
[32] 'Natural Right and the Historical Approach', in *An Introduction to Political Philosophy: Ten Essays by Leo Strauss*, (ed.), Hilail Gildin, Detroit, Wayne State University Press, 1989, p. 105.

that makes *Architectural Principles in the Age of Historicism* so
loquacious. For instead of approaching modern politics by
acknowledging the deeply divisive issues concerning property,
power, equality and nationality, and analysing the relation of
political representation to built representation, Westfall and van
Pelt accept and embellish Strauss's opposition of classical rationalism to modern historicism, and they both proceed normatively to
inquire how architecture may *typify* (not represent) the polis, 'the
art of living together in cities . . . the political life'.[33] On principle,
architecture does not represent the city, it typifies it: 'it embodies
the truth of the city', specifically, humanity's preoccupation with
and refusal of its mortality (letter from van Pelt to the author,
July 1992). This perspective, which aims to restore contingency,
presupposes the autonomy of architecture – with the results that
van Pelt comes to abhor.

Classical art is enlisted by Westfall to produce an idealization of
the American city, which, I will argue, van Pelt implicitly accepts
in spite of his own stress on 'the ideality and the actuality of
Athens'.[34] Under the cover of Straussian rationalism, Westfall
produces an eternal city which enshrines Burkean liberty, without
rights and without beauty. This polis can only be conceived as a
mix of authoritarianism and liberty. From this unassailable vision,
van Pelt turns to *the prophetic method* and presents the classical city
as axial and actual, that is, as born out of crisis and rebirth and
with its own violence and foolhardiness. Yet this founding of
architecture on crisis and rebirth so misunderstands the meaning
of Kierkegaardian repetition that no distinction can be made between faith and idolatry: so that Auschwitz as built form can only
be understood as the abject remainder of history, interrupted by
caesura and reborn as the spirit of Heidegger's 'Rectoral Address'.
Westfall's logic of validity is completed by van Pelt's logic of
repetition, as the former's arch-rationalism is completed by the
latter's self-proclaimed dejection. Both idealize types as repetition
– the one eternal, the other incursive – and therefore neither provide
any analysis of architectural representation. Auschwitz cannot
be analysed as a system of architectural representation because no
theory is conceivable within the world-view of either author that

[33] Van Pelt and Westfall, *Architectural Principles*, p. 63.
[34] Ibid., p. 125.

could provide a theory of any modern social and political system. Van Pelt compresses into an enigmatic footnote the germ of a social psychology of alienation and lack of identity against Westfall, which, if developed, would reveal the inadequacies of his own account.[35]

Westfall presents his building types as a general logic of validity which solves the political problem, the nature of citizenship, as well as the problem of its built form. In spite of his claim that his types possess eternal validity, his initial survey passes with celerity from the Greek founding of the city and invention of politics, to the Roman city and to the American city as the example of the classical city. This fast itinerary to the modern, American city is justified because the American city 'places the civic life above that of the market'.[36] Yet Westfall fails to make any distinction between Greek democratic citizenship based on allocated property, and Roman and American private property law separated from liberal citizenship. The elision of politics with city building and architecture draws attention away from the lack of any theory of sovereignty and its translation into government by means of representative institutions, that is, there is no conceivable difficulty of relating particular wills to the general will. It is simply asserted as one of three 'basic propositions' that 'politics is more important than architecture',[37] while both are said to be concerned with liberty. This defence of liberty but not of positive rights is what I refer to as the Burkean commitment of Westfall's position. The implicit argument against modern formal rights is then conducted as the methodological problem of the priority of content over form; 'the legacy of the eighteenth century *philosophes* [is] the imputation of meaning on the basis of formal qualities'.[38] Against the formalism of rights and of historicism, Westfall justifies the logic of origin and eternal validity which recognizes the atemporality or the validity of types.[39]

Even though in their mutual 'Introduction: Heraclitean Heritage',

[35] Ibid., pp. 388–9, n. 41.
[36] Ibid., p. 47.
[37] Ibid., p. 49.
[38] Ibid., p. 50.
[39] According to Quatremère, a type is 'the original reason of the thing', ibid., p. 149; and see Chapter Four, 'Building Types'. pp. 138–67.

written by van Pelt, Burke is presented as a thinker who invents historicism by his appeal to custom against the French Revolution,[40] Westfall revealingly makes Burke the spokesman for 'the method of nature in the conduct of the state',[41] which refers to Burke's defence, in the *Reflections on the Revolution in France*, of a natural law of liberty, associated with the American Revolution, and asserted against the ideas of individual autonomy and of human and political rights associated with the French Revolution. Drawing on the natural law of liberty, Westfall affirms a natural, necessary, classical, and original knowledge of 'the means by which the individual perfects his nature',[42] which it is the task of both politics and building to fulfil. This idea of liberty, which is presented without any discusssion of modern property, sovereignty, inequality or power, is completed by an authoritarian taxonomy of social institutions. The polity exercises its authority by the constitution which distinguishes between primary, political, religious and civic activities – a modern view presented as atemporal.[43] These civic activities are themselves divided into *institutions* which serve moral edification, and *arrangements* which merely train (building trades, hospitals, hotels).[44] Museums are said to be based on criteria of 'the sensate aesthetic',[45] and are merely *arrangements* (while the disdain for building trades may cast doubt on the author's disinterest in his eternal types, the relegation of museums to such a low position in human perfectibility downgrades some of the greatest achievements of modern architecture and civic imagination).

This spirit of authoritarian prescription to guarantee the ethic of liberty which allows 'the individual to perfect his nature and take his pleasure as a person'[46] (the latter activity in debased 'arrangements'), the whole presented as legitimated by the unaddressable authority of 'the atemporal, universal, enduring and true',[47] provides evidence of *the anxiety of modernity* – the mix of inner autonomy and outer heteronomy which arises from the prevalence of formal

[40] Ibid., p. 15.
[41] Ibid., p. 57.
[42] Ibid., p. 63.
[43] Ibid., pp. 67–71.
[44] Ibid., p. 71.
[45] Ibid., pp. 71–2.
[46] Ibid., p. 74.
[47] Ibid., p. 73.

legality and systematic inequality, and which Westfall seeks to avoid acknowledging at all costs by ordering and legislating its symptoms.

While van Pelt questions Westfall's methodology with its eternal claims, nowhere does he address the latter's mix of natural law of liberty with authoritarian organizational prescriptions, which both evince and evade private and corporate property, contract, inequality and bureaucracy. It can therefore be argued that the prophetic method which van Pelt develops as the antipode of Westfall's monopoly of general validity is continuous with it. For it is the same anxiety of modernity presupposed by Westfall's 'Politics' that is to be overcome by van Pelt's appeal to pseudo-Kierkegaardian repetition, but which abandons him to the worse fate of dejection at the abject outcome of repetition. For, on van Pelt's own diagnosis, if Westfall repeats backwards, that is, recollects, in his zeal to present atemporal and enduring types, then he (van Pelt) is determined to repeat, that is, to recollect forward – which is why he names his method 'prophetic remembrance'. However, the accent on crisis, rupture, axiality and rebirth does not capture the meaning of Kierkegaardian repetition. Van Pelt's prophecy presupposes the Protestant spirituality implicit in Westfall's American political individuality: outwardly assertive but protesting inner faith – just the kind of scoundrel with a good conscience that Kierkegaard thought Lutheran spirituality inadvertently legitimated, and from which he distinguished the meaning of repetition which justifies nothing – neither the angelic nor the demonic.

Van Pelt introduces the idea of Jerusalem versus Athens as the difference between destiny and fortune,[48] but then argues that Athens may be understood as Jerusalem, that is, within the prophetic fullness of time, by adopting Karl Jaspers's idea of Athens as axial, 'a city of crisis'.[49] This path of theorizing is then itself revealed to have been prompted by Jaspers's confrontation with the evidence available to him of the camp Auschwitz. Together with Fackenheim's and Wiesel's reflections on 'Auschwitz', this emphasis on contingency and crisis serves retrospectively to introduce the idea of the city as such.[50] Because it was designed by professional architects, Auschwitz is defined as a city which

[48] Ibid., pp. 77–84.
[49] Ibid., p. 117.
[50] Ibid., pp. 115–22.

negates the intelligibility of meaning, orientation and personhood, the basic properties of the design of the ancient city.[51]

Since, from Chapter Three, and retrospectively within that chapter, 'Auschwitz' as crisis introduces the prophetic idea of the city, van Pelt's discovery that the model of rupture and repetition justifies Auschwitz as a city should not be a devastating blow to his argument but confirmation of its circularity. The existential typology was initially established on the basis of crisis or caesura extrapolated from Lacoue-Labarthe's Heideggerianizing of Hölderlin's reading of Sophocles.[52] It should not come as a surprise that Auschwitz may be understood as heralded by Heidegger's apostrophe to National Socialism as the spirit of Germany reborn.[53] Furthermore, when van Pelt declares from the pit of his apocalyptic abjection that Auschwitz as a city is 'fundamentally incomprehensible' yet 'typologically apprehensible',[54] he is untrue to his own conceptualization, according to which cities and types arise from traumas, and can only be as apprehensible or incomprehensible as each other.

The 'prophetic method' should expose Nazi idolatry of race and nation not justify it, even by default, and show that the laws or types of architecture do not make a city – *the making of a city depends on the rule of law*. Van Pelt's antinomianism means that he has no criterion for distinguishing between a city and a social system run by terror and collusion. Repetition, taken from Kierkegaard's pseudonymous authorship, cannot pertain to any collectivity nor serve any political ambition; it cannot change the past, and it cannot affirm infinite possibility nor mythic or national rebirth.[55] And if van Pelt's riposte would be that the very unrepresentability of repetition means that it may be harnessed to any evil end, then he has reduced the political meaning of 'Auschwitz' to Nazi racist idealism, a represented and realized ideal, by defining the Nazis' architectural design of Auschwitz as *ipso facto* proof of the meaning of the city throughout history.[56]

[51] Ibid., p. 121.
[52] Ibid., pp. 225–9, 340–5.
[53] Ibid., pp. 317–21.
[54] Ibid., p. 340.
[55] Ibid., pp. 242–5. For the meaning of *repetition* in Kierkegaard's authorship, see Rose, *The Broken Middle: Out of Our Ancient Society*, Oxford, Blackwell, 1992, pp. 19–29.
[56] *Architectural Principles*, pp. 120–1.

This is to repeat, on the scale of a totalizing and abject philosophy of history, the architectural illusion that architecture produces the city when it is the city which produces architecture.[57] Instead this illusion should be retraced to the equivocation and anxiety which arises from the broken promises of the modern, liberal city, and their violent overcoming in Nazi pseudo-rationalization. Otherwise the renunciation of the debate as much as its unwitting and false prophecies colludes in the repetition of 'Auschwitz'.

This extraordinarily dense and challenging book, which should transform what passes for debate in architectural theory and enlarge the culture of anyone who reads it, depends on the opposition between politically salvific arch-reason and salvific but demonic anti-reason. Taken as the potential theoretical underpinning for van Pelt's *Architecture of Perdition, Architectural Principles in the Age of Historicism* reveals what happens when 'Auschwitz', the built form, is made *the measurement* of architecture as such, the anti-reason to the arch-reason associated with the architectural tradition. This is why the project considered as a whole provides an illustration of what happens when the emblem 'Auschwitz' is made *the measure* of history as such, of truth as such, of reason as such, in the attempt to reverse the role whereby history, truth and reason, now seen as colluders and criminals, would have provided the measure and explanation for the possibility of 'Auschwitz'. The result is a reductionism and determinism far more extreme and politically dangerous than any *Marxisant* explanation. For it posits an unequivocal and unnegotiable meaning for 'Auschwitz' from which all others meanings are derived (from the architectural tradition to history and truth as such). This expiation is demonic in its retrospection, for it prevents any acknowledgement of our implication as agents and as actors, as flexibly rational as well as abjectly irrational, as ambivalent – capable of succumbing to the promise of a violent overcoming but also of resisting and taking on the difficulty of living politically.

[57] See Rose, 'Social Utopianism – Architectural Illusion', in *The Broken Middle*, pp. 296–307.

Bibliography

Adorno, Theodor, 'A Portrait of Walter Benjamin', 1950, in *Prisms*, trans. Samuel and Shierry Weber, London, Neville Spearman, 1967, pp. 227–42.

Adorno, Theodor, *Minima Moralia: Reflexionen aus den beschädigten Leben*, 1951, Frankfurt am Main, Suhrkamp, 1969; trans. *Minima Moralia*, E. F. N. Jephcott, London, New Left Books, 1974.

Adorno, Theodor, 'Erziehung nach Auschwitz', 1966, in *Erziehung zur Mündigkeit: Vorträge mit Hellmut Becker 1959–1969*, ed. Gerd Kadelbach, Frankfurt am Main, Suhrkamp, 1972, pp. 88–104.

Adorno, Theodor, *Negative Dialectics*, 1966, in *Gesammelte Schriften*, VI ed. Rolf Tiedemann, Frankfurt am Main, Suhrkamp, 1973; trans. E. B. Ashton, London, Routledge and Kegan Paul, 1973.

Adorno, Theodor, *Aesthetic Theory*, 1970, trans. C. Lenhardt, London, Routledge and Kegan Paul, 1984.

Adorno, Theodor, *Kierkegaard: Construction of the Aesthetic*, 1933, trans. Robert Hullor-Kentor, Minneapolis, University of Minnesota Press, 1989.

Aesthetics and Politics, trans. Ronald Taylor, London, New Left Books, 1977.

Agnon, S. Y., 'Agunot', 1908, in Nahum N. Glatzer (ed.), *Twenty-One Stories*, New York, Schocken, 1970, pp. 30–44.

Agnon, S. Y., *A Guest for the Night*, 1939, trans. Misha Louvish, New York, Schocken, 1968.

Alter, Robert, *Necessary Angels: Tradition and Modernity in Kafka, Benjamin and Scholem*, Cambridge, Harvard University Press, 1991.

Altmann, Alexander, *Moses Mendelssohn: A Biographical Study*, London, Routledge and Kegan Paul, 1973.

Altmann, Alexander, 'Franz Rosenzweig on History', in Paul Mendes-Flohr (ed.), *The Philosophy of Franz Rosenzweig*, Hanover, University Press of New England, 1988, pp. 124–38.

Altwegg, Jürg (ed.), *Die Heidegger Kontroverse*, Frankfurt am Main, Athanäum, 1988.

Arendt, Hannah, *The Origins of Totalitarianism*, 1951, New York, Harcourt Brace Jovanovich, 1973.

Arendt, Hannah, *The Human Condition*, 1958, Chicago, The University of Chicago Press, 1973.

Arendt, Hannah, 'Walter Benjamin: 1892–1940', 1968, in *Men in Dark Times*, trans. Harry Zohn, Harmondsworth, Penguin, 1973, pp. 151–203.

Arendt, Hannah, *The Jew as Pariah: Jewish Identity and Politics in the Modern Age*, ed. Ron H. Feldman, New York, Grove Press, 1978.

Arendt, Hannah, *The Life of the Mind, Two, Willing*, London, Secker and Warburg, 1978.

Arnold, Edwin (trans.), *The Song Celestial or Bhagavad-Gîtâ*, 1885, London, Routledge and Kegan Paul, 1972.

The Babylonian Talmud, trans. H. Freedman, London, The Soncino Press, 1935.

Bacon, Francis, *The New Organon and Related Writings* 1620, ed. Fulton H. Anderson, Indianapolis, Library of Liberal Arts, 1979.

Bainton, Roland, *Here I Stand*, Tring, Lion, 1978.

Banham, Reyner, 'The Quality of Modernism', *The Architectural Review*, CLXXX, 1076 (1986), pp. 54–6.

Bataille, Georges, *The Accursed Share*, vol. III, trans. Robert Hurley, New York, Zone Books, 1991.

Bauman, Zygmunt, *Modernity and the Holocaust*, Oxford, Polity Press, 1989.

Baumgarten, Edward, *Max Weber, Werk und Person*, Tübingen, 1964.

Benjamin, Andrew (ed.), *The Problems of Modernity: Adorno and Benjamin*, Routledge, London, 1989.

Benjamin, Walter, 'Über Sprache über die Sprache des Menschen', 1916, in *Walter Benjamin: Gesammelte Schriften*, vol. II.1, ed. Rolf Tiedemann and Hermann Schweppenhäuser, Frankfurt am Main, Suhrkamp, vols I–VI, 1974–85, pp. 144; trans. Edmund Jephcott and Kingsley Shorter, in *One-Way Street and Other Writings*, London, New Left Books, 1979, p. 111.

Benjamin, Walter, 'Über das Programm der Kommenden Philosophie', 1918, in *Walter Benjamin: Gesammelte Schriften*, vol. II.1, ed. Rolf Tiedemann and Hermann Schweppenhäuser, Frankfurt am Main, Suhrkamp vols I–VI, 1974–85, pp. 157–71, trans. 'On the Program of the Coming Philosophy', Mark Ritter, in *Benjamin: Philosophy, History, Aesthetics*, ed. Gary Smith, Chicago, University of Chicago Press, 1989, pp. 1–12.

Benjamin, Walter, 'Schicksal und Charakter', 1919, in *Walter Benjamin: Gesammelte Schriften*, vol. II.1, ed. Rolf Tiedemann and Hermann Schweppenhäuser, Frankfurt am Main, Suhrkamp, vols I–VI, 1974–85, pp. 173–9, trans. 'Fate and Character', in *One-Way Street, and Other Writings*, Edmund Jephcott and Kingsley Shorter, London, New Left Books, 1979, pp. 127–30.

Benjamin, Walter, 'Zur Kritik der Gewalt', 1920–1, in *Walter Benjamin: Gesammelte Schriften*, vol. II.1, ed. Rolf Tiedemann and Hermann Schweppenhäuser, Frankfurt am Main, Suhrkamp, vols I–VI, 1974–85, pp. 179–203; trans. 'Critique of Violence', in *One Way Street and Other Writings*, Edmund Jephcott and Kingsley Shorter, London, New Left Books, 1979, pp. 132–54.

Benjamin, Walter, 'Theologisch – Politisches Fragment', 1921, *Gesammelte Schriften*, vol. II.1, ed. Rolf Tiedemann and Hermann Schweppenhäuser, Frankfurt am Main, Suhrkamp, vols I–VI, 1974–85, pp. 203–4, trans. 'Theologico – Political Fragment' in *One-Way Street, and Other Writings*, Edmund Jephcott and Kingsley Shorter, London, New Left Books, 1979, p. 155.

Benjamin, Walter, 'Goethes Wahlverwandschaften', 1921–2, in *Walter Benjamin: Gesammelte Schriften*, vol. I.1, ed. Rolf Tiedemann and Hermann Schweppenhäuser, Frankfurt am Main, Suhrkamp, vols I–VI, 1974–85, pp. 125–201.

Benjamin, Walter, 'Die Aufgabe des Übersetzers', 1923, in *Walter Benjamin: Gesammelte Schriften*, vol. IV.1, ed. Rolf Tiedemann and Hermann Schweppenhäuser, Frankfurt am Main, Suhrkamp, vols I–VI, 1974–85, pp. 9–21; trans. 'The Task of the Translator', *Illuminations*, Harry Zohn, ed. Hannah Arendt, London, Fontana, 1973, pp. 69–82.

Benjamin, Walter, 'Goethe', 1926–8, *Walter Benjamin: Gesammelte Schriften*, vol. II.2 pp. 705–39; ed. Rolf Tiedemann and Hermann Schweppenhäuser, Frankfurt am Main, Suhrkamp, vols I–VI, 1974–85, trans. 'Goethe: The Reluctant Bourgeois', Rodney Livingstone, *New Left Review*, 133 (1982), pp. 67–93.

Benjamin, Walter, *Ursprung des deutschen Trauerspiels*, 1928, in *Walter Benjamin: Gesammelte Schriften*, vol. I.1, ed. Rolf Tiedemann and Hermann Schweppenhäuser, Frankfurt am Main, Suhrkamp, vols I–VI, 1974–85, trans. *The Origin of German Tragic Drama*, John Osborne, London, New Left Books, 1977.

Benjamin, Walter, 'Zum Bilde Proust', 1929, in *Walter Benjamin:*

Gesammelte Schriften, vol. II.2, ed. Rolf Tiedemann and Hermann Schweppenhäuser, Frankfurt am Main, Suhrkamp, vols I–VI, 1974–85, pp. 310–24; trans. 'The Image of Proust' in *Illuminations*, Harry Zohn, ed. Hannah Arendt, London, Fontana, 1973, 203–17.

Benjamin, Walter, 'Theorien des deutschen Faschismus: Zu der Sammelschrift "Krieg und Krieger"', 1930, in *Walter Benjamin: Gesammelte Schriften*, vol. III, ed. Rolf Tiedemann and Hermann Schweppenhäuser, Frankfurt am Main, Suhrkamp, vols I–VI, 1974–85, pp. 238–50; trans. 'Theories of German Fascism: On the Collection of Essays *War and Warrior*, ed. by Ernst Junger', Jerolf Wikoff, *New German Critique*, Special Walter Benjamin Issue, 17 (1979), pp. 120–8.

Benjamin, Walter, 'Franz Kafka: Beim Bau der Chinesischen Mauer', 1931, in *Walter Benjamin: Gesammelte Schriften*, vol. II.2, ed. Rolf Tiedemann and Hermann Schweppenhäuser, Frankfurt am Main, Suhrkamp, vols I–VI, 1974–85.

Benjamin, Walter, 'Lehre vom Ähnlichen', 1933, in *Walter Benjamin: Gesammelte Schriften*, vol. II.1, ed. Rolf Tiedemann and Hermann Schweppenhäuser, Frankfurt am Main, Sukrhamp, vols I–VI, 1974–85, pp. 204–10; trans. 'Doctrine of the Similar', Knut Tarnowski, *New German Critique*, 17 (1979) pp. 65–9.

Benjamin, Walter, Über das mimetische Vermögen', 1933, *Walter Benjamin: Gesammelte Schriften*, vol. II. 1, ed. Rolf Tiedemann and Hermann Schweppenhäuser, Frankfurt am Main, Suhrkamp, vols I–VI, 1974–85, pp. 210–13; trans. 'On the Mimetic Faculty' in *One Way Street, and Other Writings*, Edmund Jephcott and Kingsley Shorter, London, New Left Books, 1979, pp. 160–3.

Benjamin, Walter, 'Das Kunstwerk im Zeitalter seiner technischen Reproduzierbarkeit', 1936, in *Walter Benjamin: Gesammelte Schriften*, vol. I.2, ed. Rolf Tiedemann and Hermann Schweppenhäuser, Frankfurt am Main, Suhrkamp, vols I–VI, 1974–85, pp. 435–69; trans. 'The Work of Art in the Age of Mechanical Reproduction', *Illuminations*, Harry Zohn, ed. Hannah Arendt London, Fontana, 1973, pp. 219–53.

Benjamin, Walter, 'Der Erzähler: Betrachtungen zum Werk Niokolai Lesskovs', 1936, in *Walter Benjamin: Gesammelte Schriften*, vol. II.2, ed. Rolf Tiedemann and Hermann Schweppenhäuser, Frankfurt am Main, Suhrkamp, vols I–VI, 1974–85, pp. 438–65, trans. 'The Storyteller: Reflections on the Works of Nikolai Leskov', *Illuminations*, Harry Zohn, ed. Hannah Arendt, London, Fontana, 1973, pp. 83–109.

Benjamin, Walter, 'Franz Kafka: Zur zehnten Wiederkehr series Todestages', 1939, in *Walter Benjamin: Gesammelte Schriften*, vol. II.2, ed. Rolf Tiedemann and Hermann Schweppenhäuser, Frankfurt am Main, Suhrkamp, vols I–VI, 1974–85, pp. 409–38, trans. 'Franz Kafka: On the Tenth Anniversary of His Death', in *Illuminations*, Harry Zohn, ed. Hannah Arendt London, Fontana, 1973, pp. 111–40.

Benjamin, Walter, 'Some Motifs in Baudelaire', 1939, trans. Harry Zohn, in *Charles Baudelaire: A Lyric Poet in the Era of High Capitalism*, London, New Left Books, 1973, pp. 107–54.

Benjamin, Walter, 'Über einige Motive bei Baudelaire', 1939, in *Walter Benjamin: Gesammelte Schriften*, vol. I.2, ed. Rolf Tiedemann and Hermann Schweppenhäuser, Frankfurt am Main, Suhrkamp, vols I–VI, 1974–85, pp. 605–53; trans. 'On Some Motifs in Baudelaire', *Illuminations*, Harry Zohn, ed. Hannah Arendt, London, Fontana, 1973, pp. 157–202.

Benjamin, Walter, *Briefe*, vol. 2, ed. Gershom Scholom and Theodor W. Adorno, Frankfurt am Main, Suhrkamp, 1966.

Benjamin, Walter, 'Über den Begriff der Geschichte', in *Walter Benjamin: Gesammelte Schriften*, vol. I.2, ed. Rolf Tiedemann and Hermann Schweppenhäuser, Frankfurt am Main, Suhrkamp, vols I–VI, 1974–85, pp. 691–704, trans. 'Theses on the Philosophy of History', *Illuminations*, Harry Zohn, ed. Hannah Arendt, London, Fontana, 1973, pp. 255–65.

Benjamin, Walter, 'Max Brod, Franz Kafka', in *Walter Benjamin: Gesammelte Schriften*, vol. III, ed. Rolf Tiedemann and Hermann Schweppenhäuser, Frankfurt am Main, Suhrkamp, vols I–VI, 1974–85, pp. 526–9; trans. 'Max Brod's Book on Kafka: And Some of My Own Reflections', in *Illuminations*, Harry Zohn, ed. Hannah Arendt, London, Fontana, 1993, pp. 141–8.

Bernstein, J. M., *The Fate of Art: Aesthetic Alienation from Kant to Derrida and Adorno*, Oxford, Polity, 1992.

Berry, Philippa and Wernick, Andrew (eds), *Shadow of Spirit: Postmodernism and Religion*, London, Routledge, 1993.

Binion, Rudolf, *Frau Lou: Nietzsche's Wayward Disciple*, Princeton, Yale University Press, 1968.

Bleich, David J., 'The Thirteenth Principle: Resurrection', in *With Perfect Faith: The Foundations of Jewish Belief*, New York, Ktav, 1983, pp. 619–88.

Bolz, Norbert, 'Charisma und Souveränität: Carl Schmitt und Walter Benjamin im Schatten Max Webers', in Jacob Taubes (ed.), *Religionstheorie und Politische Theologie*, vol. 1, *Der Furst dieser Welt: Carl Schmitt und die Folgen*, Munich, Wilhelm Fink, 1993, pp. 249–62.

Borowitz, Eugene B., 'The Authority of the Ethical Impulse in "Halakha"', 1981, in Norbert M. Samuelson (ed.), *Studies in Jewish*

Philosophy: Collected Essays of the Academy of Jewish Philosophy, 1980–1985, Lanham, University Press of America, 1987, pp. 489–505.

Braudel, Fernand, *Capitalism and Material Life 1400–1800*, trans. Miriam Kocha, Glasgow, Fontana, 1974.

Buber, Martin, *Daniel: Gespräche von der Verwirklichung*, 1913, *Werke*, vol. I, *Schriften zur Philosophie*, Munich, Lambert-Schneider, 1962, pp. 11–76.

Buber, Martin, 'The Holy Way: A Word to the Jews and to the Nations', 1918, in *On Judaism*, trans. Eva Jospe and I. M. Lask, New York, Schocken, 1972, pp. 108–48.

Buber, Martin, 'Nationalism', 1921, in *Israel and the World: Essays in a Time of Crisis*, New York, Schocken, 1963, pp. 214–26.

Buber, Martin, *Ich und Du*, 1922, 11th edn (1957), Heidelberg, Lambert Schneider, 1983; trans. *I and Thou*, Walter Kaufmann, Edinburgh, T. & T. Clark, 1983.

Buber, Martin, 'Revelation and Law (Martin Buber and Franz Rosenzweig)', 1922–5, in Franz Rosenzweig, *On Jewish Learning*, ed. Nahum N. Glatzer, New York, Schocken, 1965, pp. 109–118.

Buber, Martin, *On Judaism*, 1909–51, trans. Eva Jospe and I. M. Lask, New York, Schocken, 1972.

Buber, Martin, 'Dialogue', 1929, in *Between Man and Man*, trans. Ronald Gregor Smith, London, Collins, 1979, pp. 17–59.

Buber, Martin, *Kingship of God*, 1932, trans. Richard Scheiman, New Jersey, 1990.

Buber, Martin, 'The Question to the Single One', 1936, in *Between Man and Man*, trans. Ronald Gregor Smith, London, Collins, 1979, pp. 60–108.

Buber, Martin, 'What is Man?', 1938, in *Between Man and Man*, trans. Ronald Gregor Smith, London, Collins, 1979, pp. 148–247.

Buber, Martin, 'The Spirit of Israel and the World of Today', 1939, in *Israel and the World: Essays in a Time of Crisis*, New York, Schocken, 1963, pp. 183–94.

Buber, Martin, 'The Gods of the Nations and God', 1941, in *Israel and the World: Essays in a Time of Crisis*, New York, Schocken, 1963, pp. 197–213.

Buber, Martin, *Moses: The Revelation and the Covenant*, 1946, ed. Michael Fishbane, New Jersey 1988.

Buber, Martin, *Paths in Utopia*, 1946, trans. R. F. C. Hull, London, Routledge and Kegan Paul, 1949.

Buber, Martin, 'Zwischen Gesellschaft und Staat', 1950, in *Werke*, vol. 1, *Schriften zur Philosophie*, Munich, Lambert-Schneider, 1962, pp. 1006–20.

Buber, Martin, 'Distance and Relation', 1951, in *The Knowledge of Man: A Philosophy of the Interhuman*, trans. Maurice Friedman and Ronald Gregor Smith, New York, Harper, 1966, pp. 59–71.

Buber, Martin, 'On the Suspension of the Ethical', 1952, in *Eclipse of God: Studies in the Relation between Religion and Philosophy*, ed. Robert M. Seltzer, New Jersey, Humanities Press, 1988, pp. 113–20.

Buber, Martin, 'Geltung und Grenze des politischen Prinzips', 1953, in *Werke*, vol. 1, Kösel, Lambert-Schneider, 1962, pp. 1095–108.

Buber, Martin, 'Dialogue between Martin Buber and Carl R. Rogers', 1957, in *The Knowledge of Man: A Philosophy of the Interhuman*, trans. Maurice Friedman and Ronald Gregor Smith, New York, Harper, 1966, pp. 166–84.

Buber, Martin, 'Elements of the Interhuman', 1957, in *The Knowledge of Man: A Philosophy of the Interhuman*, trans. Maurice Friedman and Ronald Gregor Smith, New York, Harper, 1966, pp. 1096–108.

Buber, Martin, 'Replies to My Critics', 1965, in Paul Arthur Schilpp and Maurice Friedman, *The Philosophy of Martin Buber*, La Salle, Illinois, Open Court, 1967, pp. 689–744.

Calderón, P., *Plays: One*, trans. Gwynne Edwards, London, Methuen, 1991.

Cohen, Arthur A. 'Resurrection of the Dead', in Arthur A. Cohen and Paul Mendes-Flohr (eds), *Contemporary Jewish Religious Thought*, New York, The Free Press, 1987, pp. 807–13.

Cohen, Hermann, 'Deutschtum und Judentum', 1915, repr. in *Hermann Cohens Jüdische Schriften*, vol. II, ed. Bruno Strauss Berlin, C. A. Schwetschte und Sohn, 1924, pp. 237–301.

Cohen, Hermann, *Logic der reinen Erkenntnis*, Berlin, Bruno Cassirer, 1902.

Cohen, Hermann, *Ethik des reinen Willens*, Berlin, Bruno Cassirer, 1904.

Cohen, Hermann, *Ästhetik des reinen Gefühls*, 2 vols, Berlin, Bruno Cassirer, 1912.

Cohen, Hermann, *Reason and Hope: Selections from the Jewish Writings of Hermann Cohen*, ed. and trans. Eva Jaspe, New York, W.W. Norton & Co., 1971.

Cohen, Hermann, *Der Begriff der Religion im System der Philosophie*, Giessen, Alfred Töpelmann, 1915.

Cohen, Hermann, 'Spinoza über Staat und Religion', 1915, in *Jüdische Schriften*, vol. III, ed. Bruno Strauss, Berlin, C. A. Schwetsche und Sohn, 1924, pp. 290–372.

Cohen, Hermann, *Religion der Vernunft aus den Quellen des Judentums*, 1919, Wiesbaden, Fourier, 1978; trans. *Religion of Reason out of the Sources of Judaism*, Simon Kaplan, New York, Frederick Unger, 1972.

Cohen, Hermann, 'Innere Beziehungen der Kantischen Philosophie zum Judentum', 1910, in *Hermann Cohens Jüdische Schriften*, vol. I, *Ethische und religiöse Grundfragen*, ed. Bruno Strauss, Berlin, C. A. Schwetsche und Sohn, 1924, pp. 284–305; trans. 'Affinities between the Philosophy of Kant and Judaism', in *Reason and Hope: Selections from the Jewish Writings of Hermann Cohen*, ed. and trans. Eva Jospe, New York, W. W. Norton & Co., 1971, pp. 77–89.

Cohen, Hermann, 'Religiöse Postulate', 1907, in *Hermann Cohens Jüdische Schriften*, vol. I, ed. Bruno Strauss, Berlin, C. A. Schwetschte und Sohn, 1924, pp. 1–17.

Cohen, Stuart A., *The Three Crowns: structures of communal politics in early rabbinic Jewry*, Cambridge, Cambridge University Press, 1990.

Corbusier, Le, *Towards a New Architecture*, 1923, trans. Frederic Etchells, London, Architectural Press, 1982.

Cornford, F. M., *From Religion to Philosophy: A Study in the Origins of Western Speculation*, 1912, Brighton, Harvester, 1980.

Cupitt, Don, 'Unsystematic Ethics and Politics', in Philippa Berry and Andrew Wernick (eds), *Shadow of Spirit: Post-modernism and Religion*, London, Routledge, 1993, pp. 149–55.

Daube, David, *Appeasement or Resistance And Other Essays on New Testament Judaism*, Berkeley, University of California Press, 1987.

Davidson, Robert, *Genesis 1–11: The Cambridge Bible Commentary on the New English Bible*, Cambridge, Cambridge University Press, 1980.

Davies, W. D., *Paul and Rabbinic Judaism: Some Rabbinic Elements in Pauline Theology*, London, SPCK, 1970.

Deleuze, Gilles, *Différence et Répétition*, 1968, Paris, Presses Universitaires de France, 1972.

Deleuze, Gilles, *Nietzsche and Philosophy*, trans. Hugh Tomlinson, London, Athlone, 1983.

Derrida, Jacques, 'Of an Apocalyptic Tone recently adopted in philosophy', trans. John P. Leavey, Jr, *Oxford Literary Review*, 6: 2 (1984), pp. 3–37.

Derrida, Jacques, *Glas*, Paris, Galilée, 1974; trans. John P. Leavey, Jr, and Richard Rand, Lincoln, University of Nebraska Press, 1986.

Derrida, Jacques, *De l'espirit: Heidegger et la question*, Paris, Galilée, 1987; trans. *Of Spirit: Heidegger and the Question*, Geoffrey Bennington and Rachel Bowlby, Chicago, Chicago University Press, 1989.

Derrida, Jacques, 'Force of Law: The "Mystical Foundation of Authority"', *Cardozo Law Review, Deconstruction and the Possibility of Justice*, II, 5–6 (1990), pp. 919–73, 973–1039.

Derrida, Jacques, 'Interpretations at War: Kant, the Jew, the German', *New Literary History*, 22 (1991), pp. 39–95.

Derrida, Jacques and Meyer, Eva, 'Labyrinth und Archi/Textur: ein Gespräch mit Jacques Derrida', in *Das Abenteuer der Ideen: Architektur and Philosophie seit der industriellen Revolution*, Berlin, Frölich und Kaufmann, 1984.

Dietz, Mary G., *Between the Human and the Divine: The Political Thought of Simone Weil*, New Jersey, Rowman and Littlefield, 1988.

Duffy, Michael F. and Mittelman, Willard, 'Nietzsche's attitudes toward the Jews' *Journal of the History of Ideas*, XLIX, 2, (1988), pp. 301–17.

Durkheim, Émile, *The Division of Labour in Society*, 1893, trans. George Simpson, New York, The Free Press, 1964.

Durkheim, Émile, *Suicide: A Study in Sociology*, 1895, trans. J. A. Spaulding and G. Simpson, London, Routledge and Kegan Paul, 1952.

Eco, Umberto, 'Function and Sign: The Semiotics of Architecture', in G. Broadbent, R. Bunt and C. Jencks (eds), *Signs, Symbols and Architecture,* Chichester, Wiley, 1973, pp. 11–69.

Ellis, Marc H., *Beyond Innocence and Redemption: Confronting the Holocaust and Israeli Power*, San Francisco, Harper and Row, 1990.

Elshtain, Jean Bethke, 'The Vexation of Weil', *Telos Special Issue on Religion and Politics*, 58 (1983–4), pp. 195–203.

Fackenheim, Emil, *The Jewish Return into History: Reflections in the Age of Auschwitz and a New Jerusalem*, New York, Schocken, 1978.

Fackenheim, Emil, *To Mend the World: Foundations of Future Jewish Thought*, New York, Schocken, 1982.

Fackenheim, Emil, 'The Holocaust and Philosophy', *Journal of Philosophy*, LXXXII, 10 (1985), pp. 505–14.

Fichte, J. G., *Versuch einer Kritik aller Offenbarung*, 1792, trans. *Attempt at a Critique of all Revelation*, Garrett Green, Cambridge, Cambridge University Press, 1978.

Fielder, Leslie, 'Simone Weil: Prophet out of Israel', *Commentary*, II (1951), pp. 36–46.

Foster, Hal (ed.), *Post-modern Culture*, London, Pluto, 1985.

Foucault, Michel, 'Nietzsche, Genealogy, History', in *Language, Counter-Memory, Practice*, ed. Donald F. Bouchard, Ithaca, Cornell, 1977, pp. 139–69.

Fox, Marvin, (ed.), *Modern Jewish Ethics: Theory and Practice*, Ohio, Ohio University Press, 1975.

Frampton, Kenneth, 'New Brutalism and the Architecture of the Welfare State: England 1949–59', in *Modern Architecture: A Critical History*, London, Thames and Hudson, 1985, pp. 262–8.

Gibbs, Robert, 'The Limits of Thought: Rosensweig, Shelling and Cohen', *Zeitschrift für philosophische Forschung*, 43 (1989), pp. 618–40.

Gilman, Sander L., 'Heine, Nietzsche and the Idea of the Jew: The Other and the Self', in *Inscribing the Other*, Lincoln, University of Nebraska Press, 1991, pp. 121–42.

Gilman, Sander L., 'Heine: Nietzsche's Other', in *Inscribing the Other*, Lincoln, University of Nebraska Press, 1991, pp. 99–119.

Glatzer, Nahun N., *Franz Rosenzweig: His Life and Thought*, New York, Schocken, 1961.

Goethe, *Wilhelm Meister's Apprenticeship*, trans. Thomas Carlyle, London, Chapman and Hall, 1899.

Golomb, Jacob, 'Nitezsche's Judaism of Power', *Revue des études juives*, 147 (1988), pp. 353–85.

Guttman, Julius, 'Hermann Cohen', in *Philosophies of Judaism: A History of Jewish Philosophy from Biblical Times to Franz Rosenzweig*, trans. David W. Silverman, New York, Schocken, 1973, pp. 400–15.

Habermas, Jürgen, 'Consciousness-Raising or Redemptive Criticism: The Contemporaneity of Walter Benjamin', 1972, trans. Philip Brewster and Carl Howard Buchner, *New German Critique*, 17 (1979), pp. 30–59.

Habermas, Jürgen, *Knowledge and Human Interests*, trans. Jeremy J. Shapiro, London, Heinemann, 1972.

Habermas, Jürgen, 'Modernity versus Post-modernity', *New German Critique*, 22 (1981), pp. 3–14.

Habermas, Jürgen, 'Moderne und post-moderne Architektur', in *Die Neue Unübersichtlichkeit: Kleine Politische Schriften V*, Frankfurt am Main, Suhrkamp, 1985.

Habermas, Jürgen, *The Philosophical Discourses of Modernity*, trans. Frederick G. Laurence, Oxford, Polity, 1987.

Harrison, Jane, *Prolegomena to the Study of Greek Religion*, 1903, London, Merlin, 1980.

Hegel, G. W. F., *Differenz des Fichte'schen und Schelling'schen System der Philosophie*, 1801, Hamburg, Felix Meiner, 1962; trans. *The Difference between Fichte's and Schelling's System of Philosophy*, H. S. Harris and Walter Cerf, Albany, State University of New York Press, 1977.

Hegel, G. W. F., *Phänomenologie des Geistes*, 1807, ed. Eva Moldenhauer and Karl Markus Michel, Frankfurt am Main, Suhrkamp, 1973; trans. *Phenomenology of Spirit*, A. V. Miller, Oxford, Clarendon, 1979.

Hegel, G. W. F., *Wissenschaft der Logik*, 1812–16, vol. II, Hamburg, Felix Meiner, II 1969; trans. *Science of Logic*, A. V. Miller, London, Allan & Unwin, 1969.

Hegel, G. W. F., *Aesthetics: Lectures on Fine Art*, 1835, vol. 1, trans. T. M. Knox, Oxford, Clarendon Press, 1975.

Hegel, G. W. F., *The Letters*, trans. Clark Butler and Christine Seiler, Bloomington, Indiana University Press, 1984.

Heidegger, Martin, *Die Selbstbehauptung der deutschen Universität: Das Rektorat 1933/34*, Frankfurt am Main, Klostermann, 1983; trans. Rectoral Address, *Review of Metaphysics*, XXXVIII, 3 (1985), pp. 470–80.

Heidegger, Martin, *Einführung in die Metaphysik*, 1935, Tübingen, Niemeyer, 1987; trans. *An Introduction to Metaphysics*, Ralph Manheim, New York, Anchor, 1959.

Heidegger, Martin, *Schellings Abhandling über das Wesen der Menschlichen Freiheit [1809]*, 1936, Tübingen, Max Niemeyer, 1971; trans. *Schelling's Treatise on the Essence of Human Freedom (1809)*, Joan Stambaugh, Athens, Ohio, Ohio University Press, 1985.

Heidegger, Martin, 'Building Dwelling Thinking', 1951, in *Poetry, Language, Thought*, trans. Albert Hofstadter, New York, Harper, 1971, pp. 143–61.

Heidegger, Martin, 'Letter on Humanism', in *Martin Heidegger: Basic Writings*, trans. Frank A. Capuzzi, London, Routledge and Kegan Paul, 1978, pp. 189–242.

Heidegger, Martin, *Die Selbstbehauptung der deutschen Universität*, Frankfurt am Main, Klostermann, 1983; trans. *The Self-Assertion of the German University*.

Heidegger, Martin, *Martin Heidegger: Basic Writings*, trans. Frank A. Capuzzi, London, Routledge and Kegan Paul, 1978.

Hillach, Ansgar, 'The Aesthetics of Politics: Walter Benjamin's Theories of German fascism', *New German Critique*, 17 (1979), pp. 99–119.

Hirsch, Samson Raphael, *The Nineteen Letters on Judaism*, 1836, trans. Bernard Drachman, Jerusalem, Feldheim, 1969.

Hirsch, Samson Raphael, *Horeb: Essays on Israel's Duties in the Diaspora*, trans. Isidor Grunfeld, New York, The Soncino Press, 1981.

Hirsch, Samson Raphael, *The Pentateuch*, trans. Gertrude Hirschler, New York, The Judaica Press, 1986.

'Historikerstreit': Die Dokumentation der Kontroverse um die Einzigartigkeit der national-sozialistischen Judenvernichtung, Munich, Piper, 1987.

Hitchcock, Henry-Russell and Johnson, Philip, *The International Style*, 1932, New York, Norton, 1966.

Horkheimer, Max and Adorno, Theodor W., *Dialectic of Enlightenment*, 1944, trans. John Cumming, New York, Herder and Herder, 1972.

Jencks, Charles, *Modern Movements in Architecture*, Harmondsworth, Penguin, 1973.

Kafka, Franz, 'The Great Wall of China', in *Metamorphosis and Other Stories*, trans. Willa and Edwin Muir, Harmondsworth, Penguin, 1976, pp. 65–82.

Kant, I., *Critique of Pure Reason*, 1781, trans. N. Kemp Smith, New York, St. Martin's Press, 1965.

Kant, I., *Die Religion innerhalb der Grenzen der blossen Vernunft*, 1793, trans. *Religion within the Limits of Reason Alone*, Theodore M. Greene and Hoyt H. Hudson, New York, Harper and Row, 1960.

Kant, I., *Lectures on Ethics*, trans. Louis Infield, London, Methuen, 1979.

Kierkegaard, Søren, *Fear and Trembling: Dialectical Lyric by Johannes de Silentio*, 1843, trans. Alastair Hannay, Harmondsworth, Penguin, 1985.

Kristeva, Julia, *Powers of Horror: An Essay on Abjection*, 1980, trans. Leon S. Roudiez, New York, Columbia University Press, 1982.

Lacoue-Labarthe, Philippe, *La fiction du politique*, Paris, Christian Bourgeois, 1990; trans. *Heidegger, Art, Politics: The Fiction of the Political*, Chris Turner, Oxford, Blackwell, 1990.

Lang, Berel, *Act and Idea in the Nazi Genocide*, Chicago, Chicago University Press, 1990.

Lessing, Gotthold Ephraim, *Nathan der Weise*, 1779, Stuttgart, Reclam, 1979; trans. *Nathan the Wise*, in *Laocöon*, London, Dent, 1930.

Levinas, Emmanuel, 'Simone Weil against the Bible', 1952, in *Difficult Freedom*, trans. Séan Hand, London, The Athlone Press, 1990, pp. 133–41.

Levinas, Emmanuel, 'Aimer la Thora plus que Dieu', 1955, in *Difficile Liberté: Essais sur le judaïsm*, Paris, Albin, Michel; trans. 'Loving the Thora more than God', in *Difficult Liberty: Essays on Judaism*, trans. Séan Hand, London, The Athlone Press, 1990, pp. 142–5.

Levinas, Emmanuel, *Totalité et infini: essai sur l'exteriorité*, 1961, The Hague, Martinus Nijhoff, 1980; trans. *Totality and Infinity: An Essay on Exteriority*, Alphonso Lingis, The Hague, Martinus Nijhoff, 1979.

Levinas, Emmanuel, 'Dialogue avec Martin Buber', 1965, in *Noms propres*, Paris, Fata Morgana, 1976, pp. 51–5.

Levinas, Emmanuel, 'Martin Buber and the theory of knowledge', in Paul Arthur Schilpp and Maurice Friedman (eds), *The Philosophy of Martin Buber*, La Salle, Illinois, Open Court, 1967, pp. 133–50.

Levinas, Emmanuel, 'Le Tentation de la tentation', in *Quatre lectures Talmudiques*, Paris, Les éditions de minuit, 1968 pp. 65–109; trans. 'The Temptation of the Temptation, Annette Aronowicz, *Nine Talmudic Readings*, Bloomington, Indiana University Press, 1990, pp. 30–50.

Levinas, Emmanuel, 'Ideology and Idealism', 1975, in *The Levinas Reader*, trans. and ed. Séan Hand, Oxford, Blackwell, 1989, pp. 235–48.

Levinas, Emmanuel, *Autrement qu'être ou au delà de l'essence*, 1974, The

Hague, Martinus Nijhoff, 1978; trans. *Otherwise than Being or Beyond Essence*, 1974, trans. Alphonso Lingis, The Hague, Martinus Nijhoff, 1981.

Levinas, Emmanuel, 'Ethics as First Philosophy', 1984, in *The Levinas Reader*, trans. and ed. Séan Hand, Oxford, Blackwell, 1989, pp. 75–87.

Levinas, Emmanuel, 'Ethics and Spirit', in *Difficult Freedom: Essays on Judaism*, trans. and ed. Séan Hand, London, The Athlone Press, 1990, pp. 3–10.

Levy, Ze'ev, *Between Yahfeth and Shem: On the Relationship between Jewish and General Philosophy*, Bern, Peter Lang, 1987.

Lichtenstein, Aharon, 'Does Jewish Tradition Recognize an Ethic Independent of Halacha?', repr. in Marvin Fox (ed.), *Modern Jewish Ethics: Theory and Practice*, Columbus, Ohio University Press, 1975, pp. 102–23.

Lovelock, James, 'Gaia', in William Bloom (ed.), *The New Age: An Anthology of Essential Writings*, London, Rider, 1991, pp. 164–7.

Lowith, Karl, 'Joachim', *Meaning in History*, Chicago, Chicago University Press, 1949, pp. 145–59.

Lukacs, George, 'What is Orthodox Marxism?', in *History and Class Consciousness*, trans. Rodney Livingstone, London, Merlin, 1971, pp. 27–45.

Lynton Norbert, 'Icon of the Revolution', in *The Times Higher Educational Supplement*, 4 April 1986.

Lyotard, Jean-François, *The Postmodern Condition: A Report on Knowledge*, 1979, trans. Geoff Bennington and Brian Massumi, Manchester, Manchester University Press, 1984.

Lyotard, Jean-François, *Le Post-moderne expliqué aux enfants*, Paris, Galilée, 1986.

Lyotard, Jean-François, *Heidegger and 'the jews'*, 1988, trans. Andreas Michel and Mark S. Roberts, Minneapolis, University of Minnesota Press, 1990.

Lyotard, Jean-François, 'An Interview with Jean-François Lyotard', in *Theory Culture and Society*, 5 (1988), pp. 277–310.

Lyotard, Jean-François, *The Differend: Phrases in Dispute*, 1983, trans. George van Den Abbeele, Manchester, Manchester University Press, 1988.

McLellan, David, *Simone Weil: Utopian Pessimist*, London, Macmillan, 1989.

Maimonides, Moses, *The Guide of the Perplexed*, 1190, vol. trans. Shlomo Pines, Chicago, Chicago University Press, 1963.

Maimonides, Moses, 'Introduction' to the *Mishneh Torah*, in Isadore

Twersky (ed.), *A Maimonides Reader*, New York, Behrman House, 1972.

Mann, Thomas, *Joseph and his Brothers*, trans. H. T. Lowe-Porter, Harmondsworth, Penguin, 1978.

Marx, Karl, *Grundrisse der Kritik der politischen Ökonomie*, Wien, Europa, n.d., trans. Martin Nicolaus, Harmondsworth, Penguin, 1973.

Marx, Karl, *Capital*, trans. Ben Fowkes, Harmondsworth, Penguin, 1976.

Mendelssohn, Moses, *Morgenstunden oder Vorlesungen über das Dasein Gottes*, 1785, ed. Dominique Bourel, Stuttgart, Reclam, 1979.

Mendes-Flohr, Paul, *From Mysticism to Dialogue: Martin Buber's Transformation of German Social Thought*, 1978, Detroit, Wayne State University Press, 1989.

Mendes-Flohr, Paul, 'Franz Rosenzweig and the Crisis of Historicism', in Paul Mendes-Flohr (ed.), *The Philosophy of Franz Rosenzweig*, Hanover, University Press of New England, 1988, pp. 138–61.

Mendes-Flohr, Paul (ed.), *The Philosophy of Franz Rosenzweig*, Hanover, University Press of New England, 1988.

Mendes-Flohr, Paul, 'Nationalism as a Spiritual Sensibility: the Philosophical Suppositions of Buber's Hebrew Humanism', in *Divided Passions: Jewish Intellectuals and the Experience of Modernity*, Detroit, Wayne State University Press, 1991, pp. 181–93.

Mendes-Flohr, Paul, 'Rosenzweig and Kant: Two Views of Ritual and Religion', in *Divided Passions: Jewish Intellectuals and the Experience of Modernity*, Detroit, Wayne State University Press, 1991, pp. 283–310.

Mendes-Flohr, Paul, 'The Politics of Covenantal Responsibility: Martin Buber and Hebrew Humanism', in *Divided Passions,: Jewish Intellectuals and the Experience of Modernity*, Detroit, Wayne State University Press, 1991, pp. 194–206.

Mendes-Flohr, Paul, '"The Stronger and the Better Jews": Jewish Theological Responses to Political Messianism in the Weimar Republic', *Studies in Contemporary Jewry*, VII (1991), pp. 154–85.

Midrash Rabba, vol. I, *Genesis* (Noach), trans. H. Freedman, London, The Soncino Press, 1983.

Milbank, John, *Theology and Social Theory: Beyond Secular Reason*, Oxford, Blackwell, 1990.

Mitzman, Arthur, *The Iron Cage: An Historical Interpretation of Max Weber*, New York, Alfred Knopf, 1970.

Montesquieu, Charles de, *The Spirit of the Laws*, trans. Thomas Nugent, New York, Hafner, 1949.

Morgan, Janet, *Agatha Christie: A Biography*, London, Fontana, 1985.

Mosés, Stéphane, *Système et Révélation: la philosophie de Franz Rosenzweig*, Paris, Editions du Seuil, 1982.

Mosés, Stéphane, 'Walter Benjamin and Franz Rosenzweig', *The Philosophical Forum*, XV, 1–2 (1983–4), pp. 188–205.

Nevin, Thomas R., *Simone Weil: Portrait of a Self-Exiled Jew*, Chapel Hill, University of North Carolina Press, 1991.

Nevo, Ruth, 'Introduction' to trans. *Chaim Nachman Bialik: Selected Poems*, Jerusalem, Dvir and *The Jerusalem Post*, 1981, pp. vii–xix.

Newman, John Henry, *The Idea of a University*, ed. Martin J. Svaglic, Notre Dame, Indiana, University of Notre Dame Press, 1982.

Nietzsche, Friedrich, *Human all too Human: A Book for Free Spirits*, 1878–80, trans. R. J. Hollingdale, Cambridge, Cambridge University Press, 1986.

Nietzsche, Friedrich, 'Thoughts on the prejudices of morality', in *Daybreak*, 1881, trans. W. Kaufmann, New York, Vintage, 1979.

Nietzsche, Friedrich, *Thus Spoke Zarathustra, Werke II*, 1883–4, trans. R. J. Hollingdale, Harmondsworth, Penguin, 1961.

Nietzsche, Friedrich, *Beyond Good and Evil: Prelude to a Philosophy of the Future*, 1886, trans. Walter Kaufmann, New York, Vintage, 1966.

Nietzsche, Friedrich, 'The Free Spirit', *Beyond Good and Evil: Prelude to a Philosophy of the Future*, 1886, trans. Walter Kaufmann, New York, Vintage, 1966.

Nietzsche, Friedrich, *On the Genealogy of Morals,* 1887, *Werke III*, trans. W. Kaufman, New York, Vintage, 1969.

Nietzsche, Friedrich, *On the Genealogy of Morals and Ecce Homo,* 1887/1908, trans. W. Kaufman, New York, Vintage, 1969.

Nietzsche, Friedrich, *The Anti-Christ*, 1895, trans. R. J. Hollingdale, Harmondsworth, Penguin, 1968.

Nietzsche, Friedrich, *Werke I–V*, ed. Karl Schlechta, Frankfurt am Main, Ullstein, 1976.

Novak, David, 'Is There a Concept of Individual Right in Jewish Law?' paper presented to the Jewish Law Association Biennial Conference, Paris, 15 July 1992.

O'Brien, Conor Cruise, *The Siege: The Saga of Israel and Zionism*, London, Paladin, 1986.

O'Flaherty, James C., Sellner, Timothy F. and Helm, Robert M., (eds), *Studies in Nietzsche and the Judaeo-Christian Tradition*, Chapel Hill, University of North Carolina, 1985.

Payot, Daniel, *Le Philosophe et l'architecte: Sur quelques determinations philosophiques de l'idée d'architecture*, Paris, Aubier Montaigne, 1982.

Pétrement, Simone, *Simone Weil: A Life*, trans. Raymond Rosenthal, London, Mowbrays, 1976.

Plastow, Judith, *Standing Again at Sinai: Judaism from a Feminist Perspective*, San Francisco, HarperSanFrancisco, 1990.

274 *Judaism and Modernity*

Poggeler, Otto, 'Between Enlightenment and Romanticism: Rosenzweig and Hegel', in Paul Mendes-Flohr (ed.), *The Philosophy of Franz Rosenzweig*, Hanover, University Press of New England, 1988, pp. 107–23.

Prawer, S. S., 'Review of Robert Alter, *Necessary Angels: Tradition and Modernity in Kafka, Benjamin and Scholem*', *Times Literary Supplement*, 2 August 1991.

Pulzer, Peter, *The Rise of Political Anti-Semitism in Germany and Austria*, London, Peter Halban, 1988.

Radhakrishnan, S., *The Bhagavadgîtâ*, Bombay, Blackie and Son, 1977.

Rahel-Freund, Else, *Franz Rosenzweig's Philosophy of Existence: An Analysis of the Star of Redemption*, 1933, trans. Stephen L. Weinstein and Robert Israel, The Hague, Martinus Nijhoff, 1979.

Rickels, Laurence A., *Aberrations of Mourning: Writing on German Crypts*, Detroit, Wayne State University Press, 1988.

Rose, Gillian, *The Melancholy Science: An Introduction to the Thought of Theodor W. Adorno*, London, Macmillan, 1978.

Rose, Gillian, *Hegel contra Sociology*, London, Athlone, 1981.

Rose, Gillian, *The Broken Middle: Out of Our Ancient Society*, Oxford, Blackwell, 1992.

Rose, Gillian, *Dialectic of Nihilism: Post-Structuralism and Law*, Oxford, Blackwell, 1984.

Rosenzweig, Franz, '"Urzelle" des Stern der Erlösung', 1917, *Gesammelte Schriften*, vol. III, Berlin, Schocken, 1937, pp. 125–38.

Rosenzweig, Franz, *Der Stern der Erlösung*, 1921 (2nd edn 1930), *Gesammelte Schriften* vol. II, The Hague, Martinus Nijhoff, 1976; trans. *The Star of Redemption*, William W. Hallo, London, Routledge and Kegan Paul, 1971.

Rosenzweig, Franz, 'The Builders: Concerning the Law', 1923, in *On Jewish Learning*, ed. N. N. Glatzer, New York, Schocken, 1965, pp. 72–92.

Rosenzweig, Franz, 'Einleitung in die Akademieausgabe der Jüdischen Schriften Hermann Cohens', 1924, in *Zweistromland, Gesammelte Schriften*, vol. III ed. Reinhold and Anne Marie Meyer, Berlin, Schocken, 1937, pp. 177–224.

Rosenzweig, Franz, 'Das neue Denken', 1925, *Zweistromland: Kleinere Schriften zur Glauben, Gesammelte Schriften* III, Dordrecht, Martinus Nijhoff, 1984.

Rosenzweig, Franz, 'Vertauschte Fronten', 1929, *Zweistromland: Kleinere Schriften zu Glauben und Denken, Gesammelte Schriften*, vol. III, Dordrecht, Martinus Nijhoff, 1984; trans. of the Davos Disputation, see 'Appendices' to Heidegger, *Kant and the Problem of Metaphysics*, trans.

Richard Taft, Bloomington, Indiana University Press, 1990, pp. 71–85.

Rosenzweig, Franz, *On Jewish Learning*, ed. N. N. Glatzer, New York Schocken, 1965.

Rosenzweig, Franz, *Der Mensch und Sein Werk, Gesammelte Schriften* vols. *1–IV*, The Hague, Martinus Nijhoff, 1976.

Rossi, Aldo, *The Architecture of the City*, 1966, trans. Diane Ghirardo and Joan Ockman, New York, MIT Press, 1989.

Rotenstreich, Nathan, 'The Right and the Limitation of Buber's Dialogical Thought', in Paul Arthur Schilpp and Maurice Friedman (eds), *The Philosophy of Martin Buber*, La Salle, Illinois, Open Court, 1967, pp. 97–132.

Rotenstreich, Nathan, 'Hermann Cohen: Judaism in the Context of German Philosophy', in Jehuda Reinharz and Walter Schatzberg (eds), *The Jewish Response to German Culture: From the Enlightenment to the Second World War*, London, University Press of New England, 1985, pp. 51–63.

Rotenstreich, Nathan, 'Rosenzweig's Notion of Metaethics', in Paul Mendes-Flohr (ed.), *The Philosophy of Franz Rosenzweig*, Hanover, University Press of New England, 1988, pp. 69–88.

Rotenstreich, Nathan, *Immediacy and its Limits: A Study in Martin Buber's Thought*, Chur, Harwood Academic Publishers, 1991.

Rousseau, Emile, *Du contrat social, ou principes du droit politique*, 1762, ed. C. E. Vaughan, Manchester, Manchester University Press, 1962; trans. *The Social Contract and Discourses*, G. D. H. Cole, London, Dent, 1973.

Rubenstein, Richard R., 'Buber and the Holocaust: Some Reconsiderations on the 100th Anniversary of his Birth', *Michigan Quarterly Review*, September (1978), pp. 382–402.

Rykwert, Joseph, 'Review of Robert Jan van Pelt and Carroll William Westfall, *Architectural Principles in the Age of Historicism, The Times Higher Educational Supplement*, 30 August 1991.

Sanders, E. P., *Paul and Palestinian Judaism: A Comparison of Patterns of Religion*, London, SCM Press, 1981.

Sanders, E. P., *Jesus and Judaism*, London, SCM Press, 1985.

Sandmell, Samuel, *Judaism and Christian Beginnings*, New York, Oxford University Press, 1978.

Schelling, Friedrich W. J., *Of Human Spirit*, trans. James Gutmann, Chicago, Open Court, 1936.

Schmitt, Carl, *Political Theology: Four Chapters on the Concept of Sovereignty*, 1922, trans. George Schwab, Cambridge, Mass., MIT Press, 1988.

Schmitt, Carl, 'On the Barbaric Character of Shakespearean Drama: A Response to Walter Benjamin on the Origin of German Tragic Drama', which is an Appendix to 'The source of the Tragic', ch. 3 of *Hamlet oder Hecuba: Der Einbruch der Zeit in das Spiel*, 1956, trans. David Pan, in *Telos*, Special Issue, *Carl Schmitt Friend or Foe?* 72 (1987), pp. 146–51.

Scholem, Gershom, 'Religious Authority and Mysticism', in *On the Kabbalah and its Symbolism*, 1960, trans. Ralph Manheim, New York, Schocken, 1969, pp. 166–84.

Scholem, Gershom, 'Revelation and Tradition as Religious Categories in Judaism', 1962 in *The Messianic Idea in Judaism and Other Essays on Jewish Spirituality*, New York, Schocken, 1971, pp. 292–303.

Scholem, Gershom, 'Walter Benjamin', 1964, in *On Jews and Judaism in Crisis: Selected Essays*, trans. Lux Furtmüller, New York, Schocken, 1978, pp. 172–97.

Scholem, Gershom, 'The Crisis of Tradition in Jewish Messianism', in *The Messianic Idea in Judaism and Other Essays on Jewish Spirituality*, New York, Schocken, 1971, pp. 49–77.

Scholem, Gershom, 'The Messianic Idea in Kabbalism', in *The Messianic Idea and Other Essays on Jewish Spirituality*, New York, Schocken, 1971, pp. 37–48.

Scholem, Gershom, 'Towards an Understanding of the Messianic Idea in Judaism', in *The Messianic Idea in Judaism and Other Essays on Jewish Spirituality*, New York, Schocken, 1971, pp. 1–36.

Scholem, Gershom, 'Walter Benjamin and his angel', 1972, in *On Jews and Judaism in Crisis: Selected Essays*, trans. Werner J. Dannhauser, New York, Schocken, 1978, pp. 198–236.

Scholem, Gershom, *Walter Benjamin: The Story of a Friendship*, trans. Harry Zohn, London, Faber and Faber, 1982.

Schwarzschild, Steven, '"Germanism and Judaism" – Hermann Cohen's Normative Paradigm of German–Jewish Symbiosis', in David Bronsen (ed.), *Jews and Germans from 1860–1933: The Problematic Synthesis*, Heidelberg, Carl Winter, 1979, pp. 129–72.

Schwarzschild, Steven, 'Authority and Reason Contra Gadamer', 1981, in Norbert M. Samuelson (ed.), *Studies in Jewish Philosophy: Collected Essays of the Academy for Jewish Philosophy 1980–1985,* New York, The Free Press, 1987, 161–90.

Schwarzschild, Steven, 'An Agenda for Jewish Philosophy in the 1980s', in Norbert M. Samuelson (ed.), *Studies in Jewish Philosophy: Collected Essays of the Academy for Jewish Philosophy, 1980–1985*, Lanham, University Press *of America*, 1987, pp. 101–26.

Schwarzschild, Steven, 'Modern Jewish Philosophy', in Arthur A. Cohen and Paul Mendes-Flohr (eds), *Contemporary Jewish Religious Thought*, New York, The Free Press, 1987, pp. 629–34.

Shapira, Avraham, 'A divided heart and a man's double', *Journal of Jewish Thought and Philosophy*, 1, 1 (1991), pp. 115–39.

Shaw, Marion and Vanacker, Sabine, *Reflecting on Miss Marple*, London, Routledge, 1991.

Soloveitchik, Joseph B., *On Repentance*, ed. Pinchas H. Peli, Jerusalem, Oroth, 1980.

Steiner, George, *After Babel: Aspects of Language and Translation*, Oxford, Oxford University Press, 1975.

Steinsaltz, Adin, *The Essential Talmud*, trans. Chaya Galai, New York, Basic Books, 1976.

Strauss, Leo, *Spinoza's Critique of Religion*, 1930, trans. E. M. Sinclair, (1962), New York, Schocken, 1982.

Strauss, Leo, *Philosophy and Law: Essays towards the Understanding of Maimonides and His Predecessors*, 1935, trans. Fred Baumann, Philadelphia, The Jewish Publication Society, 1987.

Strauss, Leo, *Natural Right and History*, 1953, Chicago, The University of Chicago Press, 1971.

Strauss, Leo, 'Jerusalem and Athens: Some Preliminary Reflections', 1967, in Thomas L. Pangle (ed.), *Studies in Platonic Political Philosophy*, Chicago, Chicago University Press, 1983, pp. 147–73.

Strauss, Leo, 'Natural Right and the Historical Approach', in *An Introduction to Political Philosophy: Ten Essays by Leo Strauss*, ed. Hilail Gildin, Detroit, Wayne State University Press, 1989, pp. 99–124.

Strauss, Leo, 'Exoteric Teaching', repr. in *The Rebirth of Classical Political Rationalism: An Introduction to the Thought of Leo Strauss*, ed. Thomas L. Pangle, Chicago, Chicago University Press, 1989.

Strauss, Leo, *The Rebirth of Classical Political Rationalism: An Introduction to the Thought of Leo Strauss*, ed. Thomas L. Pangle, Chicago, Chicago University Press, 1989.

Taylor, Mark C., *Erring: A Post-modern A/theology*, Chicago, University of Chicago Press, 1984.

Taylor, Mark C., *Altarity*, Chicago, University of Chicago Press, 1987.

Thompson, Stith, *Tales of the North American Indians*, Bloomington, Indiana University, 1966.

Twersky, Isadore, *A Maimonides Reader*, New York, Behrman House, 1972.

Ulmen, G. L., *Politischer Mehrwert: Eine Studie über Max Weber und Carl Schmitt*, trans. Ursula Ludz, Weinheim, VCH Acta Humaniora, 1991.

van Pelt, Robert Jan, 'After the Walls Have Fallen Down', *Queen's Quarterly*, 96, 3 (1989), pp. 641–60.

van Pelt, Robert Jan, 'Into the Suffering City: Considerations of the German Series [by Melvin Charney]', in Phyllis Lambert (ed.), *Parables and Other Allegories; The Work of Melvin Charney, 1975–1990*, Montreal, Canadian Centre for Architecture, 1991, pp. 35–53.

van Pelt, Robert Jan, 'Prospectus: Architecture of Perdition', unpublished.

van Pelt, Robert Jan and Westfall, Carroll William, *Architectural Principles in the Age of Historicism*, New Haven, Yale University Press, 1991.

Venturi, Robert, Scott-Brown, Denise and Izenour, Steven, *Learning from Las Vegas: The Forgotten Symbolism of Architectural Form*, Cambridge, MIT Press, 1982.

Webber, Jonathan, *The Future of Auschwitz: Some Personal Reflections*, The First Frank Green Lecture, Oxford, Oxford Centre for Postgraduate Hebrew Studies, 1992.

Weber, Max, *The Protestant Ethic and the Spirit of Capitalism*, 1905, trans. Talcott Parsons, London, Unwin, 1968.

Weber, Max, 'Politics as a Vocation', 1918, *From Max Weber: Essays in Sociology*, trans. and ed. H. H. Gerth and C. Wright Mills, London, Routledge and Kegan Paul, 1967, pp. 77–128.

Weber, Max, *Economy and Society: An Outline of Interpretative Sociology*, 1922, 2 vols, ed. Guenther Roth and Claus Wittich, Berkeley, University of California Press, 1978.

Weil, Simone, *Réflexions sur les causes de la liberté et de l'oppression sociale*, 1934, Paris, Gallimard, 1955; in *Oppression and Liberty*, trans. Arthur Wills and John Petrie, London, Ark, 1988, pp. 37–124.

Weil, Simone, *L'enracinement: Prélude á une déclaration des devoirs envers l'être humain*, Paris, Gallimard, 1949; trans. *The Need for Roots: Prelude to a Declaration of Duties towards Mankind*, A. F. Wills, London, Routledge and Kegan Paul, 1978.

Weil, Simone, 'The Three Sons of Noah', 1950, in *Attente de Dieu*, Paris, Fayard, 1966, pp. 229–46; trans. Emma Craufurd, *Waiting on God*, London, Fount, 1983, pp. 177–91.

Weil, Simone, *Gravity and Grace*, 1952, trans. Emma Craufurd, London, Routledge and Kegan Paul, 1963.

Weil, Simone, *The Notebooks of Simone Weil*, vol. I, trans. Arthur Wills, fasimile edition, London, Routledge and Kegan Paul, 1956.

Weil, Simone, 'Human Personality', 1957, trans. in *Simone Weil: An Anthology*, ed. Sian Miles, London, Virago, 1986, pp. 69–98.

Witte, Bernd, *Walter Benjamin – Der Intellekuelle als Kritiker: Untersuchungen zu seinem Frühwerk*, Stuttgart, Metzier, 1976.

Witte, Bernd, *Walter Benjamin: An Intellectual Biography*, trans. James Rolleston, Detroit, Wayne State, 1991.

Wittkower, Rudolf, *Architectural Principles in the Age of Humanism*, 1949, 3rd edn, London, Alec Tiranti, 1962.

Wohlfarth, Irving, 'On Some Jewish Motifs in Benjamin', in Andrew Benjamin (ed.), *The Problems of Modernity: Adorno and Benjamin*, Routledge, London, 1989, pp. 157–215.

Wolf, Christa, *Kindheitsmuster*, 1979, trans. *A Model Childhood,* Ursule Molinaro and Hedwig Rappolt, London, Virago, 1983.

Wood, David, (ed.), *Derrida, Heidegger and Spirit*, Chicago, Northwestern University Press, 1993.

Yerushalmi, Yosef Hayim, *Zakhor: Jewish History and Jewish Memory*, Seattle, University of Washington Press, 1982.

Young, James E., *Writing and Rewriting the Holocaust: Narrative and the Consequences of Interpretation*, 1988, Bloomington, Indiana University Press, 1990.

Zohar, *The Zohar*, vol. I, trans. Harry Sperling and Maurice Simon, London, The Soncino Press, 1984.

Glossary of Hebrew Terms

Agunah   a deserted wife who, according to Jewish law, cannot remarry until the husband has been proved dead or has sent her a bill of divorce; adopted as the pen name of the Hebrew writer S. Y. Agnon (1888–1970), who used the term attributively to describe the *Shekhinah*.

Shekhinah   (according to *Kabbalah*) the Divine Presence in the world; the feminine element in God.

Kabbalah   ('tradition') applied to Jewish mysticism.

Zakhor   ('Remember!') the commandment to remember.

Torah   ('teaching') the five books of Moses (*Written Law*).

Talmud   ('learning') consolidation of *Oral Law* in the 5th century CE (Common Era).

Halakah   ('going', the way in which one should go) passages of law in the *Talmud*.

Haggada   ('saying') passages of lore in the *Talmud*: (i) anecdotes, parables, proverbs; (ii) any non-halakic passage (e.g. geography, medicine, astrology).

Index